Second Edition

Topics in Applied Psychology

Compiled by

Doug Hazlewood
University of Western Ontario

Leslie Janes
Brescia University College

Taken from:

Psychology & Work Today, Ninth Edition
by Duane Schultz and Sydney Ellen Schultz

Social Psychology, Third Canadian Edition
by Elliot Aronson, Timothy D. Wilson, Robin M. Akert, and Beverley Fehr

Educational Psychology, Third Canadian Edition
by Anita E. Woolfolk, Philip H. Winne, and Nancy E. Perry

Forensic Psychology
by Joanna Pozzulo, Craig Bennell, and Adelle Forth

Sport Psychology: A Canadian Perspective
by Peter R.E. Crocker

PEARSON

Custom
Publishing

Cover Art: *Pattern 8/Interface*, by Angela Sciaraffa.

Taken from:

Psychology & Work Today, Ninth Edition
by Duane Schultz and Sydney Ellen Schultz
Copyright © 2006, 2002, 1998 by Duane P. Schultz and Sydney Ellen Schultz
Published by Pearson Prentice Hall
Upper Saddle River, New Jersey 07458

Social Psychology, Third Canadian Edition
by Elliot Aronson, Timothy D. Wilson, Robin M. Akert, and Beverley Fehr
Copyright © 2007, 2004, 2001 by Pearson Education Canada, Inc.
Toronto, Ontario

Educational Psychology, Third Canadian Edition
by Anita E. Woolfolk, Philip H. Winne, and Nancy E. Perry
Copyright © 2006, 2003 by Pearson Education Canada, Inc.

Forensic Psychology
by Joanna Pozzulo, Craig Bennell, and Adelle Forth
Copyright © 2006 by Pearson Education Canada, Inc.

Sport Psychology: A Canadian Perspective
by Peter R.E. Crocker
Copyright © 2006 by Pearson Education Canada, Inc.

Copyright © 2006, 2005 by Pearson Custom Publishing
All rights reserved.

This copyright covers material written expressly for this volume by the editor/s as well as the compilation itself. It does not cover the individual selections herein that first appeared elsewhere. Permission to reprint these has been obtained by Pearson Custom Publishing for this edition only. Further reproduction by any means, electronic or mechanical, including photocopying and recording, or by any information storage or retrieval system, must be arranged with the individual copyright holders noted.

Grateful acknowledgment is made to the following sources for permission to reprint material copyrighted or controlled by them:

Chapter 10: "Military Psychology," reprinted from "The War Room," by D. A. Bekerian and A. B. Levey in *Applied Psychology*: Putting Theory into Practice (2005), Oxford University Press.

Printed in Canada

10 9 8 7 6 5 4 3 2

ISBN 0-536-29279-5

2006500186

ED/CH

Please visit our web site at *www.pearsoncustom.com*

PEARSON CUSTOM PUBLISHING
75 Arlington Street, Suite 300, Boston, MA 02116
A Pearson Education Company

Contents

Chapter 1
Psychology and the Law

Chapter 1

Psychology and the Law

Two days before Christmas in 1981, Barbara Stoppel, a beautiful 16-year-old girl, was found strangled in the Winnipeg doughnut shop where she worked. Several people reported that they had seen a tall, lanky man wearing a cowboy hat near the doughnut shop around the time she was killed. Police artists composed a sketch of the suspect based on the descriptions offered by these eyewitnesses. The police sketch looked a lot like Thomas Sophonow, a tall, lanky hotel doorman from Vancouver who was in Winnipeg at the time. Moreover, several witnesses testified that they had seen him leaving the doughnut shop around the time that Stoppel was strangled.

On the basis of this evidence, Sophonow was charged with murder. His trial in 1982 resulted in a hung jury (jury members were unable to reach a verdict). He was tried a second time in 1983; that jury found him guilty of second-degree murder after only four hours of deliberation. Sophonow appealed the conviction and was tried a third time in 1985. This time, after five days of deliberation (which was a record in Canada), a "problematic" juror was removed, after which the 11 remaining jurors rendered their verdict: guilty of second-degree murder. Sophonow again appealed. In all, he spent four years in prison for a murder he claimed he did not commit. In December 1985, after conducting an extensive examination of this case, the Manitoba Court of Appeal argued that he should not face a fourth trial and set him free—but did not declare him innocent. Many people, including Winnipeg's chief of police, continued to believe that Sophonow was Stoppel's killer.

In 1998, Winnipeg police reopened the case because Sophonow lobbied for DNA testing of gloves that had been found at the scene of the crime. DNA testing had not been available at the time of his trials. It is unclear whether this turned out to be useful evidence, because many people, including Sophonow and a Crown attorney, had tried on the gloves in court. However, police did finally reach the conclusion that Sophonow was not Stoppel's killer and announced that they had a new suspect. On June 8, 2000, after more than 18 years of agony, a sobbing Sophonow accepted apologies from the Winnipeg police and the Crown for sending him to prison for a crime he had not committed.

◄ Thomas Sophonow (*left*) endured three trials and spent four years in jail for a murder he did not commit. His wrongful conviction was due in part to his resemblance to the police sketch circulated at the time. Terry Samuel Arnold (*right*), who became the prime suspect in the Barbara Stoppel case, bore a striking resemblance to Sophonow. While we will probably never know whether he was Stoppel's killer, Arnold had a long history of violent crime. He committed suicide on March 29, 2005, before his case went to trial.

Life did not return to normal for Sophonow, however. The following year he had to relive the trauma of his arrest, wrongful conviction, and imprisonment during an inquiry into what went wrong. The judge presiding over the inquiry awarded Sophonow $2.6 million in compensation. However, collecting the compensation was an uphill battle. In June 2002, more than a year after the inquiry, Sophonow found himself in the middle of a fight between the city of Winnipeg and the province of Manitoba over whose responsibility it was to pay up. A cheque was eventually issued to Mr. Sophonow on February 22, 2003. He decided to accept the settlement so that he could begin to get on with his life.

The case of Thomas Sophonow raises a number of important questions. If he was innocent, why did eyewitnesses say that he was the person leaving the scene of the crime? And why did two juries believe them? How common are such miscarriages of justice? In this module, we will discuss the answers to these and other questions, focusing on the role that social psychological processes play in the legal system.

The Canadian Justice System

Let's begin with a brief review of the Canadian justice system, which consists of criminal and civil law. In civil cases, one party (the plaintiff) brings a complaint against another (the defendant) for violating the former's rights in some way. In this module, we are mostly interested in criminal law. When someone commits a crime and the police arrest a suspect, the Crown attorney's office usually decides whether there is enough evidence to press formal charges. (Sometimes at a preliminary hearing, a judge decides whether there will be a trial.) If there is adequate evidence to press charges, lawyers for the defence and the prosecution gather additional evidence and negotiate with each other. As a result of these negotiations, the defendant may plead guilty to a lesser charge. About a quarter of the cases go to trial, during which a jury or a judge decides the defendant's fate.

All of these steps in the legal process are intensely social psychological. In criminal cases, first impressions of the accused and of witnesses have a powerful effect on police investigators and jurors. Attributions about what caused the criminal behaviour are made by police, lawyers, jurors, and the judge; prejudiced beliefs and stereotypical ways of thinking affect those attributions. Attitude change and persuasion techniques abound in the courtroom, as lawyers for each side (i.e., the public and the accused) argue their case and as jurors later debate with one another; and the processes of social cognition affect the jurors' decision making when deciding guilt or innocence. Social psychologists have studied the legal system a great deal in recent years, both because it offers an excellent applied setting in which to examine basic psychological processes and because of its immense importance in daily life. If you, through no fault of your own, are accused of a crime—as Thomas Sophonow was, what do you need to know to convince the system of your innocence?

As we progress through this module, we will from time to time refer to the Thomas Sophonow case, which vividly illustrates many of the points we want to make. We will begin our discussion with the most troubling aspect of the Sophonow case: eyewitness testimony. How accurate are people at identifying someone who has committed a crime?

Eyewitness Testimony

In countries such as Canada, the legal system assigns a great deal of significance to eyewitness testimony. If you are fingered by an eyewitness as the culprit, you are quite likely to be convicted, even if considerable circumstantial evidence indicates you are innocent. Thomas Sophonow was convicted largely because of the testimony of eyewitnesses who claimed that they had seen him near the doughnut shop at about the time of the murder. There were, however, reasons to be suspicious of this testimony, as some witnesses admitted that they had come forward because of the rewards being offered for information on the case. One witness told a dramatic tale of having chased Sophonow after the murder, finally catching him on a bridge, where a fight ensued between them. This story was never corroborated. Numerous witnesses claimed that with each trial, their initially sketchy memories had become sharper and more accurate. There also should have been skepticism about the clarity with which witnesses could have seen Sophonow, given that the murder occurred between 8:15 and 8:45 P.M. on a winter evening. Moreover, witnesses offered conflicting reports of the direction in which he had headed. Despite the lack of physical evidence linking Sophonow to the scene of the crime, the eyewitness testimony that he had been in the vicinity of the doughnut shop was enough to convict him—twice.

Systematic experiments have confirmed that jurors rely heavily on eyewitness testimony when they are deciding whether someone is guilty. Unfortunately, jurors also tend to overestimate the accuracy of eyewitnesses (Ellsworth & Mauro, 1998; Loftus, 1979; Potter & Brewer, 1999; Wells & Olson, 2003). Rod Lindsay and his colleagues (1981) conducted a clever experiment that illustrates both of these points. The researchers staged the theft of a calculator in front of unsuspecting University of Alberta students, and then tested how accurately the students could pick out the "thief" from a set of six photographs. In one condition, it was difficult to identify the "thief" because he had worn a knitted cap pulled over his ears and was in the room for only 12 seconds. In the second condition, the "thief" had worn the knitted cap higher on his head, revealing some of his hair, so it was easier to identify him. In the third condition, the "thief" had worn no hat and had stayed in the room for 20 seconds, making it easiest to identify him. The first set of results was as we'd expect: The more visual information available about the "thief," the higher the percentage of students who correctly identified him in the photo lineup (see Figure 1.1).

In the next stage of the experiment, a researcher playing the role of lawyer questioned the students about their eyewitness identifications, just as a real lawyer would cross-examine witnesses in a trial. These question-and-answer sessions were videotaped. A new group of participants, playing the role of jurors, watched the videotapes of these cross-examinations and rated the extent to which they believed the witnesses had correctly identified the "thief." As shown by the upper line in Figure 1.1, the jurors overestimated the accuracy of the witnesses, especially in the condition where the thief was difficult to identify.

How accurate are eyewitnesses to real crimes? While it is impossible to say exactly what percentage of the time eyewitnesses are accurate, there is reason to believe that they often make mistakes. Researchers have documented many cases of wrongful arrest and, in a remarkably high proportion of these cases, the wrong person was convicted because

▶ **FIGURE 1.1**

THE ACCURACY OF
EYE-WITNESS IDENTIFICATION

The accuracy of eyewitness identification
depends on the viewing conditions at
the time the crime was committed. As in
this study, however, most jurors believe
that witnesses can correctly identify the
criminal even when viewing conditions
are poor.

(Adapted from Lindsay, Wells, &
Rumpel, 1981)

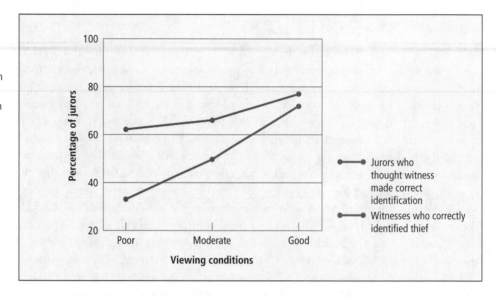

an eyewitness mistakenly identified him or her as the criminal (Penrod & Cutler, 1999;
Sporer, Koehnken, & Malpass, 1996; Wells, Wright, & Bradfield, 1999; Yarmey, 2001a; for
a review of this literature in the context of Canadian law, see Read, Connolly, & Turtle,
2001). Gary Wells and his colleagues (1998), for example, examined 40 cases in which
DNA evidence—obtained after the conviction of a suspect—indicated that the suspect
was innocent. In 36 of these cases, an eyewitness had falsely identified the suspect as the
criminal, and 5 of these falsely accused people were on death row when they were exonerated. University of Guelph psychologist A. Daniel Yarmey has observed that,
"Mistaken eyewitness identification is responsible for more wrongful convictions than all
other causes combined" (Yarmey, 2001a).

Why Are Eyewitnesses Often Wrong?

The problem is that our minds are not like video cameras, which can record an event,
store it over time, and play it back later with perfect accuracy. The study of how we form
impressions of and make inferences about other people. We saw that a number of distortions can occur. Because eyewitness testimony is a form of social perception, it is subject
to similar problems, particularly those involving memory. To be an accurate witness, a
person must successfully complete three stages of memory processing: acquisition,
storage, and retrieval of the events witnessed.

Acquisition refers to the process whereby people notice and pay attention to information in the environment. Because people cannot perceive everything that is happening
around them, they acquire only a subset of the information available in the environment.
Storage refers to the process by which people store in memory information they have
acquired from the environment, whereas **retrieval** refers to the process by which people
recall information stored in their memory (see Figure 1.2). Eyewitnesses can be inaccurate because of problems at any of these three stages.

ACQUISITION No one doubts that people accurately perceive a great deal of information about the world around them. Nonetheless, our ability to take in information is
limited, particularly when we observe unexpected, complex events. The psychologist
Hugo Münsterberg (1908), for example, described an incident that occurred at a

Acquisition the process by which
people notice and pay attention
to information in the environment;
people cannot perceive everything
that is happening around them,
so they acquire only a subset of
the information available in the
environment

Storage the process by which
people store in memory
information they have acquired
from the environment

Retrieval the process by which
people recall information stored
in their memory

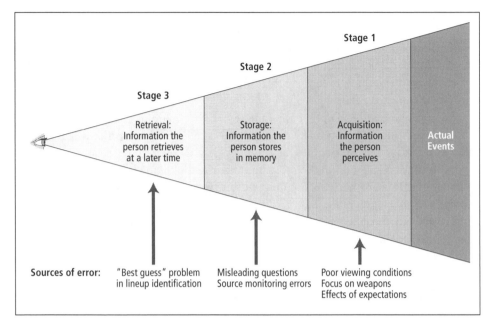

◀ **FIGURE 1.2**
ACQUISITION, STORAGE, AND
RETRIEVAL

To be an accurate eyewitness, people
must complete these three stages of
memory processing. There are sources
of error at each of the three stages.

scientific meeting attended by psychologists, lawyers, and physicians. In the middle of the meeting, a clown burst into the room, followed closely by a man with a revolver. The two men shouted wildly, grabbed each other, then fell to the ground in a fierce struggle. One of them fired a shot; then both men ran out of the room. All of the witnesses were asked to write down an exact account of what they had just seen—which was actually an event staged by two actors. Even though the eyewitnesses were educated, with (presumably) a good memory, their accounts were surprisingly inaccurate. Most of the witnesses omitted or wrote mistaken accounts of about half of the actions they had observed. Most made errors about how long the incident had occurred: while the two men were in the room for about 20 seconds, the witnesses' estimates ranged from a few seconds to several minutes. Recent research conducted at the University of Guelph shows that in general, witnesses overestimate the length of the incident they have observed (Yarmey, Jacob, & Porter, 2002).

Patricia Tollestrup, John Turtle, and John Yuille (1994) found similar eyewitness errors in actual criminal cases. They examined records of robbery and fraud cases handled by the RCMP in Vancouver, in which a suspect was caught and confessed to the crime. The researchers compared the descriptions of the criminals given by eyewitnesses and victims with the criminals' actual physical characteristics (e.g., were witnesses correct that a criminal had blond hair and a moustache?). Eyewitnesses weren't too bad at remembering some details—100 percent of bystanders correctly remembered whether the criminal had facial hair—although crime victims correctly remembered this only 60 percent of the time. However, only 48 percent of the bystanders and 38 percent of the victims correctly remembered the suspect's hair colour. Most importantly, neither bystanders nor victims did a very good job of picking the criminal out of a lineup; overall, they correctly identified the criminal only 48 percent of the time.

A number of factors limits the amount of information about a crime that people take in, such as how much time they have to watch an event and the nature of the viewing conditions. As obvious as this may sound, people sometimes forget how these factors limit eyewitness reports of crimes (Read, Connolly, & Turtle, 2001; Yarmey, Jacob, & Porter, 2002). Crimes usually occur under the very conditions that make acquisition difficult: quickly, unexpectedly, and under poor viewing conditions, such as at night. As we have already mentioned, Barbara Stoppel's murder took place after dark on a winter evening. Presumably, it would have been quite difficult for eyewitnesses to get a good look at the murderer making his getaway.

We should also remember that eyewitnesses who are victims of a crime will be terribly afraid, and this alone can make it difficult to take in everything that is happening. Further, victims tend to focus their attention on any weapon they see and less on the suspect's features (Christianson, 1992; Loftus, Miller, & Burns, 1987; Pickel, 1998; Shaw & Skolnick, 1999). If someone points a gun at you and demands your money, your attention is likely to be on the gun rather than on whether the robber has blue or brown eyes. Note that this is also true for people who witness crimes: Tollestrup, Turtle, and Yuille (1994) found that 73 percent of eyewitnesses correctly identified a police suspect when no weapon was present during a crime; this figure dropped to 31 percent when a weapon was present. Thus, it is not surprising that victims of crimes such as robbery have been found to make more eyewitness identification mistakes than do bystanders (Tollestrup, Turtle, & Yuille, 1994).

Finally, the information people notice and pay attention to is also influenced by what they expect to see. Consider our friend Alan, a social psychologist who is an expert on social perception. One Sunday, Alan was worried because his neighbour, a frail woman in her eighties, did not appear for church. After knocking on her door repeatedly and receiving no response, Alan jimmied open a window and searched her house. Soon his worst fears were realized: The woman was lying dead on the floor of her bedroom. Shaken, Alan returned to his house and telephoned the police. After spending a great deal of time in the woman's house, a detective came over and asked Alan increasingly detailed questions, such as whether he had noticed any suspicious activity in the past day or two. Alan was confused by this line of questioning and finally burst out, "Why are you

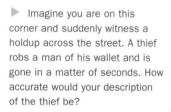

▶ Imagine you are on this corner and suddenly witness a holdup across the street. A thief robs a man of his wallet and is gone in a matter of seconds. How accurate would your description of the thief be?

asking me these questions? Isn't it obvious that my neighbour died of old age? Shouldn't we be notifying her family?" Now it was the detective's turn to look puzzled. "Aren't you the one who discovered the body?" he asked. Alan said he was. "Well," said the detective, "didn't you notice that her bedroom had been ransacked, that there was broken glass everywhere, and that there was a belt tied around her neck?"

It turned out that Alan's neighbour had been strangled by a man who had come to spray her house for insects. There had been a fierce struggle, and the fact that the woman was murdered could not have been more obvious. But Alan saw none of the signs. He was worried that his elderly neighbour had passed away. When he discovered that she had in fact died, he was quite upset, and the furthest thing from his mind was that she had been murdered. As a result, he saw what he expected to see and failed to see the unexpected. When the police later showed him photographs of the crime scene, he felt as though he had never been there. He recognized almost nothing. Alan's experiences are consistent with our discussion in Chapter 1 of how people use theories and schemas. We have many theories about the world and the people in it, and these theories influence what we notice and remember.

> When an actual perceptual fact is in conflict with expectation, expectation may prove a stronger determinant of perception and memory than the situation itself.
> —Gordon Allport and Leo Postman, *The Psychology of Rumor*, 1947

Similarly, the information we take in is influenced by how familiar we are with it. Unfamiliar things are more difficult to remember than familiar things. For example, people are better at recognizing faces within their own race, a phenomenon known as **own-race bias**. White people are better at recognizing White faces than Black or Asian faces, Black people are better at recognizing Black than White faces, and Asians are better at recognizing Asian than White faces (Levin, 2000; Meissner & Brigham, 2001a; Ng & Lindsay, 1994; Shapiro & Penrod, 1986). Daniel Levin (2000) explains that when we see the face of a person of another race, we tend to classify the face in terms of race and stop at that. In contrast, when perceiving the face of a person from our own race, we are more likely to focus on the specific features of the person. Levin observes that, "When a White person looks at another White person's nose, they're likely to think to themselves, 'That's John's nose.' When they look at a Black person's nose, they're likely to think, 'That's a Black nose'" (2000). In a series of studies, Levin demonstrated that, when people are required to move beyond their initial snap judgments and pay attention to individuating information, they are actually quite capable of discriminating between cross-race faces.

Own-race bias the finding that people are better at recognizing faces of their own race than those of other races

STORAGE Many people think that memory is like a collection of photographs. We record a picture of an event, such as the face of a robber, and place it in our memory "album." The picture may not be perfect—after all, few of us have a photographic memory. Further, memories, like real photographs, fade with age. However, it is tempting to believe that the picture, once stored, cannot be altered or retouched, and that details cannot be added to or subtracted from the image. If the robber we saw was clean-shaven, surely we will not pencil in a moustache at some later time.

Unfortunately, our memories are far from indelible. People can become confused about where they heard or saw something; memories in one "album" get confused with memories in another. As a result, people can have quite inaccurate recall about what they saw. In the case of Thomas Sophonow, the police—who were under extreme pressure to make an arrest—arranged for a key witness to meet Sophonow "accidentally" at the remand centre where he was being held. Is it possible that actually seeing Sophonow altered the witness's memory of the appearance of the "tall, lanky man with a cowboy hat" whom he allegedly had seen the night of the murder? The answer to this question is yes.

Reconstructive memory the process whereby memories for an event become distorted by information encountered after the event has occurred

classic research

> Give us a dozen healthy memories, well-formed, and...we'll guarantee to take any one at random and train it to become any type of memory we might select—hammer, screwdriver, wrench, stop sign, yield sign, Indian chief—regardless of its origin or the brain that holds it.
> —Elizabeth Loftus and Hunter Hoffman (1989)

This answer is based on years of research conducted by Elizabeth Loftus and her colleagues on **reconstructive memory**, the distortion of memories of an event by information encountered after the event has occurred (Loftus, 1979; Loftus & Hoffman, 1989; McDonald & Hirt, 1997; Weingardt, Toland, & Loftus, 1994). According to Loftus, information we obtain after witnessing an event can change our memory of the event. For example, in one study, Loftus and colleagues (Loftus, Miller, & Burns, 1978) showed students 30 slides depicting different stages of an automobile accident. The contents of one slide varied; some students saw a car stopped at a stop sign, whereas others saw the same car stopped at a yield sign (see the photos on page 11). After the slide show, the students were asked several questions about the car accident they had "witnessed." In one version, the key question was "Did another car pass the red Datsun while it was stopped at the stop sign?" In another version, the question was "Did another car pass the red Datsun while it was stopped at the yield sign?" Thus, for half of the participants, the question described the traffic sign as they had in fact seen it. But for the other half, the wording of the question subtly introduced new information—for example, if they had seen a stop sign, the question described it as a yield sign. Would this small change—akin to what might occur when witnesses are being questioned by police investigators or attorneys—have an effect on people's memory of the actual event?

All of the students were shown the two pictures (see page 11) and were asked which one they had originally seen. Most people (75 percent) who were asked about the sign they had actually seen chose the correct picture; that is, if they had seen a stop sign and were asked about a stop sign, most of them correctly identified the stop-sign photograph. Note that 25 percent made a crucial mistake on what would seem to be an easy question. Of those who had received the misleading question, however, only 41 percent chose the correct photograph. In subsequent experiments, Loftus (1979) found that misleading questions can change people's minds about how fast a car was going, whether broken glass was at the scene of an accident, whether a traffic light was green or red, or whether a robber had a moustache.

In more recent research along the same lines, Jennifer Tomes and Albert Katz (1997) showed students at the University of Western Ontario crime episodes from various films. For example, one episode from *Talons of the Eagle* showed a woman at an airport, putting her luggage in a red convertible car. A man in a truck drove up and stole her luggage and coat. The woman screamed at him and he drove away. Later, when questioned about the incident, some participants received incorrect information. For example, one question made reference to the assailant's blue truck, when in fact the truck was rust-coloured; in another question it was mentioned that the woman dropped her purse—even though she had not carried one. When participants were again questioned about the crimes, those who had been exposed to misinformation were more likely to have incorporated it into their memory of the event compared to a control group that had not been exposed to misinformation.

Researchers at Dalhousie University have found that people are especially likely to incorporate misinformation into their memories when the event they have witnessed produces negative emotion—which is likely to be the case whenever people witness crimes (Porter, Spencer, & Birt, 2003). Studies such as these show that the way in which the police and lawyers question witnesses can change the witnesses' reports about what they saw. But, we might ask: Do misleading questions alter what is stored in eyewitnesses' memories, or do the questions change only what these people are willing to report, without

Students saw one of these pictures and then tried to remember whether they had seen a stop sign or a yield sign. Many of those who heard leading questions about the street sign made mistaken reports about which sign they had seen.

(From Loftus, Miller, & Burns, 1978)

retouching their memories? While some controversy exists over the answer to this question (Koriat, Goldsmith, & Pansky, 2000; Loftus & Hoffman, 1989; McCloskey & Zaragoza, 1985; Smith & Ellsworth, 1987), most researchers endorse the following position: Misleading questions cause a problem with **source monitoring**, the process by which people try to identify the source of their memories (Johnson, Hashtroudi, & Lindsay, 1993; Mitchell & Johnson, 2000; Mitchell, Johnson & Mather, 2003).

Source monitoring the process whereby people try to identify the source of their memories

In research conducted at Bishop's University, for example, when participants received information about a crime via a radio broadcast and in written form, there was a tendency to confuse the source of these statements. Most frequently, this took the form of thinking they'd heard something on the radio that they had actually read about (Eberman & McKelvie, 2002). Similarly, in the Tomes and Katz (1997) study we discussed earlier, people who saw a rust-coloured truck but received the misleading question about a blue truck now have two pieces of information in memory: the rust-coloured truck and the blue truck. This is all well and good, as long as they remember where these memories came from: the rust-coloured truck from the crime they saw earlier, and the blue truck from the question they were asked later. The problem is that people often become mixed up about where they heard or saw something—in this case, mistakenly believing that the truck in the crime scene was blue. In short, when information is stored in memory, it is not always well tagged as to where it came from.

The implications for legal testimony are sobering. Eyewitnesses who are asked misleading questions often report seeing things that were not really there. In addition, eyewitnesses might be confused as to why a suspect looks familiar. Thomas Sophonow might have looked familiar to eyewitnesses because he happened to resemble the police sketch or because they had seen him in the earlier trials or, as in the case of one witness, because he had seen Sophonow at the remand centre.

RETRIEVAL Suppose the police have arrested a suspect and want to see if you, the eyewitness, can identify the person. Typically, the police arrange a lineup at the police station, where you will be asked whether one of several people is the perpetrator. Sometimes you will be asked to look through a one-way mirror at an actual lineup of the suspect and some foils (i.e., people known not to have committed the crime). Other times you will be asked to examine videotapes of a lineup or photographs of the suspect and the foils. In each case, if a witness identifies a suspect as the culprit, the suspect is likely to be charged and convicted of the crime. After all, the argument goes, if an eyewitness saw the suspect commit the crime and then picked the suspect out of a lineup later, that's pretty good evidence the suspect is the guilty party.

Do lineups result in correct identifications? Research conducted with people living in southern Ontario suggests that lineups have a higher success rate than the alternative of showing eyewitnesses only one person (Yarmey, Yarmey, & Yarmey, 1996). More specifically, Yarmey and colleagues found that if only one person was shown and that person was innocent, a mistaken identification was four times more likely than when the same person appeared in a six-person lineup. Errors were especially likely if the innocent person wore clothing similar to that worn by the person who committed the crime. Thus, the use of lineups appears to be better than the alternative of presenting only one person and asking eyewitnesses whether that person committed the crime.

That is not to say, however, that lineups are without problems. Just as there are problems with acquisition and storage of information, so too can there be problems with how people retrieve information from their memory (Ellsworth & Mauro, 1998; Koehnken, Malpass, & Wogalter, 1996). A number of things other than the image of a person that is stored in memory can influence whether eyewitnesses will pick someone out of a lineup. Witnesses often choose the person in a lineup who most resembles the criminal, even if the resemblance is not strong.

Suppose, for example, that a 19-year-old woman committed a robbery and the police mistakenly arrest you, a 19-year-old woman, for the crime. They put you in a lineup and ask witnesses to pick out the criminal. Which do you think would be more fair: if the other people in the lineup were a 20-year-old man, a 3-year-old child, and an 80-year-old woman, or if the other people were all 19-year-old women? In the former case, the witnesses might pick you only because you are the one who most resembles the actual criminal (Buckhout, 1974). In the latter case, it is much less likely that the witnesses will mistake you for the criminal, because everyone in the lineup is the same age and sex as the culprit (Wells, 1993; Wells & Luus, 1990).

In the Thomas Sophonow case, apparently witnesses were asked by police to identify the man with the cowboy hat they had seen outside the doughnut shop from a photographic lineup. Nine of the photographs had been taken indoors and none of the people wore hats. The tenth photo—the photo of Thomas Sophonow—was larger than the others, was taken outdoors, and showed him wearing a cowboy hat. Police later admitted that the photo gallery was biased and presented a less biased lineup to the witnesses.

According to Elizabeth Loftus, who testified at the inquiry into Sophonow's wrongful conviction, it is highly unlikely that the new, fairer lineup would have reversed the damage done by the first one: "That's like trying to squeeze toothpaste back in the tube" (Loftus, quoted in Janzen, 2001).

To avoid this "best guess" problem wherein witnesses pick the person who looks most like the suspect, social psychologists recommend that police follow these steps:

1. Ensure that everyone in the lineup resembles the witness's description of the suspect. Doing so will minimize the possibility that the witness will simply choose the person who looks most like the culprit (Wells et al., 1998).

2. Tell the witnesses that the person suspected of the crime may or may not be in the lineup. If witnesses believe that the culprit is present, they are much more likely to choose the person who looks most like the culprit, rather than saying that they aren't sure or that the culprit is not present. In short, false identifications are more likely to occur when people believe that the culprit is in the lineup (Gonzalez, Ellsworth, & Pembroke, 1993; Malpass & Devine, 1981; Wells et al., 1998, 2000).

3. Do not always include the suspect in an initial lineup. If a witness picks out someone as the culprit from a lineup that includes only foils (i.e., a blank lineup), you will know the witness is not reliable. In a study conducted at the University of Alberta, for example, 61 percent of the research participants who made an identification from a blank lineup failed to identify the correct person later when he was actually present in a photo lineup. In contrast, of participants who correctly indicated that the suspect was not in the blank lineup, only 31 percent later made a mistaken identification when shown a lineup containing the suspect (Wells, 1984).

4. Make sure that the person conducting the lineup does not know which person in the lineup is the suspect. This avoids the possibility that the person will unintentionally communicate to the witness who the suspect is (Wells et al., 1998).

5. Present pictures of people sequentially instead of simultaneously. Doing so makes it more difficult for witnesses to compare all of the pictures, choosing the one that most resembles the criminal, even when the criminal is not actually in the lineup. For example, in a study conducted at Queen's University, 35 percent of research participants exposed to a simultaneous lineup mistakenly identified an innocent person as the perpetrator, whereas only 18 percent of those exposed to a sequential lineup make a mistaken identification (Lindsay & Wells, 1985; Sporer, 1994; Steblay et al., 2001).

6. Present witnesses with photographs of people and sound recordings of their voices. Witnesses who both see and hear members of a lineup are much more likely to identify the person they saw commit a crime than are people who only see the pictures or only hear the voice recordings (Melara, DeWitt-Rikards, & O'Brien, 1989). In fact, Yarmey and colleagues (2001) found that people are really quite inaccurate when identifying voices—much less accurate than they think they are. For example, if a voice was unfamiliar to the participants, the false identification rate was 45 percent (Yarmey et al., 2001).

7. Try to minimize the time between the crime and the identification of suspects. Studies based on staged crimes (Yarmey, Yarmey, & Yarmey, 1996) and actual crimes reported in RCMP records (Tollestrup, Turtle, & Yuille, 1994) have found that the longer the time that elapses between seeing a suspect and being asked to identify the person from a lineup, the greater the likelihood of error (Read, Connolly, & Turtle, 2001).

Judging Whether Eyewitnesses Are Mistaken

Suppose you are a police detective or a member of a jury who is listening to a witness describe a suspect. How can you tell whether the witness's memory is accurate or whether he or she is making one of the many mistakes in memory we have just documented? It might seem that the answer to this question is pretty straightforward: pay careful attention to how confident the witness is. Suppose the witness stands up in the courtroom, points her finger at the defendant, and says, "That's the man I saw commit the crime. There's absolutely no doubt in my mind—I'd recognize him anywhere." Sounds pretty convincing, doesn't it? Compare this testimony to a witness who says, "Well, gee, I'm really not sure, because it all happened so quickly. If I had to guess, I'd say it was the defendant, but I could be wrong." Which witness would you be more likely to believe? The eyewitness who was more confident, of course. And you would not be alone—there is evidence that confident witnesses are more likely to be believed by police investigators, judges, and jurors (Read, Connolly, & Turtle, 2001).

In the Thomas Sophonow case, the eyewitnesses who identified him as the man near the doughnut shop became more confident of their descriptions with each trial. Sophonow testified that on the evening of Barbara Stoppel's murder, he had stopped at a store to buy some food. While he was there, he decided to purchase stockings filled with treats to distribute to children who would have to spend Christmas in a hospital. At the second trial, the court heard testimony from a ward clerk at a Winnipeg hospital, who testified that a man fitting Sophonow's description had arrived at her desk between 8:10 and 8:30 P.M. on December 23 with Christmas stockings for sick children. The clerk had told him that her hospital didn't have a children's ward, but she gave him directions to three hospitals that did. Employees of those hospitals verified that a tall, slim man had arrived with Christmas stockings; however, none of them was certain that the man had been Sophonow, nor was any clerk certain of the exact date that the stockings had been delivered. Who did the jurors believe? The witnesses who presented their testimony with greater confidence, apparently.

▷ Lineups have to be carefully constructed to avoid mistaken identifications.

CLOSE TO HOME Copyright © 2002 John McPherson. Reprinted with permission of UNIVERSAL PRESS SYNDICATE. All rights reserved.

DOES CERTAINTY MEAN ACCURACY? The only problem—and it is a big one—is that numerous studies have shown that a witness's confidence is not strongly related to his or her accuracy (Luus & Wells, 1994; Olsson, 2000; Read, Connolly, & Turtle, 2001; Smith, Kassin, & Ellsworth, 1989; Wells, Olson, & Charman, 2002; Yarmey, Jacob, & Porter, 2002). It is dangerous to assume that because a witness is very confident, he or she must therefore be correct. For example, in the Lindsay, Wells, and Rumpel (1981) experiment we discussed earlier, witnesses who saw the crime under poor viewing conditions—in which the "thief" wore the cap over his ears—had as much confidence in their identifications as did witnesses who saw the crime under moderate or good viewing conditions, even though the former were considerably less accurate (see Figure 1.1 on page 6).

Similar results were obtained at the University of Alberta when Wells, Lindsay, and Ferguson (1978) conducted another version of the calculator theft study described earlier (Lindsay, Wells, & Rumpel, 1981). These researchers again staged the theft of a calculator from a laboratory. Participants in this study were asked to identify the "thief" from a photo lineup as well as to indicate how certain they were that they had identified the correct person. The correlation between participants' confidence that they had made a correct identification and the accuracy of their identifications was only .29 (recall that a perfect correlation is 1.00). Participants also were asked questions about the event, as if under cross-examination in a trial. Other research participants, serving as jurors, observed the cross-examinations. It turned out that jurors were more likely to believe confident, rather than unconfident, witnesses—a disturbing finding, given the weak relation between accuracy and confidence.

SIGNS OF ACCURATE TESTIMONY How, then, can we tell whether a witness's testimony is correct? It is by no means easy, but research by David Dunning and Lisa Beth Stern (1994; Stern & Dunning, 1994) suggests some answers. They showed participants a film in which a man stole some money from a woman's wallet, asked participants to pick the man out of a photo lineup, and then asked participants to describe how they had made up their minds. Dunning and Stern found some interesting differences between the reports of people who accurately identified the man and the reports of people who did not. Accurate witnesses tended to say that they didn't really know how they recognized the man, that his face just "popped out" at them. Inaccurate witnesses tended to say that they used a process of elimination whereby they deliberately compared one face to another. Ironically, taking more time and thinking more carefully about the pictures was associated with making more mistakes. We should, therefore, be more willing to believe a witness who says, "I knew it was the defendant as soon as I saw him in the lineup" than one who says, "I compared everyone in the lineup, thought about it, and decided it was the defendant."

The research by Dunning and Stern, while intriguing, leaves unanswered an important question: Did taking more time on the identification task make people less accurate, or did people who were less accurate to begin with simply take more time? Maybe some people did not pay close attention to the film of the robbery, and therefore, had difficulty recognizing the robber in the lineup. Consequently, they had to spend more time thinking about it and comparing the faces, such that inaccuracy caused a longer decision time. Alternatively, there might have been something about making identifications thoughtfully and deliberately that impaired accuracy.

> No subjective feeling of certainty can be an objective criterion for the desired truth.
> —Hugo Münsterberg, *On the Witness Stand*, 1908

classic research

THE PROBLEM WITH VERBALIZATION Some fascinating studies by Schooler and Engstler-Schooler (1990) support this second possibility and suggest that trying to put an image of a face into words can cause problems. They showed students a film of a bank robbery. In the verbalization condition, they asked some of the students to write detailed descriptions of the robber's face. Other students, in the no-verbalization condition, spent the same amount of time completing an unrelated task. All students then tried to identify the robber from a photo lineup of eight faces. It might seem that writing a description of the robber would be a good memory aid and make people more accurate. In fact, the reverse was true: only 38 percent of the people in the verbalization condition correctly identified the robber, compared to 64 percent of the people in the no-verbalization condition.

Schooler and Engstler-Schooler (1990; see also Meissner & Brigham, 2001b; Schooler, Fiore, & Brandimonte, 1997) suggest that trying to put a face into words is difficult and impairs memory for that face. Using the word *squinty* to describe a robber's eyes, for example, might be a general description of what his eyes looked like but probably does not capture the subtle contours of his eyes, eyelids, eyelashes, eyebrows, and upper cheeks. When you see the photo lineup, if you look for eyes that are squinty, doing so interferes with your attention to the finer details of the faces. If you ever witness a crime, then, you should not try to put into words what the criminal looked like. And if you hear someone say she or he wrote down a description of the criminal and then deliberated long and hard before deciding whether the person was present at a lineup, you might doubt the accuracy of the witness's identification.

To sum up, several factors make eyewitness testimony inaccurate, leading to all too many false identifications. Perhaps the criminal law system in Canada should rely less on eyewitness testimony than it now does. This might mean that some guilty people go free, but it would avoid many false convictions. To see how accurate you and your friends are at eyewitness testimony, and to illustrate some of the pitfalls we have discussed, tackle Try It! on page 17.

Judging Whether Eyewitnesses Are Lying

There is yet another reason eyewitness testimony can be inaccurate. Even if witnesses have very accurate memories for what they saw, they might deliberately lie when on the witness stand. In the Thomas Sophonow case, some witnesses admitted that they testified because they wanted a reward. The man who told the wild tale of chasing and catching Sophonow was found to be lying. The Crown also relied on jailhouse informants who claimed that Sophonow had confessed to them that he was Barbara Stoppel's killer. Deals had been struck with these informants in exchange for their testimony. Why couldn't two different sets of jurors see through these stories?

Sadly, the Sophonow case is not unique in this regard. In other cases of wrongful conviction, such as those of David Milgaard and Donald Marshall, police and jury members believed the false stories of the acquaintances who testified against them. Sometimes, the truth is never established. How can we tell whether witnesses are lying or telling the truth?

Several studies have tested people's ability to detect deception (Bond, Jr., & Atoum, 2000; DePaulo & Friedman, 1998; Ekman, 2002; Gordon & Miller, 2000). When people watch a videotape of actors who are either lying or telling the truth, their ability to tell who is lying is only slightly better than chance guessing (DePaulo, 1994; DePaulo,

> If falsehood, like truth, had only one face, we would be in better shape. For we would take as certain the opposite of what the liar said. But the reverse of truth has a hundred thousand shapes.
> —Montaigne, *Essays*, 1595

try it!   The Accuracy of Eyewitness Testimony

Try this demonstration with a group of friends who you know will be gathered in one place, such as a dorm room or an apartment. The idea is to stage an incident in which someone comes into the room suddenly, acts in a strange manner, and then leaves. Your friends will then be asked to recall as much as they can about this person, to see if they are good eyewitnesses. Here are some specific instructions about how you might do this:

1. Take one friend, whom we will call the actor, into your confidence before you do this exercise. Ideally, the actor should be a stranger to the people who will be the eyewitnesses. The actor should suddenly rush into the room where you and your other friends are gathered and act in a strange (but nonthreatening) manner. For example, the actor could hand someone a flower and say, "The flower man cometh!" Or, he or she could go up to each person and say something unexpected, such as, "Meet me in Moscow at New Year's." Ask the actor to hold something in his or her hand during this episode, such as a pencil, a shoelace, or a banana. Keep track of how long the episode takes. Remember: The actor should not act in a violent or threatening way, or make the eyewitnesses uncomfortable. The goal is to act in unexpected and surprising ways, not to frighten people.

2. After a few minutes, the actor should leave the room. Inform your friends that you staged this event as a demonstration of eyewitness testimony and that, if they are willing, they should try to remember, in as much detail as possible, what occurred. Ask them to write down answers to these questions:

   (a) What did the actor look like? Write down a detailed description.
   (b) What did the actor say? Write down his or her words as best you can remember.
   (c) How much time passed between the time the actor entered the room and the time he or she left?
   (d) Did the actor touch anyone? If so, whom did he or she touch?
   (e) What was the actor holding in his or her hand?

3. After everyone has answered these questions, ask them to read their answers out loud. How much did they agree? How accurate were people's answers? Discuss with your friends why they were correct or incorrect in their descriptions.

   Note: This demonstration will work best if you have access to a video camera and can record the actor's actions. That way, you can play the tape to assess the accuracy of the eyewitnesses' descriptions. If you cannot videotape it, you can ask the actor to repeat his or her actions.

Stone, & Lassiter, 1985). And, as with eyewitness testimony, confidence is not strongly correlated with accuracy, as was recently demonstrated by researchers at Dalhousie University (Porter et al., 2002). In other words, even people who feel certain that they can tell whether someone is lying are actually not much better than chance at correctly picking out the liars.

But surely some people must be very good at detecting deception; after all, some jobs require exactly that skill. Law enforcement officials, for example, most of whom have spent years with suspects who concoct stories professing their innocence, may be much more skilled than the average person at seeing through these stories to the underlying truth.

Unfortunately, research suggests otherwise. For example, Bella DePaulo and Roger Pfeiffer (1986) tested the ability of experienced law enforcement officers—including members of the U.S. Customs Service, the Secret Service, the armed forces, police detectives, and judges—to detect deception. In general, these officials were no better at telling whether someone was lying than were untrained university students. Porter, Woodworth, and Birt (2000) obtained similar findings when comparing Canadian federal parole officers with Dalhousie University students—both groups performed at, or

Polygraph a machine that measures people's physiological responses (e.g., heart rate); polygraph operators attempt to tell if someone is lying by observing how that person responds physiologically while answering questions

> A man's most valuable trait is a judicious sense of what not to believe.
> —Euripides, playwright, 480?–406 BC

below, chance levels. The problem is that both untrained people and experts tend to think that there are reliable cues to deception, such as whether a person refuses to look you in the eye (Akehurst et al., 1996). Unlike Pinocchio with his lengthening nose, human beings do not show obvious signs of lying that are the same for every person in every situation. If people are lying, they often get away with it, regardless of whether they are talking to law enforcement experts, friends, or strangers (DePaulo & Friedman, 1998; Ekman, O'Sullivan, & Frank, 1999; Kashy & DePaulo, 1996). Recent research suggests that if people—in this case, parole officers and university students—are given extensive training, their accuracy at detecting deception can improve—but their performance remains far from perfect (Porter, Woodworth, & Birt, 2000).

ARE POLYGRAPH MACHINES ACCURATE? If people are poor lie detectors, perhaps machines can do better. You've probably heard of a **polygraph**, a machine that measures people's physiological responses, such as their heart rate and breathing rate. Polygraph operators attempt to tell if someone is lying by observing how that person responds physiologically while answering questions. In one version, called the *control question test*, the operator asks people both relevant questions about a crime (e.g., "Did you steal money from the cash register of the restaurant?") and control questions that are known to produce truthful responses (e.g., "Have you ever stolen anything in your whole life?") The assumption is that, when people lie, they become anxious and this anxiety can be detected by increases in heart rate, breathing rate, and so on. Thus, the operator monitors whether you have more of a physiological response to the relevant question than to the control question.

Another version is called the *guilty knowledge test*. Here, people answer multiple-choice questions about specific aspects of a crime, the answers to which are known only by the police and the culprit. A suspect might be asked, for example, "Was the amount stolen from the cash register $10, $23, $34, $54, or $110?" The idea is that only the criminal would know the correct answer and would, therefore, be anxious when that answer is read. The thief who knows that he stole $23 will probably be more anxious when this amount is read than will an innocent person who does not know how much money was stolen.

Polygraphs have both strong supporters (e.g., Raskin, Honts, & Kircher, 1997) and steadfast critics (e.g., Lykken, 1998). How well do these tests actually work? First, polygraph results are only as good as the person operating and interpreting the test. With several responses being measured, it is not always easy to tell whether a person has had more of a physiological response to one question than to another. One disturbing finding is that operators often disagree with one another, suggesting that the test is by no means infallible (Ellsworth & Mauro, 1998). Moreover, recent research conducted at the University of New Brunswick has shown that even the order in which questions are asked can influence the results. Cullen and Bradley (2004) found that when a control question was presented before a crime-relevant question, the test did a better job of identifying those who were guilty than when the reverse order was used (i.e., crime-relevant question followed by a control question).

Granted, when the test is administered under optimal conditions by an experienced examiner, it does reveal whether someone is lying or telling the truth at levels better than chance. But even then it is not perfect (Ben-Shakhar & Elaad, 2003; Ellsworth & Mauro, 1998; Iacono & Patrick, 1999; Saxe, 1994). The error rates vary somewhat, depending on the technique used to administer the test. Some studies have found that false negatives—in which liars are found to be telling the truth—are the most common kind of error (Honts,

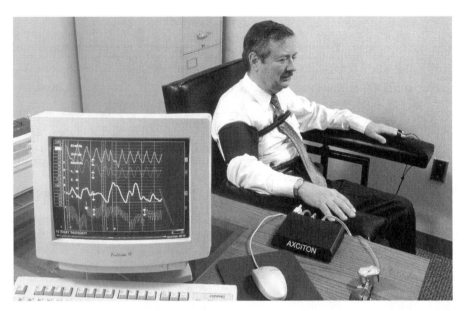

Although polygraphs can detect whether someone is lying at levels better than chance, they are by no means infallible. Because of the rate of error, Canada does not allow the results of polygraph tests to be used in court.

1994). In contrast, research conducted with inmates in a B.C. prison found that there was a tendency for the test to mistakenly classify as liars those who were actually telling the truth (Patrick & Iacono, 1989). One review concluded that averaging across all the different techniques, the polygraph typically misidentifies between 10 and 15 percent of liars as truth tellers (false negatives) and between 10 and 15 percent of truth tellers as liars (false positives); (Ekman, 2002). Because of the rate of error, Canada does not allow the results of polygraph tests to be used in court. In Thomas Sophonow's third trial, his defence lawyer attempted to have him take a lie detector test in court, but the judge refused. We might note that after Sophonow was acquitted, he took a lie detector test when he was interviewed on the television program *W-5* in 1986 and passed with flying colours.

Psychologists continue to look for the perfect lie detection machine. One approach tried a camera that records blood flow in the face using high definition thermal imaging technology (Pavlidis, Eberhardt, & Levine, 2002). The researchers hypothesized that, when people are lying, they might show a specific "thermal signature" around their eyes, reflecting the fact that there was increased blood flow, possibly from nervousness. An initial study showed that the thermal imaging technique did distinguish liars from truth tellers at a better than chance rate, but the technique was by no means perfect: 15 percent of the people were mislabelled as liars or truth tellers—about the same error rate as is found with the polygraph.

A concern with all physiological measures of deception is whether guilty people can learn to beat the tests. There is some evidence that people can deliberately act in ways that reduce the validity of the results of polygraph tests, such as biting their tongue and doing mental arithmetic. The search continues, but there is still no perfect lie detection machine that can always differentiate lies from the truth (Iacono, 2000; Kleiner, 2002).

To see how well you and your friends can tell whether someone is lying, do Try It! on page 20. How did you do? It would be nice if there were a foolproof method of telling whether someone is lying. If so, people such as David Milgaard, Stephen Truscott, Donald Marshall, and Thomas Sophonow—to name a few—would not have had to

try it!   Lie Detection

The purpose of this exercise, which should be done with a group of friends, is to see how well people can tell if someone is lying. Ask for a volunteer to be the speaker and the others to be the audience. The speaker's job will be to lie about how much he or she likes five high school acquaintances, and to tell the truth about how much he or she likes five other high school acquaintances. The audience's job is to try to guess when the speaker is telling the truth and when he or she is lying. Here are some specific instructions:

Instructions for the speaker: Make a list of 10 people you knew in high school and think about how much you liked each person. Randomly choose five people and put a *T* next to their names. These are the people about whom you will be truthful. Put an *L* next to the other names. These are the people about whom you will lie. Take a few minutes to think about what you will say. When you are ready, describe your feelings toward each person (truthfully or not) to the audience. Give a few sentences about each person.

Instructions for the audience: The speaker will be describing his or her feelings about 10 high school acquaintances. He or she will be telling the truth about half of the people and lying about the other half. Listen carefully and try to guess when the speaker is telling the truth and when he or she is lying. You may use any cues you want to make your decision. Write down the numbers

1 to 10, and put "Truth" or "Lie" next to the number of each person the speaker describes.

Scoring: The speaker, when done, should reveal when he or she was telling the truth versus lying. The audience members should tally how often they were right. People should be correct half of the time just by guessing; scores that are substantially above 50 percent may indicate that that person is good at detecting deception (or that the speaker is poor at lying!). Trade notes about what kinds of cues people paid attention to in the speaker. What did the speaker do that made you think he or she was telling a lie?

Variation: Here is an interesting variation you can try. Have half of the audience sit with their backs to the speaker so they can hear but not see him or her. The other half of the audience should sit facing the speaker. Which group was better at detecting when the speaker was lying? Bella DePaulo, Dan Lassiter, and Julie Stone (1983) found that people who were instructed to pay special attention to a speaker's tone of voice did better at lie detection than did people instructed to pay attention to how the speaker looked. When people can see a speaker, they tend to focus on facial cues that they think are good indications of lying but which, in fact, are not. Therefore, the group of people who cannot see the speaker might rely more on tone of voice and may, as a result, be more accurate.

spend years in prison for crimes they did not commit. Many psychologists doubt, though, that such a test will ever be developed; the nuances of human behaviour are too rich and complex to allow foolproof tests of honesty.

Can Eyewitness Testimony Be Improved?

We have seen a number of ways in which eyewitness testimony can go wrong. Given the importance of such testimony in criminal trials, are there ways to improve it? Two general approaches have been tried but, unfortunately, neither has proven to be very successful.

The first involves hypnosis. You may have seen movies in which a witness to a terrible crime has no memory of what occurred—until he or she is put under hypnosis. Then, while in a trance-like state, the person is able to describe the murderer in great detail. Unfortunately, this is a case in which the movies do not reflect real life. University of Toronto psychologist Marilyn Smith (1983) conducted a careful review and analysis of the literature and concluded that there is no hard evidence that people's memories improve when they are hypnotized. Subsequent research supports this conclusion (Ellsworth & Mauro, 1998; Erdelyi, 1994; Kebbell & Wagstaff, 1998; see review by Read, Connolly, & Turtle, 2001). In fact, there is some evidence that when people are under hypnosis they are more susceptible to suggestion, coming to believe they saw things that they did not

(Lynn et al., 2003; Scoboria et al., 2002). Even worse, people tend to become more confident in their memories after they have been hypnotized, even if they are no more accurate (Spiegel & Spiegel, 1987). This is dangerous because, as we saw earlier, juries often interpret a witness's confidence as a gauge of a witness's accuracy, even though confidence is not strongly related to accuracy.

The second way people have tried to increase eyewitness accuracy is with the use of the **cognitive interview** (Geiselman & Fischer, 1989). With this technique, a trained interviewer tries to improve an eyewitness's memory by focusing the individual's attention on the details and context of the event. This is done chiefly by asking the person to recall the event several times from different starting points (e.g., from the beginning of the event and from the middle of the event) and by asking the person to create a mental image of the scene. Some research using this technique looks promising (Brock, Fisher, & Cutler, 1999; Holliday, 2003). Other research, however, has been more sobering, finding that the cognitive interview may increase errors and confabulations of memory, especially when used with children (Finger & Pezdek, 1999; Fisher, Brennan, & McCauley, 2001). One reason for this is that repeatedly imagining an event has been found to increase source monitoring errors, whereby people become confused about whether they actually witnessed an event or simply imagined it later (Johnson et al., 1979). So far, then, there is no tried-and-true way to improve eyewitnesses' memories—other than by trying to avoid the pitfalls we have discussed.

THE RECOVERED MEMORY DEBATE Another form of eyewitness memory has received a great deal of attention: the case in which a person recalls having been the victim of a crime, typically sexual abuse, after many years of being consciously unaware of that fact. Not surprisingly, the accuracy of such **recovered memories** has been hotly debated (McNally, 2003; Pezdek & Banks, 1996; Schooler & Eich, 2000).

In 1992, John Popowich, a Saskatoon police officer, was charged with sexually assaulting children at a daycare centre. The children claimed that he and other adults had forced them to drink blood, perform sexual acts, and watch people having their eyes plucked out. These charges came at a time when recovered memory syndrome was receiving a lot of attention in the media and the courts; as a result, the children's testimony was believed. After a 10-year fight that took a tremendous toll on his personal and professional life, Popowich managed to establish his innocence. In the summer of 2002, Saskatchewan's justice minister issued an apology to Popowich for his wrongful conviction and agreed to pay $1.3 million in compensation (Millin, 2002).

The question of the accuracy of recovered memories is controversial. On one side are writers such as Ellen Bass and Laura Davis (1994), who claim that it is not uncommon for women who were sexually abused to repress these traumas so that they have absolutely no memory of them. The abuse and its subsequent repression, according to this view, are responsible for many psychological problems, such as depression and eating disorders. Later in life, often with the help of a psychotherapist, these events can be "recovered" and brought back into memory. On the other side of the controversy are academic psychologists who argue that the accuracy of recovered memories cannot be accepted on faith (e.g., Loftus, 2003; Schacter, 1996; Schooler, 1999). These psychologists acknowledge that sexual abuse and other childhood traumas are a terrible problem and more common than we would like to think. They further agree that claims of sexual abuse should be taken very seriously and fully investigated, and that, when sufficient evidence of guilt exists, the person responsible for the abuse should be prosecuted.

Cognitive interview a technique whereby a trained interviewer tries to improve eyewitnesses' memories by focusing their attention on the details and context of the event

Recovered memories recollections of an event, such as sexual abuse, that had been forgotten or repressed

False memory syndrome
Remembering a past traumatic experience that is objectively false but nevertheless accepted as true

But here's the problem: What is "sufficient evidence"? Is it enough that someone remembers, years later, that he or she has been abused, in the absence of any other evidence of abuse? According to many researchers, the answer is no. The reason is **false memory syndrome**, in which people can recall a past traumatic experience that is objectively false but that they believe is true (Kihlstrom, 1996). There is evidence that people can acquire vivid memories of events that never occurred, especially if another person—such as a psychotherapist—suggests that the events occurred (Johnson & Raye, 1981; Loftus, 1993; Schooler & Eich, 2000). In addition to numerous laboratory demonstrations of false memories, evidence from everyday life also indicates that memories of abuse can be false. Often these memories are contradicted by objective evidence (e.g., no evidence of satanic murders can be found); sometimes people who suddenly acquire such memories decide later that the events never occurred; and sometimes the memories are so bizarre (e.g., that people were abducted by aliens) as to strain credulity. Unfortunately, some psychotherapists do not sufficiently consider that by suggesting past abuse, they may be planting false memories rather than helping clients remember real events.

This is not to say, however, that all recovered memories are inaccurate. While scientific evidence for repression and recovery—the idea that something can be forgotten for years and then recalled with great accuracy—is sparse, there may be instances in which people do suddenly remember traumatic events that really did occur (Schooler, 1999). Therefore, any claim of abuse should be taken with the utmost seriousness. Unfortunately, it is very difficult to distinguish the accurate memories from the false ones in the absence of any corroborating evidence. For this reason, claims of abuse cannot be taken on faith, especially if they are the result of suggestions from other people.

Are there other kinds of evidence that can be used by the legal system that might be less susceptible to the kinds of inaccuracies that plague eyewitness testimony? We turn to this issue next.

Other Kinds of Evidence

There are a number of other kinds of evidence that police investigators, judges, and juries can rely on in reaching decisions about the guilt or innocence of people accused of crimes. They can turn to experts for information (e.g., about an accused's mental state). They also can rely on physical evidence such as fingerprints or DNA tests conducted on hair samples or blood. Legal professionals and juries also can base their verdicts on statistical evidence—the probability that the accused committed the crime. As we shall see, juries find some of these kinds of evidence more persuasive than others.

Expert Testimony

A number of thorny issues surrounds the use of expert testimony in court (Pfeifer, 1997). Research conducted at York University suggests that jurors may not always understand judges' instructions about the kinds of evidence that are permissible from an expert witness and the kinds of evidence that should be disregarded (Schuller & Paglia, 1999; see Schuller & Yarmey, 2001 for a review). It is important that jurors know how to properly evaluate expert testimony, because research has shown that jurors are influenced by such information.

In one study, for example, students at York University and visitors to the Ontario Science Centre were presented with a transcript of a homicide case based on an actual case, in which an abused woman shot and killed her husband (Schuller & Hastings, 1996).

Participants in the expert testimony condition read that a psychologist had testified that the woman's behaviour should be understood in terms of battered wife syndrome. The psychologist explained that battered wife syndrome resembles post-traumatic stress disorder in terms of its emotional and psychological consequences. Participants in the control condition were not exposed to any expert testimony. Did expert testimony have an effect on the mock jurors' verdicts? The answer is Yes. Participants who received expert testimony were more likely to conclude that the woman acted out of self-defence than were participants who did not hear expert testimony. Importantly, those who received expert testimony also rendered a more lenient verdict.

In Canada, the courts have shown a tendency to move away from expert testimony (Peters, 2001; Yarmey, 2001b; but see Saunders [2001] for a different opinion). Why is this the case? According to Martin Peters, a Toronto criminal lawyer, some judges believe that much of what experts—in particular, psychological experts—have to offer is common sense. In other words, jury members are assumed to already know whatever a psychologist might have to offer. Other judges are concerned that jury members will rely too heavily on what the experts say, rather than critically evaluate information themselves (Peters, 2001). Not surprisingly, psychologists argue that they do have something to offer the legal system. As A. Daniel Yarmey (2001b) points out, research on the accuracy of eyewitness testimony and on identification of suspects from lineups has revealed important information that is not part of common sense knowledge. Given that wrongful convictions are generally a result of mistaken eyewitness identification, experts can provide the kind of information that would enable jurors to properly evaluate such evidence. Fortunately, some judges agree. According to the Honourable Mr. Justice Jamie W. S. Saunders of the Nova Scotia Court of Appeal, expert testimony does have a place in Canadian courts, provided that certain guidelines are followed (e.g., experts must be independent and objective).

Physical Evidence

When crimes occur, forensic experts scrutinize the scene for footprints, fingerprints, and samples of hair or fibres. In addition, in recent years DNA testing has become much more accurate, and courts increasingly rely on this kind of evidence. When Larry Fisher was tried for the murder of Gail Miller—the murder for which David Milgaard had been wrongfully convicted—DNA testing proved that he had raped Miller. The jury then used this information to infer that he had killed her as well. The same kind of evidence that was used to convict Larry Fisher was used to exonerate Guy Paul Morin. Morin was wrongfully convicted of sexually assaulting and killing his neighbour's nine-year-old daughter in 1986. In 1995, he was exonerated on the basis of DNA evidence.

What about other kinds of physical evidence that might not be as conclusive as DNA testing? Research conducted by Elizabeth Loftus (1974, 1983) suggests that other kinds of physical evidence tend not to be very persuasive. In one study, for example, Loftus (1974) presented research participants with a description of a robbery of a grocery store and the murder of its owner. Participants in the physical evidence condition read that the defendant had been found with large sums of cash and that traces of the cleaning solution used on the store's floor had been found on his shoes. Those in the eyewitness testimony condition read that a store clerk had identified the defendant as the killer. Participants in a third condition received both physical and eyewitness evidence, but the eyewitness testimony was discredited; specifically, participants were told that the eyewitness had poor vision. It turned out that physical evidence alone was not very convincing to these mock jurors—only 18 percent of them rendered a guilty verdict. In sharp contrast, 72 percent of

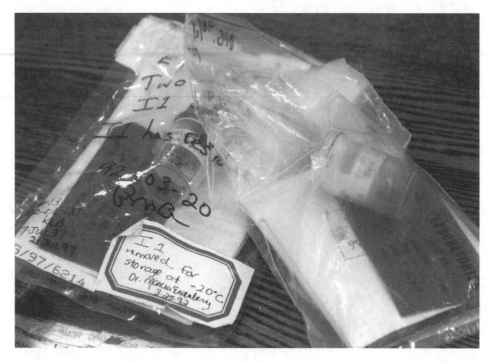

▶ A vial of melted snow containing semen samples found at the scene where Gail Miller was murdered in 1969 was the source of DNA evidence used to exonerate David Milgaard and to convict Larry Fisher. In 2005, a public inquiry began into Milgaard's wrongful conviction and imprisonment.

participants who received eyewitness testimony believed that the defendant was guilty. Perhaps most disturbing, 68 percent of participants who received eyewitness testimony that was later discredited nevertheless considered the defendant to be guilty.

In the Thomas Sophonow case, physical evidence was presented at the third trial that made it unlikely that he could have been at the doughnut shop at the time of Barbara Stoppel's murder. Sophonow testified that he had telephoned his mother in Vancouver before delivering the Christmas stockings to hospitals. Telephone records confirmed that he had placed the call at 7:56 P.M. from a location that would have made it difficult to reach the doughnut shop by the time the murder took place (between 8:15 and 8:45 P.M.). Consistent with Loftus's research, jurors obviously did not find this evidence very convincing, however, choosing instead to believe the reports of people who claimed to have seen Sophonow at the scene of the crime.

Statistical Evidence

Consider a hypothetical case that legal scholars have frequently debated. A bus hits and kills a dog. Although it is not known to which company the bus belongs, 80 percent of the buses on the route where the dog was killed are owned by the Blue Bus company. The key question is this: whether the Blue Bus company be held liable for this accident based on this statistical information alone. According to civil law—which applies to cases such as this—the Blue Bus company should be held responsible if it is "more likely than not" that a Blue Bus killed the dog.

Gary Wells (1992) presented this case to students at the University of Alberta. He found that participants who were told that 80 percent of the buses on the route were owned by the Blue Bus company were extremely reluctant to assign guilt to the Blue Bus company on this basis; only 8 percent of them held the Blue Bus company liable. In another condition, participants were told that a weigh station attendant had seen a Blue Bus on that road earlier that day but that his reports tended to be only 80 percent accurate; remarkably, in this case, 67 percent of participants assigned responsibility for the accident to the Blue Bus company. Even though the probabilities were the same in each condition (80 percent), participants were much more swayed by eyewitness testimony than by statistical evidence (i.e., 67 percent versus 8 percent convictions). Interestingly, when Wells presented the Blue Bus case to experienced judges, he found that they were no more likely than university students to assign guilt based on statistical evidence alone.

Might there be conditions under which people would be willing to place more weight on statistical evidence? Edward Wright and colleagues (1996) designed a study to answer this question. They presented the Blue Bus case to students at St. Francis Xavier University, varying the amount of time participants had before presenting their verdict, to determine whether having a lot of time to think about this kind of evidence might cause people to rely on it more. Some participants were also given the opportunity to discuss the evidence with others, to see if group discussion might increase reliance on statistical evidence. However, neither extended decision-making time nor group discussion made participants more likely to assign guilt to the Blue Bus company (Wright et al., 1996).

Based on these findings, it appears that when considering different kinds of evidence, juries and judges tend to be persuaded by the kind of evidence that is most likely to be unreliable—the reports of other people. If eyewitnesses claim that they saw the person (or bus) in question, juries are likely to render a guilty verdict based on that testimony. The testimony of an expert witness—another kind of report from a person—is likely to be persuasive as well. Physical evidence and especially statistical evidence apparently are not very persuasive at all. In short, it seems that what is most likely to convince us of something is hearing another person say that it is so.

Juries: Group Processes in Action

Juries are of particular interest to social psychologists because the way they reach verdicts is directly relevant to social psychological research on group processes and social interaction. The right to be tried by a jury of one's peers has a long tradition in Canadian law. Trial by jury was an established institution in England at the beginning of the seventeenth century, and this tradition was adopted by Canada in 1867. Despite this tradition, the jury system has often come under attack. We have already discussed several cases in which juries in Canada have reached the wrong decision and convicted innocent people. A former dean of the Harvard Law School has noted, "Why should anyone think that 12 persons brought in from the street, selected in various ways for their lack of general ability, should have any special capacity for deciding controversies between persons?" (Kalven & Zeisel, 1966).

The jury system also has been criticized on grounds that jurors may lack the ability to understand complex evidence and reach a dispassionate verdict (Arkes & Mellers, 2002; Devine et al., 2001). According to research conducted at Simon Fraser University by Rose and Ogloff (2001), jury members' comprehension of the instructions given to them by judges is remarkably low. One of their studies revealed, for example, that participants acting as mock jurors understood just over 60 percent of what they had been told. Given that the fate of people's lives rests in jurors' hands, one would hope that jurors would clearly comprehend instructions from the judge.

'Tis with our judgments
as our watches,
None go just alike,
yet each believes his own.
—Alexander Pope, *Essay on
Criticism*, 1711

The jury system has its staunch supporters, of course, and few people argue that it should be abolished altogether. The point is that it is not a perfect system and that based on research in social psychology, there are ways we might expect it to go wrong. Problems can arise at each of three phases of a jury trial: the way in which jurors use information they obtain before the trial begins; the way in which they process information during the trial; and the way in which they deliberate in the jury room after all of the evidence has been presented.

Effects of Pretrial Publicity

Because the murder of Barbara Stoppel received considerable attention in the media, it is possible that members of the jury were influenced by media reports before the trial began. Even when the information reported by the media is accurate, it is often stacked against a suspect. The reason is simple: the press gets much of its information from the police and the Crown prosecutor, who are interested in presenting as strong a case as they can against the suspect (Imrich, Mullin, & Linz, 1995). Thus, it is not surprising that the more people hear about a case in the media, the more they believe that the suspect is guilty (Fulero, 2002; Kerr, 1995; Steblay et al., 1999).

The kind of emotional publicity that arouses public passions, such as lurid details about a murder, is especially biasing. In one study, researchers contacted people who had just finished serving on juries in Michigan and asked them to watch a videotaped trial of a man accused of robbing a supermarket. Before the jurors viewed the trial, the researchers exposed them either to emotional publicity (reports that a car matching the one used in the robbery struck and killed a seven-year-old girl after the robbery), to factual publicity (a report that the suspect had an extensive prior criminal record), or to no publicity. After watching the trial and deliberating in 12-member mock juries, the participants rated whether they would vote to convict the suspect. The emotional publicity biased jurors the most, significantly increasing the percentage of jurors who gave guilty

Estate of Mischa Richter and Harald Bakken

"Since you have already been convicted by the media, I imagine we can wrap this up pretty quickly."

verdicts—even though the jurors knew they were not supposed to be influenced by any information they had learned before viewing the trial (Kramer, Kerr, & Carroll, 1990).

What can be done to counter the effects of pretrial publicity? Judges and lawyers have a variety of strategies they use to try to remedy this problem. First, lawyers for both sides (i.e., the public and the accused) are allowed to question prospective jurors before the trial. The lawyers ask people whether they have heard anything about the case and, if so, whether they feel they can render an unbiased verdict. One problem with this approach, however, is that people are often unaware that they have been biased by pretrial publicity (Ogloff & Vidmar, 1994). In the Kramer, Kerr, and Carroll (1990) study just presented, for example, the researchers removed any jurors who said that because of the pretrial publicity, they could not form an unbiased opinion. Nonetheless, the emotional publicity still influenced the verdicts given by the remaining jurors.

Second, judges can instruct jurors to disregard what they have heard in the media. But these instructions do little to erase the effects of pretrial publicity and may even *increase* the likelihood that jurors use it (Fein, McCloskey, & Tomlinson, 1997; Kramer, Kerr, & Carroll, 1990; Shaw & Skolnick, 1995). It's very difficult to erase something from our minds once we have heard it. In fact, as discussed in Chapter 1, the more we try not to think about something, the more that very thing keeps popping into consciousness (Wegner, 1989, 1992, 1994).

Another problem with pretrial publicity is that linking a person's name with incriminating events can cause negative impressions of the person, even if the media explicitly deny any such connection. In one study, when participants read a headline denying any wrongdoing on someone's part—"Bob Talbert Not Linked with Mafia"—they had a more negative impression of the person than did participants who read an innocuous headline—"Bob Talbert Arrives in City" (Wegner et al., 1981). The mere mention of Bob Talbert and the Mafia in the same headline was enough to plant seeds of doubt in readers' minds, despite the headline's explicit denial of a connection. Thus, media reports can have unintended negative effects and, once there, those effects are hard to erase.

A study conducted at the University of Toronto found that pretrial publicity had the strongest effect when mock jurors were asked to pronounce a verdict right after hearing the publicity. When participants were given the opportunity to view a videotape of the trial, their decisions were more likely to be influenced by the evidence presented in the trial (Freedman, Martin, & Mota, 1998). One can only hope that the same holds true in actual trials. Obviously, the best solution is to include only jurors who have heard nothing about the case.

How Jurors Process Information during the Trial

How do individual jurors think about the evidence they hear during a trial? As we saw in Chapter 1, people often construct theories and schemas to interpret the world around them, and the same is true of jurors. Some psychologists suggest that jurors decide on one story that best explains all of the evidence; they then try to fit this story to the possible verdicts they are allowed to render. If one of those verdicts fits well with their preferred story, they are likely to vote to convict on that charge (Hastie & Pennington, 2000; Pennington & Hastie, 1992, 1993). This finding has important implications for how lawyers present their cases. Lawyers typically present the evidence in one of two ways. In the first, called *story order,* they present the evidence in the sequence in which events occurred, corresponding as closely as possible to the story they want the jurors to believe. In the second, called *witness order,* they present witnesses in the sequence they think will

"Your Honor, we're going to go with the prosecution's spin."

have the greatest impact, even if this means that events are described out of order. A lawyer might save his or her best witness for last, for example, so that the trial ends on a dramatic and memorable note, even if this witness describes events that occurred early in the alleged crime.

If you were a lawyer, in which order would you present the evidence? You probably can guess which order Pennington and Hastie hypothesized would be most successful. If jurors are ultimately swayed by the story or schema they think best explains the sequence of events, the best strategy should be to present the evidence in story order and not in witness order. To test this hypothesis, Pennington and Hastie (1988) asked mock jurors to listen to a simulated murder trial. The researchers varied the order in which the defence attorney and the prosecuting attorney presented their cases. In one condition, both used the story order, whereas, in another condition, both used the witness order. In other conditions, one attorney used the story order, whereas the other used the witness order.

The results provided clear and dramatic support for the story order strategy. As seen in Table 1.1, when the prosecutor used the story order and the defence used the witness order, the jurors were most likely to believe the prosecutor, as 78 percent voted to convict the defendant. When the prosecutor used the witness order and the defence used the story order, the tables were turned and only 31 percent voted to convict. Pennington and Hastie speculated that one reason the conviction rate in felony trials in the United States is so high—approximately 80 percent—is that, in real trials, prosecutors usually present evidence in story order, whereas defence attorneys usually use witness order. To those of our readers who are budding lawyers, remember this when you are preparing for your first trial!

Deliberations in the Jury Room

As any lawyer can tell you, a crucial part of the jury process occurs out of sight, when jurors deliberate before deciding on the verdict. Even if most jurors are inclined to vote to convict, there might be a persuasive minority that changes their fellow jurors' minds. Sometimes this can be a minority of one, as in the classic movie *12 Angry Men*. When this film begins, a jury has just finished listening to the evidence in a murder case and all of

Table 1.1	How should lawyers present their cases?

Lawyers can present their cases in a variety of ways. This study by Pennington and Hastie (1988) found that *story order*—in which lawyers present the evidence in the order that corresponds most closely to the "story" they want the jurors to believe—works better than *witness order*—the presentation of the evidence by witnesses.

Percentage of people voting to convict the defendant

Prosecution evidence	Defence evidence	
	Story order	Witness order
Story order	59%	78%
Witness order	31%	63%

(Adapted from Pennington & Hastie, 1988)

the jurors except one vote to convict the defendant. Over the next 90 minutes, however, the lone holdout—played by Henry Fonda—persuades his peers that there is reason to doubt that the young Hispanic defendant is guilty. At first, the other jurors pressure Fonda to change his mind using techniques of normative and informational conformity, but in the end reason triumphs and the other jurors come to see that the Fonda character is right.

As entertaining as this movie is, research indicates that it does not reflect the reality of most jury deliberations (Devine et al., 2001; Ellsworth & Mauro, 1998). Researchers have found that in 97 percent of cases, the jury's final decision was the same as the one favoured by a majority of the jurors on the initial vote (Kalven & Zeisel, 1966). Majority opinion usually carries the day, bringing dissenting jurors into line. And what happens if a dissenting juror does not succumb to pressure to go along with the majority opinion? This may have been the case in the third Sophonow trial, where jurors were unable to reach a unanimous verdict after five long days of deliberation—apparently because one juror refused to go along with the rest of the group. In a startling move, the judge dismissed this juror because she supposedly had claimed to possess "psychic powers and special gifts." The juror who was removed maintains that she said no such thing. Once the problematic juror was removed, the remaining 11 members swiftly rendered their guilty verdict.

If jury deliberation is stacked toward the initial, majority opinion, why not just abandon the deliberation process, letting the jury's initial vote determine a defendant's guilt or innocence? For two reasons, this would not be a good idea. First, forcing juries to reach a unanimous verdict makes them consider the evidence more carefully, rather than simply assuming that their initial impressions of the case were correct (Hastie, Penrod, & Pennington, 1983). Second, even if minorities seldom succeed in persuading the majority to change their minds about guilt or innocence, minorities often do change people's minds about how guilty a person is. In criminal trials, juries usually have some discretion about the type of guilty verdict they can reach. In a murder trial, for example, they can often decide whether to convict the defendant of first-degree murder, second-degree murder, or manslaughter. Pennington and Hastie (1990) found that people on a jury who have a minority point of view often convince the majority to change their minds about the specific verdict to render. Thus, while a minority of

> A court is no better than each ... of you sitting before me on this jury. A court is only as sound as its jury, and a jury is only as sound as the [people] who make it up.
> —Harper Lee, *To Kill a Mockingbird*, 1960

In the classic movie *12 Angry Men*, Henry Fonda convinces the rest of his fellow jurors to change their minds about a defendant's guilt. In real life, however, such cases of a minority in a jury convincing the majority to change the verdict are rare.

jurors is unlikely to convince a majority to change its verdict from first-degree murder to not guilty, they may well convince the majority to change the verdict to second-degree murder.

Why Do People Obey the Law?

Ultimately, the success of the legal system depends on keeping people out of it. We should, of course, find ways to improve the accuracy of eyewitness testimony and help juries make better decisions. Even more important, though, is finding ways to prevent people from committing crimes in the first place. We therefore close with a discussion of how to get people to obey the law.

Do Severe Penalties Deter Crime?

Crime rates have been dropping. For example, according to Statistics Canada (2005), the crime rate in 2004 was 12% lower than a decade ago (Statistics Canada, 2005). Analysts have attributed the decrease in crime to the aging of the population (most violent crimes are committed by adolescents and young adults), Canada's healthy economy, and new approaches to preventing and solving crimes. Similar reasons have been given for the decline in violent crime that has been observed in the United States; however, in 1997 the U.S. Attorney General at the time believed that stiffer penalties for crimes were at least partly responsible (Juveniles committing fewer violent crimes, 1997). It seems to make perfect sense that the harsher the penalty for a crime, the less likely people would be to commit it. As we have seen many times in this book, however, common sense is not always correct, and in the case of crime and prison sentences, the story is not as straightforward as it might seem.

Let's begin with a theory that stiff penalties do prevent crimes. **Deterrence theory** argues that people refrain from criminal activity because of the threat of legal

Deterrence theory the theory that people refrain from criminal activity because of the threat of legal punishment, as long as the punishment is perceived as relatively severe, certain, and swift

punishment, as long as the punishment is perceived as severe, certain, and swift (Carlsmith, Darley, & Robinson, 2002; Gibbs, 1985; Williams & Hawkins, 1986). Undoubtedly this theory is correct under some circumstances. As we mentioned in Chapter 11, Manitoba and Ontario have set up special family violence courts to ensure that penalties for domestic violence are relatively severe, certain, and swift. While it is too soon to tell whether these courts are effective in reducing family violence, the early signs are encouraging. Note that, because these courts combine certain, swift punishment with rehabilitation, it is difficult to determine whether reductions in violence are attributable to punishment or to rehabilitation, or to both.

Consider another example. Imagine you are heading to downtown Edmonton for an important interview one day and become ensnarled in a traffic jam. At last the traffic clears but, unless you hurry, you will be late. "Maybe I'll speed up just a little," you think, as the speedometer creeps up to 125 kilometres per hour. Your decision to exceed the speed limit was probably based on a consideration of the fact that you are unlikely to get caught and, if you are, the penalty won't be too severe. However, suppose you knew that the Yellowhead Trail is always patrolled by the Edmonton Police Service and that the penalty for speeding is a five-year prison sentence. Chances are, you would not dare to press too hard on the accelerator.

In this example, we have made a couple of important assumptions. First, we assumed that you know the penalties for speeding. Second, we assumed that you have control over your behaviour and that whether you speed is a rational decision that you make after reflecting on the consequences. For many crimes, however, these assumptions do not hold. Surveys have found that many people are ignorant of the penalties for different crimes; if they do not know what the penalties are, the penalties cannot act as a deterrent. (To see how well you know the penalties for various federal crimes, complete Try It! on page 32). Further, other types of crimes are not based on a rational decision-making process. Many murders, for example, are impulsive crimes of passion committed by people in highly emotional states, not by people who carefully weigh the pros and cons. In general, severe penalties will only work as a deterrent when people know what the penalties are, believe that they are relatively certain to be caught, and weigh the consequences before deciding whether to commit a crime.

> American legislators suffer from a monumental illusion in their belief that long prison sentences will reduce the crime rate.
> —Jack Gibbs, 1985

To illustrate these points, let's consider two different kinds of crimes: drunk driving and murder. The decision about whether to drink and drive is one that most of us can control; when we go to a party or a bar and know that we will be driving home afterward, we can decide how much we will drink. Given that this decision is a fairly rational one—at least, under most circumstances—we would expect that certain, severe penalties would act as a deterrent. Researchers in the United States have found some support for this conclusion by comparing states with different drunk driving laws. (Such research conducted in Canada, where penalties should be the same from province to province, given that drunk driving falls under the Criminal Code of Canada.) These U.S. studies have found that increasing the severity of penalties for drunk driving is not related, by itself, to lower alcohol-related, motor vehicle fatalities. Consistent with deterrence theory, however, increasing the certainty of being caught for drunk driving—by checking the blood alcohol level of all motorists stopped at sobriety checkpoints—is associated with lower alcohol-related accidents (Evans, Neville, & Graham, 1991; Stuster & Blowers, 1995; Voas, Holder, & Gruenewald, 1999). These results suggest that severity of the penalty itself does not act as a deterrent but that an increase in the certainty of being caught does.

try it! Are You Aware of the Penalties for Crimes?

Deterrence theory holds that legal penalties will prevent crimes if perceived to be severe, certain, and swift. If people are unaware that a crime has a severe penalty, however, those penalties cannot act as a deterrent. Are you aware of the penalties specified in the Criminal Code of Canada for the following crimes? Take the following quiz to find out.

What Are the Penalties for the Following Crimes?

1. First-degree murder (deliberate, planned murder). Note that first-degree murder charges also apply if someone dies as a result of another crime being committed (e.g., a bank teller or store clerk is killed during a robbery).

2. Second-degree murder (deliberate, but unplanned, murder)

3. Manslaughter (causing the death of another person accidentally or through carelessness)

4. Communication for prostitution

5. Break and enter

6. Drug trafficking

7. Impaired driving (or having a blood-alcohol content of more than 0.08)

8. False pretence (e.g., forging a cheque)

9. Assisting suicide

10. Sexual assault

ANSWERS

According to the Criminal Code of Canada, the following are the maximum and minimum penalties for the crimes listed above. (Note that, if a minimum penalty is not specified, there is no minimum penalty for that crime.)

1. First-degree murder. Maximum sentence: life imprisonment; minimum sentence: 25 years' imprisonment without parole

2. Second-degree murder. Maximum sentence: life imprisonment; minimum sentence: 10 years' imprisonment without parole

3. Manslaughter. Maximum sentence: Life imprisonment

4. Communication for prostitution. You may be surprised to learn that prostitution itself is not illegal in Canada, but communicating about it either verbally or nonverbally is illegal. The person offering sexual services or the person seeking sexual services can be charged. Maximum sentence: 6 months' imprisonment and $2000 fine

5. Break and enter. Of a home, the maximum sentence is life imprisonment; of another kind of building, the maximum sentence is 10 years' imprisonment.

6. Drug trafficking. Sentences vary depending on the drug being sold. For cocaine, the maximum sentence is life imprisonment. For steroids, the maximum sentence is 3 years' imprisonment.

7. Impaired driving. The maximum penalty is 5 years' imprisonment. If it is a first offence, the minimum penalty is a $300 fine. If it is a second offence, the minimum penalty is 14 days' imprisonment.

8. False pretence. Maximum sentence: 10 years' imprisonment

9. Assisting suicide. Maximum sentence: 14 years' imprisonment

10. Sexual assault. The maximum penalty is 10 years' imprisonment; minimum penalty: 4 years' imprisonment. If a firearm is used, the maximum penalty is 14 years' imprisonment.

Now consider a very different crime and a very different penalty—murder and capital punishment. Canadians who favour capital punishment tend to believe that it has a deterrent effect (Haddock & Zanna, 1998; Vidmar, 1974), even though capital punishment has been abolished in Canada. A majority of Americans support the death penalty for murder, in part, because they believe that it acts as a deterrent. Of course, there is no more severe penalty than death, and if the death penalty prevents even a few murders, it might be worth it—or so the argument goes. To see if this argument is valid, several

◀ Increasing the certainty of being caught for drunk driving—by checking the blood alcohol level of every motorist stopped at a sobriety checkpoint like this one—is associated with fewer alcohol-related accidents.

studies have compared the murder rates in states that have the death penalty with those that do not; the murder rates in states before and after they adopted the death penalty; and the murder rates in other countries before and after they adopted the death penalty. The results are clear: There is no evidence that the death penalty prevents murders (Archer & Gartner, 1984; Bedau, 1997; Ellsworth & Mauro, 1998; Sorenson et al., 1999).

Opponents of the death penalty point out, as we mentioned earlier, that most murders are crimes of passion that are not preceded by a rational consideration of the consequences. Because people are not considering the consequences of their actions, the death penalty does not act as a deterrent. Further, the mistakes made whereby innocent people have been sentenced to death add up to an astonishing number.

Proponents of the death penalty say that severity of the crime is not enough; as argued by deterrence theory, severe penalties must be applied with certainty and speed. The last of these conditions is almost never met in the United States. The time between a conviction for murder and the execution of the murderer is often many years, because of the slowness of the judicial system and the many avenues of appeal open to prisoners on death row. Were the process speeded up, this argument goes, the death penalty *could* act as a deterrent.

While this is an empirical question, there is reason to doubt that the death penalty would act as a deterrent, even if it were applied swiftly. We refer to a few studies that have found that executions are followed not by a decrease but by an *increase* in murders (Archer & Gartner, 1984; Bailey & Peterson, 1997). This might seem like a bizarre finding; why would the execution of a convicted murderer *increase* the likelihood that someone else would commit a murder? As we saw, observing someone else commit a violent act weakens people's inhibitions against aggression, leads to imitation of aggression, and numbs their sense of horror over violence. Could it be that observing the government put someone to death lowers other people's inhibitions, making them more likely to commit murders? While the data are not conclusive, this argument makes eminent social psychological sense—and there is some evidence to support it (Bailey & Peterson, 1997).

Procedural Justice: People's Sense of Fairness

We have just seen that one reason people obey the law is their fear of being caught and punished. An even more important reason, however, is their moral values about what constitutes good behaviour. People will obey a law if they think that it is just, even if they are unlikely to be caught breaking it. For example, many people are honest on their tax returns because they think that cheating is wrong, not because they fear being caught for cheating. Thus, if you were a lawmaker, you could try to prevent crime in two ways. You could increase the penalties for breaking the law and the probability that people will be caught, or you could try to convince people that the law is just and fair. As we have seen, the former approach is difficult and sometimes ineffective. If we wanted to prevent people from driving through red lights, we could increase the penalties for doing so and station a police officer at every intersection; it would be far simpler, however, to convince people that it is wrong to run red lights, so that they comply with the law even when no police officers are around.

What determines whether people think a law is just? One important factor is their perception of the fairness of legal proceedings. **Procedural justice** is defined as people's judgments about the fairness of the procedures used to determine outcomes, such as whether they are innocent or guilty of a crime (Blader & Tyler, 2003; Heuer et al., 2002; Kelley & Thibaut, 1978; Miller & Ratner, 1996; Skarlicki, Ellard, & Kelln, 1998; Tyler et al., 1997; Wenzel, 2000). People who feel that they have been treated fairly are more likely to comply with the law than are people who feel that they have been treated unfairly (Tyler, 1990). Consider, for example, what happens when the police are called because of a domestic assault. What determines whether the person accused of assault will repeat this crime in the future? It turns out that one factor is whether suspects feel that they were treated fairly by the police (Misconceptions about why people obey laws, 1997).

As another example, imagine that you receive a traffic ticket for failing to stop at a stop sign. You believe that the ticket is unfair because your view of the stop sign was obstructed by branches from a large tree that should have been trimmed by the city. You decide to go to court to protest the ticket. You take photographs of the tree, make careful diagrams of the intersection, and spend hours practising your testimony before your friends. Finally, your day in court arrives. Now, imagine that one of two things occurs. In the first scenario, your ticket is dismissed without a hearing because the officer who gave you the ticket could not appear in court that day. In the second scenario, you get to present your case. The judge listens carefully, asks you a number of questions, and compliments you on your photographs and diagrams. After carefully considering all the facts, however, she rules against you, arguing that the stop sign, while obstructed, was still visible. Which outcome would you prefer—the first or the second? Surely, the first one, you might think, because there you receive a positive outcome: no fine, no points on your driving record, no increase in your insurance rates. Research by Tom Tyler (1990), however, suggests that people prefer the second scenario. There, even though the outcome was negative, people have a greater sense of procedural justice—they had their day in court and were treated with fairness and respect. It is often more important to people to maintain a sense of procedural justice than to receive positive outcomes.

In summary, social psychological research indicates that the Canadian legal system can go wrong in a number of ways. Juries rely heavily on eyewitness testimony, when in fact

Procedural justice people's judgments about the fairness of the procedures used to determine outcomes, such as whether they are innocent or guilty of a crime

such testimony is often in error. Determining when witnesses are telling the truth is difficult, even with the use of polygraphs. And because juries are groups of people who try to reach consensus by discussing, arguing, and bargaining. By illuminating these problems in their research, however, social psychologists can help initiate change in the legal system—change that will lead to greater fairness and equity and to a greater sense of procedural justice. Most important of all, heeding psychological research on these questions might reduce the number of cases in which people like Thomas Sophonow languish in prison for crimes they did not commit.

Summary

Many social psychological principles predict how people will respond in the legal arena. Because of the limitations of memory, eyewitness testimony is often inaccurate. Several factors bias the **acquisition, storage,** and **retrieval** of what people observe, sometimes leading to the false identification of criminals. For example, research on the **own-race bias** shows that people find it more difficult to recognize members of other races than members of their own race. Research on **reconstructive memory** indicates that errors in **source monitoring** can occur, whereby people become confused about where they saw or heard something. Jurors often place a great deal of faith in eyewitness testimony, even though memories can be unreliable or influenced by later suggestions, and jurors are not very good at determining when someone is lying. The **polygraph** is also an imperfect measure of lie detection. As a result, false testimony by eyewitnesses and others sometimes goes undetected. Researchers have tried to develop ways of improving eyewitness testimony, but neither hypnosis nor the **cognitive interview** has been very successful at improving eyewitness accuracy.

There is a great deal of controversy over another form of eyewitness testimony, namely the accuracy of people's memories about their own past traumatic experiences. How valid are **recovered memories**—the sudden recollection of events, such as sexual abuse, that had been forgotten or repressed? Though recovered memories may be true in some instances, they can also be the result of **false memory syndrome,** whereby people come to believe the memory is true when actually it is not. False memories are especially likely to occur when an authoritative person suggests to us that an event occurred.

Other kinds of evidence are admitted in court as well, including expert testimony, physical evidence, and statisti-cal evidence (i.e., information on the probability that the accused committed the crime). People generally do not find physical or statistical evidence convincing, preferring instead to rely on eyewitness testimony, despite its inaccuracies.

Juries are of particular interest to social psychologists because the way they reach verdicts is directly relevant to social psychological research on group processes and social interaction. Jurors are susceptible to the same kinds of biases and social pressures we documented in earlier chapters. They are sometimes biased by pretrial publicity, even when trying to put it out of their minds. During a trial, jurors attempt to make sense of the testimony and often decide on one story that explains all of the evidence. Juries are thus most swayed by lawyers who present the evidence in a way that tells a consistent story. During deliberations, jurors with minority views are often pressured into conforming to the view of the majority; as a result, verdicts usually correspond to the initial feelings of the majority of jurors.

It is also important to examine people's perceptions of the legal system, because these perceptions have a lot to do with how likely people are to obey the law. **Deterrence theory** holds that people refrain from criminal activity if they view penalties as severe, certain, and swift. Deterrence theory may be correct about crimes that are the result of rational thought about the consequences, but it is unlikely to apply to crimes of passion that are not rational, such as many murders. There is no evidence that the death penalty deters murder, and there is even some evidence that it leads to an increase in the murder rate. Finally, people are more likely to obey the law if their sense of **procedural justice** is high; that is, if they believe that the procedures used to determine guilt or innocence are fair.

Thinking Critically

1. List several ways in which people can be falsely convicted of a crime, according to psychological research. What can be done to prevent such false convictions?

2. Take three key concepts from this module and discuss how they are related to theories and research from previous chapters in the text. In what ways does basic research in social psychology speak to legal issues?

3. If you could design your own society, what would you do to keep the crime rate low? What are the pros and cons of different approaches, according to social psychological research?

If You Are Interested

Anderson, B., with Anderson, D. (1998). *Manufacturing guilt: Wrongful convictions in Canada*. Halifax, NS: Fernwood Books. This book recounts the cases of six wrongful convictions in Canada, including those of Guy Paul Morin, David Milgaard, and Donald Marshall, and takes a critical look at the Canadian justice system.

Canadian Psychology (2001). Special section—Expert testimony, *42*, 2. This special issue of *Canadian Psychology* presents different perspectives on the use of expert testimony in legal proceedings, with contributions by psychologists, a lawyer, and a Supreme Court judge.

Hafer, C. L., & Olson, J. M. (2003). An analysis of empirical research on the scope of justice. *Personality and Social Psychology Review, 7,* 311–323. This review article, written by two prominent Canadian social psychologists, addresses the important question: "Why do people behave in negative and seemingly unjust ways toward others?" Three perspectives on this issue are offered. Research relevant to these perspectives is discussed and evaluated. A very thought-provoking analysis of the concept of justice.

Lumet, Sydney (Director). (1957). *12 Angry Men* [Film]. A classic film in which a character, played by Henry Fonda, convinces all of his fellow jurors that a defendant accused of murder is innocent. As discussed in the chapter, the film is an interesting depiction of jury decision making but does not reflect actual jury outcomes. In real life, a lone juror seldom succeeds in changing the minds of the other 11 jurors.

Roesch, R., Hart, S. D., & Ogloff, J. R. P. (Eds.). (1999). *Psychology and the law: The state of the discipline*. New York: Kluwer Academic/Plenum. A collection of chapters about law and psychology by leading researchers in the field. Topics include eyewitness testimony, jury decision making, predicting violence in mentally disordered populations, and issues concerning children and the law. Several chapters were contributed by Canadian psychologists, including the editors, who are all at Simon Fraser University.

Schuller, R. A., & Ogloff, J. R. P. (Eds.). (2001). *Introduction to psychology and law: Canadian perspectives*. University of Toronto Press. A state-of-the-art synopsis of research on psychology and the law, particularly as it applies to the Canadian legal system. Regina Schuller is a professor of psychology at York University, and James Ogloff is a professor and the director of the program in law and forensic psychology at Simon Fraser University. Individual chapters were written by prominent Canadian scholars of psychology and the law. A must-read for any student interested in psychology and law.

Spanos, N. P. (1996). *Multiple identities and false memories*. Washington, DC: American Psychological Association Press. This book, written by a Carleton University psychologist, illustrates the extreme ways in which memories for events can become distorted. Section II of the book, Creating False Memories, is especially relevant to this module.

Williams, Stephen (Director). (1999). *Hardtime: The David Milgaard story* [Docudrama]. This acclaimed CTV film, winner of six Gemini awards in 1999, depicts the tragic, moving story of the wrongful conviction of David Milgaard, who spent 23 years in prison for a murder he did not commit. The film also documents the long, difficult fight to prove Milgaard's innocence.

Weblinks

www.acjnet.org
Access to Justice Network

This site contains very useful links to Canadian law and justice resource material, including legislation, organizations, databases, and discussions.

www.sarmac.org
The Society for Applied Research in Memory and Cognition (SARMAC)

This site contains abstracts of SARMAC conference papers and links to journals, including studies dealing with eyewitness testimony.

www.skeptic.com/02.3.hochman-fms.html
Recovered Memory Therapy and False Memory Syndrome

This site discusses recovered memory therapy and false memory syndrome.

www.brown.edu/Departments/Taubman_Center/Recovmem/Archive.html
The Recovered Memory Project

A detailed look at the operation of recovered memory in legal proceedings and case studies. Includes links to other studies and criticisms of theories of recovered memory, including ideas about false memory syndrome.

www.psychologymatters.org
Psychology Matters

On this site posted by the American Psychological Association, you can click on "Law/Justice" for articles pertaining to the topics discussed in this module.

Chapter 2
The Psychology of Police Investigations

The Psychology of Police Investigations

Mark Jackson was arrested for shooting a man inside a convenience store. Upon his arrest, he was taken to the police station for questioning. Over the course of a 24-hour period, Mark was interrogated on five separate occasions. The last interrogation took place at 2:00 A.M. Although Mark stated he was exhausted, he was told the interrogation would not take long and that it was best to get things over with. In reality, the interrogation lasted for more than three hours.

Initially, Mark maintained that, although he was at the store on the day of the shooting, he had nothing to do with the crime. However, throughout his interrogations the police challenged him, stating they had hard evidence proving he was the killer. This evidence not only included a security video but several eyewitnesses. None of this evidence actually existed. In addition, the police minimized the seriousness of the crime stating that the victim was a known drug dealer who "had it coming" and that Mark "did everyone a favour."

> *Over the course of his interrogations, the police continually pressured Mark to stop denying his involvement in the crime and said that if he told the truth "all of this would end." Finally, during his last interrogation, Mark admitted to the shooting. The case went to court and Mark was convicted, largely on the basis of his confession. Months later it was discovered that he had not committed the crime. Mark Jackson had confessed to a crime he had nothing to do with.*

PSYCHOLOGY AND THE INVESTIGATIVE PROCESS

Forensic psychology plays an important role in many aspects of police work. One aspect we have yet to discuss, however, is psychology's role in criminal investigations, such as the investigation described above. Many people are aware that psychology is used in criminal investigations and recent movies have done much to promote this fact. However, as you will see throughout this chapter, psychology played an important role in the investigative process long before Hollywood became interested in the topic, and it continues to do so today.

Psychologists have identified a number of key investigative tasks where psychology is particularly relevant. One of these tasks relates to the collection and evaluation of investigative information—information that is often obtained from suspects. Another relates to investigative decision making, especially decisions that require an in-depth understanding of criminal behaviour. This chapter will focus on how psychology contributes to these tasks by looking first at how the police interrogate suspects, and some possible consequences of their interrogation practices, and then by examining the practice of profiling the characteristics of criminals based on the way they commit their crimes.

POLICE INTERROGATIONS

Confession evidence is often viewed as "a prosecutor's most potent weapon" (Kassin, 1997, p. 221). In some countries, people may be convicted solely on the basis of their confession, although in Canada and the United States, a confession usually has to be backed up by some other form of evidence (Gudjonsson, 1992a). Regardless of whether corroborative evidence is required, it is a well-established fact that people who confess to a crime are more likely to be prosecuted and convicted than those who do not. Indeed, some legal scholars have gone so far as to claim that a confession makes other aspects of a trial unnecessary, because "the real trial, for all practical purposes, occurs when the confession is obtained" (McCormick, 1972, p. 316). Given the importance of confession evidence, it should come as no surprise that, although one of the goals of a **police interrogation** is to gain information that furthers the investigation, such as the location of important evidence, the other goal is to obtain a confession from the suspect (Kassin, 1997).

Being interrogated by the police for the purpose of extracting a confession is often considered to be inherently coercive. Imagine yourself being interrogated for the very first time. You would probably be in an environment that is foreign to you, faced with one, possibly two, police officers whom you have never met. You would know little of what the police officers are going to do to you and would have no one to turn to for support. Even if you were innocent of the crime in question, the situation would no doubt be an extremely intimidating one. In large part, this is due to the fact that police interrogators are part of a system that gives them certain powers over the suspect (Gudjonsson, 1992a).

There is no question that police interrogations were coercive in the past. Consider police tactics in the mid-twentieth century, for example, when whipping suspects was a common method used to obtain confessions (e.g., *Brown v. Mississippi*, 1936). Or consider a more recent episode occurring in the 1980s, where New York City police officers jolted a suspect with a stun gun in order to extract a confession (Huff, Rattner, & Sagarin, 1996). Although these overt acts of physical coercion have become much less frequent with time, they have been replaced with more subtle psychologically based interrogation techniques (Leo, 1992), such as lying about evidence, promising lenient treatment, and implying threats to loved ones. Although not all interrogators use these strategies, police officers often view these techniques as a necessary evil in order to obtain confessions from guilty persons. Indeed, leading authorities in the field of interrogation training openly state that, because offenders are so reluctant to confess, they must often be tricked into doing so (Inbau et al., 2001).

The extent to which some police officers use trickery and deceit in their interrogations has recently been made clear by Wakefield and Underwager (1998, p. 428):

> Police freely admit deceiving suspects and lying to induce confessions. Police have fabricated evidence, made false claims about witnesses to a crime, and falsely told suspects whatever they thought would succeed in obtaining a confession. They have lied about the suspect's culpability, assuring him that his behaviour was understandable and not really blameworthy, or telling him that if he described what happened, the victim could be helped. They have falsely told suspects that they had physical evidence such as footprints, fingerprints, or semen, that a co-defendant had confessed, that the weapon used in the crime had been found, that the suspect failed a lie detector, and that there was medical proof of sexual molestation.

Police officers around the world now receive specialized training in exactly how to extract confessions from suspects. Depending on where this training is provided, different approaches are taught. For example, as discussed later in this chapter, police officers in England are trained to use interrogation techniques that are far less coercive than those used in North America (Sear & Williamson, 1999). This is primarily because courts in England have begun to recognize some of the potential problems associated with coercive interrogation practices, such as increasing the likelihood of false confessions (Meissner & Russano, 2003).

Before moving on to discuss these potential problems and exploring some possible ways they can be prevented, let us look closely at the format of police interrogations as they typically take place across North America.

The Reid Model of Interrogation

The most common interrogation training program offered to U.S. and Canadian police officers is based on a book written by Inbau, Reid, Buckley, and Jayne (2001) called *Criminal Interrogation and Confessions*. Within this manual, the authors describe the now-famous **Reid model** of interrogation, a technique originally developed by John E. Reid, a polygrapher from Chicago, that has been taught to more than 300 000 police investigators since 1974 (Meissner & Russano, 2003).

A police officer interrogating a suspect

At a general level, the Reid model consists of a three-part process. The first stage is to gather evidence related to the crime and to interview witnesses and victims. The second stage is to conduct a nonaccusatorial interview of the suspect to assess any evidence of deception (i.e., to determine whether the suspect is guilty or not). The third stage is to conduct an accusatorial interrogation of the suspect (if he or she is perceived to be guilty) in which a nine-step procedure is implemented, with the primary objective being to secure a confession (Inbau et al., 2001).

This nine-step procedure in stage three consists of the following steps:

1. The suspect is immediately confronted with his or her guilt. If the police do not have any evidence against the suspect at this time, this fact can be hidden and, if necessary, the interrogator can pretend that such evidence exists.

2. Psychological themes are then developed that allow the suspect to justify, rationalize, or excuse the crime. For example, a suspected rapist may be told that the victim must have been asking for it.

3. Any statements of denial by the suspect are interrupted by the interrogator to ensure the suspect does not get the upper hand in the interrogation.

4. The interrogator overcomes the suspect's objections to the charges to a point at which the suspect becomes quiet and withdrawn.

5. Once the suspect has become withdrawn, the interrogator ensures that the suspect does not tune out of the interrogation by reducing the psychological distance between the interrogator and the suspect, such as by physically moving closer to the suspect.

6. Sympathy and understanding are then exhibited by the interrogator and the suspect is urged to come clean. For example, the interrogator might try to appeal to the suspect's sense of decency.

7. The suspect is offered face-saving explanations for the crime, which makes self-incrimination easier to achieve.

8. Once the suspect accepts responsibility for the crime (typically by agreeing with one of the face-saving explanations), the interrogator develops this admission into a full confession.

9. Finally, the interrogator gets the suspect to write and sign a full confession.

The Reid model of interrogation is based on the idea that suspects do not confess to crimes they have committed because they fear the potential consequences that await them if they do (Inbau et al., 2001). In addition, their fear of the potential consequences is not sufficiently outweighed by their internal feelings of anxiety associated with remaining deceptive (i.e., by maintaining they did not commit the crime in question). The goal of the Reid model, therefore, is to reverse this state of affairs, by making the "perceived consequences of a confession … more desirable than the anxiety generated by the deception" (Gudjonsson, 1992a, p. 62). It is assumed that the consequences of confessing and the anxiety of remaining deceptive can be manipulated by the interrogator through the use of psychologically based techniques, such as the ones described above (Jayne, 1986). For example, many believe that providing the suspect with a way to rationalize his or her behaviour can reduce the perceived consequences of confessing. Conversely, focusing on feelings of guilt can increase the anxiety associated with deception.

Police Interrogation Techniques

Techniques used in the Reid model of interrogation can be broken down into two general categories. These categories are often referred to by different names, including friendly and unfriendly techniques, Mutt and Jeff techniques, and minimization and maximization techniques. You will probably know them as good cop/bad cop techniques. Throughout this chapter, the labels minimization and maximization will be used to refer to the categories, since these terms are the most commonly accepted.

Minimization techniques refer to "soft sell" tactics used by police interrogators that are designed to "lull the suspect into a false sense of security" (Kassin, 1997, p. 223). These tactics include the use of sympathy, excuses, and justifications. For example, when the interrogator in the opening scenario suggested to Mark Jackson that the victim "had it coming" because he was a drug dealer, and that Mark "did everyone a favour" by shooting the victim, that interrogator was using minimization techniques. In contrast to minimization techniques, **maximization techniques** refer to "scare tactics" that interrogators often use "to intimidate a suspect believed to be guilty" (Kassin, 1997, p. 223). This intimidation is typically achieved by exaggerating the seriousness of the offence and by making false claims about evidence the police supposedly have.

The use of the nonexistent eyewitnesses in the opening scenario is an example of such a scare tactic.

Kassin and McNall (1991) showed that the use of these techniques might send a message to the suspect that he or she will be treated in a particular way. Specifically, they found that the use of minimization techniques "implies an offer of leniency," while the use of maximization techniques "communicates an implicit threat of punishment" (Kassin, 1997, p. 224). This is an extremely important finding because the courts regularly disregard confession evidence if the confession is obtained using explicit threats (i.e., maximization tactics), but they often accept confession evidence if it is obtained through more implicit means (i.e., minimization tactics) (Kassin, 1997). This happens even though the message being sent by a police officer using minimization tactics might not be so implicit to the suspect.

Potential Problems with the Reid Model of Interrogation

Because the Reid model of interrogation is used so extensively in North America, it has been the subject of much research. This research indicates that a number of potential problems are associated with the technique. Three problems in particular deserve our attention. The first two relate to the ability of investigators to detect deception (Ekman & O'Sullivan, 1991) and to biases that may result when an interrogator believes a suspect is guilty (Kassin, Goldstein, & Savitsky, 2003). The third problem, which has received much more attention from researchers, has to do with the coercive nature of certain interrogation practices and the possibility that these practices will result in false confessions (Ofshe & Leo, 1997). We will discuss the first two problems here and reserve our discussion of false confessions for the next section of this chapter.

DETECTING DECEPTION A more thorough discussion of **deception detection** will be provided, so our discussion here will be limited to how deception detection relates to police interrogations. The issue of whether investigators are effective deception detectors is an important one, especially when using the Reid model of interrogation, because the actual interrogation of a suspect begins only after an initial interview has allowed the interrogator to determine whether the suspect is guilty (Inbau et al., 2001). The decision to commence a full-blown police interrogation, therefore, relies on an accurate assessment of whether the suspect is being deceptive when he or she claims to be innocent.

There is currently very little research available to suggest that police officers can detect deception with any degree of accuracy (e.g., Ekman & O'Sullivan, 1991). This often appears to be true even after police officers receive specialized training (Köhnken, 1987), but there have been some recent exceptions in Canada (e.g., Porter, Woodworth, & Birt, 2000). As a result, it seems likely that the decision to interrogate a suspect when using the Reid model of interrogation will often be based on an incorrect determination that the suspect is guilty (Kassin et al., 2003).

INVESTIGATOR BIAS The second related problem with the Reid model of interrogation is that the police begin their interrogation believing that the suspect is guilty. The problem here is that when people form a belief about something before they enter a situation, they often unknowingly seek out and interpret information in that situation in a way that verifies their initial belief (Kassin et al., 2003). A recent study by Kassin and his colleagues (2003) demonstrates some of the potential dangers that can result from this particular form of **investigator bias**.

In a mock interrogation study, the researchers had students act as interrogators or suspects. Some of the interrogators were led to believe the suspect was guilty of a mock crime (finding a hidden key and stealing $100 from a locked cabinet), while others were led to believe the suspect was innocent. In reality, some of the suspects were guilty of the mock crime whereas others were innocent. Interrogators were instructed to devise an interrogation strategy to use on the suspects, and the suspects were told to deny any involvement in the crime and to convince the interrogator of their innocence. The interrogation was taped and a group of neutral observers then listened to the tape and were asked questions about the interrogator and the suspect.

A number of important results emerged from this study:

1. Interrogators with guilty expectations asked more questions that indicated their belief in the suspect's guilt. For example, they would ask, "How did you find the key that was hidden behind the VCR?" instead of "Do you know anything about the key that was hidden behind the VCR?"

2. Interrogators with guilty expectations used a higher frequency of interrogation techniques compared with interrogators with innocent expectations, especially at the outset of the interrogation.

3. Interrogators with guilty expectations judged more suspects to be guilty, regardless of whether the suspect was actually guilty.

4. Interrogators indicated that they exerted more pressure on suspects to confess when, unbeknownst to them, the suspect was innocent.

5. Suspects had fairly accurate perceptions of interrogator behaviour (i.e., innocent suspects believed their interrogators were exerting more pressure).

6. Neutral observers viewed interrogators with guilty expectations as more coercive, especially against innocent suspects, and they viewed suspects in the guilty expectation condition as more defensive.

In sum, these findings indicate that "investigative biases led to coercive and pressure-filled interrogations that, in turn, caused suspects to appear more 'defensive' and 'guilty' even when they were not guilty of the crime being investigated" (Meissner & Russano, 2003, p. 57).

Interrogation Practices and the Courts

The decision to admit confession evidence into court rests on the shoulders of the trial judge. Within North America, the key issues a judge must consider when faced with a questionable confession are whether the confession was made voluntarily and whether the defendant was competent when he or she provided the confession (Wakefield & Underwager, 1998). The reason for using these criteria is that involuntary confessions and confessions provided when a person's mind is unstable are more likely to be unreliable.

What is meant by "voluntary" and "competent" is not always clear, which is why debate continues over the issue. What does seem clear, however, is that confessions resulting from overt forms of coercion will not be admitted in court. As Kassin (1997) states, "A confession is typically excluded if it was elicited by brute force; prolonged isolation; deprivation of food or sleep; threats of harm or punishment; promises of immunity or leniency; or, barring exceptional circumstances, without notifying the suspect of his or her constitutional rights" (p. 221).

Conversely, confessions that result from more subtle forms of psychological coercion are regularly admitted into court, both in Canada and the United States. For example, in the recent Canadian case of *R. v. Oickle* (2000), Richard Oickle confessed to seven counts of arson occurring in and around Waterville, Nova Scotia, between 1994 and 1995. On appeal, the Supreme Court of Canada ruled that his confession was properly admitted by the trial judge, and therefore his conviction should stand, despite the use of some questionable interrogation techniques. These interrogation tactics included exaggerating the infallibility of a polygraph exam, implying that psychiatric help would be provided if the defendant confessed, minimizing the seriousness of the crimes, and suggesting that a confession would spare Oickle's girlfriend from having to undergo a stressful interrogation.

So, if these sorts of interrogation practices are condoned by the court, what sorts of practices are not? Box 2.1 on the next page provides a brief account of another recent Canadian case, *R. v. Hoilett* (1999), in which the Ontario Court of Appeals did rule that the defendant's confession was involuntary and therefore should not have been admitted at his trial. This ruling gives some indication as to how far Canadian police officers can go with their coercive interrogation tactics before it is considered too far by the courts.

Recent Changes to Interrogation Procedures

Due to the potential problems that can result from using coercive interrogation tactics, police agencies in several countries have recently introduced changes to their procedures. Perhaps more than anywhere else, these changes have been most obvious in England, where courts have restricted the use of many techniques found in the Reid model of interrogation (Gudjonsson, 1992a).

Over the last 20 years, police agencies in England have gone through several phases of change in an attempt to reduce oppressive interrogation practices. Currently, these agencies use the so-called PEACE model to guide their interrogations (PEACE is an acronym for *planning* and *preparation, engage* and *explain, account, closure,* and *evaluation*). According to Meissner and Russano (2003), this model provides an inquisitorial framework within which to conduct police interrogations (compared

BOX 2.1 WHEN THE POLICE GO TOO FAR: THE CASE OF *R. V. HOILETT*

Hoilett was arrested for sexual assault in Toronto at 11:25 P.M. on November 28, 1997. At the time of his arrest, Hoilett was under the influence of alcohol and crack cocaine. He was taken to the police station and placed in a cell. At 1:24 A.M. on November 29, police officers came to Hoilett's cell to remove his clothing in order for them to be forensically examined. All of his clothing was taken, including his underwear, shoes, and socks, and he was left naked in his cell with only a metal bed to sit on for one-and-a-half hours.

Shortly before 3:06 A.M., Hoilett was awakened and given some light clothes, but no underwear, and shoes that did not fit. When he asked for a tissue to wipe his nose, the police officers did not provide him with one. Hoilett was then taken from his cell to be interrogated. The interviewing officer was aware that Hoilett had consumed alcohol and crack cocaine that evening but believed the suspect was not impaired during the interrogation, only tired, which was why he kept nodding off. Although Hoilett was detained and under arrest, the interviewing officer testified that "the reason he proceeded with the interview at that hour . . . was because he was not sure he would have another opportunity to do so" (*R. v. Hoilett*, 1999, para. 5).

Hoilett made an incriminating statement to the police at this time, and the trial judge ruled that the statement was made voluntarily and knowingly and therefore it was admis-sible. In his ruling, the trial judge recognized and openly disapproved of the inhumane conduct of the police in this case. However, the judge concluded that the free will of the defendant was not affected by this treatment, and Hoilett was convicted on one count of sexual assault.

On appeal before the Ontario Court of Appeals, the court pointed out that, in reaching his conclusion that Hoilett's confession was voluntary, "the trial judge made no reference to . . . the accused's testimony where he said that his decision to speak was influenced by how cold he was and that he needed a tissue, and that the officers suggested these things could be made available to him after the interrogation" (para. 23). The Court of Appeals went on to state that "virtually everyone would have their . . . will to say no to the police significantly influenced by . . . receiving inhumane treatment . . . " (para. 25).

Referring to whether Hoilett was competent at the time he made his statement, the Court of Appeals added that there was substantial evidence he was not (e.g., Hoilett was awakened and interviewed at 3:00 A.M., he stated he was tired, and on several occasions the interrogators had to ask him whether he was awake).

As a result of their findings, the Ontario Court of Appeals reversed the decision of the trial judge, ruled that the statement of the accused was involuntary, and ordered that a new trial be held.

with the accusatorial framework used in the Reid model) and is based on an interview method known as conversation management that encourages information gathering more so than securing a confession. Although little research has been conducted to examine the impact of this new model, some research indicates that a decrease in the use of coercive interrogation tactics does not necessarily result in a substantial reduction in the number of confessions that can be obtained (Meissner & Russano, 2003).

Although North American police agencies appear more hesitant to modify their interrogation techniques, videotaping interrogations is a growing practice (Kassin, 1997). Indeed, according to Kassin (1997), approximately one third of all large police agencies in the United States videotape at least some interrogations, and 97% of police agencies that have videotaped confessions have found the videotapes useful. In addition, since various court rulings in the mid-1990s (e.g., *R. v. Barrett*, 1993), the videotaping of interrogations by the police has become common practice in Canada. Videotaping police interrogations seems a wise move for a variety of reasons. For example, White (1997) suggests that, by videotaping an interrogation, the police can protect themselves against false allegations of coercive practices, suspects can be assured they will not be subjected to interrogation methods that potentially lead to false confessions, and the courts can make more informed judgments about the appropriateness of police tactics.

FALSE CONFESSIONS

Perhaps the biggest problem that people have with the use of coercive interrogation tactics is that these techniques can contribute to the likelihood of suspects making **false confessions** (Gudjonsson, 1992a). False confessions can be defined in a number of ways. However, Ofshe (1989) provides a definition that appears to be well accepted. He suggests that a confession should be considered false "if it is elicited in response to a demand for a confession and is either intentionally fabricated or is not based on actual knowledge of the facts that form its content" (p. 13). When false confessions do occur, they should be taken seriously, especially considering the weight that juries put on confessions when determining the guilt or innocence of a defendant (Kassin & Sukel, 1997). Research indicates that when people have been wrongfully convicted of a crime, a false confession is often to blame. For example, Scheck, Neufeld, and Dwyer (2000) discovered that, in the 70 cases of wrongful convictions they examined, 21% included confession evidence that was later found to be false.

Before moving on to examine the extent of this problem, it is important to define two additional terms that are often confused with false confessions: **retracted confessions** and **disputed confessions**. As defined by Gudjonsson (1992a), "A retracted confession consists of a suspect or defendant declaring that the self-incriminating admission or confession he made is false . . . . This does not necessarily mean that the confession that the suspect made is false, because guilty people as well as innocent people may retract their confession" (p. 220). Disputed confessions, however, are confessions that are disputed at trial. This does not necessarily mean the confession is false or that it was retracted. Instead, disputed confessions may arise due to legal technicalities, or because the suspect disputes the confession was ever made (Gudjonsson, 1992a).

The Frequency of False Confessions

Most researchers readily admit that no one knows how frequently false confessions are made (e.g., Kassin, 1997). The major problem is that in most cases it is almost impossible to determine whether a confession is actually false. The fact that a confession is coerced does not mean the confession is false, just as a conviction based on confession evidence does not mean the confession is true (Kassin, 1997). As a result of this problem, researchers come up with drastically different estimates of how frequently false confessions occur. Regardless of the exact number, most researchers believe there are enough cases to treat the issue very seriously.

Different Types of False Confessions

One thing researchers do agree on is that there are different types of false confessions. According to Kassin and Wrightsman (1985), these consist of voluntary false confessions, coerced-compliant false confessions, and coerced-internalized false confessions.

VOLUNTARY FALSE CONFESSIONS Voluntary false confessions occur when someone voluntarily confesses to a crime he or she did not commit without any elicitation from the police. Research has indicated that people voluntarily false confess for a variety of reasons. For example, Gudjonsson (1992b) suggests that such confessions may arise out of (1) a morbid desire for notoriety, (2) the person being unable to distinguish fact from fantasy, (3) the need to make up for feelings of guilt by receiving punishment, or (4) a desire to protect somebody else from harm (which may be particularly prevalent among juveniles).

Although it may seem surprising, many highly publicized cases do result in voluntary false confessions. Perhaps the most famous case was the kidnapping and murder of Charles Lindbergh's baby son. (Charles Lindbergh was famous for being the first pilot to fly solo across the Atlantic Ocean in 1927.) On March 1, 1932, Charles Lindbergh Jr., at the age of 20 months, was kidnapped. Two-and-a-half months later, the decomposed body of the baby was found with a fractured skull. It is estimated that some 200 people falsely confessed to the kidnapping and murder (Note, 1953). In the end, only one man was convicted for the crime, a German immigrant named Bruno Richard Hauptman, who was executed for the crime in 1936. However, to this day, questions are still raised about Hauptman's guilt (e.g., Jones, 1997).

COERCED-COMPLIANT FALSE CONFESSIONS Coerced-compliant false confessions are those in which the suspect confesses to a crime, even though the suspect is fully aware he or she did not commit it. This type of false confession is perhaps the most common (Gudjonsson & MacKeith, 1988). Unlike voluntary false confessions, these confessions are caused by the use of coercive interrogation tactics on the part of the police, such as the maximization techniques described earlier. Specifically, coerced-compliant confessions may be given so the suspect can (1) escape further interrogation, (2) gain a promised benefit, or (3) avoid a threatened punishment (Gudjonsson, 1992b).

As with voluntary false confessions, there are a number of reported cases of coerced-compliant false confessions. For example, the 1993 movie *In the Name of the Father* starring Daniel Day Lewis is based on such a case. Gerry Conlon, along with three other Irishmen, falsely confessed to bombing two pubs in Surrey, England, as a result of coercive police interrogations. The coercive tactics included making up false evidence and threatening to harm members of Conlon's family unless he confessed. Conlon and his acquaintances were subsequently convicted and sent to prison but were later released (Gudjonsson, 1992a). Box 2.2 on page 52 provides an example of a recent coerced-compliant false confession that occurred in Canada.

COERCED-INTERNALIZED FALSE CONFESSIONS The third, and perhaps the most bizarre, type of false confession proposed by Kassin and Wrightsman (1985) is the **coerced-internalized false confession**. Here, individuals recall and confess to a crime they did not commit, usually after they are exposed to highly suggestive questions, such as the minimization techniques described earlier in the chapter (Gudjonsson, 1992a). In contrast to the coerced-compliant false confessor, however, these individuals actually end up believing they are responsible for the crime. According to Gudjonsson (1992b), there are several vulnerability factors associated with this type of false confession, including (1) a history of substance abuse or some other interference with brain function, (2) the inability of people to detect discrepancies between what they observed and what has been erroneously suggested to them, and (3) factors associated with mental state, such as severe anxiety, confusion, or feelings of guilt.

Perhaps the most frequently cited case of a false confession falls under the heading of a coerced-internalized false confession (Ofshe & Watters, 1994). The case involves Paul Ingram, who, in 1988, was accused by his two adult daughters of committing crimes against them, crimes that included sexual assault, rape, and satanic ritual abuse that involved slaughtering newborn babies. As if some of these allegations were not strange enough, Ingram confessed to the crimes after initially being adamant he had never committed them. In addition, he was eventually able to recall the crimes in vivid detail despite originally claiming he could not remember ever abusing his daughters. Ingram ended up pleading guilty to six counts of rape and was sentenced to 20 years in prison. In prison, Ingram came to believe he was not guilty of the crimes he confessed to. After having initial appeals rejected, Ingram was released from prison on April 8, 2003.

Many people feel that Ingram falsely confessed to the crimes he was sentenced for. Supporters of this position typically draw on two related pieces of evidence (see Olio & Cornell, 1998, for evidence to the contrary). First, it is known that Ingram was exposed to highly suggestive interrogation techniques that have been shown to adversely influence people's memory of events. For example, over the course of five

BOX 2.2 FALSE CONFESSION IN A CHILD-ABUSE CASE

In the case *R. v. M.J.S.* (2000), M.J.S. was accused of aggravated assault on his baby son (J.S.) and, after supplying the police with a written confession, was charged with the crime. But was M.J.S. responsible for the crime, or was this a case of a coerced-compliant false confession?

J.S. was one to three months old at the time the abuse was supposed to have happened. The boy had been admitted to the hospital for a suspected chest infection and vomiting problems. While in the hospital, X-rays were taken, and it was later discovered that the baby had several rib fractures. The injuries were unusual for a baby so young, leading the baby's pediatrician to notify Child Welfare. The testimony of an expert suggested that the most likely cause of the fractures was that the baby was shaken.

A police investigation was begun. Both M.J.S and his wife cooperated with the police throughout the investigation. On four occasions, the police interrogated the accused. During these interrogations, the police used techniques similar to those used in the Reid model of interrogation, which eventually led the accused to confess. Fortunately, all of the interrogations were videotaped, which provided the courts with a means to determine whether the confession was coerced.

Much of the interrogation consisted of developing various psychological themes to justify the crime. For example, one of the interrogating officers stated that "No doubt it was probably accidental on your part. . . . I don't believe it was intentional. . . . Children's bones are so fragile. . . . You made a mistake" (*R. v. M.J.S.*, para. 16). In addition, every time the accused denied his involvement in the crime, the officers interrupted with statements such as, "We are beyond that point—we know you did it" (para. 19).

The officers also lied to the accused, stating they had talked to everyone else who may have been involved with the incident and they were all cleared. This had not happened. Furthermore, the interviewing officers appealed to the accused's sense of honour and decency, and stressed how much better he would feel if he confessed. For example, one officer stated, "You'll be able to say to yourself ... I'm going to sleep tonight, knowing that I told the truth" (para. 20). Still denying his involvement in any wrongdoing, the accused was presented with threatening statements. One interrogator stated, "If you run from this mistake, your family disintegrates, your family falls apart.... If you want your kids to be raised in a foster home, or adopted somewhere, that is a decision that you have to make" (para 25).

In ruling on the confession evidence, the judge stated that the alleged confession in this case was extracted by threats and implied promises. The judge decided that the techniques employed by the investigators were coercive and that the accused confessed to the crime in order to escape the oppressive atmosphere created by the interrogations. The judge concluded by stating, "This case is a classic illustration of how slavish adherence to a technique can produce a coerced-compliant false 'apology' [confession] even from an accused who has denied 34 times that he did anything wrong when caring for his child" (para. 45). As a result of these findings, the confession evidence was deemed inadmissible.

months, Ingram took part in 23 interrogations in which he was instructed (on some of these occasions) to visualize scenes of satanic cult activity that he could not remember (Wrightsman, 2001). Second, a psychologist hired to evaluate the case, Dr. Richard Ofshe from the University of California, concluded that Ingram had been brainwashed into believing he was responsible for the crimes (Ofshe & Watters, 1994). To demonstrate this belief, Ofshe conducted an experiment where he presented Ingram with a fabricated scenario, that Ingram had forced his son and daughter to have sex together while he watched (Olio & Cornell, 1998). According to Olio and Cornell (1998), phase 1 of the experiment consisted of Ofshe asking Ingram if he could remember the incident (Ingram indicated he could not). Ofshe then instructed Ingram to use the same techniques he had used during his previous interview sessions. The next day, Ingram informed Ofshe he could now remember the incident and he produced a written confession providing details of his involvement. In phase 2 of the experiment, Ofshe pressured Ingram to retract his confession, but Ingram was not willing to do so.

Interrogative Suggestibility and Compliance

As we have already mentioned, the major difference between coerced-compliant and coerced-internalized false confessions is that coerced-compliant false confessors are fully aware they are not responsible for the crimes they are confessing to. Research indicates that two psychological characteristics play a key role in these two types of confessions—compliance and suggestibility. **Compliance** refers to a tendency to go along with demands made by people perceived to be in authority, even though the person may not agree with them (Gudjonsson, 1989). **Suggestibility** refers to the tendency to accept (i.e., internalize) information communicated during questioning (Gudjonsson, 1984). Dr. Gisli Gudjonsson, from the Institute of Psychiatry in London, has developed standardized scales for measuring both compliance and suggestibility.

THE GUDJONSSON COMPLIANCE SCALE The Gudjonsson Compliance Scale (GCS) is a self-report questionnaire consisting of 20 true-false questions that tap into two aspects of compliance: a person's eagerness to please others and a person's desire to avoid conflict and confrontation with people (Gudjonsson, 1989). For example, the section measuring a person's eagerness to please others includes questions such as "I try hard to do what is expected of me" and "I generally believe in doing as I am told." In contrast, the section measuring a person's desire to avoid conflict and confrontation includes questions such as "I give in easily to people when I am pressured" and "I tend to give in to people who insist that they are right" (Gudjonsson, 1992a).

Although the GCS has not been the subject of much research, there is some evidence that it is useful for identifying suspects who can be characterized as compliant. For example, Gudjonsson (1989) compared the GCS scores for "resisters" (suspects who did not confess even though there was evidence they were guilty) with "false confessors" (suspects who retracted confessions they had previously made). The results suggested that the former group had significantly lower GCS scores than the latter group, providing one possible reason that these individuals performed the way they did during their police interrogations (a practical example of this scale in use is presented in Box 2.3).

THE GUDJONSSON SUGGESTIBILITY SCALE The Gudjonsson Suggestibility Scale (GSS1) measures two distinct types of interrogative suggestibility (Gudjonsson, 1984). First, it measures susceptibility to give in to leading questions, which is known as **yield**. It also measures the tendency to alter answers after being put under pressure by an interviewer, which is known as **shift**. This scale is based on a short story, which is read to a subject. The subject is then asked to recall details from the story. The subject is asked 20 questions, 15 of which are misleading (trial 1). Next, the subject is told that he or she has made a number of errors in answering the questions (even if no errors have been made), that it is necessary to ask all the questions again, and that the subject should try to be more accurate (trial 2). The extent to which the subject gives in to the misleading questions on the first trial is scored as *yield*. Any change in answers between the first and second trial is scored as *shift*. Yield and shift are added together to make up the total suggestibility score.

Research has indicated that the GSS1 is a potentially important diagnostic tool for assessing the degree to which a suspect can be characterized as suggestible. In a study similar to what was done with the GCS, Gudjonsson (1984) compared the GSS1 scores for resisters and false confessors and, as hypothesized, found that resisters had significantly lower GSS1 scores than did false confessors. Research has also been conducted to examine the various correlates of interrogative suggestibility. Many of these correlations are consistent with what would be expected. For example, certain forms of anxiety correlate positively with suggestibility (as anxiety increases, suggestibility increases), while intelligence correlates negatively (as intelligence increases, suggestibility decreases) (Gudjonsson, 1992a).

Studying False Confessions in the Lab

It is obviously difficult to study if, and how, false confessions occur. Even in the research laboratory it is not an easy task because of obvious ethical constraints (Kassin & Kiechel, 1996). Nowadays, no university ethics committee would allow research participants to be led to believe they had committed crimes of the sort that Paul Ingram was accused of. As a result, researchers have attempted to develop innovative laboratory paradigms that allow them to study the processes that may cause false confessions to occur without putting their participants at risk. One such paradigm was proposed by Dr. Saul Kassin and his student.

In their study, Kassin and Kiechel (1996) tested whether individuals would confess to a "crime" they did not commit. They had participants take part in what they thought was a reaction time study. A co-conspirator read a list of letters out loud to a participant who had to type these letters into a computer. However, before each

BOX 2.3 USING THE GUDJONSSON COMPLIANCE AND SUGGESTIBILITY SCALES

Gudjonsson (1992a) describes the following case of the Birmingham Six. In November 1974, two pubs in Birmingham, England, were bombed by the Irish Republican Army (IRA) killing 21 people. Six Irishmen were arrested for the bombings and interrogated. Two of the suspects did not sign any confession, and the other four did sign a confession. Although the defendants argued that the police had beaten their confessions out of them, their confessions were admitted as evidence in court and the six men were convicted. They were imprisoned until 1990 at which time they were released based on new evidence.

Thirteen years after their interrogation, Gudjonsson was asked to assess all six defen-dants. Part of the assessment protocol included the GCS and GSS1. Figure 2.1 indi-cates that the six men differed dramatically in their level of compliance and suggestibility. Two of the defendants scored very high on both scales, two scored very low, and two scored in the middle. Interestingly, the two defendants who scored lowest on the scales were the same two men who did not sign a written confession in 1974. Gudjonsson (1992a) is careful to point out that there is no way to know what the defendants' com-pliance and suggestibility scores were in 1974. Nevertheless, it is intriguing that these scores correspond so well with the behaviour exhibited by the Birmingham Six in their original police interrogations.

FIGURE 2.1

THE COMPLIANCE (GCS) AND SUGGESTIBILITY (GSS1) SCORES OF THE BIRMINGHAM SIX

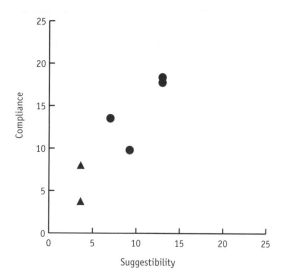

The two defendants who did not sign written confessions are indicated by triangles.

Source: Adapted from Gudjonsson, 1992a.

session began, the participant was warned that, if he or she hit the ALT key on the keyboard while typing in the letters, all the data would be lost. Sixty seconds after beginning the task, the computer automatically crashed, which brought the head researcher into the lab with accusations that the participant had hit the key.

Kassin and Kiechel were specifically interested in how two factors would affect participant reactions to the allegations. Participant vulnerability (defined as the participant's certainty concerning his or her own innocence) was manipulated by varying the speed that participants had to type. In the "not vulnerable" condition, letters were read at a rate of 43 letters per minute; in the "vulnerable" condition, letters were read at a rate of 67 letters per minute. The researchers also varied whether false evidence was presented. In the "no false evidence" condition, the co-conspirator stated she did not see what happened; in the "false evidence" condition, she stated she saw the participant hit the ALT key. The results from the study are presented in Table 2.1.

To measure the degree to which participants complied with the allegations, the researchers presented each participant with a written confession and recorded how many participants signed it. As indicated in Table 2.1, many participants accepted responsibility for the crime despite the fact they were innocent, particularly the vulnerable participants presented with false evidence. To measure the degree to which participants internalized their confession, the researchers recorded comments made by participants to another co-conspirator outside the lab who asked them what had happened. If the participant accepted blame for the crime, he or she was recorded as exhibiting **internalization**. As indicated in Table 2.1, many participants also internalized their confession. Again, this was especially true for vulnerable participants presented with false evidence. Finally, to measure the degree to which participants made up details to fit with their confession, known as **confabulation**, the researchers brought the participant back into the lab, read the list of letters again, and asked the participant to try to reconstruct where things had gone wrong. As indicated in Table 2.1,

TABLE 2.1 COMPLIANCE, INTERNALIZATION, AND CONFABULATION IN KASSIN AND KIECHEL'S STUDY

	No False Evidence (No Witness)		False Evidence (Witness)	
	Not Vulnerable (Slow Pace)	*Vulnerable (Fast Pace)*	*Not Vulnerable (Slow Pace)*	*Vulnerable (Fast Pace)*
Compliance	35%	65%	89%	100%
Internalization	0%	12%	44%	65%
Confabulation	0%	0%	6%	35%

Source: Adapted from Kassin and Kiechel, 1996.

vulnerable participants presented with false evidence were once again found to be particularly susceptible to confabulation.

In sum, these findings suggest that it is possible to demonstrate, under laboratory conditions, that people can admit to acts they are not responsible for and come to believe in their guilt to such a point that they can reconstruct details of an act that never occurred (Kassin & Kiechel, 1996). However, whether these findings can be generalized to actual police interrogations, in which people are falsely confessing to much more serious crimes, is clearly open to debate. Indeed, given the triviality of their mock crime, even Kassin and Kiechel raise this issue about their findings. Perhaps in the future, forensic psychologists will find a way to conduct laboratory studies of false confessions that are not so problematic in this regard.

The Consequences of Falsely Confessing

There are at least two major consequences of a false confession. The most obvious consequence is the impact on the individual making the confession, in particular if the confession is admitted as evidence in court. As mentioned previously, research indicates that false confessions do sometimes lead people to be convicted for crimes they did not commit (Leo & Ofshe, 1998). This finding has led some researchers to examine the impact that coerced confessions have on jurors.

In one study, Kassin and Sukel (1997) presented participants with transcripts of a mock murder trial. One group of participants received a transcript in which the defendant immediately confessed to the police during questioning (the low-pressure condition). A second group of participants received a transcript in which the defendant was coerced into confessing by having his hands cuffed behind his back and being threatened by the interrogator (the high-pressure condition). A third group of participants received a transcript in which the defendant never confessed to the murder (the control condition). The results of the study indicate that those participants presented with a confession obtained in the high-pressure condition recognized the confession was involuntary and said it would not affect their decisions. However, when actual verdicts were examined across the three groups, the presence of a confession was found to significantly increase the conviction rate, even for those participants in the high-pressure condition. Thus, not only can people be convicted of crimes they did not commit based on their false confession, but this can happen even when the confession appears to have been obtained through coercive interrogation tactics.

A second consequence of false confessions that is not as commonly recognized usually comes from people voluntarily confessing to crimes they did not commit. Although such a confession no doubt has consequences for the false confessor, it also has unappreciated consequences for the police and, therefore, the public. When somebody volunteers a false confession, the police are diverted down a false trail that may waste valuable time, time that could be used to identify and apprehend the real offender. Howitt (2002) provides an example of this happening in the Yorkshire Ripper serial murder investigation that took place in England during the 1970s. At one point in the investigation, the police were sent several tape recordings supposedly from the Ripper himself. Howitt states that senior police officers on the case, believing the tapes to be genuine, used up valuable resources investigating the tapes. However, the tapes were not genuine and these actions probably delayed the eventual arrest of Peter Sutcliffe and allowed further murders to take place.

CRIMINAL PROFILING

In order for the police to be able to conduct their interrogations, they need to have a viable suspect in custody. In some instances, the identification of probable suspects is relatively straightforward, because in many crimes the victim and the offender know each other and there is often a clear motivation for the crime, such as passion, greed, or revenge. But what about those crimes in which it is more difficult to identify a suspect, crimes in which the victim and offender are strangers and there is no clear motive? In these cases, the police often rely on unconventional investigative techniques, such as **criminal profiling**.

WHAT IS A CRIMINAL PROFILE?

There is no single definition of criminal profiling (Alison et al., 2002). Indeed, there is still little agreement as to what the technique should even be called. Numerous terms are used to describe the technique, including criminal profiling, psychological profiling, offender profiling, and investigative profiling (Wilson, Lincoln, & Kocsis, 1997). However, the definition proposed by John Douglas and his former colleagues from the Federal Bureau of Investigation (FBI) fairly accurately describes them all: profiling is "a technique for identifying the major personality and behavioural characteristics of an individual based upon an analysis of the crimes he or she has committed" (Douglas et al., 1986, p. 405).

Although criminal profiling is now used in a range of contexts, it is most commonly used in cases of serial homicide and rape (Holmes & Holmes, 2002). In particular, profiling is thought to be most applicable in cases in which extreme forms of psychopathology are exhibited by the offender, including sadistic torture and ritualistic behaviour (Geberth, 1990). Criminal profiling was originally intended to help the police identify the criminal in these sorts of cases, either by narrowing down a list of suspects or by providing new lines of inquiry. However, criminal profiling is now used for a number of purposes including the following (Homant & Kennedy, 1998):

- To help set traps to flush out an offender
- To determine whether a threatening note should be taken seriously
- To give advice on how best to interrogate a suspect
- To tell prosecutors how to break down defendants in cross-examination

Although every criminal profile will undoubtedly be different in terms of the information it contains, some of the most common personality and behavioural characteristics that profilers try to predict include the offender's age, sex, race, level of intelligence, educational history, hobbies, family background, residential location, criminal history, employment status, psychosexual development, and post-offence behaviour (Holmes & Holmes, 2002). Often these predictions are made by forensic psychologists and psychiatrists who have either clinical or research experience with offenders (Wilson et al., 1997). In North America, however, the majority of profilers are experienced and specially trained law enforcement officers (Rossmo, 2000).

The Origins of Criminal Profiling

Criminal profiling is usually thought to have been developed by agents from the FBI in the 1970s. However, there are numerous examples of profiling techniques being used long before that time (Canter, 2000). Woodsworth and Porter (1999), for example, suggest that the documented history of profiling can be traced back at least to the publication of the *Malleus Maleficarum*, "a text from the late 1400s written by contractors to the Catholic Church for the purpose of accurately identifying and eradicating witches" (p. 243). According to these researchers, this was one of the first systematic approaches for identifying and making inferences about the characteristics of supposedly guilty individuals. Beyond this example, there are other early instances of profiling techniques, which were often used for the specific purpose of inferring the background characteristics of an unknown offender from the behaviours he or she exhibited at the crime scene. The investigation that you may be most familiar with is the famous case of Jack the Ripper (Harrison, 1993).

EARLY ATTEMPTS AT CRIMINAL PROFILING In 1888, a series of murders were committed in the east end of London, around an area known as Whitechapel. The victims were all women, and all were mutilated by the offender. At one point, the unknown offender sent a letter to the newspapers, and at the end of it he signed his name, Jack the Ripper (Holmes & Holmes, 2002). A police surgeon involved with the investigation of the murders engaged in a form of criminal profiling. As Woodworth and Porter (1999, p. 244) reveal:

> Dr. George Phillips attempted to create a reconstruction of various crime scenes and describe the wounds of the victims for the purpose of gaining a greater insight into the offender's psychological make-up. In particular, Phillips believed that a circumspect examination of the wound patterns of murder victims could provide clues about both the behaviour and personality of the offender who committed the crimes.

This is probably one of the first times that criminal profiling was used in a criminal investigation. Unfortunately, it assisted little, evidenced by the fact that we still have no idea who Jack the Ripper actually was.

Another well-known case, often cited as an example of how accurate some profilers can be, is the case of New York City's Mad Bomber. Starting in 1940, an unknown offender began detonating bombs in public places around New York (Wrightsman, 2001). Stumped, the New York City Police Department turned to a local forensic psychiatrist, Dr. James Brussel, to assist with the case. By examining the actions of the bomber, Brussel began to develop a profile of the unknown offender. Dr. Brussel's profile included characteristics such as the following: the offender would be a middle-aged male, he would suffer from paranoia, he would be pathologically self-centred, he would be reasonably educated, he would be unmarried and possibly a virgin, he would be Roman Catholic, and he would wear buttoned-up double-breasted suits (Turvey, 2002). In 1957, almost 17 years after the bombings started, the police finally arrested George Metesky. Metesky fit most of the characteristics that Dr. Brussel had profiled, even down to the double-breasted suit he wore to the police station (Holmes & Holmes, 2002). Metesky was subsequently sent to a mental institution for the criminally insane. He was released in 1973 and died in 1994.

THE FBI AND BEYOND The next big milestone in the history of criminal profiling was the development of a criminal profiling program at the FBI in the 1970s (Turvey, 2002). Not only was this the first time that profiles were produced in a systematic way by a law enforcement agency, but it was also the first time that training was provided in how to construct criminal profiles. Subsequent to the development of the FBI's Behavioral Sciences Unit in 1972, the National Center for the Analysis of Violent Crime (NCAVC) was opened for the purpose of conducting research in the area of criminal profiling and providing formal guidance to police agencies around the United States that were investigating serial crimes, in particular serial murder. Similar units have now sprung up in police agencies around the world, including Canada, Germany, and England. These units typically provide operational support to police agencies in cases in which profiling may be useful, and many conduct their own research into criminal profiling. See Box 2.4 for an example of how the RCMP is moving the criminal profiling field forward.

How Is a Criminal Profile Constructed?

Once a crime series has been detected that warrants a criminal profile, profilers must go through a process of profile construction. Despite the fact that profiling has been regularly used by the police since the 1980s, very little is actually known about this process. Indeed, the descriptions of the profiling process provided by researchers and profilers are incredibly vague. For example, in a now-classic study of criminal profiling, Pinizzotto and Finkel (1990) describe the process of profiling as an equation in the form: WHAT + WHY = WHO. The WHAT of the crime refers to the material that profilers collect at the start of an investigation, such as crime scene photos, autopsy reports, and descriptions of victims. The WHY of the crime refers to the motivation for the crime and each crime scene behaviour. The WHO of the crime refers to the actual profile that is eventually constructed once the WHAT and the WHY components have been determined.

Obviously, although this conceptual model may make sense at a general level, it is much too vague to be useful. As Pinizzotto and Finkel (1990) themselves point out,

BOX 2.4 THE RCMP'S VIOLENT CRIME LINKAGE ANALYSIS SYSTEM (VICLAS)

In recent years, the RCMP has played a pivotal role in developing the field of criminal profiling. In large part, they have been able to do this by drawing on the best of modern computer technology. One of the RCMP's most significant advances has been the development in the mid-1990s of an automated system for linking serial crimes, the Violent Crime Linkage Analysis System, or **VICLAS**. One of the biggest problems the police encounter when they are faced with a possible crime series is **linkage blindness**, which refers to an inability on the part of the police to link geographically dispersed serial crimes committed by the same offender because of a lack of communication among police agencies (Egger, 2002). VICLAS was developed, in part, to prevent such linkage blindness.

The backbone of VICLAS is a booklet that police officers fill out. The questions in this booklet are supposed to capture crucial behavioural information on crimes of a serious nature. These crimes include motiveless homicides, sexual assaults, missing persons, and nonparental abductions (Collins et al., 1998). The booklet contains more than 200 questions about the offender's behaviour, the victim, and any forensic information that is available. This information is then entered into a computer and downloaded into a centralized database where it is carefully compared with other crimes. Specially trained VICLAS analysts determine if there are any possible crime linkages. If any potential links are identified, the crimes are highlighted as a series and the relevant police agencies are notified and encouraged to share information (Collins et al., 1998).

According to Woodsworth and Porter (1999), as of the year 2000, "there were more than 30 000 cases in the system, and although there are no official statistics on its success rate, there were 3200 known linkages" (p. 253). These encouraging results, in addition to anecdotal evidence that suggests the system holds promise, have earned VICLAS a reputation as one of the best crime linkage analysis systems in existence (Collins et al., 1998). Police from around the world, including agencies in England, Australia, and Germany, are currently using VICLAS to help solve their serial crimes. Following the conviction of Paul Bernardo in 1995 for the brutal murders he committed, VICLAS reporting was made mandatory for police agencies in Ontario, and it may soon be mandatory in other provinces.

the model "does not tell us precisely how ... the profiler gets from the WHAT to the WHY, or from the WHY to the WHO" (p. 217). Other conceptual models have also been produced, particularly by profilers from the FBI, but these models also lack the degree of specificity required to truly understand the process by which a criminal profile is constructed (e.g., Douglas & Burgess, 1986). Undoubtedly, part of the problem with providing such detail is that profiling is still viewed primarily as an art, not a science (Homant & Kennedy, 1998). Although some are making an effort to change this (e.g., Canter, 2000), profiling is currently based to a large extent on the profiler's experience and intuition (Douglas & Olshaker, 1995). As a result, asking a profiler to provide specific details of how he or she constructs a criminal profile may be similar to asking Picasso to explain how he paints.

Different Types of Profiling Methods

Although it is not clear how criminal profilers construct their profiles, it is clear that they can draw on different types of profiling methods. Specifically, two approaches can be used by profilers—the deductive profiling method and the inductive profiling method. **Deductive criminal profiling** involves the prediction of an offender's background characteristics generated from a thorough analysis of the evidence left at the crime scenes by that particular offender (Holmes & Holmes, 2002). This deductive method of profiling largely relies on logical reasoning. This is indicated in an example provided by Canter (2000), in which the victim of an unidentified assailant noticed that the offender had short fingernails on his right hand and long fingernails on his left hand. According to Canter, "Somebody with specialist knowledge suggested that this was a characteristic of people who are serious guitar players. It was therefore a reasonable deduction that the assailant was somebody who played the guitar" (p. 24). The primary disadvantage of this profiling method is that the underlying logic of the argument can sometimes be faulty. Take the prediction we just described. Although the argument appears to be logical, it is in fact wrong. The offender in this case did not play the guitar at all. Instead, the reason he had short fingernails on his right hand was that he had a job repairing old tires.

In contrast to deductive profiling, **inductive criminal profiling** involves the prediction of an offender's background characteristics generated from a comparison of that particular offender's crimes with similar crimes committed by other, known offenders. This method is based on the premise that "if certain crimes committed by different people are similar, then the offenders must also share some common personality traits" (Holmes & Holmes, 2002, p. 5). The inductive method of profiling relies largely on a determination of how likely it is an offender will possess certain background characteristics given the prevalence of these characteristics among known offenders who have committed similar crimes. An example of the inductive profiling method is provided by Aitken et al. (1996), who developed a statistical profile of a child sex murderer. Based on their analysis of similar crimes committed by known offenders, they predicted that there was a probability of .96 that the offender would know the victim, a probability of .92 that the offender would have a previous criminal conviction, a probability of .91 that the offender would be single, a probability of .79 that the offender would live within five miles (eight kilometres) of the crime scene, and a probability of .65 that the offender would be under the age of 20. In this case, the profile turned out to be very accurate.

In contrast to deductive profiling, the major problem with the inductive method of profiling is with sampling issues (Turvey, 2002). The key problem is that it will never be possible to have a representative sample of serial offenders from which to draw profiling conclusions from. That is, if we encounter a serial crime with behaviours A, B, and C, but no crimes in our database have behaviours A, B, and C, how do we construct an accurate profile? One reason for this problem is that many offenders are never caught for their crimes and, therefore, these offenders can never be included in a database of solved offences.

THE ORGANIZED-DISORGANIZED MODEL Many profilers today use an inductive profiling approach developed by the FBI in the 1980s. This model was largely developed through interviews with incarcerated serial murderers and has come to be called the **organized-disorganized model** (Hazelwood & Douglas, 1980). The model suggests that an offender's crime scene can be classified as either organized or disorganized (see Table 2.2). Organized crime scene behaviours reflect a well-planned and controlled crime, while disorganized behaviours reflect an impulsive crime, which is chaotic in nature. Similarly, an offender's background can be classified as either organized or disorganized (see Table 2.3 on page 64). Organized background characteristics reflect a methodical individual, while disorganized characteristics reflect a disturbed individual, who is usually suffering from some form of psychopathology. The basic idea is that, when encountering a disorganized crime scene, the investigator should profile the background characteristics of a disorganized offender, and likewise for organized crime scenes and organized background characteristics. Although little research has examined whether the organized-disorganized model actually works, the research that does exist raises serious doubts (e.g., Canter et al., 2004). Indeed, even the FBI has refined this model to account for the many offenders who display mixtures of organized and disorganized features (Douglas et al., 1992).

TABLE 2.2 ORGANIZED AND DISORGANIZED CRIME SCENE BEHAVIOURS

Organized Behaviours	Disorganized Behaviours
Planned offence	Spontaneous offence
Use of restraints on the victim	No restraints used on the victim
Ante-mortem sexual acts committed	Post-mortem sexual acts committed
Use of a vehicle in the crime	No use of a vehicle in the crime
No post-mortem mutilation	Post-mortem mutilation
Corpse not taken	Corpse (or body parts) taken
Little evidence left at the scene	Evidence left at the scene

Source: Adapted from Ressler et al., 1986.

TABLE 2.3 ORGANIZED AND DISORGANIZED BACKGROUND CHARACTERISTICS	
Organized Characteristics	**Disorganized Characteristics**
High intelligence	Low intelligence
Skilled occupation	Unskilled occupation
Sexually adequate	Sexually inadequate
Lives with a partner	Lives alone
Geographically mobile	Geographically stable
Lives and works far away from crimes	Lives and works close to crimes
Follows crimes in media	Little interest in media
Maintains residence and vehicle	Does not maintain residence or vehicle

Source: Adapted from Ressler et al., 1986.

The Validity of Criminal Profiling

Because the police frequently use profiling, it is important to consider whether the technique is actually reliable and valid. The view of some researchers is that profiling is generally accepted as a useful investigative technique (e.g., Homant & Kennedy, 1998), but others are more cautious (e.g., Alison et al., 2002). Many profilers claim they have experienced much success with their profiles, but these claims are typically based on personal observations, not empirical research (Woodsworth & Porter, 1999). The few empirical studies that do exist suggest that profiling may be beneficial, but not necessarily for the reasons we might expect. For example, in one of the most recent evaluation studies, Copson (1995) found that profiles were viewed as operationally useful by 82.6% of the police officers he surveyed, but only 2.7% of that sample said that this was because the profile led to the identification of the offender. Most of the police officers indicated that profiling was useful because it either furthered their understanding of the case (60.9%) or it reassured them of their own judgments about the offender (51.6%).

Despite the relatively high figures indicating that criminal profiling may be useful, the practice is still often criticized. Three criticisms in particular have received attention from researchers:

1. Many forms of profiling are based on a theoretical model of personality that lacks strong empirical support.

2. Many profiles contain information that is so vague and ambiguous they can potentially fit many suspects.

3. Professional profilers may be no better than untrained individuals at constructing accurate criminal profiles.

Let's now look at each of these criticisms in turn.

DOES PROFILING HAVE A STRONG THEORETICAL BASE? There seems to be general agreement that most forms of profiling, including the FBI's organized-disorganized approach, rely on a **classic trait model** of personality that was popular in psychology before the 1970s (Alison et al., 2002). In this model, the primary determinants of behaviour are stable, internal traits (Mischel, 1968). These traits are assumed to result in the expression of consistent patterns of behaviour over time and across situations. In the criminal context, this consistency is thought to persist across an offender's crimes and into the offender's noncriminal lifestyle, thus allowing him or her to be accurately profiled (Homant & Kennedy, 1998). Thus, an offender characterized by a trait of "organization" is expected to exhibit organized behaviours across his or her crimes (e.g., the offender will consistently plan the crimes, use restraints, and use weapons), as well as in his or her noncriminal life (e.g., the offender will be highly intelligent, sexually adequate, and geographically mobile) (Alison et al., 2002).

Although some researchers believe this classic trait model provides a solid basis for criminal profiling (e.g., Homant & Kennedy, 1998), other researchers disagree (e.g., Alison et al., 2002). Those who disagree draw on research from the field of personality psychology, which demonstrates that traits are not the only (or even primary) determinant of behaviour (Cervone & Shoda, 1999). Rather, situational influences are also known to be very important in shaping our behaviour, and some researchers argue that there is no reason to suspect that serial offenders will be any different (Bennell & Canter, 2002). From a profiling perspective, the impact of various situational factors (e.g., an extremely resistant victim, being interrupted during a crime, or having a bad day at work) may create behavioural inconsistencies across an offender's crimes, and between different aspects of his or her life, making it very difficult to create an accurate profile.

Those who believe the classic trait model forms a strong basis for criminal profiling also acknowledge the "checkered past" that this model has experienced (e.g., Homant & Kennedy, 1998). However, these individuals refer to instances in which behavioural consistency has been found in the noncriminal context and highlight the fact that higher levels of behavioural consistency typically emerge when we examine pathological populations (Pinizzotto & Finkel, 1990). Assuming that most serial offenders do in fact fall into this pathological population, these supporters argue that the level of behavioural consistency that they express may be adequate to develop accurate criminal profiles. Clearly, more empirical research dealing with this issue is required before any firm conclusions can be made. Until then, the debate over the validity of criminal profiling will continue.

WHAT IS THE IMPACT OF AMBIGUOUS PROFILES? Another common criticism of criminal profiling is that many profiles are so ambiguous that they can fit many suspects. If one of the goals of profiling is to help prioritize potential suspects, this concern clearly needs to be addressed. To examine this issue, Alison, Smith, Eastman, and Rainbow (2003) examined the content of 21 profiling reports and found that almost one-quarter (24%) of all the profiling opinions provided in these reports could be considered ambiguous (i.e., the opinion could be interpreted differently by different people). Of more direct relevance to the ambiguity criticism, however, is an interesting follow-up study conducted by Alison, Smith, and Morgan (2003), where they examined whether ambiguous profiles could in fact be interpreted to fit more than one suspect.

Alison and his colleagues provided details of a genuine crime to two groups of forensic professionals, including senior police detectives. The crime involved the murder of a young woman. Each group of participants was then provided with a criminal profile constructed for this case by the FBI. They were asked to read the profile and compare it to the description of a suspect. Unbeknownst to the participants, each group was provided with a different suspect description. One group was provided with the description of the genuine offender, while the other group was provided with a suspect constructed by the researchers, who was different from the genuine offender on a number of key points. For example, the genuine offender had no previous criminal convictions whereas the bogus offender had several previous convictions for assault and burglary. After comparing the profile with their suspect, each participant was asked to rate the accuracy of the profile and to state if (and why) he or she thought the profile would be operationally useful.

Despite the fact that each group received different suspect descriptions, both groups of participants rated the profile as fairly accurate, with no significant difference between the groups. In addition, both groups viewed the profile as generally useful and indicated they thought it would allow the police to narrow down the list of potential suspects and develop new lines of inquiry. This study, therefore, provides preliminary support for the criticism that ambiguous profiles can in fact be interpreted to fit more than one suspect, even when those suspects are quite different from one another. However, although such a finding could have serious implications, we must be careful in interpreting these results. For example, it would be important to know how closely the profile used in this study matches the typical criminal profile provided in the field. In addition, it should be emphasized that this study is far from realistic. For example, the crime scene details and suspect descriptions provided to the participants in this study contained much less information than would be the case in an actual police investigation. Until a more realistic study is conducted, it is difficult to know what the practical implications of the study are, but it does raise some very interesting and potentially important questions.

HOW ACCURATE ARE PROFESSIONAL PROFILERS? The last criticism that we will deal with here is the possibility that professional profilers may be no more accurate in their profiling predictions than are individuals who have received no specialized training. In early writings on criminal profiling, claims were even made that profilers may be no better than bartenders at predicting the characteristics of unknown offenders (Campbell, 1976). If this is in fact the case, the police must consider how much weight they will put on statements made by professional profilers. Unlike the previous two criticisms, this issue has been examined on numerous occasions and the results have been mixed (Kocsis et al., 2000). In other words, profilers are sometimes found to be more accurate than other groups when asked to construct profiles under laboratory conditions but, at other times, they are found to be no more accurate.

In a fairly representative study, Kocsis and his colleagues (2000) compared profile accuracy across five groups of individuals—profilers, psychologists, police officers, students, and psychics. All participants were provided with the details of a genuine crime, which they were asked to review. The participants were then given a series of questionnaires that dealt with various aspects of the offender's background, including his or her physical characteristics, cognitions related to the offence, pre- and post-offence behaviours, social history, and personality characteristics. The participants' task with these questionnaires was to select the alternatives that best described the unknown offender. Accuracy was determined for each group by comparing the responses from the participants with the correct answers. The results from this study are presented in Table 2.4, which indicates the mean number of questions that each group got correct for each subset of characteristics.

As you can see from this table, professional profilers were the most accurate when it came to profiling cognitive processes (e.g., degree of planning) and social history (e.g., marital status). Therefore, they have received the highest total accuracy score,

TABLE 2.4 COMPARING PROFILERS, PSYCHOLOGISTS, POLICE OFFICERS, STUDENTS, AND PSYCHICS*

Measure	Profilers	Psychologists	Police	Students	Psychics
Cognitions	3.20	2.27	2.49	2.03	2.60
Physical	3.60	3.63	3.43	3.42	2.80
Offence	4.00	4.03	3.09	3.64	3.65
Social	3.00	2.63	2.60	2.94	2.25
Total	13.80	12.57	11.60	12.03	11.30
Personality	24.60	34.03	22.03	26.84	27.70

Source: Adapted from Kocsis et al., 2000.

*Numbers refer to the mean number of correct questions. The number of correct questions that participants could have predicted was 7 for cognitions, 6 for physical characteristics, 7 for offence behaviours, and 10 for social history (total accuracy is, therefore, out of 30). Kocsis and his colleagues did not provide information relating to the total number of correct predictions for personality characteristics.

which is an aggregate score for all subsets of characteristics, excluding personality predictions. On the other hand, psychologists were the most accurate when it came to profiling physical characteristics (e.g., offender age), offence behaviours (e.g., degree of control), and personality features (e.g., temperament). When the results of the four non-profiler groups were combined, Kocsis and his colleagues found that the combined score of the nonprofiler groups was lower than the profilers, leading them to conclude that "the collective skills of profilers are superior to the individual skills represented by each of the comparison groups" (p. 325). However, given the preliminary nature of this study, the marginal accuracy differences between groups, and the fact that other researchers have sometimes found little support for the accuracy of professional profilers (e.g., Pinizzotto & Finkel, 1990), it seems likely that the debate over whether professional profilers can provide more accurate profiles than untrained individuals will continue.

OTHER TYPES OF PROFILING

In addition to criminal profiling, two other forms of profiling are commonly used by the police—geographic profiling and racial profiling—though the widespread use of racial profiling has just recently been uncovered.

Geographic Profiling

Geographic profiling is used frequently by the police to help them investigate serial crimes more efficiently. In simple terms, geographic profiling uses crime scene locations to predict the most likely area where the offender resides (Rossmo, 2000). As is the case with criminal profiling, geographic profiling is used most often in cases of serial homicide and rape, though it has also been used in cases of serial robbery, arson, and burglary. Geographic profiling is used primarily for prioritizing potential suspects. This is accomplished by rank ordering the suspects based on how close they live to the predicted home location, so the suspect who lives closest to the predicted home location would be focused on first (Rossmo, 2000). This is an important task considering the number of suspects who can enter a serial crime investigation. For example, in the recently solved Green River serial murder case in Washington state, the police collected more than 18 000 suspect names (Rossmo, 1995).

The basic assumption behind geographic profiling is that most serial offenders do not travel far from home to commit their crimes and, therefore, it should be possible to make a reasonably accurate prediction about where an offender lives. Fortunately for the geographic profiler, research supports this assumption. Perhaps surprisingly, it turns out that serial offenders tend to be consistent in their crime site selection choices, often committing their crimes very close to where they reside (Rossmo, 2000). Indeed, even many of the most bizarre serial killers commit their crimes close to home, but there are certainly some high-profile offenders, such as Ted Bundy and Henry Lee Lucas, who travel long distances (Canter et al., 2000). For travelling offenders, geographic profiling is typically not a useful investigative strategy but, for the majority of serial offenders who do commit their crimes locally, a number of profiling strategies can be used (Snook et al., in press).

One of the first cases in which geographic profiling techniques were used was the case of the Yorkshire Ripper in England. After five years of unsolved murders, an advisory team was set up to review the investigation. Although some on the investigative team felt the offender lived in a different part of the country from where the crimes were happening (due largely to one of the voluntary false confessions discussed earlier), the advisory team believed the offender was a local man. To provide support for this claim, the advisory team constructed a type of geographic profile (Kind, 1987). They plotted the 17 Ripper murders onto a map and calculated the centre of gravity for the points. That is, by adding up the x-y coordinates for each crime and dividing by the 17 crimes, they could calculate the x-y coordinate for the centre of gravity. In this case, the centre of gravity was near Bradford, a city close to where the majority of the murders had taken place. When Peter Sutcliffe was eventually arrested for the crimes, he was found to reside in a district of Bradford.

During the 1990s, a number of individuals built computerized **geographic profiling systems** that could assist with the profiling task. One of these individuals was Dr. Kim Rossmo, who is profiled in Box 2.5 on page 70. The locations of linked crime sites are input into these systems represented as points on a map. The systems then perform calculations using mathematical models of offender spatial behaviour, which reflect the probability that the offender lives at particular points in the area where the offences have taken place. Every single location on the map is assigned an overall probability and these probabilities are designated a colour. For example, the top 10% of probabilities might be assigned the colour red, and so on. The eventual output is a coloured map, in which each colour band corresponds to the probability that the offender lives in the area (see Figure 2.2 on page 71). The police use this map to prioritize their investigative activities. Geographic profilers also consider other factors that may affect an offender's spatial behaviour, such as the density of suitable victims in an area, but this probability map forms the basis of their prediction.

Racial Profiling

Recently, it has also become clear that the police engage in another form of profiling—**racial profiling**. Unlike criminal profiling or geographic profiling, racial profiling refers to any police-initiated action that relies on the race or ethnicity of an individual, rather than that individual's criminal behaviour (Ramirez, McDevitt, & Farrell, 2000). According to Harris (1999a), one of the most common forms of racial profiling is the police practice of stopping and searching vehicles (for drugs and weapons usually) because the driver does not "match" the vehicle he or she is driving (see Box 2.6 on page 72 for a Canadian example).

BOX 2.5 CANADIAN RESEARCHER PROFILE: DR. KIM ROSSMO

Dr. Kim Rossmo had been a police officer with the Vancouver Police Department for 16 years when he became the first Canadian police officer to get his Ph.D. in criminology. At Simon Fraser University in Burnaby, B.C., Dr. Rossmo began his doctoral studies with Paul Brantingham, a well-known environmental criminologist. Drawing on his background in mathematics and his experience as a street-wise police officer, Dr. Rossmo decided to take what was known about offender spatial behaviour from fields like environmental criminology and put them to practical use by developing an investigative tool for predicting where unknown serial offenders are likely to live.

After years of research, Dr. Rossmo developed an approach he called criminal geographic targeting and designed a geographic-profiling system called Rigel, which is now one of the most sought-after investigative tools by police agencies around the world. Dr. Rossmo is regularly called in to assist with serial crime investigations by the RCMP, the FBI, and Scotland Yard. Based on his most recent estimation, he has consulted on about 200 cases, ranging from murders to bombings to robberies. One of his most recent cases was the high-profile Washington sniper case, which proved to be a particularly difficult case for geographic profiling because of the transient nature of the suspects.

After working as a detective inspector in charge of the Geographic Profiling Section of the Vancouver Police Department for a number of years, Dr. Rossmo moved on to serve a two-year term as the director of research for the prestigious Police Foundation in Washington, D.C. Dr. Rossmo now calls Texas State University home, where he directs the newly established Advanced Criminal Investigative Research Center in the Department of Criminal Justice.

In addition to his ongoing consultancy work, Dr. Rossmo continues to conduct research on geographic profiling and is expanding his focus to deal with other issues of importance. For example, he is currently engaged in research on the geographic patterns of illegal land border crossing, and he is getting involved in studies related to his long-term interest in criminal investigative failures and the factors that lead to these failures. When asked where he sees the field going in the future, he indicates that research in his area will have to start relating to more immediate, practical concerns, such as counterterrorism issues.

Dr. Rossmo has been the recipient of many awards for his achievements as a police officer and an academic, and he recently made a guest appearance as a character in the crime novel *Burnt Bones* by Michael Slade. He is the author of numerous articles and has recently published *Geographic Profiling*, the first book on the subject. This book provides an excellent example of how academic research can successfully be applied to help with real-world policing problems.

FIGURE 2.2

A COMPUTERIZED GEOGRAPHIC PROFILE

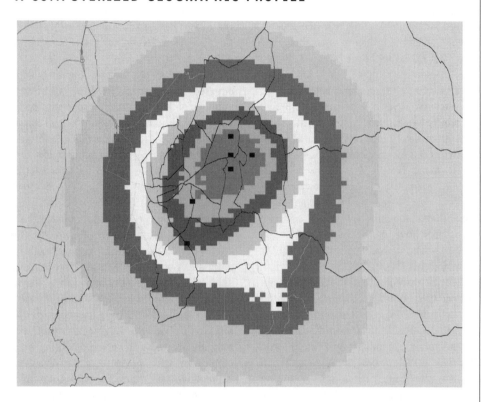

The black dots represent the crime locations and the different coloured bands (represented here by different shades of grey) correspond to the probability that the offender resides in that particular geographic area. The high priority search area in this case centres on the four crimes in the upper half of the map.

Due to some high-profile cases in the United States (e.g., *Wilkins v. Maryland State Police*, 1999), racial profiling is beginning to get more attention from researchers, the police, and the media. This attention appears to be warranted, given the results of recent public surveys. These surveys confirm that the majority of U.S. citizens believe the police actively engage in racial profiling. This seems to be the case regardless of the respondent's race. For example, a recent Gallup Poll indicated that 56% of whites and 77% of blacks believe that racial profiling is pervasive (Gallup Poll, 1999). What appears to differ by race, however, is the percentage of people who believe they have been the target of racial profiling. For example, results from the same Gallup Poll

BOX 2.6 A CANADIAN EXAMPLE OF RACIAL PROFILING

On November 1, 1999, Decovan Brown, a former Toronto Raptors basketball player, was arrested in Toronto for driving a motor vehicle while under the influence of alcohol (*R. v. Brown*, 2002). Before he was stopped, Brown was speeding slightly in his Ford Expedition. Brown is a young black man. At trial, Brown's lawyer alleged that "Mr. Brown was arbitrarily stopped by the investigating officer because of racial profiling rather than for driving at a speed slightly in excess of the posted speed limit" (*R. v. Brown*, 2002, para. 2). According to Brown's lawyer, "the arrest ... was based on the stereotypical assumption that young black men who are driving expensive motor vehicles obtained them by crime or are implicated in recent criminal activity" (para. 2).

Despite the fact that the defence had evidence to support their allegation that the police officer in this case had used racial profiling, the trial judge dismissed it, indicating that he found the allegations "nasty" and "malicious" (*R. v. Brown*, 2002, para. 2). In addition, the judge's remarks made during sentencing referred to his "distaste for the matters that were raised during the course of the trial" (para. 20), and he suggested that the defendant "might extend an apology to the officer because [the judge was] satisfied the allegations [were] completely unwarranted" (para. 20).

On appeal, the Ontario Supreme Court stressed that judges "must be particularly vigilant in their efforts to impartially determine applications like this one" (*R. v. Brown*, 2002, para. 18). The court also indicated that "judges must be particularly sensitive to the need to ... be fair to all Canadians of every race, religion, nationality and ethnic origin" (para. 19). On Brown's appeal, the Ontario Supreme Court ruled that many of the trial judge's comments to Brown and his lawyer during the trial were completely inappropriate and that the trial judge did not appear to understand the importance of some of the evidence. For example, the Court stated that for a judge to regard an application as distasteful "is materially inconsistent with the duty of a judge to hear and determine the application with an open mind" (para. 20). Ultimately, the Ontario Supreme Court ruled that the appeal by Brown should be allowed and a new trial was ordered.

indicate that only 6% of white men believe they have been stopped by the police based on their race alone, versus 42% of black men, and this percentage increases further for black men between the ages of 18 and 34.

Anecdotal accounts and empirical research also confirm that racial profiling is practised by some police agencies (Ramirez et al., 2000). For example, Lamberth (1999) conducted an analysis of police stop and searches in Maryland. Using data from the Maryland State Police, he compared the drivers who were stopped and searched along a major highway in Maryland with those who were actually violating traffic laws. According to Harris (1999b), who discussed Lamberth's study in some detail, approximately 74% of Lamberth's "law violator" sample consisted of white individuals while only 17.5% were black individuals. More important, a staggering

79.2% of the drivers who were stopped and searched were black. Studies in other countries provide similar findings (Home Office, 1998).

Of course, the possibility exists that such behaviour simply reflects an accurate perception on the part of the police that members of some minority groups are more likely to carry drugs and weapons. Existing research, however, does not support this assumption. In Lamberth's (1999) study, for example, he found that a similar percentage of black and white drivers who were stopped and searched were actually found with drugs in their possession (28.4% and 28.8%, respectively) (cited by Harris, 1999b). Other research also supports these findings (Fitzgerald, 1999). It appears, therefore, that racial profiling is not a valid police procedure, and some police forces have started to implement policies in an attempt to reduce the use of this sort of profiling.

SUMMARY

1. The police attempt to achieve two things when conducting interrogations—to gain information that furthers the investigation and to obtain a confession from the suspect. Police officers in North America use the Reid model of interrogation to interrogate suspects. This model advocates the use of psychologically based interrogation tactics to break down a suspect's resistance to telling the truth. The tactics used in the Reid model of interrogation can be broken down into minimization and maximization techniques.

2. The three potential problems with the Reid model of interrogation are (1) the inability of police officers to accurately detect deception, (2) biases that result from presuming a suspect is guilty, and (3) an increased likelihood that suspects will make false confessions.

3. False confessions must be differentiated from retracted confessions and disputed confessions. A false confession is one that is either intentionally fabricated or is not based on actual knowledge of the facts in a case. A retracted confession is simply someone declaring that his or her confession is false. A disputed confession is one that is disputed at trial, often because of a legal technicality or because the suspect disputes the confession was ever made.

4. There are three types of false confessions, each having its own set of vulnerability factors. Voluntary false confessions occur when someone voluntarily confesses to a crime he or she did not commit without any elicitation from the police. Coerced-compliant false confessions are those in which the suspect confesses to a crime, even though the suspect is fully aware that he or she did not commit it. Coerced-internalized false confessions consist of individuals confessing to a crime they did not commit—and subsequently coming to the belief they committed the crime—usually after they are exposed to highly suggestive questions.

5. Criminal profiling is used frequently by the police in serial crime investigations. They use it for prioritizing suspects, developing new lines of inquiry, setting traps to flush out offenders, determining whether an offender's actions should be taken seriously, giving advice on how to interrogate suspects, and developing courtroom strategies.

   Despite its widespread use, criminal profiling is often criticized. One major criticism centres on the lack of a strong theoretical base underlying the approach. A second criticism relates to the fact that many profiles contain ambiguous information and this may cause problems when police officers are asked to interpret the profile. A third criticism is that professionally trained profilers may be no better than other individuals at constructing accurate profiles.

6. The police also use two other types of profiling. Geographic profiling is defined as any technique that uses crime scene locations to predict the most likely area where the offender resides. Racial profiling refers to any police-initiated action that relies on the race or ethnicity of an individual, rather than that individual's criminal behaviour.

KEY CONCEPTS

DISCUSSION QUESTIONS

1. You have been called in by the police to give them advice on how to conduct a police interrogation. In particular, they want to know how far they can go to get a confession from a suspect, while at the same time making sure the confession will be admissible in court. What advice would you give to them?

2. Many police agencies now videotape their police interrogations, presenting potential advantages for the police, suspects, and the courts. Do you see any potential problems with using this procedure? What are some other possible ways to minimize the problems that result from modern-day interrogation practices?

3. Because the Reid model of interrogation can increase the degree to which people falsely confess to crimes, people seem to agree that it should not be used with particular individuals (e.g., those who have a severe learning disability). However, few police agencies have policies in place to indicate when it is not appropriate to use the Reid model. Develop a set of recommendations for when the technique should and shouldn't be used.

4. Researchers are now using laboratory-based studies in an attempt to understand the processes involved when people confess to crimes they did not commit. Do you think this is problematic? Why or why not?

5. You are a criminal profiler who uses the inductive approach to profiling. You encounter a series of crimes in which the offender consistently attacks elderly women in their apartments at night. How would you go about constructing a profile in this case? What sorts of problems would a deductive profiler have with your profile? How could you attempt to counter some of the arguments?

6. A number of studies have found that people view ambiguous criminal profiles as accurate even when they are asked to rate their accuracy against different suspects. Researchers have claimed that this occurs because people are able to creatively re-interpret ambiguous profiles to make them fit any number of potential suspects. What other factors could contribute to this finding?

7. Geographic profiling works in large part because offenders commit most of their crimes close to home. Why do you think offenders do this?

ADDITIONAL INFORMATION

Readings

Gudjonsson, G.H. (2003). *The psychology of interrogations and confessions: A handbook.* West Sussex, UK: John Wiley & Sons.

Holmes, R.M., & Holmes, S.T. (2002). *Profiling violent crimes: An investigative tool* (3rd edition). Thousand Oaks, CA: Sage.

Kassin, S.M. (1997). The psychology of confession evidence. *American Psychologist, 52,* 221–233.

Web Sites

The Homepage of the Reid Model of Interrogation
www.reid.com/index.html

Police Interrogations and Confessions
www.williams.edu/Psychology/Faculty/Kassin/research/confessions.htm

Criminal Profiling Site
www.corpus-delicti.com/

Chapter 3
Psychology and Health

Chapter 3

Psychology and Health

Meet Erika (Katy) Simons, a vivacious, energetic woman. Katy was born in 1911 in Amsterdam, Holland, where her family offered sanctuary to Jews during World War II. Whenever there was a knock on the door, Jews who were staying with them had to be quickly hidden. Katy and her family were well aware that they were placing their lives at risk. "I don't remember if I was ever afraid," she says. "It didn't matter. You just did what you needed to do." For Katy, this also entailed delivering food and supplies to Jews. She was eventually captured by the Nazis and imprisoned. Katy and the other prisoners took turns sleeping on a single straw mattress and comforted one another by singing and reminiscing. During this time, she didn't know whether her family members also had been captured or if they were even still alive. Her mother eventually managed to have a note smuggled into the prison letting her know that they were fine. When Katy was released from prison, she immediately resumed her acts of compassion, becoming a courier for the underground resistance movement.

In April 2002, at the age of 91, Katy Simons became the first Canadian to receive the Righteous among the Nations award from the Holocaust memorial centre in Jerusalem. This award is bestowed on non-Jews who risked their lives to save Jews from the Holocaust. Although Katy Simons is honoured to be the recipient of this award, she accepts it with her usual modesty: "It is simple. If you can save a life, you do it" (Elvers, 2002).

World War II prevented Katy Simons from following her dream of attending university. She had hoped to begin university before the war started, but her father died and she was needed at home to help take care of her younger siblings. When she left home, she took nurse's training in a college in England because she needed to get into a career quickly in order to support herself financially. While she longed to attend university, it wasn't an option; she never married and needed to keep working to make ends meet. But Katy never let go of her dream. As soon as she retired—by then in Canada—she registered for courses at the University of Winnipeg. She was a little worried that the other students might wonder what that "old lady" was doing there and one day asked a fellow student if the others minded having her in class. "Oh, no!" said the student. "Not at all! You ask the questions I'd be too afraid to ask." Katy then knew that she was welcome.

Shortly after Katy started attending university, she required hip surgery. She recalls not wanting to miss her evening history class, so she obtained special permission to leave the hospital. In her usual unstoppable way, she walked from the hospital to the university—a distance of at least 1 kilometre. (She did, however, accept a ride back to the hospital from her professor!) Katy became a familiar sight at the university and eventually graduated. Her infectious enthusiasm, humour, and warmth gained her instant popularity among students, staff, and faculty. Her age was never an issue.

The enthusiasm with which Katy embraced her university studies is characteristic of her approach to life. She still finds pleasure in the many activities in her life, which include origami and reciting poetry in any of the four languages she speaks fluently. As Katy's experiences would suggest, her life has not been easy. Quite the contrary. Health problems have reduced her mobility to the point where she had to move into an assisted-living apartment. Remarkably, she manages to get around with the use of arm crutches and is thankful for the independence she has. When she was interviewed for

▲ Katy Simons, age 92, maintains her zest for life, despite the health difficulties she faces.

this textbook, at age 92, she passed by the elevator and insisted on taking two flights of stairs up to the coffee shop in her building! People who know Katy are struck by the fact that her feisty spirit, her pleasant smile, and the sparkle in her eyes have not dimmed with age. Why has Katy Simons lived such a long and rewarding life? Is her positive outlook on life related to her longevity, or is she simply blessed with good genes and good luck? As you will see, it may be more than a coincidence that Katy is so upbeat and in control of her life and in such good health for someone in her nineties.

This module is concerned with the application of social psychology to physical and mental health, which is a flourishing area of research (Bailis & Segall, 2004; Cohen & Herbert, 1996; Salovey, Rothman, & Rodin, 1998; Taylor, 1995). We will focus on topics on the interface of social psychology and health: how people cope with stress in their lives, the relationship between their coping styles and their physical and mental health, and how we can get people to behave in healthier ways.

Stress and Human Health

There is more to health than germs and disease—we also need to consider the amount of stress in our lives and how we deal with that stress (Inglehart, 1991). A great deal of anecdotal evidence indicates that stress can affect the body in dramatic ways. Consider these examples, reported by the psychologist W. B. Cannon (1942):

- After eating some fruit, a New Zealand woman learns that it came from a forbidden supply reserved for the chief. She is horrified and her health deteriorates, and the next day she dies—even though it was a perfectly fine piece of fruit.
- A man in Africa has breakfast with a friend, eats heartily, and goes on his way. A year later, he learns that his friend made the breakfast from a wild hen, a food strictly forbidden in the man's culture. The man immediately begins to tremble and is dead within 24 hours.
- An Australian man's health deteriorates after a witch doctor casts a spell on him. He recovers only when the witch doctor removes the spell.

These examples probably sound pretty bizarre. But let's fast-forward to the beginning of the twenty-first century, where many similar cases of sudden death occur following a psychological trauma. When people undergo a major upheaval in their lives, such as losing a spouse, declaring bankruptcy, or being forced to resettle in a new culture, their chance of dying increases (Morse, Martin, & Moshonov, 1991). Or consider the plight of an older person who is institutionalized in a long-term health care facility. In many such institutions in Canada, the residents have little responsibility for or control over their own lives: they cannot choose what to eat, what to wear, or even when to go to the bathroom. Residents in such institutions often become passive and withdrawn, and fade into death as if they have simply given up. This is quite a contrast to the zest shown by Katy Simons as she begins her tenth decade of life!

Stress also takes a toll on its victims in other ways. According to research conducted at McGill University, Holocaust survivors—particularly those who were adolescents or young adults at the end of World War II—continue to experience negative psychological effects such as paranoia and depression, more than 40 years after they were persecuted (Sigal & Weinfeld, 2001). Similarly, the cruelty and abuse some First Nations children suffered in residential schools continue to have traumatic effects on the survivors (Hanson & Hampton, 2000). And many people experienced psychological and physical problems after the terrorist attacks on September 11, 2001, in the United States (Schlenger et al., 2002; Silver et al., 2002). One study measured the heart rates of a sample of adults in New Haven, Connecticut, the week after the attacks. Compared to a control group of people studied before the attacks, the people studied after the attacks showed lower heart rate variability, which is a risk factor for sudden death (Lampert et al., 2002). Finally, as you know all too well, university life is fraught with stress. A large-scale study of university students across Canada found that psychological distress (e.g., anxiety, depression) was significantly higher among students than in Canada's general population (Adlaf et al., 2001). The good news was that distress declined with each successive year in university. Rest reassured that things will get better as you go along!

As these examples suggest, our physical and psychological health is closely tied to the amount of stress in our lives. As we will see, we need to consider not only the amount of stress in our lives, but also how we deal with that stress.

Effects of Negative Life Events

Among the pioneers in research on stress was Hans Selye (1956, 1976), who defined stress as the body's physiological response to threatening events. He focused on how the human body adapts to threats from the environment, regardless of the source of a threat, be it a psychological or physiological trauma. Later researchers have examined what it is about a life event that makes it threatening. Holmes and Rahe (1967), for example, suggested that stress is the degree to which people have to change and readjust their lives in response to an external event. The more change required, the more stress occurs. Thus, if a spouse or partner dies, just about every aspect of a person's life is disrupted, leading to a great deal of stress. This definition of stress applies to happy events in one's life as well, if the event causes a person to change his or her daily routine. Graduating from university is a happy occasion, but it can be stressful because of the major changes it sets in motion in one's life. Similarly, many people look forward to retirement, failing to anticipate the extent of life change that occurs as a result of this transition. A study of Bell Canada retirees, for example, found that, for many people, retirement brings with it considerable instability and stress (Marshall, Clarke, & Ballantyne, 2001).

To assess such life changes, Holmes and Rahe (1967) developed a measure called the Social Readjustment Rating Scale (see Table 3.1). Some events, such as the death of a spouse or partner, have many "life change units," because they involve the most change in people's daily routines. Other events, such as getting a traffic ticket, have relatively few life change units. Here's how the scale works. Participants check all events that have occurred to them in the preceding year and then get a score for the total number of life change units caused by those events. The scores are then correlated with the frequency with which the participants become sick or have physical complaints. Several studies have found that the higher the score people report, the worse their physical and mental health (Seta, Seta, & Wang, 1990; Tesser & Beach, 1998).

These findings probably don't come as much of a surprise; it seems pretty obvious that people who are experiencing a lot of change and upheaval in their lives are more likely to feel anxious and get sick. A closer look reveals, however, that these findings aren't all that straightforward. One problem, as you may have recognized, is that most studies in this area use correlational designs rather than experimental designs. Just because life changes are correlated with health problems does not mean that the life

Table 3.1 The Social Readjustment Rating Scale

Rank	Life Event	Life Change Units*	Rank	Life Event	Life Change Units*
1	Death of spouse	100	23	Son or daughter leaving home	29
2	Divorce	73	24	Trouble with in-laws	29
3	Marital separation	65	25	Outstanding personal achievement	28
4	Jail term	63	26	Spouse begins or stops work	26
5	Death of a close family member	63	27	Begin or end school	26
6	Personal injury or illness	53	28	Change in living conditions	25
7	Marriage	50	29	Revision of personal habits	24
8	Fired at work	47	30	Trouble with boss	23
9	Marital reconciliation	45	31	Change in work hours or conditions	20
10	Retirement	45	32	Change in residence	20
11	Change in health of a family member	44	33	Change in school	20
12	Pregnancy	40	34	Change in recreation	19
13	Sex difficulties	39	35	Change in church activities	19
14	Gain of new family member	39	36	Change in social activities	18
15	Business readjustment	39	37	Mortgage or loan less than $10 000	17
16	Change in financial state	38	38	Change in sleeping habits	16
17	Death of close friend	37	39	Change in number of family get-togethers	15
18	Change to different line of work	36	40	Change in eating habits	15
19	Change in number of arguments with spouse	35	41	Vacation	13
20	Mortgage over $10 000	31	42	Christmas	12
21	Foreclosure of mortgage or loan	30	43	Minor violations of the law	11
22	Change in responsibilities at work	29			

* According to Holmes and Rahe (1967), the greater the number of "life change units" you have experienced within the past year, the greater the likelihood of physical illness.

(Adapted from Holmes & Rahe, 1967)

changes *caused* the health problems. Some researchers have argued persuasively that it is not life changes that cause health problems, but rather, that people with certain personality traits, such as the tendency to experience negative moods, are more likely to experience life difficulties and to have health problems (Schroeder & Costa, Jr., 1984; Watson & Pennebaker, 1989).

Another problem with inventories such as Holmes and Rahe's is that it focuses on stressors experienced by the middle class and under-represents stressors experienced by the poor and members of minority communities. Variables such as poverty and racism are potent causes of stress (Clark et al., 1999; Jackson & Inglehart, 1995; Jackson, et al, 1996). To understand the relationship between stress and health, we need to understand better such community-level and cultural-level variables as poverty and racism.

Perceived Stress and Health

Simply totting up the number of negative life events that people experience—such as divorcing or losing one's job—violates a basic principle of social psychology: subjective situations have more of an impact on people than objective situations (Griffin & Ross, 1991). Of course, some situations are objectively bad for our health, regardless of how we interpret them (Jackson & Inglehart, 1995; Taylor, Repetti, & Seeman, 1997). Still, there are events that seem to have negative effects only on the people who construe them in

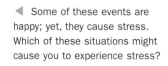
◀ Some of these events are happy; yet, they cause stress. Which of these situations might cause you to experience stress?

negative ways. Some people view getting a traffic ticket as a major hassle, whereas others view it as a minor inconvenience. Some people view a major life change such as getting divorced as a liberating escape from an abusive relationship, whereas others view it as a devastating personal failure. As recognized by Richard Lazarus (1966, 1993, 2000) in his pioneering work on stress, it is subjective, not objective, stress that causes problems. An event is stressful for people only if they interpret it as stressful; thus, we can define **stress** as the negative feelings and beliefs that occur whenever people feel unable to cope with demands from their environment (Lazarus & Folkman, 1984).

Stress the negative feelings and beliefs that occur whenever people feel unable to cope with demands from their environment

Consider, for instance, our opening example of Katy Simons. If she were filling out the Social Readjustment Rating Scale, she would check "personal injury or illness," given that she is experiencing a number of health problems, as well as "begin or end school" and "change in living conditions," to name a few. As a result, she would receive a large number of life change units. According to the theory, she should be at high risk for further physical problems from the stress caused by her hip surgery, completing university, and other changes to her life. But as we saw, Katy is not particularly bothered by these events. With her characteristic optimism, she looks on the bright side, welcoming the fact that she is able to get about with crutches. Katy finds these events possible to cope with; therefore, these events do not fit our definition of stress.

Studies using this subjective definition of stress confirm the idea that it is the life experiences that we perceive as negative that are bad for our health. Lefrançois and colleagues (2000), for example, administered a French version of the Holmes and Rahe (1967) Social Readjustment Rating Scale (modified to focus on the life changes associated with aging) to elderly people in Quebec. As expected, life changes that were regarded as negative were associated with the greatest psychological distress (Lefrançois et al., 2000).

Stress caused by negative interpretations of events can even affect our immune systems, making us more susceptible to disease. Consider, for example, the common cold. When people are exposed to the virus that causes a cold, 20 to 60 percent of them become sick. Is it possible that stress is one determinant of who will become ill? To find out, Cohen, Tyrrell, and Smith (1991, 1993) asked volunteers to spend a week at a research institute in southern England. As a measure of stress, the participants listed recent events that had had a negative impact on their lives. That is, consistent with our definition of stress, the participants listed only events they perceived to be negative. The researchers then gave participants nasal drops that contained either the virus that causes the common cold or saline (saltwater). The participants were subsequently quarantined for several days so that they had no contact with other people. The results?

How much stress people experienced determined how likely they were to catch a cold from the virus (see Figure 3.1). Among people who reported the least amount of stress, about 27 percent came down with a cold. This rate increased steadily the more stress people reported, topping out at a rate of nearly 50 percent in the group that was experiencing the most stress. This effect of stress was found even when several other factors that influence catching a cold were taken into account, such as the time of year people participated and the participant's age, weight, and gender. This study, along with others like it, shows that the more stress people experience, the lower their immunity to diseases (Cohen, 2001; Stone et al., 1993).

The results from Cohen, Tyrrell, and Smith's correlational study have been confirmed by research using experimental designs. For example, there are studies in which people's immune responses are measured before and after undergoing mildly stressful tasks in the laboratory, such as solving mental arithmetic problems continuously for 6 minutes or giving speeches on short notice. It turns out that even relatively mild stressors such as these can lead to a suppression of the immune system (Cacioppo, 1998; Cacioppo et al., 1998).

The finding that stress has negative effects on people's health raises an important question: What exactly is it that makes people perceive a situation as stressful? One important determinant, as we will now see, is the amount of control they believe they have over the event.

▶ **FIGURE 3.1**

STRESS AND THE LIKELIHOOD OF CATCHING A COLD

People were first exposed to the virus that causes the common cold, then isolated. The greater the amount of stress they were experiencing, the greater the likelihood that they caught a cold from this virus.

(Adapted from Cohen, Tyrell, & Smith, 1991)

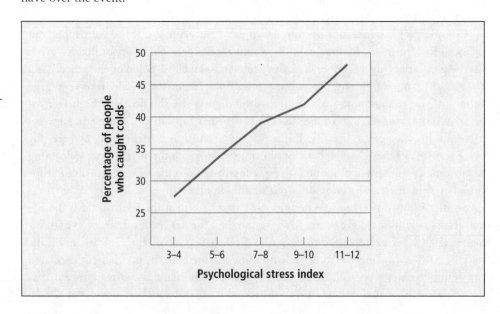

Feeling in Charge: The Importance of Perceived Control

How much control do you have over your own life? Are you able to decide what to do with each day? When and what to eat? When to study? When to go out with friends? Is it possible that the amount of control you have over your life is related to your health?

Studies with the chronically ill suggest that it is. Shelley Taylor and her colleagues (1984), for example, interviewed women with breast cancer and found that many of them believed they could control whether their cancer returned. Here is how one man described his wife: "She got books, she got pamphlets, she studied, she talked to cancer patients. She found out everything that was happening to her and she fought it. She went to war with it. She calls it 'taking in her covered wagons and surrounding it'" (quoted in Taylor, 1989). The researchers found that women who believed that their cancer was controllable were better adjusted psychologically (see also Folkman & Moskowitz, 2000). Moreover, there is some evidence that people who try to control their cancer and its treatment live slightly longer than those who do not (Taylor, 1989).

Subsequent studies have found that a high sense of **perceived control**—defined as the belief that we can influence our environment in ways that determine whether we experience positive or negative outcomes—is associated with good mental and physical health (Burger, 1992; Skinner, 1995, 1996; Thompson, 1999). The benefits of perceived control have been demonstrated in a variety of domains. For example, Helgeson and Fritz (1999) interviewed patients who had undergone a coronary angioplasty because of diseased arteries. The people who had a high sense of control over their futures were less likely to experience subsequent heart problems than those with a low sense of control (Helgeson, 2003; Helgeson & Fritz, 1999).

Perceived control the belief that we can influence our environment in ways that determine whether we experience positive or negative outcomes

Such effects are not limited to physical health. A study conducted with clients at sexual assault centres in southern Ontario found that rape victims who believed that they generally had control over outcomes in their lives experienced less depression and showed fewer symptoms of post-traumatic stress 6 months or more after the event compared to rape victims who felt that they had little control (Regehr, Cadell, & Jansen, 1999). In a very different vein, longitudinal research conducted by the Canadian Aging Research Network with elderly residents of Manitoba has found that those who perceived that they have control over housework and outdoor work were more likely to see themselves as having good health—more so than elderly people who perceived less control. Importantly, those who perceived control actually were in better health (Chipperfield, Perry, & Menec, 1999) and tended to live longer (Menec & Chipperfield, 1997). Finally, research conducted at the University of Manitoba found that first-year students who felt that they had control over their academic performance reported less anxiety and boredom and actually received better grades than those who perceived less control (Perry et al., 2001; Perry, 2003). Students who were high in perceived control and who used failure experiences as a motivation to do better in the future, rather than dwelling on the failure, were especially likely to do well.

Of course, studies such as these are using correlational, rather than experimental, designs. Researchers measure the amount of control people are experiencing and correlate this with their psychological and physical adjustment. Such studies cannot prove that feelings of control *cause* good physical or emotional health; for example, it is possible that good physical or emotional health causes one to feel more in control. Indeed, Menec, Chipperfield, and Perry (1999) found that elderly people who believed that they were in good health were also more likely to perceive control over their lives and engage in control-enhancing strategies. To address the question of whether feelings of control have beneficial causal effects, we need to conduct experimental studies in which people are randomly assigned to conditions of "high" versus "low" perceived control. Fortunately, a number of such experimental studies have been conducted (Heckhausen & Schulz, 1995; Rodin, 1986).

INCREASING PERCEIVED CONTROL IN NURSING HOMES Some of the most dramatic effects of perceived control have been found in studies of older people in nursing homes. Many people who live in nursing homes and hospitals feel that they have lost control of their lives (Raps et al., 1982). People are often placed in long-term care facilities against their wishes and, once there, have little say in what they do, whom they see, or what they eat. For example, an observational study of residents at a nursing home in Alberta found that patients tended to sit passively and to rely on nursing staff to initiate contact (Intrieri & Morse, 1997).

Ellen Langer and Judith Rodin (1976) believed that it would be beneficial for residents of a nursing home if their feelings of control were increased. They asked the director of a nursing home in Connecticut to convey to the residents that contrary to what they might think, they had a lot of responsibility for their own lives. Here is an excerpt of his speech:

> Take a minute to think of the decisions you can and should be making. For example, you have the responsibility of caring for yourselves, of deciding whether or not you want to make this a home you can be proud of and happy in. You should be deciding how you want your rooms to be arranged—whether you want it to be as it is or whether you want the staff to help you rearrange the furniture. You should be deciding how you want to spend your time.... If you are unsatisfied with anything here, you have the influence to change it.... These are just a few of the things you could and should be deciding and thinking about now and from time to time every day (Langer & Rodin, 1976).

The director went on to say that a movie would be shown on two nights the following week and that the residents should decide which night they wanted to attend. Finally, he gave each resident a gift of a houseplant, emphasizing that it was up to the resident to take care of it.

The director also gave a speech to residents assigned to a comparison group. This speech was different in one crucial way—all references to making decisions and residents being responsible for themselves were deleted. The director emphasized that he wanted the residents to be happy, but he did not say anything about the control they had over their lives. He said that a movie would be shown on two nights the next week and that the residents would be assigned to see it on one night or the other. He gave plants to these residents as well, but said that the nurses would take care of the plants.

The director's speech might not seem like a major change in the lives of the residents. The people in the induced control group heard one speech about the responsibility they had for their lives and were given one plant to water. That doesn't seem like very strong stuff, does it? But to an institutionalized person who feels helpless and constrained, even a small boost in control can have a dramatic effect. Indeed, residents in the induced control group became happier and more active than did residents in the comparison

Giving senior citizens a sense of control over their lives has been found to have positive benefits, both physically and psychologically.

group (Langer & Rodin, 1976). Most dramatic of all, the induced control intervention affected the residents' health and mortality. By 18 months after the director's speech, 30 percent of residents in the comparison condition had died, compared to only 15 percent of residents in the induced control group (Rodin & Langer, 1977; see left side of Figure 3.2).

Richard Schulz (1976) increased feelings of control in residents of nursing homes in a different way. Schulz started a program in a North Carolina nursing home wherein undergraduates visited the residents once a week for 2 months. In the induced control condition, the residents decided when the visits would occur and how long they would last. In a randomly assigned comparison condition, it was the students, not the residents, who decided when the visits would occur and how long they would last. While residents received visits in both conditions, in only one could they control the visits' frequency and duration. This may seem like a minor difference, but, again, giving the residents some semblance of control over their lives had dramatic effects. After 2 months, those in the induced control condition were happier, healthier, more active, and were taking fewer medications than those in the comparison group. Schulz returned to the nursing home several months later to assess the long-term effects of his intervention, including its effect on mortality rates. Based on the results of the Langer and Rodin (1976) study, we might expect that those residents who could control the students' visits would be healthier and more likely to still be alive than residents who could not. However, there is a crucial difference between the two studies; the residents in the Langer and Rodin study were given an enduring sense of control, whereas the residents in the Schulz study experienced control and then lost it when the students' visits ceased. Langer and Rodin's participants could continue to choose which days to participate in different activities, to take care of their plant, and to feel they could make a difference in what happened to them—even after the study ended. By contrast, when Schulz's study was over and the students stopped visiting, the residents who could control the visits suddenly had that control removed.

Unfortunately, Schulz's intervention had an unintended effect. Once the program ended, the people in the induced control group did worse (Schulz & Hanusa, 1978). Compared to people in the comparison group, they were more likely to have experienced deteriorating health and zest for life, and they were more likely to have died (see the right side of Figure 3.2). This study has sobering implications for the many programs in which volunteers visit residents of nursing homes, prisons, and mental hospitals. These programs might be beneficial in the short run but do more harm than good after they end.

DISEASE, CONTROL, AND WELL-BEING   We end this discussion with a word of caution. First, the findings we have been describing are culturally specific. There is evidence that the relationship between perceived control and distress is much higher in Western cultures than in Asian cultures (Sastry & Ross, 1998). In Western cultures, where mastery and individualism are prized, people are much more likely to feel distressed when they cannot control their destinies. Asians are less likely to worry about lower control because of their emphasis on collectivism and putting the group ahead of the individual.

Second, even in Western societies, there is a danger in exaggerating the relation between perceived control and physical health. The social critic Susan Sontag (1978, 1988) perceptively observed that when a society is plagued by a deadly but poorly understood disease, such as tuberculosis in the nineteenth century and AIDS today, the illness is often blamed on some kind of human frailty, such as lack of faith, moral weakness, or a broken heart. As a result, people sometimes blame themselves for their illnesses, even to the point where they do not seek effective treatment. Even though it is beneficial for people to feel that they are in control of their illnesses, the downside of this strategy is that if they do not get better, they may blame themselves for failing to recover. Tragically, diseases such as cancer can be fatal no matter how much control a person feels. One of Lance

▶ **FIGURE 3.2**

PERCEIVED CONTROL AND MORTALITY

In two studies, elderly residents in nursing homes were made to feel more in control of their lives. In one (Rodin & Langer, 1977), the intervention endured over time so that people continued to feel in control. As seen in the left side of the figure, this intervention had positive effects on mortality rates. Those who received it were more likely to be alive 18 months later than those who did not. In the other study (Schulz & Hanusa, 1978), the intervention was temporary. Being given control and then having it taken away had negative effects on mortality rates, as seen in the right side of the figure.

(Adapted from Rodin & Langer, 1977, and Schulz & Hanusa, 1978)

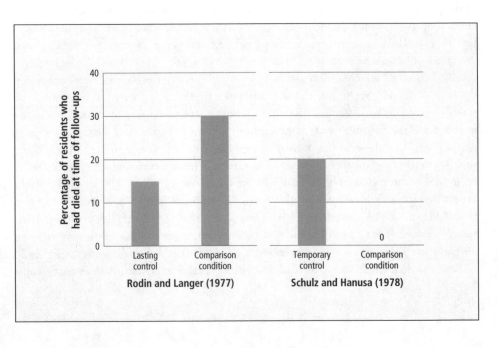

Armstrong's doctors put it this way, "I've seen wonderful, positive people not make it in the end ... and some of the most miserable, ornery people survive to resume their ornery lives" (Armstrong, 2000, p. 127). It only adds to the tragedy if people with serious diseases feel a sense of moral failure, blaming themselves for a disease that was unavoidable.

For people living with serious illness, maintaining some form of control has important benefits. Suzanne Thompson and her colleagues found that, even when people who are seriously ill with cancer or AIDS feel no control over the disease, many of them believe that they can still control the *consequences* of the disease (e.g., their emotional reactions and some of the physical symptoms, such as how tired they feel). And the more people feel they can control the consequences of their illness, the better adjusted they are, even if they know they cannot control the eventual course of the disease. In short, it is important to feel in control of something—even if it is not the disease itself (Heckhausen & Schutz, 1995; Thompson, 2002; Thompson, Nanni, & Levine, 1994).

Knowing You Can Do It: Self-Efficacy

Believing we have control over our lives is one thing; believing that we can actually execute the specific behaviours that will get us what we want is another. Sam might have a general sense that he is in control of his life, but will this mean that he will find it easy to stop smoking? According to Albert Bandura (a highly influential social psychologist who was born in Alberta and studied at the University of British Columbia), we have to examine his **self-efficacy,** which is the belief in one's ability to carry out specific actions that produce desired outcomes (Bandura, 1997; Bandura & Locke, 2003). If Sam believes that he can perform the behaviours that will enable him to quit smoking—throwing away his cigarettes, avoiding situations in which he is most tempted to smoke, distracting himself when he craves a cigarette—then chances are he will succeed. If he has low self-efficacy in this domain, believing that he can't perform the behaviour necessary to quit, then he is likely to fail.

Self-efficacy the belief in one's ability to carry out specific actions that produce desired outcomes

People's level of self-efficacy has been found to predict a number of important health behaviours, such as the likelihood that they will quit smoking, lose weight, lower their cholesterol, and exercise regularly (Bandura, 1997; Salovey et al., 2000). For example, a study of more than a thousand high school students in Toronto found that those who were high in self-efficacy in the area of exercise were more likely to engage in vigorous physical exercise than those who had low self-efficacy in this area (Allison, Dwyer, & Makin, 1999). Again, it is not a general sense of control that predicts this behaviour, but the confidence that one can perform the specific behaviour in question. A person might have high self-efficacy in one domain, such as high confidence that he or she can lose weight, but low self-efficacy in another domain, such as low confidence that he or she can quit smoking.

Self-efficacy increases the likelihood that people will engage in healthier behaviour in two ways. First, it influences people's persistence and effort at a task. People with low self-efficacy tend to give up easily, whereas people high in self-efficacy set higher goals, try harder, and persist more in the face of failure—thereby increasing the likelihood that they will succeed (Cervone & Peake, 1986; Litt, 1988). Second, self-efficacy influences the way our bodies react while we are working toward our goals. For example, people with high self-efficacy experience less anxiety while working on a difficult task, and their immune system functions more optimally (Bandura et al., 1988; Wiedenfield et al., 1990). In short, self-efficacy operates as a kind of self-fulfilling prophecy. The more you believe that you can accomplish something, such as quitting smoking, the greater the likelihood that you will.

How can self-efficacy be increased? A study by Blittner, Goldberg, and Merbaum (1978) on smoking cessation suggests one way. Adult smokers who wanted to quit smoking were randomly assigned to one of three conditions. In the self-efficacy condition, participants were told that they had been chosen for the study because they "showed that they had strong willpower and great potential to control and conquer their desires and behaviour." These participants then underwent a 14-week smoking cessation program. Participants in the treatment-alone condition underwent the same program as people in the self-efficacy condition, with one important difference—instead of being told that they had been selected because of their high potential for quitting, they were told that they had been chosen at random for the treatment program. Finally, participants in the no-treatment control condition did not receive self-efficacy instructions nor did they take part in the treatment program; they were told that they would be contacted for the study at a later time.

As seen in Figure 3.3, the self-efficacy instructions were quite effective. By the end of the treatment period, 67 percent of people in the self-efficacy condition had quit smoking, compared to only 28 percent in the treatment-alone group and 6 percent in the no-treatment control group. Remember that the only way in which these conditions differed was that in the self-efficacy condition, participants were led to believe that they had high potential for quitting smoking. Believing that we can do something is a powerful determinant of whether we actually succeed.

Explaining Negative Events: Learned Helplessness

What happens when we experience a setback? Despite our belief in ourselves, perhaps we failed to quit smoking or did poorly on a midterm. Another important determinant of our physical and mental health is how we explain to ourselves why a negative event occurred. Consider two university students who both get poor grades on their first calculus test.

▶ **FIGURE 3.3**

THE ROLE OF SELF-EFFICACY IN
SMOKING CESSATION

Adult smokers were randomly assigned to one of three conditions. In the self-efficacy condition, people were told that they were selected for the study because they had great potential to quit. They then underwent a 14-week smoking cessation program. People in the treatment-alone condition participated in the same program, but were told that they had been randomly selected for it. People in the no-treatment control condition did not take part in the program. At the end of the 14-week period, substantially more people in the self-efficacy condition had quit smoking. Believing that one has the ability to carry out beneficial behaviour—having high self-efficacy—is an important determinant of whether people succeed.

(Adapted from Blittner, Goldberg, & Merbaum, 1978)

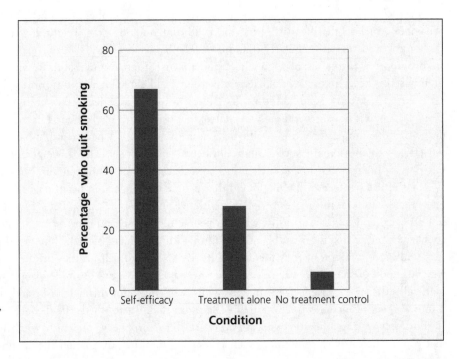

Student A says to herself, "I'll bet the professor deliberately made the test difficult, to motivate us to do better. I'll just have to study harder. If I really buckle down for the next test, I'll do better." Student B says to himself, "Wow, I guess I can't really cut it. I was worried that I wasn't smart enough to make it in university and, boy, was I ever right." Which student do you think will do better on the next test? Clearly the first one, because she has explained her poor performance in a way that is more flattering to herself and makes her feel more in control. In contrast, the second student is expressing **learned help-lessness**—pessimism that results from attributing a negative event to stable, internal, and global factors (Abramson, Seligman, & Teasdale, 1978; Overmier, 2002; Seligman, 1975).

If we think that a negative event has a stable cause—we've made a **stable attribution**—we believe that the event was caused by things that will not change over time (e.g., our intelligence), as opposed to factors that can change over time (e.g., the amount of effort we put into a task). Explaining this negative event as stemming from an internal cause—that is, making an **internal attribution**—means we believe that something about us caused the event (e.g., our own ability or effort), as opposed to factors that are external to us (e.g., the difficulty of a test). Finally, explaining an event as the result of a global or widespread cause—that is, making a **global attribution**—is the belief that the event is caused by factors that apply in a large number of situations (e.g., our general intelligence, which will influence our performance in many areas), rather than factors that are specific and apply in only a limited number of situations (e.g., how good we are at math, which will affect our performance in math courses but not in other courses). According to learned helplessness theory, making stable, internal, and global attributions for negative events leads to hopelessness, depression, reduced effort, and difficulty in learning (see Figure 3.4).

Student B, for example, believes that the cause of his poor grade is stable (being unintelligent will last forever), internal (something about him is to blame), and global (being unintelligent will affect him in many situations other than calculus classes). This kind of explanation will lead to learned helplessness, thereby producing depression, reduced effort, and the inability to learn new things. Student A, in contrast, believes that the cause of her poor grade is unstable (the professor will make the tests easier, and she can study harder next time), external (the professor intentionally made the test hard), and specific (the things that caused her poor calculus grade are unlikely to affect anything else, such as her grade in English). People who explain bad events in this more optimistic way are less likely to be depressed and more likely to do better on a broad range of tasks (Joiner & Wagner, 1995; Peterson & Seligman, 1984; Sweeney, Anderson, & Bailey, 1986).

Consider cyclist Lance Armstrong's comeback after he had recovered from cancer. In his first races, he did fairly well, finishing fourteenth in a 5-day race through Spain and nineteenth in an 8-day race from Nice to Paris. He was used to winning, however, and initially explained his failure to do so in this way: "Well, I've just been through too much. I've been through three surgeries, three months of chemo, and a year of hell, and that's the reason I'm not riding well. My body is just never going to be the same" (Armstrong, 2000, p. 188). Note that he attributed his poor performance to a cause that was internal (his lowered physical abilities), stable (a condition that would not change), and global (a condition that would influence many aspects of his life, not just one race). Had he persisted in explaining his performance in this way, surely he would not have gone on to win the Tour de France. Instead, he had the insight to recognize that every cyclist has ups and downs and that no one wins every race. "What I really should have been saying,"

Learned helplessness the state of pessimism that results from explaining a negative event as stemming from stable, internal, and global factors

Stable attribution the belief that the cause of an event is a result of factors that will not change over time, as opposed to unstable factors that will change over time

Internal attribution the belief that the cause of an event is because of things about you, as opposed to factors that are external to you (e.g., the difficulty of a test)

Global attribution the belief that the cause of an event is a result of factors that apply in a large number of situations, as opposed to the belief that the cause is specific and applies in only a limited number of situations

▲ **FIGURE 3.4**

THE THEORY OF LEARNED
HELPLESSNESS

Explaining a negative event in a pessimistic manner leads to learned helplessness (i.e., depression, lowered effort,
poor learning).

Armstrong realized, "was, 'Hey, it's just a bad day'"—an attribution to a cause that was external (the particular circumstances, not something about him), unstable (something likely to change), and specific (something limited to that one situation).

Learned helplessness theory is intimately related to attribution theory. Attribution theorists assume that your attitudes and behaviours depend on how you interpret the causes of events, an assumption that learned helplessness shares. Note that we do not know the real reason our hypothetical students did poorly on their calculus test. Instead, learned helplessness theory states that it is more important to consider people's perceptions of these causes. The real causes, of course, are not irrelevant. Students who truly lack ability in calculus are likely to do poorly on future calculus tests. In life, however, what actually causes our behaviour is often not so clear-cut or fixed. In such situations, people's attributions about the causes of their problems can be very important.

To explore this link between learned helplessness and academic performance, Tim Wilson and Patricia Linville (1982, 1985) conducted a study with first-year students at Duke University. They assumed that many first-year students experience academic difficulties because of a damaging pattern of attributions. Because of the difficulty of adjusting to a new academic and social environment, the first year of university has its rough spots for nearly everyone. The problem is that many first-year students do not realize how common such adjustment problems are and assume that their problems come from personal predicaments that are unlikely to change—just the kind of attribution that leads to learned helplessness. Wilson and Linville tried to combat this pessimism by convincing first-year students that the causes of poor performance are often temporary. In the

 People can experience learned helplessness in a variety of settings, including at work. Fortunately, most bosses do not encourage learned helplessness in the way that Dilbert's boss does.

DILBERT reprinted by permission of United Feature Syndicate, Inc.

treatment condition, the students watched videotaped interviews of four more senior students, each of whom mentioned that his or her grades had been poor or mediocre during the first year but had improved significantly since then. The students were also given statistics indicating that academic performance is often poor in the first year of university but improves thereafter. The researchers hypothesized that this simple message would help prevent learned helplessness, increasing the students' motivation to try harder and removing needless worries about their abilities. Judging by the students' future performance, this is just what happened. Compared to students in a control group who participated in the study but did not watch the videotaped interviews or see the statistics, students in the treatment condition improved their grades more in the following year and were less likely to drop out. Similar results have been found in studies in other countries, including Canada and Belgium (Menec et al., 1994; Van Overwalle & De Metsenaere, 1990; Wilson, Damiani, & Shelton, 2002).

Because people's attributions were not directly measured in the Wilson and Linville (1982) study, we can only infer that the students improved their academic performance because of a beneficial change in their attributions. Other studies have directly measured people's attributions, and found that those who explain bad events in optimistic ways are less depressed, in better health, and do better in school and in their careers (Dweck, 1999; Perry, 2003; Peterson, Seligman, & Vaillant, 1988; Seligman & Schulman, 1986; Snyder, Irving, & Anderson, 1991).

Students who realize that poor academic performance in the first year of university is common and likely to improve will probably do better than students who believe that poor performance is a result of personal shortcomings that are unlikely to change.

Finally, research by Rempel, Ross, and Holmes (2001) suggests that those who make optimistic attributions for negative events also do better in their close relationships. Married couples living in the Waterloo area were asked to discuss a problem in their relationship. The researchers then compared whether couples who were high in trust made different attributions for problems in their relationships than couples who were low in trust. Indeed, high-trust couples were found to make positive, global attributions for their partner's behaviour. Even when discussing a conflict, these couples were optimistic; they focused on the enduring, positive aspects of their partner and the relationship. In contrast, low-trust couples showed a pattern of negative, pessimistic attributions; in other words, for these couples, learned helplessness had set in.

In summary, we have seen that our feelings of control and self-efficacy, and the kinds of attributions we make for our performance, are important determinants of our psychological and physical health. The power of our minds over our bodies is, of course, limited. But research shows that perceived control, self-efficacy, and optimistic attributions are beneficial, making it easier for us to cope with the hardships life deals us.

Coping with Stress

Coping styles the ways in which people react to stressful events

No one always feels in control, of course, and sometimes it is difficult to avoid being pessimistic after something bad happens. The death of a loved one, an acrimonious divorce, and the loss of a job are extremely stressful events. Considerable research indicates that people exhibit various reactions, or **coping styles**, in the face of potentially stressful events (e.g., Aspinwall & Taylor, 1997; Lazarus & Folkman, 1984; Lehman et al., 1993; Salovey et al., 2000; Somerfield & McCrae, 2000). What are these styles and how successful are they? We will examine a few coping styles here, beginning with research on differences in the way that men and women respond to stress.

Gender Differences in Coping with Stress

One of your authors (Tim Wilson) often takes the family dog, Jackson, to a park with a fenced-in area where dogs are allowed to run free. Most of the time, the neighbourhood dogs get along quite well, romping together with abandon. Occasionally, the romping gets out of hand, and one of the more aggressive dogs goes on the attack. The other dogs react in one of two ways: sometimes they respond in kind and a dogfight occurs—soon broken up by the owners. At other times the picked-on dogs seem not to like their chances and take off as fast as they can, tails between their legs. Fortunately, Jackson is quite fast and can often be seen running just ahead of a dog with bared teeth.

Fight-or-flight response responding to stress by either attacking the source of the stress or fleeing from it

Walter Cannon (1932) termed this the **fight-or-flight response**—defined as responding to stress by either attacking the source of the stress or fleeing from it. The fight-or-flight response has been viewed as the way in which all mammals respond to stress. When under threat, mammals are energized by the release of hormones such as norepinephrine and epinephrine, and—like the dogs in the park—they either go on the attack or retreat as quickly as they can. That, at least, has been the accepted story for many years. Recently, Shelley Taylor and her colleagues (2000) pointed out a little-known fact about research on the fight-or-flight syndrome: most of it has been done on males, particularly male rats. Is it possible that females respond differently to stressful events?

Taylor and her colleagues argue that the fight-or-flight response does not work well for females because they typically play a greater role in caring for children. Neither fighting nor fleeing is a good option for a pregnant female or one tending offspring. Consequently,

Taylor and her colleagues argue, a different way of responding to stress has evolved in females, the **tend-and-befriend response**. Instead of fighting or fleeing, women respond to stress with nurturant activities designed to protect themselves and their offspring (tending), and creating social networks that provide protection from threats (befriending).

Tending has a number of benefits for both the mother and the child; for example, a quiet child is less likely to be noticed by predators, and nurturing behaviour leads to lower stress and improved immune functioning in mammals. Befriending involves the creation of close ties with other members of the species, which also confers a number of advantages. A close-knit group can exchange resources, watch out for predators, and share child care. Human females are more likely than males to develop intimate friendships, cooperate with others, and focus their attention on social relationships (Fehr, 1996). This is especially so when people are under stress. Research conducted in the United States (Tamres, Janicki, & Helgeson, 2002) and in the Canadian Maritimes (Day & Livingstone, 2003) has found that when stressed, women are more likely to seek out others, particularly other women.

It is possible that the tend-and-befriend response has a biological basis, just as the fight-and-flight response does in males. Specifically, females are more likely to show increased levels of the hormone oxytocin when under stress, and there is evidence that oxytocin has calming properties and promotes affiliation with others (Ennis, Kelly, & Lambert, 2001; Taylor et al., 2000). However, the tendency for women to seek social support could also stem from the ways in which women and men are socialized. There is evidence, for example, that women are more rewarded than men for turning to others during stress and discussing their problems (Collins & Miller, 1994).

It is easy to oversimplify gender differences such as these. While gender differences in coping do exist, the magnitude of these differences is not very large (Tamres, Janicki, & Helgeson, 2002). Further, seeking social support can benefit both women and men, as we'll see next.

Social Support: Getting Help from Others

One of the striking things about cyclist Lance Armstrong's recovery from cancer was the amount of support he received from his family and friends. His mother, to whom he was very close, took an active role in his treatment and recovery. She stayed by his side as

Tend-and-befriend response responding to stress with nurturant activities designed to protect oneself and one's offspring (tending) and creating social networks that provide protection from threats (befriending)

◀ Females are somewhat more likely than males to develop intimate friendships, cooperate with others, and focus their attention on social relationships, particularly when under stress. Shelley Taylor and her colleagues (2000) have referred to this as a *tend-and-befriend* strategy, responding to stress with nurturant activities designed to protect oneself and one's offspring (tending) and creating social networks that provide protection from threats (befriending).

much as possible and organized his schedule, prescription medicines, and diet. A close circle of friends stayed with him as well, many travelling great distances to visit him at the hospital and nurse him through the treatments. For example, 24 hours after his brain surgery, a group of friends took him to dinner at a restaurant across the street from the hospital. Armstrong also developed close friendships with many of the doctors and nurses who treated him (Armstrong, 2000).

Social support—defined as the perception that others are responsive and receptive to one's needs—is very helpful when dealing with stress (Helgeson & Cohen, 1996; Ryff & Singer, 2001; Sarason, Sarason, & Pierce, 1990; Stroebe & Stroebe, 1996; Uchino, Uno, & Holt-Lunstead, 1999). For example, after devastating hurricanes killed dozens of people and destroyed the homes and properties of thousands of others in South Carolina and Florida, researchers found that the people who coped the best were those who felt they had the most social support, such as having others to talk to and to help solve problems (Norris & Kaniasty, 1996). More recently, a study found that following the terrorist attacks on September 11, 2001, a number of people reported dealing with the sense of threat by spending time talking to others (Yum & Schenck-Hamlin, 2005).

Social support also plays an important role in the workplace, particularly for those who are employed in high-stress occupations. For example, a study of more than 800 Canadian and American firefighters found that those who received social support at work and from their families were less likely to suffer from post-traumatic stress disorder (Corneil et al., 1999). Similarly, a study of physicians, nurses, and technicians employed at cancer clinics in southern Ontario found that stress was less likely to impair job performance for those health care professionals who perceived that social support was available in their workplace (Stewart & Barling, 1996). Clearly, when we believe that we have someone to lean on, we can deal better with life's problems.

But what about in cases of life-threatening illnesses, such as Lance Armstrong's battle with cancer? Controlled studies suggest that social support plays an important role in the course of such diseases. In one study, David Spiegel and his colleagues (1989) randomly assigned women with advanced breast cancer to a social support condition or a control condition. Women in the social support condition met weekly with doctors and other patients to discuss their problems and fears, whereas people in the control group did not have access to this support system. Social support not only improved women's moods and reduced their fears but also lengthened their lives by an average of 18 months. These are certainly dramatic findings! More recently, the effects of social support were evaluated among a group of Canadian women who had been widowed in the previous two years (Stewart et al., 2001). These women met weekly in small groups led by a peer—a woman who also was widowed—and a mental health professional. At the end of the 20-week program, the women showed a number of improvements, including increased positive affect and increased hope and confidence.

Evidence for the role of social support also comes from cross-cultural studies. People who live in cultures that stress interdependence and collectivism suffer less from stress-related diseases, possibly because it is easier for people in these cultures to obtain social support. People who live in cultures that emphasize individualism are more often expected to go it alone—and their health pays the price (Bond, 1991; Brislin, 1993; Cross & Vick, 2001). For example, a study of elderly women and men from two different regions in Quebec found that those who were lacking in social support experienced greater psychological distress (e.g., depression, anxiety) than those with adequate social support (Lefrançois et al., 2000). Perhaps more dramatically, the availability of social support has

Social support the perception that others are responsive and receptive to one's needs

even been found to affect longevity. House, Robbins, and Metzner (1982) assessed the level of social support in a large sample of men and women in the years 1967 to 1969. They found that men with a low level of social support were 2 to 3 times more likely to die over the next 12 years than were men with a high level of social support; women with a low level of social support were 1.5 to 2 times more likely to die.

classic research

Does this mean that you should always seek out comfort and advice from others? Not necessarily. According to the **buffering hypothesis**, we are in greatest need of social support when we are under stress (Cohen & Wills, 1985; Koopman et al., 1998; Pierce et al., 1996). When times are tough—when you've just broken up with your girlfriend or boyfriend, or your parents have gone off the deep end again—social support helps in two ways. First, it can help you interpret an event as less stressful than you otherwise would. Suppose you've just found out that you have midterms in your psychology and calculus classes on the same day. If you have several friends in these classes who can commiserate with you and help you study, you are likely to find the tests less of a big deal than if you had to cope with them on your own. Second, even if we do interpret an event as stressful, social support can help us cope. Suppose you've just done poorly on a midterm and feel bad about it. It's best to have close friends to help you deal with this and figure out how to do better on the next test (Stroebe & Stroebe, 1996).

Buffering hypothesis the hypothesis that we need social support only when we are under stress, because it protects us against the detrimental effects of this stress

The moral? The countless popular songs you've heard are right. In times of trouble, find a friend to lean on. To get an idea of the amount of social support you feel is available in your life, complete the Try It! quiz on page 98.

Personality and Coping Styles

Some people, of course, are more likely to seek help from others or, more generally, to react in adaptive ways when under stress. Others seem to react badly when the going gets tough. As seen earlier in our discussion of learned helplessness, part of this comes from the way people explain the causes of a particular setback; explaining the setback in an optimistic way leads to better coping than explaining events in a pessimistic way. Other researchers have looked at this from the vantage point of individual differences, the aspects of people's personalities that make them different from other people.

◀ It is important to try to adopt an optimistic approach to life, because optimists have been found to be healthier and to react better to stress.

try it!   Social Support

This scale is made up of a list of statements, each of which may or may not be true about you. For each statement, choose T (for probably true) if the statement is true about you, or F (for probably false) if the statement is not true about you. You may find that many of the statements are neither clearly true nor clearly false. If so, try to decide quickly whether probably true or probably false is more descriptive of you. Although some questions will be difficult to answer, it is important that you pick one alternative or the other. Remember to circle only one of the alternatives for each statement. Read each item quickly but carefully before responding. Remember that this is not a test and there are no right or wrong answers.

1. There is at least one person I know whose advice I really trust.   T   F
2. There is really no one I can trust to give me good financial advice.   T   F
3. There is really no one who can give me objective feedback about how I'm handling my problems.   T   F
4. When I need suggestions for how to deal with a personal problem, I know there is someone I can turn to.   T   F
5. There is someone whom I feel comfortable going to for advice about sexual problems.   T   F
6. There is someone I can turn to for advice about handling hassles over household responsibilities.   T   F
7. I feel that there is no one with whom I can share my most private worries and fears.   T   F
8. If a family crisis arose, few of my friends would be able to give me good advice about how to handle it.   T   F
9. There are very few people I trust to help solve my problems.   T   F
10. There is someone I could turn to for advice about changing my job or finding a new one.   T   F

Scoring: You get one point each time you answered true (T) to questions 1, 4, 5, 6, and 10 and one point for each time you answered false (F) to questions 2, 3, 7, 8, and 9.

This scale was developed to measure what the researchers call *appraisal social support*, or "the perceived availability of someone to talk to about one's problems" (Cohen, Mermelstein, Kamarach, & Hoberman, 1985, pp. 75–76). One of their findings was that when people were not under stress, those low in social support had no more physical symptoms than those high in social support. However, when people were under stress, those low in social support had more physical symptoms than those high in social support. This is support for the buffering hypothesis. We need social support the most when times are tough. Another finding was that women scored reliably higher on the social support scale than men did. If you scored lower than you would like, you might want to consider reaching out to others more when you are under stress.

(Adapted from Cohen, Mermelstein, Kamarach, & Hoberman, 1985)

> Between the optimist and the pessimist
> the difference is droll;
> The optimist sees the doughnut,
> The pessimist the hole.
> —McLandburgh Wilson, 1915

OPTIMISM Some people, such as Katy Simons, are by nature optimistic, generally expecting the best out of life, whereas others always see the dark underside. And there is evidence that optimistic people react better to stress and are generally healthier than pessimists (Armor & Taylor, 1998; Carver & Scheier, 2003; Salovey et al., 2000). To get an idea of how optimistic you tend to be, complete the Try It! on page 99.

The good news is that most people have been found to have an optimistic outlook on life. In fact, there is evidence that most people are *unrealistically* optimistic about their lives (Armor & Taylor, 1998; Taylor & Brown, 1988, 1994). We discussed research on unrealistic optimism showing that we tend to expect that good events are more likely to happen to us than to our peers, and that negative events are less likely to happen to us than to our peers.

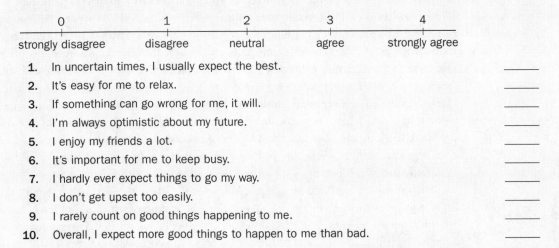

try it! The Life Orientation Test

Please indicate the extent of your agreement with each of the following 10 statements, using the scale below. Be as accurate and honest as you can on each item, and try not to let your answer to one question influence your answer to other questions. There are no right or wrong answers.

```
        0              1              2              3              4
strongly disagree   disagree      neutral         agree     strongly agree
```

1. In uncertain times, I usually expect the best. _____
2. It's easy for me to relax. _____
3. If something can go wrong for me, it will. _____
4. I'm always optimistic about my future. _____
5. I enjoy my friends a lot.
6. It's important for me to keep busy. _____
7. I hardly ever expect things to go my way. _____
8. I don't get upset too easily. _____
9. I rarely count on good things happening to me. _____
10. Overall, I expect more good things to happen to me than bad. _____

Scoring: First, reverse your answers to questions 3, 7, and 9. That is, for these questions, change 0 to 4, 1 to 3, 3 to 1, and 4 to 0. Then, total these reversed scores and the scores you gave to questions 1, 4, and 10. (Ignore questions 2, 5, 6, and 8, because they were filler items.)

This is a measure of *dispositional optimism* created by Scheier, Carver, and Bridges (1994). According to these researchers, the higher your score, the more optimistic your approach to life. The average score for university students in their study was 14.3, with no significant differences between women and men. Several studies have found that optimistic people cope better with stress and are healthier than their pessimistic counterparts.

This kind of unrealistic optimism would be a problem if it caused people to make serious mistakes about their prospects in life. Obviously, it would not be a good idea to convince ourselves that we will never get lung disease and therefore smoke as much as we want. Fortunately, most people have a healthy balance of optimism and reality monitoring. We manage to put a positive spin on many aspects of our lives, which leads to increased feelings of control and self-efficacy. At the same time, most people are able to keep their optimistic biases in check when they are faced with a real threat and need to take steps to deal with that threat (Armor & Taylor, 1998). Consider again cyclist Lance Armstrong's battle with cancer. In one sense, he was quite realistic, finding out all he could about the disease and the latest treatments and seeking the advice of many experts. He even learned to read X-rays as well as the doctors. Despite the severity of his disease, however, and the very real possibility that it might kill him, he was able to maintain a sense of optimism: "What is stronger, fear or hope?... Initially, I was very fearful and without much hope, but, as I sat there and absorbed the full extent of my illness, I refused to let the fear completely blot out my optimism" (Armstrong, 2000, p. 99).

TYPE A VERSUS TYPE B PERSONALITY Another personality variable that has received a great deal of attention is the **Type A versus Type B personality**, which is a personality typology based on how people typically confront challenges in their lives

Type A versus Type B personality a personality typology based on how people typically confront challenges in their lives; the Type A person is typically competitive, impatient, hostile, and control-oriented, whereas the Type B person is typically patient, relaxed, and noncompetitive

(Rosenman, 1993). The Type A individual is typically competitive, impatient, hostile, aggressive, and control-oriented, whereas the Type B person is typically patient, relaxed, and noncompetitive. We are all familiar with the Type A personality—this is the person who honks and yells at other drivers when they don't drive to his or her satisfaction. People with this personality type appear to deal with stress efficiently and aggressively. Their hard-driving, competitive approach to life pays off in some respects; Type A individuals tend to get good grades in university and to be successful in their careers (Kliewer, Lepore, & Evans, 1990; Ovcharchyn, Johnson, & Petzel, 1981); however, this success comes with some costs. According to research conducted at York University, Type A individuals spend relatively little time on nonwork activities (Burke & Greenglass, 1990) and have more difficulty balancing their work and family lives. For example, Esther Greenglass (1991) found that among female professors, those who were Type A had high career aspirations and reported conflict between professional and familial roles. Type A women with children were particularly hard-driven; they spent an average of 86 hours per week working on job-related and household tasks. Further, numerous studies show that Type A individuals are more prone to coronary heart disease than are Type B individuals (Matthews, 1988).

Subsequent studies have tried to pinpoint what it is about the Type A personality that links it to heart disease. The most likely culprit is hostility (Farber & Burge-Callaway, 1998; Krantz & McCeney, 2002; Salovey et al., 2000; Williams, 2002). Competitiveness and a fast-paced life might not be so bad by themselves, but people who are chronically hostile are more at risk for coronary disease. Given this risk, it would seem especially important for Type A people to maintain an exercise program. The tricky part is that Type A people turn almost every situation—even exercise—into a competitive one, with the result that exercise can actually have counterproductive effects. For example, in a recent study, Masters, Lacaille, and Shearer (2003) had Type A university students pedal an exercise bike. Participants in the competitive condition were told that the researchers would record their distance to see which participant was best. Participants in the noncompetitive condition were simply told that their distance would be recorded. Type A participants in the competitive condition later exhibited greater hostility and other negative emotions than those in the noncompetitive condition. Thus, an activity that should have been beneficial ended up putting Type A participants at even greater risk of coronary problems.

Type A personality may partially explain why Stewart McCann (2001, 2003) at the University College of Cape Breton found that people who peak early in their careers have shorter lives. This tendency to die young if you peak early was found among American and French presidents, American state governors, Canadian prime ministers, Nova Scotia premiers, and distinguished psychologists, to name a few. McCann suggests that Type A personality may play a role in the higher mortality rate among such high achievers.

What determines whether you are Type A or Type B? There are a number of factors. You are more likely to be a Type A if you are male, your parents are Type A, and you live in an urban rather than a rural area (Rosenman, 1993). The culture in which you grow up may also play a part. There is a higher rate of coronary disease in many Western cultures than in many Asian countries, such as Japan. Why? There are two reasons. First, in Western cultures where individualism and competitiveness are prized, personality types more like Type A might be encouraged (Triandis, 1995). Second, people who live in cultures that stress collectivism might have more support from other people when they experience stress and, as we have seen, such social support is a valuable way of making stress more manageable (Triandis, 1995).

HARDINESS There are other personality traits that are related to stress and coping. Kenneth Dion has examined the personality variable of hardiness in relation to a particular kind of stress, namely the stress of being a victim of prejudice and discrimination (Dion, 2002, 2003). **Hardiness** is a combination of self-esteem and a sense of control that helps people interpret and deal with stressful events in a positive, effective manner. In one study, Dion and his colleagues assessed perceptions of discrimination, stress symptoms, and hardiness among members of Toronto's Chinese community (Dion, Dion, & Pak, 1992). They found that discrimination was correlated with psychological stress—but only for those who were low in hardiness. People with hardy personalities reported just as much discrimination but much less stress.

> **Hardiness** a personality trait defined as a combination of self-esteem and a sense of control

Why might people who are hardy experience less stress in the face of discrimination? Foster and Dion (2001) wondered whether people make different attributions for negative events, depending on their level of hardiness. To find out, they conducted a study on gender discrimination and found that hardy women tended to attribute discrimination to specific, unstable factors rather than to global, stable factors. In other words, the hardy participants, unlike their less hardy counterparts, treated the discrimination they experienced as an isolated event.

RESILIENCE Finally, researchers recently have turned their attention to yet another personality trait, namely **resilience**, defined as the ability to bounce back from negative experiences and adapt to the demands of life. Frederickson, Tugade, Waugh, and Larkin (2003) measured resilience among University of Michigan students in the spring of 2001. Those who were high in resilience showed higher life satisfaction, greater optimism, more positive emotions, and less depression than those who were low in resilience. As you well know, later in that year, on September 11, 2001, terrorists hijacked and crashed four passenger airplanes in the United States, resulting in more civilian casualties in one day than any other event in American history. Frederickson and colleagues explored whether the students' reactions to this event would differ, depending on their level of resilience. They found that people experienced negative emotions in the wake of this event, regardless of how resilient they were (i.e., as measured the previous spring). Those who were high in resilience, however, experienced more positive emotions (such as gratitude and love) and less depression than those who were low in resilience. Additional analyses revealed that it was these positive emotions that were the active ingredient in protecting these participants from depression. The researchers suggest that it is the experience of positive emotions that accounts for why resilient people cope better with negative life events and experience greater life satisfaction in general (Fredrickson et al., 2003).

> **Resilience** the ability to recover from negative experiences and adapt to the demands of life

Investigations such as these are in the domain of personality psychology, in that they focus on traits that set people apart. What is it about one person that makes him or her more resistant to health problems than another person? The social psychologist takes a different tack. We ask, Can we identify ways of coping with stress that everyone can adopt to make it easier to deal with the challenges of life?

Opening Up: Confiding in Others

When something traumatic happens to you, is it best to try to bury it as deeply as you can and never talk about it, or to open up and discuss your problems with others? While folk wisdom has long held that it is best to open up, only recently has this assumption been put to the test. James Pennebaker and his colleagues (Pennebaker 1990, 1997; Niederhoffer & Pennebaker, 2002; Pennebaker & Seagal, 1999) have conducted a number of interesting

▶ Research by Pennebaker
(1990) on opening up shows that
there are long-term health benefits to writing or talking about
one's personal trauma.

classic
research

experiments on the value of confiding in others. Pennebaker and Beale (1986), for example, asked university students to write for 15 minutes on each of four consecutive nights about a traumatic event that had happened to them. Students in a control condition wrote for the same amount of time about a trivial event. The traumas they chose to write about were highly personal and in many cases quite tragic, including such events as rape and the death of a sibling. .

Writing about these events was upsetting in the short term. People who wrote about traumatic events reported more negative moods and showed greater increases in blood pressure. But there were also dramatic long-term benefits: These people were less likely to visit the student health centre during the next six months, and they reported having fewer illnesses. Similarly, Pennebaker and his colleagues found that first-year university students who wrote about the problems of entering university (Pennebaker, Colder, & Sharp, 1990) and survivors of the Holocaust who disclosed the most about their World War II experiences improved their health over the next several months (Pennebaker, Barger, & Tiebout, 1989; Pennebaker, Colder, & Sharp, 1990). Other research confirms the importance of opening up. For example, a study of more than 2000 Ontario nurses found that those who reported having a friend to confide in experienced fewer stress-related health problems, although this relation was more likely to hold for women than for men (Walters et al., 1996).

What is it about opening up that leads to better health? Pennebaker (1997) argues that people who write about negative events construct a more meaningful narrative or story that explains the events. He has analyzed hundreds of pages of writing from his participants and finds that the people who improve the most are those who began with rather incoherent, disorganized descriptions of their problem and ended with coherent, organized stories that explained the event and gave it meaning. Once people are able to gain insight into an experience and feel they understand it, they are better able to put it behind them (Hemenover, 2003; Kelly et al., 2001). Further, people might be less inclined to suppress thoughts about the event if they have written about it. Trying to suppress thoughts can lead to a preoccupation with those very thoughts, because the act of not trying to think about them can actually make us think about them more (Wegner, 1994). Thus, writing about a traumatic event may help people gain a better understanding of the event and move forward with life.

Prevention: Improving Health Habits

Beyond helping people reduce stress, social psychologists can offer some insights into how to get people to change their health habits more directly: to stop smoking, to lose weight, to eat a healthier diet, and to stop abusing alcohol or other drugs. In fact, this is an area in which social psychology can be especially helpful.

North Americans are doing a pretty good job of improving some of their health habits; for instance, the percentage of the Canadian population aged 15 and over who are smokers has been declining slowly and steadily. Currently, this figure is down to 20 percent (Statistics Canada, 2005b). People today are more likely to avoid high-cholesterol and fatty foods than they were a few years ago, and more women are getting Pap smears to detect cancer. In addition, a recent survey found an increase in seat belt usage, an increase in mammography exams for women aged 40 and over, and an increase in flu shots for people over the age 65 (Nelson et al., 2002). There is definitely room for improvement, however. The number of obese Canadian adults and children has increased substantially over the past 25 years. In 1978–79, the adult obesity rate in Canada was 14 percent; by 2004, this number had risen to 23 percent (Statistics Canada, 2005c). The largest increase in obesity has occurred for adults between the ages of 25 and 34—in this age group, obesity has nearly tripled, increasing from 9 percent to 21 percent over the last 25 years.

In addition, binge drinking on university campuses is occurring at an alarmingly high rate (Wechsler et al., 2002). A study conducted at York University found that students who drink alcohol tend to do so two to three times per week and, on each occasion, generally consume five or six standard drinks (e.g., five or six bottles of beer). For male students, this results in an average of 16 drinks per week; for female students, the weekly average is 13 drinks. According to the researchers, this level of alcohol consumption qualifies as "heavy social drinking" (Wall, Hinson, & McKee, 1998). Although most binge drinkers believe that it will be easy to stop after leaving university, many find it very hard to do so and develop serious drinking problems.

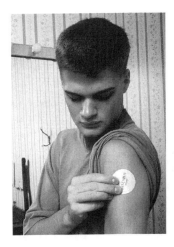

◀ Canadians are making progress in improving some areas of health; for example, more and more people are quitting smoking. However, Canadians are not doing very well in other areas. Many people find it difficult to lose weight and maintain a regular exercise program. How can social psychology help people act in healthier ways?

Finally, people who are at risk for getting AIDS are not taking as many precautions as they should. For example, a study conducted in Ontario found that only 29 percent of young adults who had engaged in casual sex over the past year had always used a condom (Herold & Mewhinney, 1993). A more recent Canada-wide health survey reported similar findings, namely that 30 percent of young people reported not having used a condom the last time they had sex. This percentage was even higher (nearly 44%) among adults aged 20 to 24 (Statistics Canada, 2005d).

How can we persuade people to change their health habits?

Message Framing: Stressing Gains versus Losses

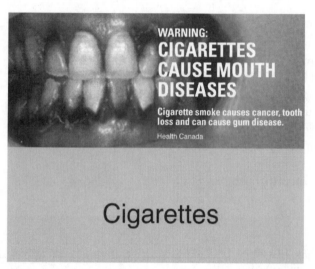

One of the graphic photos on cigarette packaging. This attempt to use fear to change people's behaviour was introduced by the Canadian government in an attempt to curb smoking.

One approach, on attitude change, is to present people with persuasive communications urging them to act in healthier ways. As we mentioned in that chapter, the Canadian government has placed graphic photographs of people suffering from lung cancer and other smoking-related diseases on cigarette packages, with the intent of frightening them into quitting, or not starting, smoking. Many public service advertisements take this approach, trying to scare people into applying sunscreen, using condoms, and wearing seat belts or helmets.

Is it always best to scare people, emphasizing what they have to lose by acting in unhealthy ways? Suppose, for example, that you were devising a public service ad to lower fatalities from skin cancer. Your goal is to get people to examine their skin regularly for cancer and to use sunscreen when they are exposed to the sun. You could frame your message in terms of what people have to lose by not performing these behaviours; for example, you might emphasize that most skin cancers are fatal if not detected at an early stage. Or you could frame your message in a more positive way by emphasizing what people have to gain; for example, you could say that skin cancers are curable if detected early and that people can decrease their chances of getting skin cancer by using sunscreen.

It might seem that these different messages would have the same effect; after all, they convey the same information—it is a good idea to examine your skin regularly and use sunscreen. It turns out, though, that framing messages in terms of losses versus gains can make a big difference (Jones, Sinclair, & Courneya, 2003; Rothman & Salovey, 1997). When trying to get people to *detect* the presence of a disease, it is best to use a loss frame, emphasizing what they have to lose by avoiding this behaviour (e.g., the costs of not examining one's skin for cancer) (Meyerowitz & Chaiken, 1987; Rothman, 2000; Wilson, Purdon, & Wallston, 1988). When trying to get people to engage in behaviour that will *prevent* disease, it is best to use a gain frame, emphasizing what they have to gain by engaging in this behaviour (e.g., using sunscreen) (Linville, Fischer, & Fischhoff, 1993; Rothman et al., 1999). Alex Rothman and his colleagues (1993), for example, found that framing a message in terms of losses increased women's intentions to examine their skin for cancer (a detection behaviour), whereas framing a message in terms of gains increased women's intentions to use sunscreen (a prevention behaviour). (See Figure 3.5.)

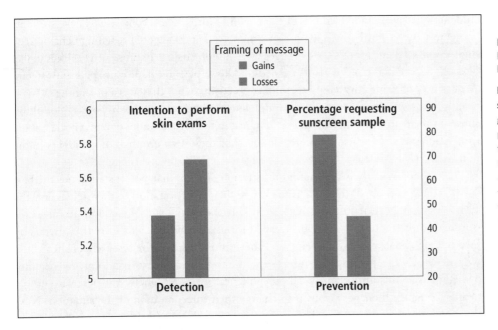

◀ **FIGURE 3.5**

FRAMING HEALTH MESSAGES
IN TERMS OF GAINS OR
LOSSES

Rothman and colleagues (1993) presented women with information trying to
get them to avoid skin cancer. Some
participants received a message that
focused on the positive benefits of
being concerned about skin cancer
(e.g., "If they are detected early, most of
these cancers are curable"). Other participants received a message framed in
terms of the negative consequences of
not being concerned about skin cancer
(e.g., "Unless they are detected and
treated early, most of these cancers are
not curable"). As seen in the left side of
the figure, the loss-framed message
worked best on detection behaviour
(i.e., people's intention to perform
exams of their skin). As seen in the right
side of the figure, the gain-framed
message worked best with prevention
behaviour (i.e., requesting a sample of
sunscreen).

(Adapted from Rothman et al., 1993)

So, before designing your public health ad, decide which kind of behaviour you are going to target—a prevention or detection behaviour—and design your ad accordingly.

Changing Health-Relevant Behaviour Using Dissonance Theory

Unfortunately, when it comes to changing ingrained health habits, public service ads may be of limited success. The problem is that with many health problems, there are over-whelming barriers to change. Consider the use of condoms. Most people are aware that AIDS is a serious problem and that using condoms provides substantial protection against AIDS. Still, a surprisingly small percentage of people use condoms. One reason is that many people find condoms to be inconvenient and unromantic, as well as a reminder of disease—something they don't want to think about when they are having sex. Where sexual behaviour is involved, there is a strong tendency to go into denial—in this case, to decide that, while AIDS is a problem, we are not at risk. What can be done to change this potentially fatal attitude?

One of the most important messages of social psychology is that to change people's behaviour, you need to challenge their self-esteem in such a way that it becomes to their advantage psychologically to act differently. By doing so, they feel good about themselves, maintaining their self-esteem. Sound familiar? This is a basic tenet of dissonance theory.

Elliot Aronson and his colleagues applied the principles of dissonance theory to get people to behave in healthier ways, including using condoms more often (Aronson, Fried, & Stone, 1991; Stone et al., 1994). To review briefly, university students were asked to compose a speech describing the dangers of AIDS and advocating the use of condoms "every single time you have sex." The students gave their speech in front of a video camera, after being informed that the resulting videotape would be played to an audience of high school students. Was giving this speech sufficient to change behaviour, making the students more likely to use condoms themselves? The answer is yes—but only when the students were also made mindful of their own failures to use condoms. These students were most aware of their own hypocrisy—namely, that they were preaching behaviour to high school students that they themselves were not practising. Because no one likes to feel like a hypocrite, these participants needed to take steps to fix their damaged self-esteem. A clear way of doing this would be to start practising what they were preaching. This is exactly what Aronson and his colleagues found. Students in the hypocrisy condition showed the greatest willingness to use condoms in the future, and when given the opportunity, purchased significantly more condoms for their own use than did students in the non-hypocrisy conditions.

The condom study is yet another illustration of a familiar point: sometimes the best way to change people's behaviour is to change their interpretation of themselves and the social situation. No attempt was made to modify the participants' behaviour (their use of condoms) directly. They were not rewarded for using condoms; nor were they given any information about what would happen if they didn't. Instead, the researchers altered the way in which the participants interpreted their failure to use condoms. We cannot overemphasize this important social psychological message: One of the best ways to get people to change their behaviour is to change their interpretation of the situation. Now that you have read about several of the factors that influence health behaviour, see if you can improve your habits by taking the advice in the Try It! below.

try it! Changing Your Health Habits

Pick a health habit of yours and try to improve it, using the principles we have discussed in this chapter. For example, you might try to lose a few kilograms, exercise more, or cut down on your smoking. We should mention right away that this is not easy. If it were, we would all be svelte, physically fit nonsmokers! We suggest that you start small with a limited goal; try to lose 2 kilograms, for example, or increase your exercise by one or two hours a week.

Here are some specific suggestions as to how to change your behaviour. Increase your feelings of control over your behaviour, particularly your self-efficacy in this domain. One way to do this is to start small. If you are trying to lose weight, for example, begin slowly with some easy-to-control behaviour. You might start by eliminating one food or beverage from your diet that you do not like all that much but that is pretty fattening. Suppose, for example, that you drink a 200-calorie fruit juice five times a week. Replacing the juice with water will save 52 000 calories a year, which is equivalent to 6 kilograms! The idea is to gain mastery over your behaviour slowly, improving your feelings of self-efficacy. When you've mastered one behaviour, try another. You can do it!

If you experience a setback, such as eating two pieces of cake at a birthday party, avoid a damaging pattern of attributions. Do not assume that the setback was a result of internal, stable, global causes—this will cause learned helplessness. Remember that almost everyone fails the first time they try to diet or quit smoking. It often takes people several attempts; therefore, a setback or two is not because of something unchangeable about you. Keep trying.

Try your own little dissonance experiment, such as the one we discussed by Elliot Aronson and colleagues (1991) on safer sex. There are two steps:

First, make a speech to others urging them to adopt the behaviour you are trying to change. For example, tell all of your friends about the dangers of obesity. The more involved and detailed you make your speech and the wider your audience, the better.

Second, make a detailed list of times when you did not practise what you preached (e.g., when you gained weight). You might find it easier to quit once you have put yourself through this "hypocrisy" procedure.

It can be stressful to change a well-ingrained habit, and it is at times of stress that social support is most important. Talk with your friends and family about your attempts to change your behaviour. Seek their advice and support. Even better, convince several friends to try these techniques with you. Make it a group project, in which you and your friends support each others' efforts to alter your behaviour.

Summary

Stress, best defined as the negative feelings that occur when people feel that they cannot cope with their environment, has been found to have a number of negative effects, such as impairment of the immune system. One key determinant of stress is how much **perceived control** people have over their environment. The less control people believe they have, the more likely it is that the event will cause them physical and psychological problems. For example, the loss of control experienced by many older people in nursing homes can have negative effects on their health and mortality. It is also important for people to have high **self-efficacy** in a particular domain, which is the belief in one's ability to carry out specific actions that produce desired outcomes. In addition, the way in which people explain the causes of negative events is critical to how stressful those events will be. When bad things happen, **learned helplessness** results if people make **stable, internal**, and **global attributions** for those events. Learned helplessness leads to depression, reduced effort, and difficulty in learning new material.

Coping styles refer to the ways in which people react to stressful events. Recent research suggests that men are more likely to react to stress with a **fight-or-flight response**, reacting to stress by either attacking the source of the stress or fleeing from it. Women are more likely to react to stress with a **tend-and-befriend response**, reacting to stress with nurturant activities designed to protect oneself and one's offspring (tending) and creating social networks that provide protection from threats (befriending). **Social support**—the perception that other people are responsive to one's needs—is beneficial for men and women. According to the **buffering hypothesis**, social support is especially helpful in times of stress by making people less likely to interpret an event as stressful and helping them cope with stressful events.

Research on personality traits, such as optimism, the **Type A versus Type B personality, hardiness**, and **resilience** focuses on how people typically deal with stress and how these styles are related to their physical health. Optimistic, hardy, and resilient people tend to react better to stress and to be healthier. Type A individuals—particularly those with high levels of hostility—are more at risk for coronary disease.

Other researchers focus on ways of coping with stress that everyone can adopt. Several studies show that opening up, which involves writing or talking about one's problems, has long-term health benefits.

It is also important to explore strategies for getting people to act in healthier ways. One strategy is to present people with persuasive communications urging them to adopt better health habits. To be successful, it is important to tailor these messages to the kinds of behaviour you want people to adopt. To get people to perform detection behaviour, such as examining their skin for cancer, it is best to use messages framed in terms of losses (the negative consequences of failing to act). To get people to perform preventive behaviour, such as using sunscreen, it is best to use messages framed in terms of gains (the positive consequences of performing the behaviour). Even more powerful are techniques that arouse dissonance that will be reduced by changing one's health habits, such as making people feel hypocritical about their failure to use condoms.

Thinking Critically

1. Think of a personal example of an event that some people found to be stressful and others did not. Why was it stressful for some people but not others? Were some of the factors mentioned in this chapter involved, such as perceived control, self-efficacy, or learned helplessness?

2. Design a program to help first-year university students adjust to the academic demands of their institution, using the principles discussed in this chapter.

3. Design a public health campaign to get university students to engage in less heavy social drinking, using the principles discussed in this chapter.

If You Are Interested

Flett, G. L., Endler, N. S., & Fairlie, P. (1999). The interaction model of anxiety and the threat of Quebec's separation from Canada. *Journal of Personality and Social Psychology, 76,* 143–150. A fascinating analysis of reactions to the threat of Quebec's separation from Canada. Data were gathered from York University students three hours before the October 1995 Quebec referendum, as well as one week after the vote. The researchers found that participants who tended to be anxious and who perceived the referendum situation as ambiguous and threatening experienced high levels of anxiety prior to the vote.

Haines, Randa (Director). (1991). *The doctor* [Film]. A surgeon discovers what it is like to be on the other side of the health care system when he develops throat cancer. The surgeon develops a close relationship with a terminally ill patient as he struggles with his own mortality. An interesting look at learned helplessness and perceived control and health.

Hanson, I., & Hampton, M. R. (2000). Being Indian: Strengths sustaining First Nations People in Saskatchewan residential schools. *Canadian Journal of Community Mental Health, 19,* 127–142. Elders who were survivors of residential schools in Saskatchewan were interviewed about their experiences and how they coped. From these interviews, the authors identify eight major strategies that the survivors used for coping with the horrific abuse they suffered as children. It is suggested that these strategies reflect traditional sources of strength for Aboriginal peoples and should be incorporated into community health programs aimed at healing the trauma of the residential school experience.

Pennebaker, J. W. (1990). *Opening up: The healing powers of confiding in others.* New York: William Morrow. An insightful, accessible presentation of research on the value of discussing one's problems with other people.

Perry, R. (2003). Perceived (academic) control and causal thinking in achievement settings. *Canadian Psychology, 44,* 312–331. This article reviews research conducted by the author and his colleagues at the University of Manitoba over the past two decades on the role of attributions and perceived control in predicting academic performance and withdrawal rates in university. Applications of this research, including which teaching strategies are most likely to be effective, are discussed.

Salovey, P., Rothman, A. J., & Rodin, J. (1998). *Social psychology and health behaviour.* In D. Gilbert, S. Fiske, & G. Lindzey (Eds.), *The handbook of social psychology* (4th ed., Vol. 2, pp. 633–683). New York: McGraw-Hill. A broad, insightful review of the emerging field of health psychology.

Seligman, M. E. P. (1990). *Learned optimism.* New York: Springer-Verlag. An interesting book on optimism and learned helplessness theory by one of its originators.

Suedfeld, P. (Ed.). (2001). *Light from the ashes: Social science careers of young Holocaust refugees and survivors.* Ann Arbor: University of Michigan Press. In this book, University of British Columbia social psychologist Peter Suedfeld presents a collection of essays written by high-profile social scientists who were Holocaust survivors. The contributors, including Peter Suedfeld, offer poignant, deeply touching accounts of their Holocaust experiences and explore the impact of these experiences on their personal and professional lives. Suedfeld raises the intriguing possibility that success of several might be attributable, at least in part, to the resiliency and coping ability that Holocaust survivors developed because of the trauma they experienced.

Weblinks

www.cpa.ca
Canadian Psychological Association

This is the home page for the Canadian Psychological Association, and provides information and articles on health psychology, conferences, and career opportunities.

http://healthpsych.com
Health Psychology & Rehabilitation

This site offers research, viewpoints, and practical suggestions about the practice of health psychology in medical and rehabilitation settings, and links to many other health psychology resources.

http://userpage.fu-berlin.de/~health/lingua5.htm
Self-Efficacy across Cultures

The paper by Schwarter and Scholtz (2000) on this site compares perceived levels of self-efficacy across 14 different cultures.

www.psychologymatters.org
Psychology Matters

This extremely valuable resource posted by the American Psychological Association showcases the application of psychological research to real-world problems. Research articles relevant to health are listed. You can click on such key terms as health, psychological well-being, or trauma, grief, and resilience.

Chapter 4
Sports Psychology

Krista Munroe-Chandler
Craig Hall

CHAPTER 4

Sports Psychology

Chapter Objectives

After reading this chapter, you should be able to do the following:

1. Define and describe each of the five psychological skills most often used in a psychological skills training program.

2. Explain why these psychological skills work.

3. Describe the measurement and implementation of the skills.

4. Describe the components of a psychological skills training program.

Stephanie is a 13-year-old novice-level figure skater representing a Toronto club. She consistently executes a double Axel and has been working for the past season on her triple jumps. She and her coach, Dave, have decided that for her to become a top performer she needs to work not only on her physical skills but also on her mental skills. Stephanie does not have a specific problem (e.g., extreme nervousness before competition); however, both she and Dave recognize the importance of enhancing mental skills. To help her improve her mental skills, they have asked for the help of an applied sport psychology consultant. The consultant meets with them, and together they develop a psychological skills training program.

After meeting with Stephanie and Dave, the applied sport psychology consultant first conducted performance profiling. Based on the results, the consultant determined that Stephanie needed to get psyched up for practices because she tended to be sluggish when she first stepped on the ice. She also needed to improve her focus during practice since she was spending too much time talking with friends and watching other skaters, rather than focusing on what she needed to do. Finally, she needed to enhance her confidence at competitions.

To accomplish these objectives, Stephanie began to do exercises and listen to upbeat music just before a practice. She developed and followed a practice plan that outlined in detail what she had to accomplish during a practice. In addition, she started to regularly do imagery and developed and used a set of confidence-building self-statements at competitions. This initial intervention proved very effective, and Stephanie continues to work with the applied sport psychology consultant on improving the mental side of her skating.

Athletes approach applied sport psychology consultants for two general reasons: (a) to seek help with specific problems, such as performance anxiety and lack of self-confidence and (b) to work to improve the mental side of sport, such as imagery and attention control. In the above scenario, Stephanie has decided to work with a sport psychology consultant for the second reason. Rather than dealing with a specific problem, the consultant is faced with generating a psychological skills training program for Stephanie. The challenge for the consultant will be to determine what techniques should be incorporated into the psychological skills training program (or intervention) and what emphasis should be placed on each. In this chapter we will address these and other issues.

Some Common Myths about Sport Psychology Interventions

MYTH: *Psychological skills training (PST) is a band-aid solution.*
Some athletes and coaches believe that the effective use of self-talk or imagery can be learned in one or two sessions to quickly fix a problem, such as lack of confidence. Just as physical skills take time and effort to develop, so too do psychological skills. There are no quick fixes to problems, and dedicating time to PST over an extended period will enhance athletes' performance and help them reach their full potential.

MYTH: *Only elite athletes can benefit from psychological skills training.*
Successful performance at any level of sport involves technical, tactical, physical, and mental components. Although elite athletes can benefit from highly developed psychological skills, even young athletes will experience the gains garnered from improved psychological skills. Therefore, PST can be implemented at any stage of an athlete's career, but ideally it should be initiated at the grassroots level in order to ensure the most effective development of the mental side of sport.

MYTH: *Athletes need a sport psychologist only when they are performing poorly.*
The third myth is that athletes need a sport psychologist only when they are performing poorly. Most successful athletes realize that achieving peak performance requires a detailed plan that includes an understanding of physiology and nutrition, implementation of cutting-edge technology, and employment of psychological skills training. It is harder to fix a problem once it has started than to keep a problem from occurring.

Introduction

For decades, sport psychology consultants have been studying and developing psychological skills interventions to help athletes enhance their performance and psychological well-being. A **psychological skills training** program, or intervention, entails the structured and consistent practice of psychological skills and generally has three distinct phases: education, acquisition, and practice. In the education phase, athletes recognize the importance of mental skills in sport and how the skills affect performance. There are various approaches to accomplishing this; however, one of the simplest ways is to ask athletes about the importance of mental skills in sport. Although most athletes realize the importance of the mental side of sport, very few actually spend time developing these skills in comparison with the time spent on physical skills.

Athletes often have some understanding of a psychological skill, but they do not fully comprehend its complexity and its optimal use. Therefore, in the acquisition phase, the focus is placed on helping athletes acquire the various psychological skills and learn how to most effectively employ them. In the practice phase, the goals are to have the athletes automate the various psychological skills through overlearning and to implement these skills in practice and competition.

The psychological skills that have been researched most extensively and incorporated into psychological skills training programs are the following: goal setting, imagery,

> Athletes approach an applied sport psychologist to seek help with specific problems and to work to improve the mental side of sport.

Photo courtesy of Joe Patronite/Getty Images.

self-talk, arousal regulation, and attention control. Each of these five skills will be discussed in turn. We will define each skill and discuss why it works, how it can be measured, and how it can be integrated into a psychological skills training program. Measurement tools are discussed in some detail since without proper assessment there cannot be a successful psychological skills training program.

Goal Setting

Goal setting is the most commonly used performance enhancement strategy in sport psychology. Leading sport psychology consultants working with Olympic athletes have reported that goal setting is the psychological intervention most often used (Gould, Tammen, Murphy, & May, 1989); however, most athletes rate their goals as being only moderately effective in enhancing sport performance (Burton, Naylor, & Holliday, 2001).

Types of Goals

A **goal** is a target or objective that people strive to attain. There are three types of goals that athletes can set. **Performance goals** focus on improving and attaining personal performance standards, such as learning an out-turn draw in curling or giving 100% effort at all times in a lacrosse match. **Process goals** focus on specific behaviours that an athlete must engage in throughout a performance, such as snapping the wrist when stroking a squash ball or pulling the arms in tight while executing a spin in figure skating. In contrast to the first two types of goals, **outcome goals** focus on social comparison and competitive results, such as winning a race or outscoring an opponent. Thus, outcome goals are dependent on the ability and performance of one's opponents. **Goal setting**, therefore, is the practice of establishing desirable objectives for one's actions. Research suggests incorporating all three types of goals when developing a goal-setting program (Filby, Maynard, & Graydon, 1999).

<
There are three types of goals athletes can set: *outcome*—to score a goal, *process*—to make an accurate pass to the winger, and *performance*—to give 100% effort.
Photo © Michael Kevin Daly/CORBIS.

Effectiveness of Goal Setting

Research suggests that goal setting works in various ways. According to Locke and Latham (1985), goals direct attention, mobilize effort, foster persistence, and promote the development of new learning strategies. In addition, goals may influence athletes' performance by enhancing their self-confidence and their sense of satisfaction (Moran, 2004). Research has consistently demonstrated the positive effects of goal setting. Burton et al. (2001) noted that 78% of sport and exercise studies have shown moderate-to-strong effects on behaviour. For example, Wanlin, Hrycaiko, Martin, and Mahon (1997) conducted a multiple baseline design in which youth speed skaters received training in goal setting. Over the course of the intervention, the skaters made improvements in their skating as a result of their goal setting.

Most athletes rate goals as being only moderately effective (Burton et al., 2001) even though goal setting is one of the most extensively employed interventions in sport psychology. This is likely due to the fact that athletes are not certain about how to effectively set goals, and as a result they do not think that goal setting works. Additionally, a number of barriers, such as lack of time and everyday distractions, hinder the practice of goal setting among athletes (Weinberg, 2002). Later in this chapter, we shall examine some ways of setting effective goals.

Assessing Goals

Performance profiling is a flexible assessment tool that allows for the identification of athletes' performance-related strengths and weaknesses. It is often used as a first step in developing an intervention program. In addition to its utility as a general assessment procedure, it can be used as an aid to goal setting (Butler & Hardy, 1992; Jones, 1993). There are five steps in performance profiling:

Step 1: Identify key performance characteristics of an elite athlete in your sport. Think of the best person in your sport and identify the characteristics of that athlete. These can include physical, technical, tactical, and mental characteristics.

Step 2: Identify the ideal rating for each of the athlete's characteristics. On a scale from 1 to 10, with 1 being *not at all important* and 10 being *extremely important*, indicate your ideal scores. This rating is also your target.

Step 3: Rate your current ability for each characteristic on a scale of 1 to 10, with 1 being *not at all like me* and 10 being *completely like me*. Be as honest as possible.

Step 4: Find your discrepancy score by subtracting your current rating from your ideal rating. The higher the discrepancy score, the weaker you perceive your ability for that characteristic.

Step 5: Prioritize your targets. After identifying your performance weaknesses (highest discrepancy scores), pick out the two or three that are most in need of correction.

Having identified performance characteristics most in need of urgent attention, you can now implement strategies (set goals) to improve these characteristics. Take the example of a field hockey player who, through performance profiling, has identified her penalty stroke as a weakness. Accordingly, she sets two goals: to improve her shot speed by 10% and improve the height of her shot by 30 cm over the course of four weeks. How to set effective goals, such as those established by the field hockey player, is discussed next.

Recommendations for Goal Setting

The acronym SMART has been recommended to help athletes remember five important guidelines for effective goal setting (Weinberg & Gould, 2003). Goals should be specific, measurable, adjustable, realistic, and timely (see Table 4.1).

Table 4.1   Field Hockey Goal-setting Example Using SMART Guidelines

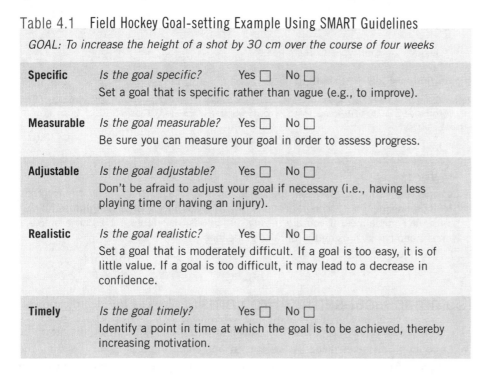

GOAL: To increase the height of a shot by 30 cm over the course of four weeks

Specific	*Is the goal specific?* Yes ☐ No ☐
	Set a goal that is specific rather than vague (e.g., to improve).
Measurable	*Is the goal measurable?* Yes ☐ No ☐
	Be sure you can measure your goal in order to assess progress.
Adjustable	*Is the goal adjustable?* Yes ☐ No ☐
	Don't be afraid to adjust your goal if necessary (i.e., having less playing time or having an injury).
Realistic	*Is the goal realistic?* Yes ☐ No ☐
	Set a goal that is moderately difficult. If a goal is too easy, it is of little value. If a goal is too difficult, it may lead to a decrease in confidence.
Timely	*Is the goal timely?* Yes ☐ No ☐
	Identify a point in time at which the goal is to be achieved, thereby increasing motivation.

There are other important goal-setting guidelines that athletes should follow. First, athletes should set goals for both practice and competition. Often athletes focus only on competition goals; however, setting practice goals is important when one considers the time spent in practice compared with the time spent in competition. Second, it is important to write down your goals and make them public. In doing so, it is more likely that you will attempt to achieve your goals, given that people around you are aware of your objectives and can be helpful in motivating you to accomplish them. Third, goals should be stated positively, rather than negatively: "I want to run the best 100-metre time possible" rather than "I don't want to come in last in the 100-metre." Fourth, for teams to maximize potential, Dawson, Bray, and Widmeyer (2002) suggested four types of goals to be considered: (a) individual athlete's goals for self, (b) individual athlete's goal for the team, (c) the team's overall goal, and (d) the team's goal for individual members. Finally, the progress toward goal achievement should be reviewed on a regular basis. Conducting this regular review allows you to identify if your goals are appropriate (see Table 4.2).

An example of an intervention using SMART goals is the Wanlin et al. (1997) study previously mentioned (under "Effectiveness of Goal Setting"). All skaters in this study receiving the goal-setting package were first shown a videotape of the instructions to be followed throughout the duration of the study. Athletes were asked to develop a mission, set long-term goals, set subgoals and practice goals, and employ self-talk and visualization to help them achieve the goals. Moreover, athletes were asked to keep a logbook in which their daily practice goals were reported and measured. Athletes were told the goals must be flexible as well as challenging. The skaters made improvements in their skating performance over the course of the goal-setting intervention.

Table 4.2   Goal-setting Guidelines

- Set SMART goals.

- Set goals for practice and competition.

- Make your goals public.

- State goals positively rather than negatively.

- Consider the four types of team goals.

- Review your goals regularly.

Note: Adapted from "The PETTLER Approach to motor imagery: A functional equivalence model for sport psychologists," by P.S. Holmes and D.J. Collins, 2001, Journal of Applied Sport Psychology, 13, pp. 60–83. Copyright 2001 by Taylor and Francis, Philadelphia.

Reflections 4.1

Consider a goal that you have set (personal, athletic, or academic). Does it follow the SMART guidelines? If so, congratulations; if not, revise your goal so that it does follow the SMART guidelines. If you are having difficulties, use Table 4.1 as an example. Now set another goal using the SMART guidelines.

Common Goal-setting Problems

There are some common problems in implementing a goal-setting program. One of the most common mistakes made by athletes in implementing a program is setting too many goals. Athletes end up setting so many goals that they cannot properly monitor them, and they find the evaluation to be overwhelming and lose interest. Those who are just beginning a goal-setting program should work on achieving a small number of goals. Performance profiling will assist the athlete in determining those few goals in need of immediate attention.

Another common problem occurs when athletes do not willingly participate in the goal-setting program. Some individuals will not be excited about goal setting and may even have a negative attitude toward it. Forcing athletes to set goals is not very effective because individual commitment is required. One solution for recognizing individual differences is to expose all athletes to goal setting and work more with those who show the most interest.

Underestimating the time it takes to implement a goal-setting program is another common problem. Often a coach will implement a program with athletes early in the season. As the season progresses, however, less and less time is spent on goal setting, and toward the end of the season the goal-setting program is completely forgotten. Coaches and athletes need to recognize the time required to undertake a goal-setting program. It is better to devote 15 minutes a week throughout the season to goal setting than to attempt to devote 15 minutes a day and not be able to follow through on it.

Finally, failure to provide follow-up is one of the major problems with goal-setting programs. Evaluation of goals is imperative and the continued use of performance profiling throughout the season is one effective way to achieve this. Without follow-up and evaluation, goal setting is simply a waste of time and effort (see Table 4.3).

Table 4.3 Common Goal-setting Problems

- Setting too many goals

- Failing to recognize individual differences in interest in goal setting

- Underestimating the time required to set goals

- Failure to provide follow-up and evaluation

Conclusions about Goal Setting

It is almost impossible to conceive of a psychological skills training program that does not include goal setting. For athletes to enhance their performance, weaknesses must be identified and corrected. In overcoming weaknesses, it is almost inevitable that goals will be set. What becomes important is ensuring that athletes set SMART goals that are supported and evaluated. Although goal setting is a complex process that requires hard work and discipline, it can be extremely effective in helping athletes achieve excellence in sport (Burton et al., 2001). Thus, it is highly recommended that athletes of all competitive levels engage in goal setting.

Imagery

Canadian Olympic speed skater, Isabelle Charest stated,

A big part of my training has been visualization—I try to put myself in race situations. It starts when I lace up my skates and I go through every possible scenario in the race, the crowd, even the people watching at home. I see the race from various angles, starting first or second, leading and sometime coming from the back of the pack. (Kingsley, 1998)

Researchers and athletes alike have long been interested in imagery and its effect on sport performance. Some have gone so far as to hail it as the "central pillar of applied sport psychology" (Perry & Morris, 1995, p. 339). In addition, coaches view imagery as one of the most important psychological skills to teach their athletes (Rodgers, Hall, & Buckolz, 1991).

The Nature of Imagery

As the above quotation from Isabelle Charest suggests, imagery should involve as many perspectives as possible; however, referring to imagery as "visualization" is somewhat misleading. Visualization suggests that only one sense is being used, that of sight. It has been documented, however, that athletes try to incorporate as many senses as possible including, sight, auditory, olfactory, tactile, and kinesthetic. The latter sense is particularly important for athletes since it involves the feel or sensation of bodily movements. The more polysensory the image, the more real it becomes, and the more effective it will be on sport performance. Given the multidimensional nature of imagery, White and Hardy (1998) have defined imagery as:

An experience that mimics real experience. We can be aware of "seeing" an image, feeling movements as an image, or experiencing an image of smell, tastes, or sounds without actually experiencing the real thing. Sometimes people find that it helps to close their eyes. It differs from dreams in that we are awake and conscious when we form an image. (p. 389)

Analytic Model of Imagery

Most of the recent imagery research has stemmed from Paivio's (1985) analytic model, which suggests that imagery has cognitive and motivational functions that operate on either a specific or a general level. Thus, **cognitive general imagery** includes images of strategies, game plans, or routines—for example, imaging a floor routine in gymnastics; **cognitive specific imagery** includes images of specific sport skills—for example, imaging a free throw in basketball; **motivational general imagery** includes images relating to physiological arousal levels and emotions—for example, imaging feeling calm and relaxed in front of a crowd; and **motivational specific imagery** includes images related to an individual's goals—for example, imaging receiving a gold medal. More recently, Hall, Mack, Paivio, and Hausenblas (1998) divided the motivational general function into a **motivational general-arousal** function, encompassing imagery associated with arousal and stress, and a **motivational general-mastery** function, representing imagery associated with being mentally tough, in control, and self-confident (see Figure 4.1).

Based on the five functions, Martin, Moritz and Hall (1999) developed an applied model for depicting how imagery works in sport. Although the model shows that athletes use imagery in three different situations, they report using imagery most in competition and, more specifically, just prior to competition (Munroe, Giacobbi, Hall, & Weinberg, 2000). According to the model, the desired sport outcome should be matched to the correct function of imagery. For example, if an athlete wanted to reduce anxiety prior to a competition, the type of imagery used should be motivational general-arousal. Athletes have been found to use all five functions of imagery; however, they report using motivational general-mastery the most (Munroe, Hall, Simms, & Weinberg, 1998).

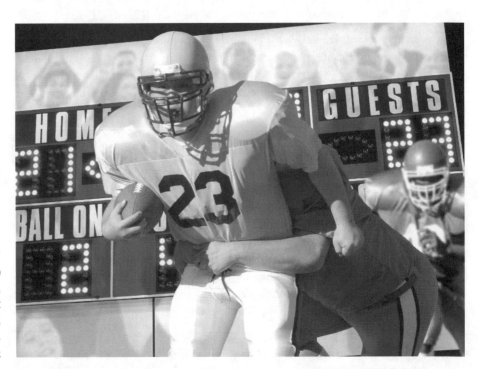

>

When you use imagery, try to make it polysensory: see the ball, feel the ball, smell the fresh-cut grass, hear the crowd cheer, taste the sweat on your lips.

Photo © Thinkstock/Alamy.

Figure 4.1   The five functions of imagery

Level	Motivational Function	Cognitive Function
General	Mastery Arousal	Strategies
Specific	Goals	Skills

Note: Adapted from "Imagery Use by Athletes: Development of the Sport Imagery Questionnaire," by C. R. Hall, D. Mack, A. Paivio, and H. A. Hausenblas, 1998, International Journal of Sport Psychology, 29, pp. 73–89, Edizioni Luigi Pozzi; and from "Cognitive and Motivational Functions of Imagery in Human Performance," by A. Paivio, 1985, Canadian Journal of Applied Sport Sciences, 10, pp. 22S–28S. Canadian Association of Sports Sciences.

The model also illustrates that the effect of imagery function on outcome is moderated by imagery ability, which includes both visual and kinesthetic imagery. Although minimal research has been conducted on imagery use by injured athletes, Sordoni, Hall, and Forwell (2002) found that such athletes use imagery for three main reasons: cognitive, motivational, and healing imagery (see Figure 4.2).

There is considerable support for the main proposal of the model that the function of imagery should match the desired outcome. With respect to the cognitive functions of imagery, numerous studies conducted in a wide variety of contexts have shown that the use of cognitive specific imagery is conducive to enhancing the learning and performance of motor skills (see Driskell, Copper, & Moran, 1994 for a review). Case studies and anecdotal evidence suggest that cognitive general imagery can be beneficial when used for the learning and performance of play strategies. For example, the performance benefits of using cognitive general imagery have been reported for rehearsing football plays (Fenker & Lambiotte, 1987), wrestling strategies (Rushall, 1988), and entire canoe slalom races (MacIntyre & Moran, 1996).

Figure 4.2   Applied model of imagery use in sport.

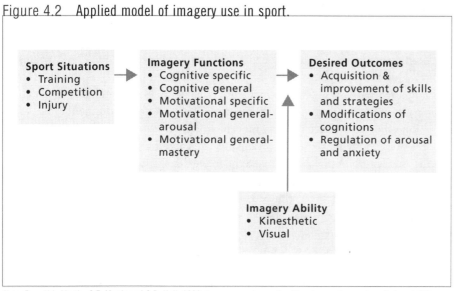

Note: From K.A. Martin, S.E. Mortiz and C.R. Hall, 1999, Imagery use in sport: a literature review and applied model, The Sport Psychologist 13(3): 248, figure 1. © 1999 by Human Kinetics Publishers, Inc. Adapted with permission from Human Kinetics (Champaign, IL).

With respect to motivational imagery, Munroe et al. (2000) reported that athletes use motivational specific imagery to develop goals, and Callow and Hardy (2001) argued that a benefit to using motivational specific imagery would be an increase in athletes' motivation to attain their goals. In another study, Callow, Hardy, and Hall (2001) investigated the effects of a motivational general-mastery intervention on the sport confidence of three elite badminton players. The researchers employed a single-subject multiple-baseline design. The two-week, six-session intervention was made up of motivational general-mastery imagery, consisting of images associated with control, confidence, and mental toughness in difficult situations. A significant increase in sport confidence was demonstrated for two of the players, and a stabilized confidence level was demonstrated for the third, thus indicating that a motivational general-mastery imagery intervention can improve sport confidence.

Lastly, research examining motivational general-arousal imagery has indicated that it can be used by athletes to regulate arousal and anxiety. More specifically, images of the emotions and arousal associated with competitive performance—for example, anger, anxiety, excitement, fear, pressure, psyched-up, etc.—are related to increased levels of state anxiety (Carter & Kelly, 1997; Hale & Whitehouse, 1998; Murphy & Woolfolk, 1987; Murphy, Woolfolk, & Budney, 1988; Vadocz, Hall, & Moritz, 1997). In contrast, images of performing in a relaxed and calm state are related to decreased levels of state anxiety (Murphy & Woolfolk, 1987; Murphy et al., 1988; Ryska, 1998).

Imagery Assessment Tools

Two types of imagery assessment tools have typically been used in sport psychology. One tool measures imagery ability, and the other assesses the frequency of imagery use. One of the most important factors influencing imagery effectiveness is imagery ability. Some athletes are better imagers than others even though most athletes report using imagery. In addition, Rodgers et al. (1991) in their intervention study with figure skaters found the imagery ability of the skaters improved with imagery practice. This suggests that imagery is not only an ability but also a skill that can be improved through regular practice.

Instruments have been developed to measure imagery ability. The Movement Imagery Questionnaire-Revised (MIQ-R; Hall & Martin, 1997) is an eight-item questionnaire that assesses an individual's visual and kinesthetic imagery ability. Participants are asked to first physically perform four different movements then visually or kinesthetically image the four movements. Each movement involves an arm, a leg, or a whole body movement. Participants then rate how well they felt they were able to visually or kinesthetically image the movement, and imagery scores are calculated separately for both subscales.

A second instrument is the Vividness of Movement Imagery Questionnaire (VMIQ; Isaac, Marks, & Russell, 1996), which assesses the vividness of visual imagery ability. Briefly, the 24-item scale has participants rating different imagined actions or movements in two ways, by watching someone else do them and by doing it themselves. Respondents then rate the vividness of each image.

Different tools assess the frequency of imagery use. There are questionnaires that provide information on imagery frequency (and other mental skills); examples are the Test of Psychological Skills (TOPS; Thomas, Murphy, & Hardy, 1999) and the Ottawa Mental Skills Assessment Tool (Durand-Bush, Salmela, & Green, 2001). These types of questionnaires provide considerable information about a number of psychological skills, but they do not provide detailed information about any one skill, such as imagery.

In comparison, other instruments have been designed to assess only imagery. The Sport Imagery Questionnaire (SIQ; Hall et al., 1998) is a 30-item self-report measure that asks athletes to rate how frequently they use the five functions of imagery as described in Figure 4.1 (see Table 4.4). A number of studies have employed the SIQ to examine and provide support for the applied model of imagery proposed by Martin et al. (1999).

Table 4.4 Sport Imagery Questionnaire Sample Items

Examples of Items in the SIQ

- I imagine my skills improving. (cognitive specific)

- I image alternative strategies in case my event/game plan fails. (cognitive general)

- I imagine winning a medal. (motivational specific)

- I imagine appearing self-confident in front of my opponents. (motivational general-mastery)

- I get psyched up when imagining performing. (motivational general-arousal)

Recommendations for Using Imagery

Holmes and Collins (2001) have provided some guidelines in their PETTLEP model that are useful when conducting imagery interventions (see Table 4.5).

For imagery use to be effective, it must be incorporated into a daily routine. Bull, Albinson, and Shambrook (1996) suggest brief sessions (five minutes) once or twice a day for athletes who are beginning imagery. As athletes become more comfortable with and better at using imagery, they should systematically increase the amount of imagery employed. Cumming and Hall (2002) argue that imagery requires deliberate practice and just as for physical practice, more is better. Because imagery is a skill and improves with practice, athletes will become better imagers over the course of an imagery intervention. The better imagers they become, the more effective their imagery will be.

Here are other recommendations for using imagery:

- Images should be positive rather than negative (Hall, 2001).

- Athletes should be in a good mood when using imagery (Gregg, Hall, & Hanton, 2004).

- Athletes need to be encouraged to use imagery during those times when imagery use is typically less frequent, such as in the off-season and early competitive season (Munroe et al., 1998).

- Less skilled athletes need to be encouraged to use imagery (Hall, 2001).

- Athletes of all ages can benefit from imagery interventions (Munroe-Chandler, Hall, Fishburne, & Strachan, 2004).

Conclusions about Imagery

Imagery is an integral part of many psychological skills training programs because of its wide range applicability and the fact that imagery can be implemented virtually

Table 4.5   The PETTLEP Model of Imagery

A Guide for Using Imagery: The PETTLEP Model	
P = Physical	The physical nature of the imagery is dependent upon the task. You must determine whether relaxation or increased arousal is helpful prior to imaging.
E = Environment	The image should be as real or as close to the actual environment as possible. If you are unfamiliar with the competition venue, perhaps video footage or pictures will enhance your image.
T = Task	Depending on the task, your imagery perspective may vary. Skills that rely heavily on form have been found to benefit most from an external imagery perspective.
T = Timing	The temporal characteristics or timing of the image should be equal to that of your physical performance (e.g., if a skating routine takes three minutes to physically execute, so too should the imagery).
L = Learning	The content of the image should change based on the learning of the skill. For example, the content of your image when you are first learning a camel spin should be different from when you have mastered the skill.
E = Emotion	Images will be more effective if you attach meaning or emotion to them. If imaging winning a gold medal, feel the excitement and the joy that is a part of it.
P = Perspective	Consider both perspectives, internal and external, when imaging.

Note: Adapted from Holmes & Collins, 2001 / Holmes, Paul S., & Collins, David J. (2001). "The PETTLEP approach to motor imagery: A functional equivalence model for sport psychologists." Journal of Applied Sport Psychology, March 1, 2001, Vol.13:1, 60–83. Taylor & Francis, Philadelphia.

anywhere and anytime. Coaches, athletes, and sport psychology consultants have all recognized imagery as an effective intervention for influencing a number of factors as evidenced in Martin et al.'s (1999) applied model. Moreover, every athlete (novice to elite) can benefit from the use of imagery, providing the imagery is built into a daily routine and fits the needs of the athlete.

Self-talk

One of the skills most highly promoted by applied sport psychology consultants and frequently included in psychological skills intervention training programs is self-talk (e.g., Bull et al., 1996; Hanton & Jones, 1999). Although many different definitions have been forwarded, Hardy (2004) recently proposed a strong definition of self-talk, following his extensive research on athletes' self-talk at the University of Western Ontario. He argued that **self-talk** should be defined as "*overt* [out loud] or *covert* [in your head] sport related statements that are addressed to the self, multidimensional and somewhat dynamic in nature, include interpretive elements associated with the content of the self-statements, and seem to serve at least two functions for the athlete, instructional and motivational" (p. 145, italics added).

Functions of Self-talk

Self-talk serves two basic functions in sport: instructional and motivational. **Instructional self-talk** is used by athletes for skill development, skill execution, strategy development, and general performance improvement (Hardy, Gammage, & Hall, 2001). For example, Landin and Hebert (1999) investigated the effectiveness of instructional self-talk by having varsity tennis players use the cue words "split" and "turn" in order to improve their volleying technique at the net. These two cue words were constructed to represent the two phases of the volleying: splitting the legs shoulder width apart for a balanced position, and then turning the shoulders in order to reduce excessive raquet head movement. Improvements in the players' volleying performance were observed, indicating that sport performance can be improved by self-talk.

According to Hardy et al. (2001a), athletes employ **motivational self-talk** for three purposes: (a) for mastery, for example, building self-confidence, staying focused, being mentally ready, coping in difficult circumstances; (b) for arousal, for example, psyching up, relaxing; and (c) for drive, for example, increasing effort, increasing drive, reaching their potential. To date, there has been little research investigating motivational self-talk in sport. Nevertheless, one of the most consistent findings in sport psychology research is the direct relationship between positive thinking and successful performance. Undoubtedly, positive thinking entails considerable positive self-talk. Applied sport psychology books often stress that athletes need to change "I can't" to "I can" and "It's difficult for me" to "It's a challenge for me" if they want to be more successful (see Bull et al., 1996).

Assessment of Self-talk

Various approaches and measures have been employed by researchers to assess athletes' use of self-talk. The Self-Talk Grid (Hardy, Hall, & Alexander, 2001) measures two dimensions of self-talk: valence (positive vs. negative) and directional interpretation (motivating vs. de-motivating). Athletes simultaneously report on both dimensions by placing a check mark on a 9×9 grid: they indicate the valence of their self-talk, from *extremely positive* to *extremely negative*, as well as how they interpret their self-statements, from *extremely motivating* to *extremely de-motivating*. A weakness of the Self-Talk Grid is that it does not provide a detailed account of athletes' self-talk. As noted in Hardy's (2004) definition, self-talk is multidimensional, and the Self-Talk Grid assesses only two of the six dimensions of self-talk, valence and directional interpretation.

A more comprehensive questionnaire for assessing athletes' self-talk was recently developed by Hardy (2004). The Self-Talk Use Questionnaire (STUQ) is a 59-item self-report instrument that assesses the frequency of athletes' use of self-talk. The

---

Reflections 4.2

You have just been scored against and trail by one goal. What could you say to yourself in order to build confidence and stay positive?

STUQ has four sections: section 1 examines *when* athletes use self-talk; section 2, *what* athletes say to themselves; section 3, *why* athletes talk to themselves in both practice and competition; and section 4, *how* athletes use self-talk (see Table 4.6). The instrument appears to be both reliable and valid.

An alternative approach to using questionnaires, developed by Van Raalte, Brewer, Rivera, and Petitpas (1994), is a tennis-specific observational method called Self-Talk and Gestures Rating Scale (STAGRS). Independent judges rate athletes' usage of overt self-talk during a competitive tennis match. The STAGRS measures the use of positive, negative, and instructional self-talk (and gestures). Positive self-talk and gestures are the summed occurrences of complimenting opponents, fist pumps, and positive self-talk. Negative self-talk and gestures are the summed occurrences of ball abuse, frustration, hitting oneself, laughing in frustration, negative self-talk, opponent abuse, and racquet abuse. Finally, instructional self-talk are the summed occurrences of giving instructions to oneself (e.g., keep raquet head up) and practice motions without the ball. There are some limitations with the STAGRS. It assesses self-talk only in tennis, and it measures only overt self-talk; however, most of athletes' self-talk is covert.

Recommendations for Using Self-talk

Hardy (2004) identified six self-talk dimensions that should be used as a guide when developing a self-talk intervention for athletes. The first dimension, valence, refers to self-talk being positive or negative. Most of the self-talk research has compared positive versus negative self-talk and has consistently shown that positive self-talk is better. For example, Dagrou, Gauvin, and Halliwell (1992) found that a positive self-talk group significantly outperformed a negative self-talk and control group on a dart-throwing task. It is recommended that interventions focus on the use of positive self-talk.

The second dimension is concerned with how athletes' self-statements are verbalized, whether overtly or covertly. To date, there has been no direct comparison between the effectiveness of overt and covert self-talk in the sport domain. Nevertheless, it is known that both coping statements and goals are more effective if they are publicly

Table 4.6   Example Items of the Self-talk Use Questionnaire

Section on the STUQ	Example of an Item
When	How often do you use self-talk in relation to your sport before a practice?
What	In your opinion, generally what percentage of your self-talk is positive in nature? _____% generally what percentage of your self-talk is neutral in nature? _____% generally what percentage of your self-talk is negative in nature? _____% **(Percentages given should total 100%)**
Why	How often do you say things to yourself in practice to refine an already learned skill?
How	How often do you combine self-talk with mental imagery when using self-talk to help learn/fine tune a skill?

<

The Self-Talk Use Questionnaire (STUQ) assesses the frequency of athletes' use of self-talk: when, what, why, and how.

Photo © Philippe Caron/Sygma/CORBIS.

known. It is recommended, therefore, that some of the self-talk in an intervention be overt.

The third dimension involves the self-determination of the statements used by athletes. Statements can be conceptualized as assigned or freely chosen. Research, such as the tennis study conducted by Landin and Hebert (1999), demonstrates that assigned self-talk can be very effective. However, Hardy (2004) has argued that self-talk freely chosen by the athlete might have a greater motivational influence. Given that there is no research comparing the effectiveness of assigned versus freely chosen self-talk in sport, it is recommended that the coach, the sport psychology practitioner, and the athlete collaborate in the development of the athlete's self-talk statements.

The fourth and fifth dimensions of self-talk are closely related and entail the motivational interpretation of self-talk. The fourth dimension, directional interpretation, is concerned with whether athletes view their self-talk as motivating or de-motivating. The fifth dimension is intensity and is concerned with the extent to which athletes interpret their self-talk to be motivating—*not at all* or *very much so*. Different from the directional interpretation dimension, intensity is achieved regardless of whether athletes view that self-talk as motivating or de-motivating. For interventions, we recommend that athletes use self-talk they perceive as very motivating.

The final dimension of self-talk is frequency (i.e., how often athletes employ self-talk). Research has found that successful athletes use more self-talk than unsuccessful athletes. For example, Mahoney and Avener (1977) found that male gymnasts who qualified for the U.S. Olympic team reported a greater use of self-talk in competition and practice than those gymnasts who did not qualify for the Olympics. Based on such findings, it is recommended that athletes be encouraged to use self-talk frequently (see Table 4.7).

Landin (1994) provided some additional guidelines for the use of verbal cues in sport. Verbal cues should be brief, phonetically simple, logically associated with the particular elements of the respective task, and be compatible with the rhythm and timing of the task.

Table 4.7   The Six Dimensions of Self-talk

1. Valence—Positive or Negative

2. Verbalization—Overt or Covert

3. Self-Determination—Assigned or Freely Chosen

4. Directional Interpretation—Motivating or De-motivating

5. Directional Intensity—Not At All or Very Much So

6. Frequency—Often or Never

Conclusions about Self-talk

It is important that athletes practise positive self-talk. We encourage athletes to analyze the content of their self-talk and be on the lookout for negatively framed statements. When negative statements enter your mind, they should be immediately replaced with positive ones. Furthermore, athletes need to ensure their self-talk incorporates both instructional and motivational statements. Athletes who invest in improving their self-talk will find their efforts well rewarded.

Arousal Regulation

The relationship between arousal and anxiety is complex. Given that athletes may require different levels of arousal for peak performance, it is important that athletes learn to identity which mental and emotional states are necessary for success. The following two quotations from Canadian athletes represent the diversity in arousal levels needed for peak performance. Tania Vincent, national level speed skater, said, "I need to be nervous before a race because it gives me that extra boost. I transfer my nervousness to adrenaline and it helps me keep going" (Wilson, 1998, ¶6).

I discovered that after a certain point of nervousness, I would start to deteriorate pretty rapidly. There was a real drop off point in my ability to perform if I got too nervous . . . so it was just being able to find that little narrow comfort zone. (Orlick & Partington, 1986, p. 69)

Once athletes can identify their optimal level of arousal, they can learn to voluntarily program these responses. Because the theories and research pertaining to the arousal-performance relationship are covered elsewhere, this section will focus on techniques to reduce and increase levels of arousal.

For the purposes of our discussion, we will adopt the definition as proposed by Zaichkowsky and Baltzell (2001). **Arousal** is a multidimensional construct containing physiological, cognitive appraisal, and affective components. Coaches and athletes would concur that performance fluctuations in sport are many times the result of being overaroused or underaroused. Given the strong relationship between arousal and performance, it is not surprising that athletes use techniques to regulate their arousal levels.

Techniques to Reduce or Increase Arousal

TECHNIQUES TO REDUCE AROUSAL   Many performance problems arise because of overarousal. In order to avoid any detrimental effects on performance, learning to relax is vital. Below we discuss various techniques that have been shown to effectively reduce arousal level.

Breathing   If done properly, breathing is a simple technique used to relax. Diaphragmatic breathing, as opposed to quick shallow breathing, increases the amount of oxygen being delivered through the body and facilitates the removal of waste. When athletes feel overaroused prior to a competition, their breathing rate usually increases and breathing becomes very shallow. By learning to breathe better, athletes can achieve deep relaxation or momentary relaxation.

Breathing Exercise: Take a deep breath (dig down into the belly) and imagine your lungs are divided into three levels. Begin by filling the lower level of the lungs with air. You will notice the diaphragm moving down slightly and forcing the abdomen out. Next, fill the middle level of the lungs by expanding the chest cavity and raising the ribcage. Finally, fill the upper level of the lungs. Notice a slight rise in the chest and shoulders. Hold the breath for several seconds; then exhale slowly. Repeat this exercise until you feel comfortable with this breathing technique. To help enhance this technique, you may want to consider rhythmic breathing, in which you inhale for a count of four and exhale for a count of eight (a 1:2 ratio). This helps to slow the breathing and allows you to focus on the exhalation (Williams & Harris, 1998).

Progressive Relaxation   Jacobson (1938) first introduced this technique as a means to relax. Progressive relaxation was based on the notion that tension and relaxation are mutually exclusive. This means one cannot be relaxed and tense at the same time. Although the initial training program devised by Jacobson was lengthy and required a substantial amount of training, abbreviated exercises that are just as effective have evolved (Carlson & Hoyle, 1993). Once the technique has been mastered, athletes can achieve a relaxed state in a matter of minutes, thereby making it useful just prior to competition or during breaks in competition.

Progressive relaxation involves systematically tensing and relaxing specific muscles in a pre-determined order: left arm, right arm, left leg, right leg, abdomen, back, chest, shoulders, neck, and face muscles. The tensing (or contraction phase) teaches awareness and sensitivity while the letting go (or relaxing phase) teaches awareness of the absence of tension. Bernstein and Carlson (1993) propose that once the athlete can achieve the abbreviated version (normally takes several weeks of practice), an even shorter version can be attained. This includes tensing the entire body, holding for 5–10 seconds, and then releasing the tension to achieve a relaxed state.

Progressive Relaxation Exercise: In the following abbreviated version of progressive relaxation, tense each group of muscles and hold for 5–10 seconds, and then relax for 30–40 seconds.

a.   Make tight fists with both hands, tighten the biceps and the forearms, hold the tension, and then relax.

b.   Tighten the muscles of both thighs; at the same time you curl your toes and tighten the calves. Hold. Relax.

c.   Take a deep breath, hold it, and raise the shoulders while making the stomach hard and tightening the buttocks. Hold. Relax.

d.   Tense all the facial muscles while employing the tension procedure for the neck. Hold. Relax.

> In order to avoid any detrimental effects on performance, learning to relax is vital; proper diaphragmatic breathing is a simple relaxation technique.

Photo courtesy of Tongro Image Stock/Maxx Images.

Meditation   **Meditation** allows for deep relaxation of the mind, which in turn, relaxes the body. Meditation has been found to facilitate athletic performance (Schaffer, 1992); however, these positive effects seem most prominent in activities involving gross motor movements, such as running. Meditation involves the uncritical focus of attention on a single thought, sound, or object (usually called the mental device). Although meditation is normally associated with eastern and western religious practice, Herbert Benson (1975) devised the relaxation response, which is a generalized version of meditation and one that is employed by athletes as a means to relax.

Meditation Exercise: Before you begin, find a quiet place where you can get comfortable and where distractions are minimal. Choose a mental device (mantra), such as the word "calm" or "warm." Adopt a passive attitude in which thoughts and images enter the mind but are not attended to. Close your eyes, and relax all your muscles, beginning at your feet and progressing up to your face. Focus on your breathing. With each exhalation, repeat your mantra. Breathe easily and naturally. Continue this for 10–20 minutes. Once finished, remain seated with your eyes closed. After a few minutes you may open your eyes. Practise the technique once or twice daily. Remember to remain passive by just letting the relaxation happen.

Autogenic Training   **Autogenic training** focuses on feelings associated with limbs and muscles of the body. More specifically, the training consists of three components: (a) warmth and heaviness of the limbs, (b) visualizing relaxing scenes at the same time as imagining the first component, and (c) specific relaxing themes in self-statements. Spigolon and Annalisa (1985) provide some anecdotal evidence that autogenic training works to improve athletic performance. Just as progressive relaxation takes time and training to master, so does autogenic training. Several months of regular training are needed to become skilled at this technique.

Autogenic Training Exercise: Autogenic training consists of six sequential stages. As described in progressive relaxation, allow the feelings to happen without interference. Allow yourself to learn each stage before progressing to the next. Repeat the suggestions in each stage six times followed by the word "quiet" once (see Table 4.8). Once the athlete has learned all the stages, the entire sequence can be practised.

TECHNIQUES TO INCREASE AROUSAL   Although the techniques mentioned thus far have dealt with relaxation, there are times when athletes need to psych themselves up and become energized. While relaxation training is used to lower arousal to optimal levels, **psyching up strategies** are used to increase arousal levels. When underaroused, athletes cannot perform effectively. Their reactions will be slowed down and their coordinations reduced. Many attempts by athletes to energize themselves or their teams have been done at the wrong time, thereby causing overarousal (Cox, 2002). Athletes and coaches must first identify the signs and symptoms of low energy, and then decide which of the following techniques is best suited to their needs. Below we discuss various techniques that have been shown to effectively increase arousal level.

Pep Talks   The pep talk is one of the most widely used and recognized energizing strategies. It is important, however, that the pep talk be meaningful and be applied at the correct time. If your player or team is already energized prior to a competition, you may want to think twice before giving the "win one for the gipper" speech.

Bulletin Boards   Catchy phrases or quotes displayed in a location that is visually prominent (e.g., locker room door, above athlete's stall) are an easy way to increase arousal (activation). Athletes seeing these on a daily basis will remember them and use them as reinforcement when needed.

Pre-competitive Workouts   A pre-competitive workout can enhance activation. It is not uncommon for athletes to feel fatigued on the day of competition. Therefore, a light workout several hours prior to competition can combat this fatigue.

Verbal Cues   Using energizing words such as "explode," "quick," or "go" can help a player or team to quickly become activated. There are situations where athletes do not have enough time to generate energy with a pre-competitive workout. In instances such as these, energizing words can be employed.

Breathing   Although breathing is a technique that can be used to relax, it can also be used as an energizer. By increasing the rhythm of breathing and imagining activation and energy with each inhalation, an athlete can increase arousal.

Table 4.8   Autogenic Training Stages, Sensations, and Suggestions

Stage	Sensation	Suggestion
Stage 1	Heaviness in the extremities	"My right (left) arm is heavy."
Stage 2	Warmth in the extremities	"My right (left) arm is very warm."
Stage 3	Regulation of cardiac activity	"My heartbeat is regular and strong."
Stage 4	Regulation of breathing	"My breathing rate is slow, calm, and relaxed: it breathes me."
Stage 5	Abdominal warmth	"My solar plexus is warm." (place hand on upper abdominal area while saying this phrase)
Stage 6	Cooling of the forehead	"My forehead is cool."

Imagery   Energizing images work in much the same way as energizing verbal cues. Be sure to formulate an image that is personally energizing. For instance, 2004 Olympic gymnastics floor champion Kyle Shewfelt stated, "The night before, I was trying to sleep, but I was going through my routine in my head. I wasn't too nervous, but I was trying to make it perfect.... [on competition day] I think I went through it about 5000 more times" ("Senior men," 2004, ¶3). As a result, he was full of energy when arriving at the competition venue.

Music   Many athletes use music to get psyched up. For many, music is part of their pre-competitive routine to help them achieve their optimal arousal level. Recently the NBA decided that athletes could no longer wear headphones and listen to music in the warm-up. Vince Carter, formerly of the NBA Toronto Raptors, noted that his pre-competitive routine would suffer as a result of this decision ("Carter told," 2004).

Measurement of Arousal Levels

Arousal can be measured in a number of ways, including physiological recordings, self-reports, and behavioural observations. A recent trend has been the construction of multidimensional self-report instruments, such as the Competitive State Anxiety Inventory-2 (CSAI-2; Martens, Burton, Vealey, Bump, & Smith, 1990).

Conclusions about Arousal Levels

Athletes' ability to effectively regulate arousal is one of the most important techniques in ensuring athletic success. Athletes need to know how and when to relax or become energized in both training and competition. Using the techniques and exercises outlined above will aid athletes in achieving optimal arousal levels.

Reflections 4.3
In previous chapters, we discussed the concepts of stress, anxiety, and coping, whereas this chapter has focused on specific psychological strategies. How would you develop a coping skills program for an athlete who reports experiencing debilitating high levels of cognitive anxiety during critical parts of a competition? Think carefully about what information you would need and the potential psychological or mental skills a trained and competent helper could teach the athlete.

Attention Control

Attention is fundamental to skilled motor performance (Abernethy, 2001). Players often attribute performing poorly to a loss of concentration or becoming distracted. Even a very temporary loss of focus can mar performance and spell the difference between winning and losing. For example, missing a short easy putt in golf as a result of simply not exerting enough concentration has cost numerous professionals tournament wins. Given the importance of attention to successful sport performance, it comes as little surprise that many psychological skills training programs include attention control training (e.g., Bull et al., 1996).

Recent research views **attention** as a multidimensional construct having at least two components (Abernethy, 2001). First, it is considered to be a limited resource. This refers to the known limitations people have in performing two or more tasks at

<

Research has shown that dual-task performance (e.g., dribbling a basketball while looking to make a pass) gets better with training.
Photo courtesy of Getty Images/ Digital Vision.

the same time. A basketball player, as an example, must dribble the ball and at the same time monitor the position of teammates and opponents. The second component of attention concerns the selective processing of specific information while ignoring other information. Alternatively, it can be considered as focusing on relevant cues while disregarding irrelevant ones. A goalie in hockey must determine from where a shot is being taken while disregarding the jostling players in front of the net.

Research has shown that performing multiple tasks, such as dribbling a basketball while looking to make a pass, gets better with training (Abernethy, 2001). In addition, performers become better with practice at selecting pertinent information or cues (e.g., the goalie determining from where the shot is taken) and are less likely to be distracted by irrelevant ones.

Assessing Attention as a Limited Resource

Probably the most common approach to measuring attention as a limited resource in experimental psychology has been the use of dual-task procedures. These procedures determine the attention demands and characteristics of two different tasks that are performed simultaneously. The **primary task** is the task for which attention demand is assessed. The **secondary task** provides the principal performance measure from which the implications concerning primary task demand are obtained. The following is an example of a dual task. A soccer player is required to dribble a ball down a field; this is the primary task. While dribbling, the player is required to change direction when a coach blows the whistle, and this reaction-time task (e.g., go right on the whistle blow) would be the secondary task. This signal could be given by the coach at various phases of the dribbling task, such as at the start, when a defender is encountered, or when the player is dribbling with no defenders nearby. Tasks similar to this one have shown that all phases of performing a skill do not require the same amount of attention. This dual-task procedure, unfortunately, has been rarely used to measure attention in sport because of the difficulty in determining an appropriate secondary task, as well as in achieving baseline measures of performance for both the primary and secondary tasks.

An alternative method of assessing attention demands has been to use physiological measures of information processing load. Researchers have used such measures as pupil diameter, cardiac acceleration or deceleration, cardiac variability, and EEG event-related potentials as indicators of information processing load. For example, researchers have proposed that when a task is performed that requires an external attentional focus, heart rate slows down immediately before the task is executed. This proposal has received some support. Boutcher (2002) found evidence of cardiac deceleration among elite rifle shooters just before they pull the trigger, which suggests they seem to be able to switch on their attention on demand. The limitations of using these physiological measures are that they can be quite costly and are only indirect measures of attention demands (i.e., they may not always be good measures of attentional resource limitations).

Assessing Selective Attention

There are multiple means to assess attention (see Table 4.9). One approach to assessing the selection of relevant information is the use of visual occlusion techniques. **Temporal occlusion** examines the amount of time people take to select the information they need in order to respond. Researchers show people a videotape of a skill. At various points during the action, the videotape is stopped and the observers are required to make a response. For example, Abernethy and Russell (1987) had badminton players watch video sequences of a player making different shots. When the video was stopped, the observers made predictions about the landing positions of the shuttle. To examine when, in the course of the observed action, accurate decisions were made, the video was stopped at different times prior to, during, and after the shuttle contact. Thus, the researchers could determine when during the action the observers could select the necessary information for making a correct decision.

Table 4.9   Summary of Selective Attention Assessment Tools

Assessing Selective Attention
Visual Occlusion Techniques: Temporal and Event
Eye Movement Recordings
Self-Report Measures
Test of Attentional and Interpersonal Style (TAIS)
Thought Occurrence Questionnaire for Sport (TOQS)

Event occlusion examines which characteristics of the performance people use to make a correct response. In this case, parts of the video are masked so the observers cannot see selected parts of the action. The logic of this approach is that if people make poorer decisions when they cannot see a specific cue (e.g., the hitting arm of a badminton player making a shot), then that cue is important for successful performance.

Another approach to investigating the selection of relevant information is the use of eye movement recordings. Sophisticated equipment tracks the movement of the eyes and records where they are looking at a particular time. The assumption is that what a person is looking at should provide insight into what information in the environment a person is attending to. The question is, can we relate eye movements to visual attention? The answer seems to be yes but with considerable caution. Although it is not possible to make an eye movement without a corresponding shift in attention, attention can be moved around the visual field without making eye movements. Therefore, visual fixation (periods when the eye remains relatively stationary) and attention are not one and the same. This means that eye movement recordings may underestimate what people are visually attending to.

A third approach to assessing selective attention is the use of self-report measures. These measures typically address how well people are able to focus their attention. Attentional focus is sometimes considered in terms of width (i.e., a broad or narrow focus) and direction (i.e., an external or internal focus). Taking a doubles tennis player as an example, the player would need a narrow external focus when volleying a ball at the net, but a broad internal focus when analyzing how to move at the net (e.g., to poach or not on a partner's upcoming serve). One of the most common measures of attentional focus is the Test of Attentional and Interpersonal Style (TAIS; Nideffer, 1976), and a number of sport-specific versions of this instrument have also been developed (e.g., baseball version (B-TAIS), Albrecht & Feltz, 1987). Research has indicated, however, that the TAIS has some inadequacies and should be employed with caution (Ford & Summers, 1992).

Although researchers have questioned the use of the TAIS, there is a promising new instrument for the assessment of concentration skills. The Thought Occurrence Questionnaire for Sport (TOQS; Hatzigeorgiadis & Biddle, 2000) is a 17-item test that measures the degree to which athletes experience cognitive interference from distracting thoughts during competition. The three subscales measure (a) task-related worries, such as "During the competition, I had thoughts that other competitors are better than I am"; (b) task-irrelevant thoughts, such as "During the competition, I had thoughts about what I'm going to do when I go home"; and (c) thoughts of escape, such as "During the competition, I had thoughts that I cannot stand it anymore."

Using Attention-control Strategies

There are different techniques for controlling attention (see Table 4.10 on next page). The most commonly used technique for learning to control attention is **attention simulation training**, in which athletes replicate the kinds of attention-demanding situations they find themselves in during competition. Players should practise simultaneously working on two tasks that typically must be performed together to produce optimal performance. Players should also practise focusing on relevant cues and disregarding irrelevant one. The practise, however, is only likely to be effective if it is sport specific. In other words, the training situations must allow the performer to practise the specific attention-sharing and cue-selection strategies required in the sport skill. A defenceman

Table 4.10   Summary of Attention-control Strategies

- Simulation Training

- Performance Routines

- Attentional Cues

- Imagery

in hockey should practise carrying the puck while looking to pass to one of the forwards, and a goalie should practise stopping shots with other players in front of the net.

Other attention-control strategies include performance routines, attentional cues, and imagery (Bull et al., 1996). **Performance routines** are a set sequence of thoughts and actions that are done before the performance of key skills. For example, professional golfer Mike Weir has a famous "waggle," which is part of a distinct pre-shot routine. What began as a physical move to counteract his hockey actions, the waggle has become part of his pre-shot routine (Wilson, 2003). It is now identical from one swing to the next. In order for performance routines to be effective in competition, they must be carefully planned and then extensively practised in training.

There are two types of routines used by athletes. Pre-event routines are the fixed thoughts and actions athletes undertake in the time leading up to competition (e.g., night before or morning of competition); pre-performance routines are the fixed thoughts and actions athletes undertake immediately before executing a skill (e.g., bouncing the ball three times before taking a foul shot). These routines work because they encourage athletes to focus on task-relevant information. They also remind athletes to remain in the present rather than dwell on past events of possible future outcomes. Finally, performance routines prevent the athlete from attending too much to skill technique instead of letting skills happen automatically.

Attentional cues are words and actions that direct the athlete's attention. These cues help athletes to focus their concentration on the task at hand and to refocus their concentration if lost. Three types of concentration cues are verbal, visual, and physical. A verbal cue is typically a single word, which is repeated at the appropriate moment. Some examples of verbal cues are *smooth*, *high*, *speed*, *ready*, and *power*. A visual cue entails focusing keenly on something in the athlete's surroundings. For example, looking at the strings of a squash racquet, staring at the logo on the shaft of a field hockey stick, and fixating on the button in curling are all visual cues an athlete may use. A physical cue involves doing an action, such as taking a deep breath, banging the stick on the ice, and slapping the thigh. Some athletes use a single cue while others prefer to use a combination. Just like performance routines, attentional cues need to be practised regularly and employed consistently before implementing them in competition.

Imagery, as a means of controlling attention, can be used in two ways. It can be used to prepare for various scenarios that ensure athletes will not be distracted by unexpected events. For example, a skater could imagine how to react if the music stops during the middle of her program. Moreover, imagery can be used as a means of parking errors in order to prevent dwelling on mistakes. For example, a volleyball player may image placing errors in the garbage can at the side of the court, or a soccer player may image placing errors in the tree at the end of the pitch. Just as with the other techniques discussed above, parking errors requires considerable practice. In doing so, the athlete creates a link between parking the image and focusing attention on relevant performance cues.

Conclusions about Attention Control

It is difficult to conceive of anything more important in sport than paying attention to the task at hand. Attention-control strategies are often perceived as inherent in elite athletes; however, the old adage "practice makes perfect" is apt when it comes to developing effective strategies. An athlete's control over attentional focus is learned through practice just like any other difficult physical skill. Using the techniques discussed above, athletes can improve their attention control and perform successfully during the critical moments in their sport.

Chapter Summary

A variety of psychological intervention strategies to enhance sport performance have been discussed in this chapter. These strategies involve the following five key psychological skills. Athletes should set SMART goals that are supported and evaluated. Imagery should be part of every psychological skills training program because of its wide application and the fact that it can be implemented virtually anywhere and anytime. Athletes should analyze the content of their self-talk and modify negatively framed statements. Athletes need to know how and when to relax or become energized during both training and competition. Athletes should improve their attention control so they can perform successfully during the critical moments in their sport.

The benefits of these strategies have been supported by research as well as by the anecdotal reports from athletes, coaches, and applied sport psychologists. It is important to remember that these psychological strategies can be learned, practised, and applied in a variety of settings, such as during training, competition, and injury rehabilitation. These strategies will be beneficial, however, only if athletes are committed to putting the time and effort into mastering them. Consider the results for Stephanie, the figure skater, in the opening vignette.

Review Questions

1. What are the five psychological skills discussed in this chapter?
2. Why are the five psychological skills effective?
3. Describe one way to measure each of these five psychological skills.
4. Describe the SMART guidelines for goal setting.
5. What are the guidelines for using imagery?
6. What are the six self-talk dimensions?
7. What are the techniques that effectively reduce arousal level?
8. What are the techniques that effectively increase arousal level?
9. Describe each of the four attentional control strategies and provide an example of each.

Suggested Reading

Abernethy, B. (2001). Attention. In R. N. Singer, H. A. Hausenblas, & C. M. Janelle (Eds.), *Handbook of sport psychology* (2nd ed., pp. 53–85). New York: Wiley.

Burton, D. (1989). Winning isn't everything: Examining the impact of performance goals on collegiate swimmers' cognitions and performance. *The Sport Psychologist, 3,* 105–132.

Butler, R. J., & Hardy, L. (1992). The performance profile: Theory and application. *The Sport Psychologist, 6*, 253–264.

Hall, C. R. (2001). Imagery in sport and exercise. In R. N. Singer, H. A. Hausenblas, & C. M. Janelle (Eds.), *Handbook of sport psychology* (2nd ed., pp. 529–549). New York: Wiley.

Williams, H. M., & Harris, D. V. (2001). Relaxation and energizing techniques for regulation of arousal. In J. M. Williams (Ed.), *Applied sport psychology: Personal growth to peak performance* (4th ed., pp. 229–246).

References

Abernethy, B. (2001). Attention. In R. N. Singer, H. A., Hausenblas, & C. M. Janelle (Eds.), *Handbook of sport psychology* (2nd ed., pp. 53–85). New York: Wiley.

Abernethy, B., & Russell, D. G. (1987). The relationship between expertise and visual search strategy in a racquet sport. *Human Movement Science, 6*, 283–319.

Albrecht, R. R., & Feltz, D. L. (1987). Generality and specificity of attention related to competitive anxiety and sport performance. *Journal of Sport Psychology, 9*, 231–248.

Benson, H. (1975). *The relaxation response.* New York: William Morrow.

Bernstein, D. A., & Carlson, C. R. (1993). Progressive relaxation: Abbreviated methods. In P. M. Lehrer & R. L. Woolfolk (Eds.), *Principles and practices of stress management* (2nd ed., pp. 58–87). New York: Guilford Press.

Boutcher, S. H. (2002). Attentional processes and sport performance. In T. Horn (Ed.), *Advances in sport psychology* (2nd ed., pp. 441–457). Morgantown, WV: Fitness Information Technology.

Bull, S. J., Albinson, J. G., & Shambrook, J. (1996). *The mental game plan: Getting psyched for sport.* Brighton, UK: Sports Dynamic.

Burton, D., Naylor, S., & Holliday, B. (2001). Goal setting in sport: Investigating the goal effectiveness paradigm. In R. N. Singer, H. A. Hausenblas, & C. M. Janelle (Eds.), *Handbook of sport psychology,* (2nd ed., pp. 497–528). New York: Wiley.

Butler, R. J., & Hardy, L. (1992). The performance profile: Theory and application. *The Sport Psychologist, 6*, 253–264.

Callow, N., & Hardy, L. (2001). Types of imagery associated with sport confidence in netball players of varying skill levels. *Journal of Applied Sport Psychology, 13*, 1–17.

Callow, N., Hardy, L., & Hall, C. (2001). The effect of a motivational general-mastery imagery intervention on the sport confidence of high-level badminton players. *Research Quarterly for Exercise and Sport, 72*, 389–400.

Carlson, C. R., & Hoyle, R. H. (1993). Efficacy of abbreviated progressive muscle relaxation training: A quantitative review of behavioral medicine research. *Journal of Consulting and Clinical Psychology, 61*, 1059–1067.

Carter, J. E., & Kelly, A. E. (1997). Using traditional and paradoxical imagery interventions with reactant intramural athletes. *The Sport Psychologist, 11*, 175–189.

Carter told to tune out. (2004, November 17). *The Windsor Star,* p. E2.

Cox, R. H. (2002). *Sport psychology: Concepts and applications* (5th ed.). New York: McGraw-Hill.

Cumming, J., & Hall, C. (2002) Deliberate imagery practice: The development of imagery skills in competitive athletes. *Journal of Sport Sciences, 20*, 137–145.

Dagrou, E., Gauvin, L., & Halliwell, W. (1992). Effets du langage positif, négatif, et neuter sur la performance motrice [Effects of positive, negative, and neutral self-talk on motor performance]. *Canadian Journal of Sports Sciences, 17*, 145–147.

Dawson, K. A., Bray, S. R., & Widmeyer, W. N. (2002). Goals setting by intercollegiate sport teams and athletes. *Avante, 8*, 14–23.

Driskell, J. E., Copper, C., & Moran, A. (1994). Does mental practice enhance performance? *Journal of Applied Psychology, 79*, 481–492.

Durand-Bush, N., Salmela, J. H., & Green, D. I. (2001). The Ottawa Mental Skills Assessment Tool (OMSAT-3). *The Sport Psychologist, 15*, 1–19.

Fenker, R. M., & Lambiotte, J. G. (1987). A performance enhancement program for a college football team: One incredible season. *The Sport Psychologist, 1*, 224–236.

Filby, W., Maynard, I., & Graydon, J. (1999). The effect of multiple-goal strategies on performance outcomes in training and competition. *Journal of Applied Sport Psychology, 11*, 230–246.

Ford, S. K., & Summers, J. J. (1992). The factorial validity of the TAIS attentional style subscales. *Journal of Sport & Exercise Psychology, 14*, 283–297.

Gould, D., Tammen, V., Murphy, S., & May, J. (1989). An examination of US Olympic sport psychology consultants and the services they provide. *The Sport Psychologist, 3*, 300–312.

Gregg, M., Hall, C., & Hanton, S. (2004). Perceived effectiveness of mental imagery. Manuscript submitted for publication.

Hale, B. D., & Whitehouse, A. (1998). The effects of imagery-manipulated appraisal on intensity and direction of competitive anxiety. *The Sport Psychologist, 12*, 40–51.

Hall, C. R. (2001). Imagery in sport and exercise. In R. N. Singer, H. A. Hausenblas, & C. M. Janelle (Eds.), *Handbook of sport psychology* (2nd ed., pp. 529–549). New York: Wiley.

Hall, C. R., Mack, D., Paivio, A., & Hausenblas, H. A. (1998). Imagery use by athletes: Development of the sport imagery questionnaire. *International Journal of Sport Psychology, 29*, 73–89.

Hall, C. R., & Martin, K. A. (1997). Measuring movement imagery abilities: A revision of the movement imagery questionnaire. *Journal of Mental Imagery, 21*, 143–154.

Hanton, S., & Jones, G. (1999). The effects of a multimodal intervention program on performers: II. Training the butterflies to fly in formation. *The Sport Psychologist, 13*, 22–41.

Hardy, J. (2004). *Describing athlete self-talk.* Unpublished doctoral dissertation, University of Western Ontario, London, Ontario.

Hardy, J., Gammage, K., & Hall, C. R. (2001a). A description of athlete self-talk. *The Sport Psychologist, 15*, 306–318.

Hardy, J., Hall, C. R., & Alexander, M. R. (2001b). Exploring self-talk and affective states in sport. *Journal of Sport Sciences, 19*, 469–475.

Hatzigeorgiadis, A., & Biddle, S. J. H. (2000). Assessing cognitive interference in sport: Development of the thought occurrence questionnaire for sport. *Anxiety, Stress and Coping, 13*, 65–86.

Holmes, P. S., & Collins, D. J. (2001). The PETTLEP approach to motor imagery: A functional equivalence model for sport psychologists. *Journal of Applied Sport Psychology, 13*, 60–83.

Isaac, A., Marks, D., & Russell, E. (1996). An instrument for assessing imagery or movement: The vividness of movement imagery questionnaire (VMIQ). *Journal of Mental Imagery, 10*, 23–30.

Jacobson, E. (1938). *Progressive relaxation.* Chicago, IL: University of Chicago Press.

Jones, G. (1993). The role of performance profiling in cognitive behavioral interventions in sport. *The Sport Psychologist, 7*, 160–172.

Kingsley, J. (1998, February 16). Canadians get back in the game. *The Canadian Press.* http://www.canoe.ca/SlamNaganoShortTrackSkatingArchive/feb16_can.html

Landin, D. (1994). The role of verbal cues in skill learning. *Quest, 46*, 299–313.

Landin, D., & Hebert, E. P. (1999). The influence of self-talk on the performance of skilled female tennis players. *Journal of Applied Sport Psychology, 11*, 263–282.

Locke, E. A., & Latham, G. P. (1985). The application of goal setting to sports. *Journal of Sport Psychology, 7*, 205–222.

MacIntyre, T., & Moran, A. (1996). Imagery use among canoeists: A worldwide survey of novice, intermediate, and elite slalomists. *Journal of Applied Sport Psychology, 8*, S132.

Mahoney, M. J., & Avener, M. (1977). Psychology of the elite athlete: An exploratory study. *Cognitive Therapy and Research, 6*, 225–342.

Martens, R., Burton, D., Vealey, R. S., Bump, L. A., & Smith, D. E. (1990). Development and validation of the competitive state anxiety inventory-2. In R. Martens, R. S. Vealey, & D. Burton (Eds.), *Competitive anxiety in sports* (pp. 117–190). Champaign, IL: Human Kinetics.

Martin, K. A., Moritz, S. E., & Hall, C. R. (1999). Imagery use in sport: A literature review and applied model. *The Sport Psychologist, 13,* 245–268.

Moran, A. P. (2004). *Sport and exercise psychology.* New York: Taylor & Francis Group.

Munroe, K. J., Giacobbi, P. R., Hall, C., & Weinberg, R. (2000). The four Ws of imagery use: Where, when, why, and what. *The Sport Psychologist, 14,* 119–137.

Munroe, K. J., Hall, C. R., Simms, S., & Weinberg, R. (1998). The influence of type of sport and time of season on athletes' use of imagery. *The Sport Psychologist, 12,* 440–449.

Munroe-Chandler, K. J., Hall, C. R., Fishburne, G., & Strachan, L. (2004, October). *Imagery use in youth sport from a developmental perspective: Current issues and future directions.* Symposium presented at the annual meeting of the Canadian Society for Psychomotor Learning and Sport Psychology, Saskatchewan, Canada.

Murphy, S. M., & Woolfolk, R. L. (1987). The effects of cognitive interventions on competitive anxiety and performance on a fine motor skill accuracy task. *International Journal of Sport Psychology, 18,* 152–166.

Murphy, S. M., Woolfolk, R. L., & Budney, A. J. (1988). The effects of emotive imagery on strength performance. *Journal of Sport & Exercise Psychology, 10,* 334–345.

Nideffer, R. M. (1976). The test of attentional and interpersonal style. *Journal of Personality and Social Psychology, 34,* 394–404.

Orlick, T., & Partington, J. (1986). *Psyched: Inner views of winning.* Gloucester, ON: Coaching Association of Canada.

Paivio, A. (1985). Cognitive and motivational functions of imagery in human performance. *Canadian Journal of Applied Sport Science, 10,* 22S–28S.

Perry, C., & Morris, T. (1995). Mental imagery in sport. In T. Morris & J. Summers (Eds.), *Sport psychology: Theory, applications and issues* (pp. 339–385). Brisbane, Australia: Wiley.

Rodgers, W. M., Hall, C. R., & Buckolz, E. (1991). The effect of an imagery training program on imagery ability, imagery use, and figure skating performance. *Journal of Applied Sport Psychology, 3,* 109–125.

Rushall, B. S. (1988). Covert modeling as a procedure for altering an elite athlete's psychological state. *The Sport Psychologist, 2,* 131–140.

Ryska, T. A. (1998). Cognitive-behavioral strategies and precompetitive anxiety among recreational athletes. *Psychological Record, 48,* 697–708.

Schaffer, W. (1992). *Stress management for wellness* (2nd ed.). New York: Harcourt Brace Jovanovich.

Senior men: Kyle Shewfelt. (n.d.). *Gymn.ca* Retrieved December 23, 2004, from http://gymn.ca/athletes/interviews/shewfelt_04.shtml

Sordoni, C., Hall, C., & Forwell, L. (2002). The use of imagery in athletic injury rehabilitation and its relationship to self-efficacy. *Physiotherapy Canada, 54,* 177–185.

Spigolon, L., & Annalisa, D. (1985). Autogenic training in frogmen. *International Journal of Sport Psychology, 16,* 312–320.

Thomas, P. R., Murphy, S. M., & Hardy, L. (1999). Test of performance strategies: Development and preliminary validation of a comprehensive measure of athletes' psychological skills. *Journal of Sport Sciences, 17,* 697–711.

Vadocz, E. A., Hall, C. R., & Moritz, S. E. (1997). The relationship between competitive anxiety and imagery use. *Journal of Applied Sport Psychology, 9,* 241–253.

Van Raalte, J. L., Brewer, B. W., Rivera, P. M., Petitpas, A. J. (1994). The relationship between observable self-talk and competitive junior tennis players' match performance. *Journal of Sport & Exercise Psychology, 16,* 400–415.

Wanlin, C. M., Hrycaiko, D. W., Martin, G. L., & Mahon, M. (1997). The effects of a goal-setting package on the performance of speed skaters. *Journal of Applied Sport Psychology, 9,* 212–228.

Weinberg, R. S. (2002). Goal setting in sport and exercise: Research to practice. In J. Van Raalte & B. Brewer (Eds.), *Exploring sport and exercise psychology* (2nd ed., pp. 25–48).

Weinberg, R. S., & Gould, D. (2003). *Foundations of sport and exercise psychology* (3rd ed.). Champaign, IL: Human Kinetics.

White, A., & Hardy, L. (1998). An in-depth analysis of the uses of imagery by high level slalom canoeists and artistic gymnasts. *The Sport Psychologist, 12*, 387–403.

Williams, J. M., & Harris, D. V. (1998). Relaxation and energizing techniques for regulation of arousal. In J. M. Williams (Ed.), *Personal growth to peak performance* (3rd ed., pp. 219–236). Mountain View, CA: Mayfield.

Wilson, L. (1998, January 31). Eyes on the prize. *The Calgary Sun.* http://www.canoe.ca/ SlamNagano ShortTrackSkatingArchive/jan31_nstss.html

Wilson, M. (2003). A master champion. Retrieved December 23, 2004, from http://www.thegolfer mag.com/the_golfer/archive/style03/story_style03_swingseq.htm

Zaichkowsky, L. D., & Baltzell, A. (2001). Arousal and performance. In R. N. Singer, H. A. Hausenblas, & C. M. Janelle (Eds.), *Handbook of sport psychology* (2nd ed., pp. 319–339). New York: Wiley.

Chapter 5
Psychology and Education

5 PSYCHOLOGY AND EDUCATION

continued

Study or *The Schoolgirl*, c. 1933–1934, by Jean Puy. © 2003 Artists Rights Society (ARS), New York/ADAGP, Paris. Copyright Giraudon/Art Resource, NY.

Teachers' Casebook

What Would You Do?

Your school district has adopted a new student-centred curriculum for grades K through 6. Quite a bit of time and money was spent on workshops for teachers; buying levelled books and good children's literature; developing manipulatives for mathematics; building comfortable reading corners; making costumes, puppets, and other reading props; designing science projects; and generally supporting the innovations. Students and teachers are mostly pleased with the program. Many students appear to be more engaged in learning—but some students seem lost. The students' written work is longer and more creative. However, standardized tests indicate a drop in scores. The principal is clearly getting worried—this was her big project, and she had to work hard to "sell it" to some members of the parent advisory committee and school board. Several parents of students in your class are complaining that they have had to hire tutors or buy commercial programs to teach their children basic skills.

Critical Thinking

As a teacher, what would you do about the parents' complaints? Would you make any changes in your approach? What information would you need to make good decisions? Who should be involved in these decisions?

Collaboration

With three or four other students in your class, role-play a staff meeting in which the principal has asked whether the move toward more student-centred teaching was hasty and needs to be reconsidered. How do you and your colleagues respond?

Much of this text has been about learning and learners. In this chapter, we focus on teachers and teaching. We look first at characteristics of effective teachers and at how teachers' expectations for and interactions with students can influence achievement. Next, we examine how teachers plan, including how they use taxonomies of learning objectives or themes as a basis for planning.

With a sense of how to set goals and make plans, we move to a consideration of some general teacher-centred strategies: direct instruction, seatwork, homework, questioning, recitation, and group discussion. The next section focuses on student-centred approaches to teaching in different subjects. These reflect the constructivist views of learning. Finally, we discuss how teachers can support self-regulated learning in their classrooms—the highly effective approach to learning.

In addition to reading about strategies for teaching described in this chapter, we encourage you to review strategies for meeting the diverse needs of learners in inclusive classrooms.

By the time you have completed this chapter, you should be able to answer these questions:

- *What are the characteristics of effective teachers?*
- *How can teachers' expectations affect student learning?*
- *When and how should teachers use instructional objectives?*
- *In what situations would each of the following formats be most appropriate: direct instruction, seatwork and homework, questioning, and group discussion?*
- *How does the teacher's role vary in direct and student-centred approaches to teaching?*
- *What are the merits of student-centred approaches to teaching reading, mathematics, and science?*
- *How can teachers promote self-regulated learning in their classrooms?*

CHARACTERISTICS OF EFFECTIVE TEACHERS

Stop/Think/Write

Think about the most effective teacher you ever had—the one that you learned the most from. What were the characteristics of that person? What made that teacher so effective?

Some of the earliest research on effective teaching focused on the personal qualities of the teachers themselves (Medley, 1979). Results revealed some lessons about three teacher characteristics: knowledge, clarity, and warmth.

Teachers' Knowledge

Do teachers who know more about their subject have a more positive impact on their students? When we look at teachers' knowledge of facts and concepts, as measured by test scores and college grades, the relationship to student learning is unclear and may be indirect. Teachers who know more facts about their subject do not necessarily have students who learn more. But teachers who know more may make clearer presentations and recognize student difficulties more readily. They are ready for any student questions and do not have to be evasive or vague in their answers. And we know from Linda Darling-Hammond's (2000) work that the quality of teachers—as measured by whether the teachers had a major in their teaching field—is related to student performance. Thus, knowledge is necessary but not sufficient for effective teaching because being more knowledgeable helps teachers be clearer and more organized.

Clarity and Organization

When Barak Rosenshine and Norma Furst (1973) reviewed about 50 studies of teaching, they concluded that clarity was the most promising teacher behaviour for future research on effective teaching. Teachers who provide clear presentations and explanations tend to have students who learn more and who rate their teachers more positively (Hines, Cruickshank, & Kennedy, 1985; Land, 1987). Teachers with more knowledge of the subject tend to be less vague in their explanations to the class. The less vague the teacher, the more the students learn (Land, 1987). See the Guidelines on page 148 for ideas about how to be clear and organized in your teaching (Berliner, 1987; Evertson et al., 2003).

Warmth and Enthusiasm

As you are well aware, some teachers are much more enthusiastic than others. Some studies have found that ratings of teachers' enthusiasm for their subject are correlated with student achievement gains (Rosenshine & Furst, 1973). Warmth, friendliness, and understanding seem to be the teacher traits most strongly related to student attitudes (Murray, 1983; Ryans, 1960; Soar & Soar, 1979). In other words, teachers who are warm and friendly tend to have students who like them and the class in general. But note that these are correlational studies. The results do not tell us that teacher enthusiasm causes student learning or that warmth causes positive attitudes, only that the two variables tend to occur together. Teachers trained to demonstrate their enthusiasm have students who are more attentive and involved, but not necessarily more successful on tests of content (Gillett & Gall, 1982). The Guidelines on page 148 include some ideas for communicating warmth and enthusiasm.

Check Your Knowledge

- What are some general characteristics of effective teachers?

Apply to Practice

- Identify one of your teachers who exemplifies good teaching.

Teachers' beliefs about students also affect students' learning. For this reason, we turn to teacher expectations next.

TEACHER EXPECTATIONS

Stop/Think/Write

When you thought about the most effective teacher you ever had, was one of the characteristics of that teacher that he or she believed in you or demanded the best from you? How did the teacher communicate that belief?

Two kinds of expectation effects can occur in classrooms. The first has been referred to as the **Pygmalion effect** (Rosenthal & Jacobson, 1968), or self-fulfilling prophecy. When teachers' beliefs about students' abilities have no basis in fact, but student behaviour comes to match the initially inaccurate expectation, the outcome may be explained as a **self-fulfilling prophecy**. The second kind of expectation effect occurs when teachers are fairly accurate in their initial reading of students' abilities and respond to students appropriately. There is nothing wrong with forming and acting on accurate estimates of student ability. The problems arise when students show some improvement but teachers do not alter their expectations to take account of the improvement. This is called a **sustaining expectation effect**, because the teacher's unchanging expectation sustains the student's achievement at the expected level. The chance to raise expectations, provide more appropriate teaching, and thus encourage greater student achievement is lost. In practice, self-fulfilling prophecy effects seem to be stronger in the early grades and sustaining effects are more likely in the later grades (Kuklinski & Weinstein, 2001). And some students are more likely than others to be the recipients of sustaining expectations. For example, children who are withdrawn provide little information about themselves, so teachers may sustain their expectations about these children for lack of new input (Jones & Gerig, 1994).

Pygmalion effect Exceptional progress by a student as a result of high teacher expectations for that student; named for the mythological king Pygmalion, who made a statue, then caused it to be brought to life.

self-fulfilling prophecy A groundless expectation that is confirmed because it has been expected.

sustaining expectation effect An effect that occurs when student performance is maintained at a certain level because teachers don't recognize improvements.

Sources of Expectations

Research indicates that there can be many sources of teachers' expectations (Van Matre, Valentine, & Cooper, 2000). Intelligence test scores are an obvious source, especially if teachers do not interpret the scores appropriately. Gender also

Teaching Effectively

Organize your lessons carefully.

EXAMPLES

1. Provide objectives that help students focus on the purpose of the lesson.

2. Begin lessons by writing a brief outline on the board, or work on an outline with the class as part of the lesson.

3. If possible, break the presentation into clear steps or stages.

4. Review periodically.

Anticipate and plan for difficult parts in the lesson.

EXAMPLES

1. Plan a clear introduction to the lesson that tells students what they are going to learn and how they are going to learn it.

2. Do the exercises and anticipate student problems—consult the teachers' manual for ideas.

3. Have definitions ready for new terms, and prepare several relevant examples for concepts.

4. Think of analogies that will make ideas easier to understand.

5. Organize the lesson in a logical sequence; include checkpoints that incorporate oral or written questions or problems to make sure the students are following the explanations.

Strive for clear explanations.

EXAMPLES

1. Avoid vague words and ambiguous phrases. Steer clear of "the somes"—*something, someone, sometime, somehow;* "the not verys"—*not very much, not very well, not very hard, not very often;* and other unspecific fillers, such as *most, not all, sort of, and so on, of course, as you know, I guess, in fact,* or *whatever,* and *more or less.*

2. Use specific (and, if possible, colourful) names instead of *it, them,* and *thing.*

3. Refrain from using pet phrases such as *you know, like,* and *Okay?* Another idea is to record a lesson on tape to check yourself for clarity.

4. Give explanations at several levels so that all students, not just the brightest, will understand.

5. Focus on one idea at a time and avoid digressions.

Make clear connections by using explanatory links such as *because, if ... then,* or *therefore.*

EXAMPLES

1. "Explorers found it difficult to get to the west coast of Canada because it was so hard to cross the Rockies."

2. Explanatory links are also helpful in labelling visual material such as graphs, concept maps, or illustrations.

Signal transitions from one major topic to another with phrases.

EXAMPLES

1. *"The next area ...,"* *"Now we will turn to ...,"* or *"The second step is...."*

2. Outline topics, listing key points, drawing concept maps on the board, or using an overhead projector.

Communicate an enthusiasm for your subject and the day's lesson.

EXAMPLES

1. Tell students why the lesson is important. Have a better reason than "This will be on the test" or "You will need to know it next year." Emphasize the value of the learning itself.

2. Be sure to make eye contact with the students.

3. Vary your pace and volume in speaking. Use silence for emphasis.

influences teachers; most teachers expect more behaviour problems from boys than from girls and may have higher academic expectations for girls. The notes from previous teachers and the medical or psychological reports found in students' permanent record files are another obvious source of expectations. Knowledge of ethnic background also seems to have an influence, as does knowledge of older brothers and sisters. Teachers hold higher expectations for attractive students. Previous achievement, socioeconomic class, and the actual behaviours of the student are also often used as sources of information. Even the student's after-school activities can be a source of expectations. Teachers tend to hold higher expectations for students who participate in extracurricular activities than for students who do nothing after school.

Expectations and beliefs focus attention and organize memory, so teachers may pay attention to and remember the information that fits the initial expectations (Fiske, 1993; Hewstone, 1989). Even when student performance does not fit expectations, the teacher may rationalize and attribute the performance to external causes beyond the student's control. For example, a teacher may assume that the student who is typically low achieving but who did well on a test must have cheated and that the typically high-achieving student who failed must have been upset that day. In both cases, behaviour that seems out of character is dismissed. It may take many instances of supposedly uncharacteristic behaviour to change the teacher's beliefs about a particular student's abilities. Thus, expectations often remain in the face of contradictory evidence (Brophy, 1982, 1998).

Do Teachers' Expectations Really Affect Students' Achievement?

The answer to this question is more complicated than it might seem. There are two ways to investigate the question. One is to give teachers unfounded expectations about their students and note if these baseless expectations have any effects. The other approach is to identify the naturally occurring expectations of teachers and study the effects of these expectations. The answer to the question of whether teacher expectations affect student learning depends in part on which approach is taken to study the question.

Rosenthal and Jacobson used the first approach—giving teachers groundless expectations and noting the effects. The study was heavily criticized for the experimental and statistical methods used (Elashoff & Snow, 1971; Snow, 1995; Weinberg, 1989). A careful analysis of the results revealed that even though grade 1 through 6 students participated in the study, the self-fulfilling prophecy effects could be traced to just five students in grades 1 to 2 who changed dramatically. When other researchers tried to replicate the study, they did not find evidence of a self-fulfilling prophecy effect, even for children in these lower grades (Claiborn, 1969; Wilkins & Glock, 1973). After reviewing the research on teacher expectations, Raudenbush (1984) concluded that these expectations have only a small effect on student IQ scores (the outcome measure used by Rosenthal and Jacobson) and only in the early years of a new school setting—in the first years of elementary school and then again in the first years of junior high school.

But what about the second approach—naturally occurring expectations? Research shows that teachers do indeed form beliefs about students' capabilities. Many of these beliefs are accurate assessments based on the best available data and are corrected as new information is collected. Even so, some teachers do favour certain students (Babad, 1995; Rosenthal, 1987). For example, in a study of 110 students followed from age 4 to age 18, Jennifer Alvidrez and Rhona Weinstein (1999) found that teachers tended to overestimate the abilities of preschool children they rated as independent and interesting and underestimate the abilities of children seen as immature and anxious. Teachers' judgments of student ability at age 4 predicted student grade-point average at age 18. The strongest predictions were for students whose abilities were *underestimated*. If teachers decide that some students are less able, and if the teachers lack effective strategies for working with lower-achieving students, then students may experience a double threat—low expectations and inadequate teaching (Good & Brophy, 2003). The power of the expectation effect depends on the age of the students (generally speaking, younger students are more susceptible) and on how differently a teacher treats students for whom he or she has high and low expectations, an issue we turn to next (Kuklinski & Weinstein, 2001).

TABLE 5.1 Six Dimensions of Teaching That Can Communicate Expectations

Dimension	Students believed to be MORE capable have:	Students believed to be LESS capable have:
Tasks assigned, procedures, task definition, pacing, qualities of environment	More opportunity to perform publicly on meaningful tasks More opportunity to think	Less opportunity to perform publicly, especially on meaningful tasks (supplying alternative endings to a story versus learning to pronounce a word correctly) Less opportunity to think, analyze (because much work is aimed at practice)
Grouping practices	More assignments that deal with comprehension, understanding (in higher-ability groups)	Less choice on curriculum assignments, and more work on drill-like assignments because they are believed to be low achievers
Locus of responsibility for learning	More autonomy (more choice in assignments, fewer interruptions)	Less autonomy (frequent teacher monitoring of work, frequent interruptions)
Feedback and evaluation practices Motivational strategies	More opportunity for self-evaluation More honest/contingent feedback	Less opportunity for self-evaluation Less honest/more gratuitous/less contingent feedback
Quality of teacher–student relationships	More respect for the learner as an individual with unique interests and needs	Less respect for the learner as an individual with unique interests and needs

Source: Adapted from Good, T., & Weinstein, R. (1986). Teacher expectations: A framework for exploring classrooms. In K. Zumwalt (Ed.), *Improving teaching* (The ASCD 1986 Yearbook). Copyright © 1986 by the Association for the Supervision and Curriculum Development. Reprinted with permission. All rights reserved.

Teacher Behaviour and Student Reaction

Table 5.1 shows six dimensions of teacher communication toward students that may be influenced by expectations. These dimensions include both instructional practices and interpersonal interactions.

Instructional Strategies. Different grouping processes may well have a marked effect on students. And some teachers leave little to the imagination; they make their expectations all too clear. For example, Alloway (1984) recorded comments such as these directed to low-achieving groups:

"I'll be over to help you slow ones in a minute." "The blue group will find this hard."

In these remarks, the teacher not only tells the students that they lack ability but also communicates that finishing the work, not understanding, is the goal.

Once teachers assign students to ability groups, they usually assign different learning activities. To the extent that teachers choose activities that challenge students and increase achievement, these differences are probably necessary. Activities become inappropriate, however, when students who are ready for more challenging work are not given the opportunity to try it because teachers believe that they cannot handle it. This is an example of a sustaining expectation effect and can result in underachievement on the part of students, since they are not expanding their knowledge and skills, or boredom.

Teacher–Student Interactions. However the class is grouped and whatever the assignments, the quantity and the quality of teacher–student interactions are likely to affect the students. Students who are expected to achieve tend to be asked more and harder questions, to be given more chances and a longer time to respond, and to be interrupted less often than students who are expected to do poorly. Teachers also give these students cues and prompts, communicating their belief that the students can answer the question (Allington, 1980; Good & Brophy, 2003; Rosenthal, 1995). When an answer on a test is "almost right," the teacher is more likely to give the benefit of the doubt (and thus the better grade) to students who are high achieving (Finn, 1972). Teachers tend to smile at these students more often and show greater warmth through such non-verbal responses as leaning toward the students and nodding their heads as the students speak (Woolfolk & Brooks, 1983, 1985).

In contrast, teachers ask easier questions, allow less time for answering, and are less likely to give prompts to students for whom they hold low expectations. Teachers are more likely to respond with sympathetic acceptance or even praise to inadequate answers from students who are low achieving but criticize them for wrong answers. Even more disturbing, students who are low achieving receive less praise than students who are high achieving for similar correct answers. This inconsistent feedback can be very confusing for low-ability students. Imagine how hard it would be to learn if your wrong answers were sometimes praised, sometimes ignored, and sometimes criticized and your right answers received little recognition (Good 1983a, 1983b).

Of course, not all teachers form inappropriate expectations or act on their expectations in unconstructive ways (Babad, Inbar, & Rosenthal, 1982). But avoiding the problem may be more difficult than it seems. In general, students for whom teachers' expectations are low also tend to be the most disruptive students. (Of course, low expectations can reinforce their desire to disrupt or misbehave.) Teachers may call on these students less, wait a shorter time for their answers, and give them less praise for right answers, partly to avoid the wrong, careless, or silly answers that can cause disruptions, delays, and digressions (Cooper, 1979). The challenge is to deal with these very real threats to classroom management without communicating low expectations to some students or fostering their own low expectations of themselves. And sometimes, low expectations become part of the culture of the school—beliefs shared by teachers and administrators alike (Weinstein, Madison, & Kuklinski, 1995). The Guidelines on page 152 may help you avoid some of these problems.

Check Your Knowledge

- What are some sources of teacher expectations?
- What are the two kinds of expectation effects, and how do they happen?
- What are the different avenues for communicating teacher expectations?

Apply to Practice

- How have teachers communicated their expectations to you in the past? What behaviours have you found most encouraging?

Next, we describe how teachers can effectively plan and implement instruction to support students' learning.

PLANNING: THE FIRST STEP IN EFFECTIVELY TEACHING

Stop/Think/Write

Greta Morine-Dershimer (2003) asks which of the following are true about teachers' planning:

Time is of the essence.	A little goes a long way.
Plans are made to be broken.	You can do it yourself.
One size fits all.	Don't look back.

Avoiding the Negative Effects of Teacher Expectations

Use information about students from tests, cumulative folders, and other teachers very carefully.

EXAMPLES

1. Some teachers avoid reading cumulative folders at the beginning of the year.
2. Be critical and objective about the reports you hear from other teachers.

Be flexible in your use of grouping strategies.

EXAMPLES

1. Review work of students often and experiment with new groupings.
2. Use different groups for different subjects.
3. Use mixed-ability groups in cooperative exercises.

Make sure that all the students are challenged.

EXAMPLES

1. Don't say, "This is easy; I know you can do it."
2. Offer a wide range of problems and encourage all students to try a few of the harder ones for extra credit. Find something positive about these attempts.

Be especially careful about how you respond to low-achieving students during class discussions.

EXAMPLES

1. Give them prompts, cues, and time to answer.
2. Give ample praise for good answers.
3. Call on low achievers as often as high achievers.

Use materials that show a wide range of ethnic groups.

EXAMPLES

1. Check readers and library books. Is there ethnic diversity?
2. If few materials are available, ask students to research and create their own, based on community or family sources.

Make sure that your teaching does not reflect racial, ethnic, or sexual stereotypes or prejudice.

EXAMPLES

1. Use a checking system to be sure you call on and include all students.

2. Monitor the content of the tasks you assign. Do boys get the "hard" math problems to work at the board? Do you avoid having students with limited English give oral presentations?

Be fair in evaluation and disciplinary procedures.

EXAMPLES

1. Make sure that equal offences receive equal punishment. Find out from students in an anonymous questionnaire whether you seem to be favouring certain individuals.
2. Try to grade student work without knowing the identity of the student. Ask another teacher to give you a second opinion from time to time.

Communicate to all students that you believe they can learn—and mean it.

EXAMPLES

1. Return papers that do not meet standards with specific suggestions for improvements.
2. If students do not have the answers immediately, wait, probe, and then help them think through an answer.

Involve all students in learning tasks and in privileges.

EXAMPLES

1. Use some system to make sure that you give each student practice in reading, speaking, and answering questions.
2. Keep track of who gets to do what job. Are some students always on the list while others seldom make it?

Monitor your non-verbal behavior.

EXAMPLES

1. Do you lean away or stand farther away from some students? Do some students get smiles when they approach your desk while others get only frowns?
2. Does your tone of voice vary with different students?

When you thought about the What Would You Do? challenge, you were planning. In the past few years, educational researchers have become very interested in teachers' planning. They have interviewed teachers about how they plan, asked teachers to "think out loud" while planning or to keep journals describing their plans, and even studied teachers intensively for months at a time. What have they found?

First, planning influences what students will learn, since planning transforms the available time and curriculum materials into activities, assignments, and tasks for students. Time is the essence of planning. When a teacher decides to devote seven hours to language arts and 15 minutes to science in a given week, the students in that class will learn more language than science. In fact, differences as dramatic as this do occur. Nancy Karweit (1989) reported that in one school the time allocated to mathematics ranged from two hours and 50 minutes a week in one class to five hours and 55 minutes a week in a class down the hall (Clark & Peterson, 1986; Clark & Yinger, 1988; Doyle, 1983). Planning done at the beginning of the year is particularly important because many routines and patterns, such as time allocations, are established early. So *a little planning does go a long way* in terms of what will be taught and what will be learned.

Second, teachers engage in several levels of planning—by the year, term, unit, week, and day. All the levels must be coordinated. Accomplishing the year's plan requires breaking the work into terms, the terms into units, and the units into weeks and days. Planning done at the beginning of the year is particularly important, because many routines and patterns are established early. For experienced teachers, unit planning seems to be the most important level, followed by weekly and then daily planning. As you gain experience in teaching, it will become easier to coordinate these levels of planning (Clark & Yinger, 1988; Morine-Dershimer, 2003).

Third, plans reduce—but do not eliminate—uncertainty in teaching. Even the best plans cannot (and should not) control everything that happens in class; planning must allow flexibility. There is some evidence that when teachers "overplan"—when they fill every minute and stick to the plan no matter what—their students do not learn as much as students whose teachers are flexible (Shavelson, 1987). So *plans are not made to be broken*—but sometimes they need to be bent a bit.

In order to plan creatively and flexibly, teachers need to have wide-ranging knowledge about students, their interests, and abilities; the subjects being taught; alternative ways to teach and assess understanding; working with groups; the expectations and limitations of the school and community; how to apply and adapt materials and texts; and how to pull all this knowledge together into meaningful activities. The plans of beginning teachers sometimes don't work because the teachers lack knowledge about the students or the subject—they can't estimate how long it will take students to complete an activity, for example, or they stumble when asked for an explanation or a different example (Calderhead, 1996).

In planning, you can *do it yourself*—but *collaboration* is better. Working with other teachers and sharing ideas is one of the best experiences in teaching. But even great lesson plans taken from a terrific website on science have to be adapted to your situation. Some of the adaptation comes before you teach and some comes after. In fact, much of what experienced teachers know about planning comes from looking back—reflecting—on what worked and what didn't, so *do look back* on your plans and grow professionally in the process.

Finally, there is no one model for effective planning. *One size does not fit all* in planning. For experienced teachers, planning is a creative problem-solving process (Shavelson, 1987). Experienced teachers know how to accomplish many lessons and segments of lessons. They know what to expect and how to proceed, so they don't necessarily continue to follow the detailed lesson-planning models they learned during their teacher-preparation programs. Planning is more informal—"in their heads." However, many experienced teachers think it was helpful to learn this detailed system as a foundation (Clark & Peterson, 1986).

"And Then, of Course, There's the Possibility of Being Just the Slightest Bit Too Organized." (By permission of Glen Dines. From *Phi Delta Kappan*.)

No matter how you plan, you must have a learning goal in mind. In the next section, we consider the range of goals that you might have for your students.

Objectives for Learning

We hear quite a bit today about visions, goals, outcomes, and standards. At a very general, abstract level are the grand goals society may have for graduates of public schools (e.g., that all graduates have effective communication and problem-solving skills). However, very general goals are meaningless as potential guidelines for instruction. Therefore, many provinces (e.g., British Columbia, Manitoba, Ontario) are developing standards that provide more specific descriptions of how students will demonstrate progress toward the attainment of grand goals (e.g., students will develop the concept of fractions, mixed numbers, and decimals and use models to relate fractions to decimals and to find equivalent fractions). Sometimes the standards are turned into indicators such as "representing equivalent fractions" (Anderson & Krathwohl, 2001, p. 18). At this level, the indicators are close to being instructional objectives.

Norman Gronlund (2000) defines **instructional objectives** as "intended learning outcomes ... the types of performance students are expected to demonstrate at the end of instruction to show that they have learned what was expected of them" (p. 4). Although there are many different approaches to writing objectives, each assumes that the first step in teaching is to decide what changes should take place in the learner—what is the goal of teaching. When people with behavioural views write objectives, they focus on observable and measurable changes in the learner. **Behavioural objectives** use terms such as *list*, *define*, *add*, or *calculate*. **Cognitive objectives**, on the other hand, emphasize thinking and comprehension, so they are more likely to include words such as *understand*, *recognize*, *create*, or *apply*. Let us look more closely at two different methods of writing instructional objectives: one that reflects behaviourist views of learning and another based on cognitive views of learning.

Mager: Start with the Specific. Robert Mager has developed a very influential system for writing instructional objectives. Mager's idea is that objectives ought to describe what students will be doing when demonstrating their achievement and how you will know they are doing it (Mager, 1975). Mager's objectives are generally regarded as *behavioural*. According to Mager, a good objective has three parts. First, it describes the intended student behaviour—what must the student do? Second, it lists the conditions under which the behaviour will occur—how will this behaviour be recognized or tested? Third, it gives the criteria for acceptable performance on the test. Figure 5.1 shows how the system works. This system, with its emphasis on final behaviour, requires a very explicit statement. Mager contends that often students can teach themselves if they are given well-stated objectives.

instructional objectives Clear statement of what students are intended to learn through instruction.

behavioural objectives Instructional objectives stated in terms of observable behaviour.

cognitive objectives Instructional objectives stated in terms of higher-level thinking operations.

Connect & Extend

To your own philosophy
What is your reaction to the following statement? "Behavioural objectives often may be appropriate for training (an end in itself) but seldom are appropriate for education (which is concerned with understanding)."

Figure 5.1 Mager's Three-Part System

Robert Mager believes that a good learning objective has three parts: the student behaviour, the conditions under which the behaviour will be performed, and the criteria for judging a performance.

Source: From Mager, R. F. (1975). *Preparing instructional objectives.* Belmont, CA: Fearon. Reprinted by permission of David S. Lake Publishers.

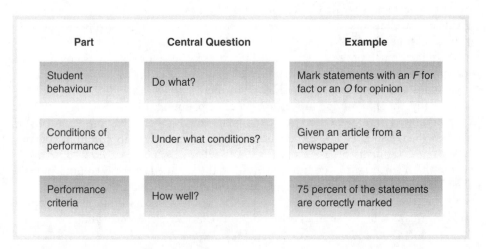

Part	Central Question	Example
Student behaviour	Do what?	Mark statements with an *F* for fact or an *O* for opinion
Conditions of performance	Under what conditions?	Given an article from a newspaper
Performance criteria	How well?	75 percent of the statements are correctly marked

Gronlund: Start with the General. Norman Gronlund (2000) offers a different approach, often used for writing cognitive objectives. He believes that an objective should be stated first in general terms (*understand*, *solve*, *appreciate*, etc.). Then the teacher should clarify by listing examples of behaviour that would provide evidence that the student has attained the objective. Look at the example in Table 5.2. The goal here is solving real-life mathematics problems that require finding surface area. The teacher does not want the student to stop with finding the area of particular figures. Instead, the teacher looks at performance on these sample tasks to decide if the student can effectively solve a real-life problem by computing surface area. The teacher could just as well have chosen different indicators.

Gronlund's emphasis on specific objectives as samples of more general student ability is important. A teacher could never list all the behaviour that might be involved in solving problems in the subject area, but stating an initial, general objective makes it clear that the ability to solve problems is the purpose. The most recent research on instructional objectives tends to favour approaches similar to Gronlund's. It seems reasonable to state a few central objectives in general terms and clarify them with examples of specific behaviour, as in Table 5.2 (Popham, 2002).

Planning involves designating learning goals, making decisions about how to help students achieve them, and assessing their success. Tactics may or may not involve written tasks.

Flexible and Creative Plans—Using Taxonomies

Stop/Think/Write

Think about your assignments for one of your classes. What kind of thinking is involved in doing the assignments?

> Remembering facts and terms?
>
> Understanding key ideas?
>
> Applying information to solve problems?
>
> Analyzing a situation, task, or problem?
>
> Creating or designing something new?
>
> Making evaluations or giving opinions?

What kind of thinking is involved in answering this Stop/Think/Write question?

TABLE 5.2 Gronlund's Combined Method for Creating Objectives

General Objective

For grade 6 mathematics: Student can efficiently solve real-life problems that require finding sizes of surface areas.

Specific Examples

1. Discriminates between the surface area of a figure and other quantitative characteristics of that figure (e.g., height and volume).
2. States the formula for the area of a rectangle.
3. Given the dimensions of a rectangle, computes its area.
4. Given the dimensions of a right triangle, computes its area.
5. Given the dimensions of a right cylinder, computes its surface area.
6. When confronted with a real-life problem, determines whether computing the area of a surface will help solve that problem.

Source: Adapted from Gronlund, N. E. (1999). *How to write and use instructional objectives* (6th ed.). Upper Saddle River, NJ: Prentice Hall. Copyright © 1999 by Prentice Hall. Reprinted by permission.

taxonomy Classification system.

Several decades ago, a group of educational evaluation experts led by Benjamin Bloom set out to improve college and university examinations. The impact of their work has touched education at all levels around the world (Anderson & Sosniak, 1994). Bloom and his colleagues developed a **taxonomy**, or classification system, of educational objectives. Objectives were divided into three domains: cognitive, affective, and psychomotor. A handbook describing the objectives in each area was eventually published. In real life, of course, behaviour from these three domains occurs simultaneously. While students are writing (psychomotor), they are also remembering or reasoning (cognitive), and they are likely to have some emotional response to the task as well (affective).

cognitive domain In Bloom's taxonomy, memory and reasoning objectives.

The Cognitive Domain. Six basic objectives are listed in Bloom's taxonomy of the thinking or **cognitive domain** (Bloom, Engelhart, Frost, Hill, & Krathwohl, 1956):

1. *Knowledge:* Remembering or recognizing something without necessarily understanding, using, or changing it.
2. *Comprehension:* Understanding the material being communicated without necessarily relating it to anything else.
3. *Application:* Using a general concept to solve a particular problem.
4. *Analysis:* Breaking something down into its parts.
5. *Synthesis:* Creating something new by combining different ideas.
6. *Evaluation:* Judging the value of materials or methods as they might be applied in a particular situation.

It is common in education to consider these objectives as a hierarchy, each skill building on those below, but such a view is not entirely accurate (Seddon, 1978). Some subjects, such as mathematics, do not fit this structure very well (Kreitzer & Madaus, 1994). Still, you will hear many references to *lower-level* and *higher-level objectives*, with knowledge, comprehension, and application considered lower level and the other categories considered higher level. As a rough way of thinking about objectives, this classification can be helpful (Gronlund, 2000).

The taxonomy of objectives can also be helpful in planning assessments because different procedures are appropriate for objectives at the various levels. Gronlund (2000) suggests that factual knowledge objectives can best be measured by true/false, short-answer, matching, or multiple-choice tests. Such tests also work with the comprehension, application, and analysis levels of the taxonomy. For measuring synthesis and evaluation objectives, however, essays, reports, projects, and portfolios are more appropriate. Essay tests also work at the middle levels of the taxonomy.

Bloom 2001. Bloom's taxonomy guided educators for more than 40 years and is considered among the most significant educational writings of the 20th century (Anderson & Sosniak, 1994). In 2001, a group of educational researchers met to discuss revising the taxonomy (Anderson & Krathwohl, 2001). The new version retains the six basic levels in a slightly different order, but the names of three levels have been changed to indicate the cognitive processes involved. The six cognitive processes are remembering (knowledge), understanding (comprehension), applying, analyzing, evaluating, and creating (synthesizing). In addition, the revisers have added a new dimension to the taxonomy to recognize that cognitive processes must process something—you have to remember or understand or apply some form of knowledge. Table 5.3 summarizes the resulting model by showing that six processes—the cognitive acts of remembering, understanding, applying, analyzing, evaluating, and creating—act on four kinds of knowledge—factual, conceptual, procedural, and metacognitive.

Consider how this revised taxonomy might suggest objectives for a social studies/language arts class. For example, an objective that targets *analysis of conceptual knowledge* might be:

TABLE 5.3 A Revised Taxonomy in the Cognitive Domain

The Knowledge Dimension	The Cognitive Process Dimension					
	1. Remember	2. Understand	3. Apply	4. Analyze	5. Evaluate	6. Create
A. Factual Knowledge						
B. Conceptual Knowledge						
C. Procedural Knowledge						
D. Metacognitive Knowledge						

Source: From Anderson, L. W., & Krathwohl, D. R. (Eds.). (2001). *A taxonomy for learning, teaching, and assessing: A revision of Bloom's taxonomy of educational objectives.* New York: Addison-Wesley Longman. Copyright © 2000 by Addison-Wesley Longman. Adapted with permission.

After reading a historical account of the framing of Canada's Constitution, students will be able to recognize the author's point of view or bias.

An objective for evaluating metacognitive knowledge might be:

Students will reflect on their strategies for identifying the biases of the author.

The Affective Domain. The objectives in the taxonomy of the **affective domain,** or domain of emotional response, range from least committed to most committed (Krathwohl, Bloom, & Masia, 1964). At the lowest level, students simply pay attention to a certain idea. At the highest level, students adopt an idea or a value and act consistently with that idea. There are five basic objectives in the affective domain.

affective domain Realm of attitudes and feelings.

1. *Receiving:* Being aware of or attending to something in the environment. This is the "I'll-listen-to-the-concert-but-I-won't-promise-to-like-it level."

2. *Responding:* Showing some new behaviour as a result of experience. At this level, a person might applaud after the concert or hum some of the music the next day.

3. *Valuing:* Showing some definite involvement or commitment. At this point, a person might choose to go to a concert instead of a film.

4. *Organization:* Integrating a new value into one's general set of values, giving it some ranking among one's general priorities. This is the level at which a person would begin to make long-range commitments to concert attendance.

5. *Characterization by value:* Acting consistently with the new value. At this highest level, a person would be firmly committed to a love of music and demonstrate it openly and consistently.

Like the basic objectives in the cognitive domain, these five objectives are very general. To write specific learning objectives, you must state what students will actually be doing when they are receiving, responding, valuing, and so on. For example, an objective for a nutrition class at the valuing level (showing involvement or commitment) might be stated as follows: "After completing the unit on food contents and labelling, at least 50 percent of the class will commit to a junk-food boycott project by giving up candy for a month."

The Psychomotor Domain. Until recently, the **psychomotor domain,** or the realm of physical ability objectives, has been mostly overlooked by teachers not directly involved with physical education. There are several taxonomies in this domain (e.g., Harrow, 1972; Simpson, 1972) that generally move from basic perceptions and reflex actions to skilled, creative movements. James Cangelosi (1990) provides a useful way to think about objectives in the psychomotor domain either as voluntary muscle capabilities that require endurance, strength, flexibility, agility, and speed or as the ability to perform a specific skill.

psychomotor domain Realm of physical ability and coordination objectives.

Objectives in the psychomotor domain should be of interest to a wide range of educators, including those in fine arts, vocational-technical education, and special education. Many other subjects, such as chemistry, physics, and biology, also require specialized movements and well-developed hand and eye coordination. Using lab equipment, the mouse on a computer, or art materials means learning new physical skills. Here are two examples of psychomotor objectives:

> Four minutes after completing a 1.6-kilometre run in eight minutes or under, your heart rate will be below 120.
>
> Use a computer mouse effectively to "drag and drop" files.

Whatever your instructional objectives for your students, Terry TenBrink (2003, p. 67) suggests the following five criteria. Objectives should be:

1. Developmentally appropriate.

2. Attainable by the students within a reasonable time limit.

3. In proper sequence with other objectives (not to be accomplished until the prerequisite objectives are met).

4. In harmony with the overall goals of the course (and curriculum).

5. In harmony with the goals and values of the institution.

The Guidelines on page 159 should help you whether you use objectives for every lesson or for just a few assignments.

Another View: Planning from a Constructivist Perspective

Stop/Think/Write

Think about the same course assignments you analyzed for thinking processes in the previous Stop/Think/Write. What are the big ideas that run through all those assignments? What other ways could you learn about those ideas besides the assignments?

constructivist approach View that emphasizes the active role of the learner in building understanding and making sense of information.

Traditionally, it has been the teacher's responsibility to do most of the planning for instruction, but new ways of planning are developing. In **constructivist approaches**, planning is shared and negotiated. The teacher and students together make decisions about content, activities, and approaches. Rather than having specific student behaviour and skills as objectives, the teacher has overarching goals—"big ideas"—that guide planning. These goals are understandings or abilities that the teacher returns to again and again.

An Example of Constructivist Planning. Vito Perrone (1994) has these goals for his secondary history students. He wants his students to be able to

- use primary sources, formulate hypotheses, and engage in systematic study;
- handle multiple points of view;
- be close readers and active writers;
- pose and solve problems.

The next step in the planning process is to create a learning environment that allows students to move toward these goals in ways that respect their individual interests and abilities. Perrone (1994) suggests identifying "those ideas, themes, and issues that provide the depth and variety of perspective that help students develop significant understandings" (p. 12). For a secondary history course, a theme might be "democracy and revolution" or "fairness concerning land claims." A theme in math or music might be "patterns"; in literature, "personal identity." Perrone suggests mapping the topic as a way of thinking about how the theme can generate learning and understanding. An example of a topic map, using the theme of ecology, is shown in Figure 5.2.

Using Instructional Objectives

Avoid "word magic"—phrases that sound noble and important but say very little, such as, "Students will become deep thinkers."

EXAMPLES

1. Keep the focus on specific changes that will take place in the students' knowledge of skills.

2. Ask students to explain the meaning of the objectives. If they can't give specific examples of what you mean, the objectives are not communicating your intentions to your students.

Suit the activities to the objectives.

EXAMPLES

1. If the goal is the memorization of vocabulary, give the students memory aids and practice exercises.

2. If the goal is the ability to develop well-thought-out positions, consider position papers, debates, projects, or mock trials.

3. If you want students to become better writers, give many opportunities for writing and rewriting.

Make sure that your tests are related to your objectives.

EXAMPLES

1. Write objectives and rough drafts for tests at the same time. Revise these drafts of tests as the units unfold and objectives change.

2. Weight the tests according to the importance of the various objectives and the time spent on each.

With this topic map as a guide, teacher and students can work together to identify activities, materials, projects, and performances that will support the development of the students' understanding and abilities—the overarching goals of the class. The teacher spends less time planning specific presentations and

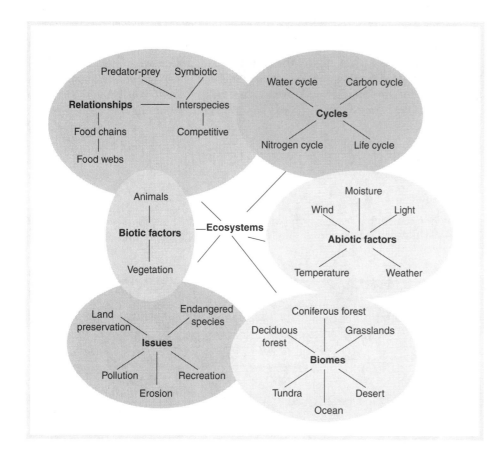

Figure 5.2 Planning with a Topic Map

With this map of the topic "ecology," a grade 6 teacher can identify themes, issues, and ideas for study. Rather than "cover" the whole map, the teacher can examine a few areas in depth.

assignments and more time gathering a variety of resources and facilitating students' learning. The focus is not so much on students' products as on the processes of learning and the thinking behind the products.

Integrated and Thematic Plans. The planning map shows a way to use the theme of ecology to integrate issues in a science class. Today, teaching with themes and with integrated content are major elements in planning and designing lessons and units, from kindergarten (Roskos & Neuman, 1995) through high school (Clarke & Agne, 1997). For example, middle school teachers Elaine Homestead and Karen McGinnis and college professor Elizabeth Pate (Pate, McGinnis, & Homestead, 1995) designed a unit on "Human Interactions" that included studying racism, world hunger, pollution, and air and water quality. Students researched issues by reading textbooks and outside sources, learning to use databases, interviewing local officials, and inviting guest speakers into class. Students had to develop knowledge in science, mathematics, and social studies. They learned to write and speak persuasively, and in the process raised money for hunger relief in Africa.

Elementary-age students can benefit from integrated planning too. There is no reason to work on spelling skills, then listening skills, then writing skills, and then social studies or science. All these abilities can be developed together if students work to solve authentic problems. Themes for younger children can include, for example, people, pets, gardens as habitats, communities, and patterns. Possibilities for older children are given in Table 5.4.

Check Your Knowledge

- What are the levels of planning, and how do they affect teaching?
- What is an instructional objective?
- Describe the three taxonomies of educational objectives.

Apply to Practice

- Identify a cognitive, affective, and psychomotor objective for yourself for this week.
- Name a theme that could organize your planning for a grade you might teach.

Let's assume you and your students have valuable and interesting plans and learning objectives. What next? You still need to decide what is happening on Monday. You need to design tasks and activities for teaching and learning that are appropriate for the objectives. You have an idea of *what* you want students to understand, but *how* do you teach to encourage understanding?

TEACHER-DIRECTED INSTRUCTION

What Would You Say?

In your interview for the last remaining opening in the district of your dreams, the principal asks, "What is the best lesson you have taught so far? Tell me all about it and especially about what made it so good."

TABLE 5.4 Some Themes for Integrated Planning for Older Children	
General Systems Theory	Graphical Representations of Patterns
The Politics of Biology	Field-Based Research
Cause and Effect	Probability and Prediction
Levels of Analysis	Diversity and Variation
Conditional and Enabling Relations	Stewardship
Darwinism	Conservation of Energy and Matter

In this section, we turn to examining a variety of strategies that reflect teacher-led, or teacher-directed, formats for turning objectives into action in the classroom. These strategies are not complete models of teaching, but rather building blocks that can be used to construct lessons and units. We begin with the strategy many people associate most directly with teaching: explanation and direct instruction.

Explanation and Direct Instruction

Some studies have found that teacher-led instruction takes up one-sixth to one-fourth of all classroom time. Teacher explanation is appropriate for communicating a large amount of material to many students in a short period of time, introducing a new topic, giving background information, or motivating students to learn more on their own. Teacher-led instruction is therefore most appropriate for cognitive and affective objectives at the lower levels of the taxonomies described earlier: for remembering, understanding, applying, receiving, responding, and valuing (Arends, 2001; Kindsvatter, Wilen, & Ishler, 1992). Student-centred approaches that rely heavily on students' active construction of meaning are more appropriate for higher levels of learning and self-regulated learning. These will be described in the next main section.

Direct Instruction. In the 1970s and 1980s, there was an explosion of research that focused on effective teaching. The results of all this work identified a model of teaching that was related to improved student learning. Barak Rosenshine calls this approach **direct instruction** (1979) or **explicit teaching** (1986). Tom Good (1983a) uses the term **active teaching** for a similar approach.

direct instruction/explicit teaching Systematic instruction for mastery of basic skills, facts, and information.

The direct instruction model fits a specific set of circumstances because it was derived from a particular approach to research. Researchers identified the elements of direct instruction by comparing teachers whose students learned more than expected (based on entering knowledge) with teachers whose students performed at an expected or average level. The researchers focused on existing practices in American classrooms. Because the focus was on traditional forms of teaching, the research could not identify successful innovations. Effectiveness was usually defined as average improvement in standardized test scores for a whole class or school. So the results hold for large groups, but not necessarily for every student in the group. Even when the average achievement of a group improves, the achievement of some individuals may decline (Brophy & Good, 1986; Good, 1996; Shuell, 1996).

active teaching Teaching characterized by high levels of teacher explanation, demonstration, and interaction with students.

Given these conditions, direct instruction applies best to the teaching of **basic skills**—clearly structured knowledge and essential skills, such as science facts, mathematics computations, reading vocabulary, and grammar rules (Rosenshine & Stevens, 1986). These skills involve tasks that are relatively unambiguous; they can be taught step-by-step and tested objectively. Direct instruction is not necessarily appropriate for objectives such as helping students write creatively, solve complex problems, or mature emotionally. Weinert and Helmke (1995) describe effective direct instruction as having the following features:

basic skills Clearly structured knowledge that is needed for later learning and that can be taught step by step.

> (a) the teacher's classroom management is especially effective and the rate of student interruptive behaviors is very low; (b) the teacher maintains a strong academic focus and uses available instructional time intensively to initiate and facilitate students' learning activities; (c) the teacher insures that as many students as possible achieve good learning progress by carefully choosing appropriate tasks, clearly presenting subject-matter information and solution strategies, continuously diagnosing each student's learning progress and learning difficulties, and providing effective help through remedial instruction. (p. 138)

But how exactly can teachers ensure that their direct instruction has these characteristics and is effective in practice?

Rosenshine's Six Teaching Functions. Rosenshine and his colleagues (Rosenshine, 1988; Rosenshine & Stevens, 1986) have identified six teaching functions based on the research on effective instruction. These can serve as a checklist or framework for teaching basic skills.

1. *Review and check the previous day's work.* Reteach if students misunderstood or made errors.

2. *Present new material.* Make the purpose clear, teach in small steps, and provide many examples and non-examples.

3. *Provide guided practice.* Question students, give practice problems, and listen for misconceptions and misunderstandings. Reteach if necessary. Continue guided practice until students answer about 80 percent of the questions correctly.

4. *Give feedback and correctives* based on student answers. Reteach if necessary.

5. *Provide independent practice.* Let students apply the new learning on their own, in seatwork, cooperative groups, or homework. The success rate during independent practice should be about 95 percent. This means that students must be well prepared for the work by the presentation and guided practice and that assignments must not be too difficult. The point is for the students to practise until the skills become overlearned and automatic—until the students are confident. Hold students accountable for the work they do—check it.

6. *Review weekly and monthly* to consolidate learning. Include some review items as homework. Test often, and reteach material missed on the tests.

These six functions are not steps to be followed in a particular order, but all of them are elements of effective instruction. For example, feedback, review, or reteaching should occur whenever necessary and should match the abilities of the students. Also, keep in mind the age and prior knowledge of your students. The younger or the less prepared your students, the briefer your explanations should be. Use more and shorter cycles of presentation, guided practice, feedback, and correctives.

There are several other models of direct instruction, but most share the elements presented in Table 5.5, which summarizes Madeline Hunter's Mastery Teaching (Hunter, 1982), another example of direct instruction.

Why Does Direct Instruction Work? What aspects of direct instruction might explain its success? Linda Anderson (1989b) suggests that lessons that help students perceive links among main ideas help them construct accurate understandings. Well-organized presentations, clear explanations, the use of explanatory links, and reviews can all help students perceive connections among ideas. If done well, therefore, a direct instruction lesson may be a resource that students use to construct understanding. For example, reviews activate prior knowledge, so that students are ready to understand. Brief, clear presentations and guided practice avoid overloading the students' information processing systems and taxing their working memories. Numerous examples and explanations give many pathways and associations for building networks of concepts. Guided practice can also give the teacher a snapshot of the students' thinking as well as their misconceptions, allowing the teacher to address them directly as misconceptions rather than simply as "wrong answers."

Every subject, even university-level English or chemistry, can require some direct instruction. Noddings (1990) reminds teachers that students may need some direct instruction in how to use various manipulative materials to get the possible benefits from them. Students working in cooperative groups may need guidance, modelling, and practice in how to ask questions and give explanations. And to solve difficult problems, students may need some direct instruction in possible problem-solving strategies.

Criticisms of Direct Instruction. Direct instruction, particularly when it involves extended teacher presentations or lectures, has some disadvantages. You may find that some students have trouble listening for more than a few minutes at a time and that they simply tune you out. Teacher presentations can put the students in a passive position by doing much of the cognitive work for them and may prevent students from asking or even thinking of questions (Freiberg & Driscoll, 1996; Gilstrap & Martin, 1975).

Connect & Extend

To the research

For another perspective, read Berg, C. A., & Clough, M. (1991). Hunter lesson design: The wrong one for science teaching. *Educational Leadership, 48*(4), 73–78. *Focus Questions*: Why do Berg and Clough believe that the Hunter design is the wrong one for science teaching? How do you think Hunter would react? Then read Hunter, M. (1991). Hunter design helps achieve the goals of science instruction. *Educational Leadership, 48*(4), 79–81. *Focus Questions*: Evaluate Hunter's defence of her model. Do you agree that the Hunter approach can achieve the goals of science instruction?

TABLE 5.5 The Hunter Mastery Teaching Programs: Selected Principles

Get students set to learn.

- Make the best use of the prime time at the beginning of the lesson.
- Give students a review question or two to consider while you call the roll, pass out papers, or do other "housekeeping" chores. Follow up—listen to their answers and correct if necessary.
- Create an *anticipatory set* to capture the students' attention. This might be an advance organizer, an intriguing question, or a brief exercise. For example, at the beginning of a lesson on categories of plants, you could ask, "How is pumpkin pie similar to cherry pie but different from sweet potato pie?" Answer: Pumpkins and cherries are both fruits, unlike sweet potatoes.
- Communicate the lesson objectives (unless withholding this information for a while is part of your overall plan).

Provide information effectively.

- Determine the basic information and organize it. Use this basic structure as scaffolding for the lesson.
- Present information clearly and simply. Use familiar terms, examples, illustrations.
- Model what you mean. If appropriate, demonstrate or use analogies, such as, "If the basketball Ann is holding were the sun, how far away do you think I would have to hold this pea to represent Pluto ...?"

Check for understanding and give guided practice.

- Ask a question and have every student signal an answer: "Thumbs up if this statement is true, down if it's false."
- Ask for a choral response: "Everyone, is this a dependent or an independent clause?"
- Sample individual responses: "Everyone, think of an example of a closed system. Jon, what's your example?"

Allow for independent practice.

- Get students started right by doing the first few questions together.
- Make independent practice brief. Monitor responses, giving feedback promptly.

One solution to this problem is **scripted cooperation**, which allows teachers to incorporate active learning into lectures. Several times during the presentation, the teacher asks students to work in pairs. One person is the summarizer and the other critiques the summary. This activity gives students a chance to check their understanding, organize their thinking, and translate ideas into their own words. Other possibilities are described in Table 5.6.

Critics also claim that direct instruction is based on a *wrong theory* of learning. Teachers break material into small segments, present each segment clearly, and reinforce or correct, thus *transmitting* accurate understandings from teacher to student. The student is viewed as an "empty vessel" waiting to be filled with knowledge, rather than an active constructor of knowledge (Anderson, 1989a; Berg & Clough, 1991; Davis, Maher, & Noddings, 1990). These criticisms of direct instruction echo the criticisms of behavioural learning theories.

There is ample evidence, however, that direct instruction and explanation can help students learn actively, not passively (Leinhardt, 2001). For younger and less prepared learners, student-controlled learning without teacher direction and instruction can lead to systematic deficits in the students' knowledge. Without guidance, the understandings that students construct may be incomplete and misleading (Weinert & Helmke, 1995). Deep understanding and fluid performance—whether in dance or mathematical problem solving or reading—require models of expert performance and extensive practice with feedback (Anderson, Reder, & Simon, 1995). Guided and independent practice with feedback are at the heart of the direct instruction model.

The message for teachers is to match instructional methods to learning goals.

scripted cooperation Learning strategy in which two students take turns summarizing material and criticizing the summaries.

Connect & Extend

To your teaching
Madeline Hunter gives these examples of instructions a teacher can give to check for student understanding (Hunter, M. [1982]. *Mastery teaching*. El Segundo, CA: TIP Publications, p. 60):

"Look at the first multiple-choice question. Decide which answer you would select and when I say 'show me,' place that number of fingers under your chin.

"Make a plus with your fingers if you agree with this statement, a minus if you don't and a zero if you have strong feelings."

Connect & Extend

To your teaching

Here are some ideas for ways to involve all students actively in a lesson. Ask them to:

1. Tell the answer to a neighbour.

2. Summarize the main idea in one or two sentences, writing the summary on a piece of paper and sharing this with a neighbour, or repeat the procedures to a neighbour.

3. Write the answer on a slate, then hold up the slate.

4. Raise their hands if they know the answer (thereby allowing the teacher to check the entire class).

5. Raise their hands if they agree with an answer someone else gave.

6. Raise different coloured cards when the answer is a, b, or c.

Taken from Rosenshine, B. (1987). Explicit teaching. In D. Berliner & B. Rosenshine (Eds.), *Talks to teachers* (pp. 75–62). New York: Random House.

TABLE 5.6 Active Learning and Teacher Presentations

Here are some ideas for keeping students cognitively engaged in lessons. They can be adapted for many ages.

Question, All Write: Pose a question, ask everyone to jot an answer, then ask several volunteers to share their answers with the class.

Outcome Sentences: After a segment of presentation, ask students to finish sentences such as "I learned ...," "I'm beginning to wonder ...," "I was surprised...." Share as above. Students may keep their outcome sentences in a learning log or portfolio.

Underexplain with Learning Pairs: Give a brief explanation, then ask students to work in pairs to figure out the process or idea.

Voting: Ask "How many of you ..." questions and take a count, e.g., "How many of you agree with Raschon?" "How many of you are ready to move on?" "How many of you got 48 on this problem?"

Choral Response: Have the whole class restate in unison important facts and ideas, such as "The environment is one whole system" or "A 10-sided polygon is called a decagon."

Speak-Write: Tell students you will speak briefly, for three or four minutes. They are to listen but not take notes. At the end of the time, ask them to write the main ideas, a summary, or questions they have about what you said.

Source: Adapted from Harmin, M. (1994). *Inspiring active learning: A handbook for teachers.* Alexandria, VA: Association for Supervision and Curriculum Development.

Seatwork and Homework

Stop/Think/Write

Think back to your elementary and high school days. Do you remember any homework assignments? What sticks in your mind about those assignments?

Seatwork. In Vancouver, some parents are pressing the school board to designate one school as a "traditional" school that will, among other things, emphasize structured seatwork and increase homework (Mickleburgh, 1999). There is little research on the effects of **seatwork**, or independent classroom-desk work, but it is clear that this technique is often overused. In fact, one study found that American elementary students spend 51 percent of mathematics time in school working alone, while Japanese students spend 26 percent and Taiwanese students spend only 9 percent (Stigler, Lee, & Stevenson, 1987). Some educators point to these differences as part of the explanation for Asian students' superiority in mathematics.

Seatwork should follow up a lesson and give students supervised practice. It should not be the main mode of instruction. Unfortunately, many workbook pages do little to support the learning of important objectives. Before you assign work, ask yourself, "Does doing this work help students learn anything that matters?" For example, consider this task, cited in the report of the Commission on Reading of the National Institute of Education (Anderson, Hiebert, Scott, & Wilkinson, 1985):

> Read each sentence. Decide which consonant letter is used the most. Underline it each time.

What's the point? This sort of activity communicates to students that reading isn't very important or useful. Students should see the connection between the seatwork or homework and the lesson. Tell them why they are doing the work. The objectives should be clear, all the materials that might be needed should be provided, and the work should be easy enough that students can succeed on their own. Success rates should be high—near 100 percent. When seatwork is too difficult, students often resort to guessing or copying just to finish (Anderson, 1985).

seatwork Independent classroom work.

Individualized instruction does not necessarily mean students working alone; it refers to the idea of tailoring the pace, learning objectives, level, and assessment approach so that each individual student benefits.

Carol Weinstein and Andy Mignano (2003) describe several alternatives to workbooks, such as reading silently and reading aloud to a partner; writing for a "real" audience; writing letters or journals; transcribing conversations and punctuating them properly; making up problems; working on long-term projects and reports; solving brain teasers and puzzles; and engaging in computer activities. One of our favourites is creating a group story. Two students begin a story on the computer. Then two more add a paragraph. The story grows with each new pair's addition. The students are reading and writing, editing and improving.

Homework. In contrast to the limited research on seatwork, educators have been studying the effects of homework for over 75 years (Cooper & Valentine, 2001a, 2001b; Corno, 2000). As you can see from the Point/Counterpoint box below, there continues to be a debate about the value of homework.

To benefit from individual or group seatwork or homework, students must stay involved and do the work. The first step toward involvement is getting students started correctly by making sure that they understand the assignment. It may help to do the first few questions as a class, to clear up any misconceptions. This is especially important for homework assignments because students may have no one at home to consult if they have problems with the assignment. A second way to keep students involved is to hold them accountable for completing the work correctly, not just for filling in the page. This means the work should be checked, the students given a chance to correct the errors or revise work, and the results counted toward the class grade (Brophy & Good, 1986). Expert teachers often have ways of correcting homework quickly during the first minutes of class by having students check each other's or their own work.

POINT >< COUNTERPOINT

Is Homework a Valuable Use of Time?

Like so many methods in education, homework has moved in and out of favour. In the early 1900s, homework was seen as an important path to mental discipline, but by the 1940s, homework was criticized as too much drill and low-level learning. Then in the 1950s, homework was rediscovered as a way for North American children to catch up with the Soviet Union in science and mathematics, only to be seen as too much pressure on students during the more laid-back 1960s. By the 1980s, homework was viewed as necessary for our students to compete with students around the world (Cooper & Valentine, 2001b). Everyone has done homework—were those hours well spent?

> Point *Homework does not help students learn.*

No matter how interesting an activity is, students will eventually get bored with it—so why give them work both in and out of school?

They will simply grow weary of learning. And important opportunities are lost for community involvement or leisure activities that would create well-rounded citizens. When parents help with homework, they can do more harm than good—sometimes confusing their children or teaching them incorrectly. And students from poorer families often must work, so they miss doing the homework; then the learning discrepancy between the rich and poor grows even greater. Besides, the research is inconsistent about the effects of homework. For example, one study found that in-class work was better than homework in helping elementary students learn (Cooper & Valentine, 2001b).

< Counterpoint *Well-planned homework can work for many students.*

Harris Cooper and Jeffrey Valentine reviewed many studies of homework

and concluded that there is little relationship between homework and learning for young students, but the relationship between homework and achievement grows progressively stronger for older students. There is recent evidence that students in high school who do more homework (and watch less television after school) have higher grades, even when other factors such as gender, grade level, ethnicity, socioeconomic status, and amount of adult supervision are taken into consideration (Cooper & Valentine, 2001b; Cooper, Valentine, Nye, & Lindsay, 1999). Consistent with these findings, the National PTA in the United States makes these recommendations:

> For children in grades K–2, homework is most effective when it does not exceed 10–20 minutes each day; older students, in grades 3–6, can handle 30–60 minutes a day; in junior and senior high school, the amount of homework will vary by subject. (Henderson, 1996, p. 1)

Making Seatwork and Homework Valuable. Seatwork particularly requires careful monitoring. Being available to students doing seatwork is more effective than offering students help before they ask for it. To be available, you should move around the class and avoid spending too much time with one or two students. Short, frequent contacts are best (Brophy & Good, 1986; Rosenshine, 1977). Sometimes you may be working with a small group while other students do seatwork. In these situations, it is especially important for students to know what to do if they need help. Nancy has observed in classrooms where students follow a rule, "Ask three, then me." Students have to consult three classmates before seeking help from the teacher. Teachers in these classrooms spend time early in the year showing students *how* to help each other—how to ask questions and how to explain.

What about monitoring homework? If students get stuck on homework, they need help at home, someone who can scaffold their work without just "giving the answer" (Pressley, 1995). But many family members don't know how to help (Hoover-Dempsey et al., 2001; Hoover-Dempsey, Bassler, & Burow, 1995). The Family and Community Partnerships box below includes ideas for helping families help with homework.

FAMILY AND COMMUNITY PARTNERSHIPS

Homework

Make sure that families know what students are expected to learn.

EXAMPLES

1. At the beginning of a unit, send home a list of the main objectives, examples of major assignments, key due dates, homework "calendar," and a list of resources available free at libraries or on the internet.

2. Provide a clear, concise description of your homework policy—how homework is counted toward class grades; consequences for late, forgotten, or missing homework; etc.

Help families find a comfortable and helpful role in their child's homework.

EXAMPLES

1. Remind families that "helping with homework" means encouraging, listening, monitoring, praising, discussing, brainstorming—not necessarily teaching and never doing the work for their child.

2. Encourage families to set aside a quiet time and place for everyone in the family to study. Make this time a regular part of the daily routine.

3. Have some homework assignments that are fun and involve the whole family—puzzles, family albums, watching a television program together and doing a "review."

4. At parent–teacher conferences, ask families what they need to play a helpful role in their child's homework.

Solicit and use suggestions from families about homework.

EXAMPLES

1. Find out what responsibilities the child has at home—how much time is available for homework.

2. Periodically, have a "homework hotline" for call-in questions and suggestions.

If no one is at home to help with homework, set up other support systems.

EXAMPLES

1. Assign study buddies who can be available over the phone.

2. If students have computers, provide lists of internet help lines.

3. Locate free help in public libraries and make these resources known.

Take advantage of family and community "funds of knowledge" to connect homework with life in the community and life in the community with lessons in school (Moll et al., 1992).

EXAMPLES

1. Create a lesson about how family members use math and reading in sewing and in housing construction (Epstein & Van Voorhis, 2001).

2. Design interactive homework projects that families do together to evaluate needed products for their home, for example, deciding on the best buy on shampoo or paper towels.

Questioning and Recitation

Teachers pose questions; students answer. This form of teaching, sometimes called *recitation*, has been with us for many years (Stodolsky, 1988). The teacher's questions generally follow some sort of plan to develop a framework for the subject matter involved. The students' answers are often followed by reactions from the teacher, such as praise, correction, or requests for further information. The pattern from the teacher's point of view consists of *structure* (setting a framework), *solicitation* (asking questions), and *reaction* (praising, correcting, and expanding) (Clark, Gage, Marx, Peterson, Staybrook, Winne, 1979). These steps are repeated over and over.

Let us consider the heart of recitation, the soliciting, or *questioning*, phase. Effective questioning techniques may be among the most powerful tools that teachers employ during lessons. An essential element of innovations such as cognitive apprenticeships, peer learning techniques, authentic learning activities, and nearly all other contemporary learning techniques is keeping students cognitively engaged—and that is where skilful questioning strategies are especially effective. Questions play several roles in cognition. They can help students rehearse information for effective recall. They can work to identify gaps in their knowledge base and provoke curiosity and long-term interest. They can initiate cognitive conflict and promote the disequilibrium that results in a changed knowledge structure. They can serve as cues, tips, or reminders. And students as well as teachers should learn to question effectively. We tell our students that the first step in doing a good research project is asking a good question.

For now, we will focus on teachers' questions, to make them as helpful as possible for students. Many beginning teachers are surprised to discover how valuable good questions can be and how difficult they are to create.

Kinds of Questions. Some educators have estimated the typical teacher asks between 30 and 120 question an hour, or about 1 5000 000 questions over a teaching career (Sadker & Sadker, 2003). What are these questions like? Many can be categorized in terms of Bloom's taxonomy of objectives in the cognitive domain. Table 5.7 offers examples of questions at the different taxonomic levels.

Another way to categorize questioning is in terms of **convergent questions** (only one right answer) or **divergent questions** (many possible answers). Questions about concrete facts are convergent: "Who ruled England in 1540?" "Who wrote the original *Peter Pan*?" Questions dealing with opinions or hypotheses are divergent: "In this story, which character is most like you and why?" "In 100 years, which of the past five prime ministers will be most admired?"

convergent questions Questions that have a single correct answer.

divergent questions Questions that have no single correct answer.

Quite a bit of space in education textbooks has been devoted to urging teachers to ask a greater number of higher-level (analysis, synthesis, and evaluation) and divergent questions. Is this really a better way of questioning? Research has provided several surprises.

Fitting the Questions to the Students. Both high- and low-level questions can be effective (Barden, 1995; Redfield & Rousseau, 1981), although whether a question is actually high- or low-level depends on the student's knowledge (Winne, 1979). Different patterns seem to be better for different students, however. The best pattern for younger students and for lower-ability students of all ages is simple questions that allow a high percentage of correct answers, ample encouragement, help when the student does not have the correct answer, and praise. For high-ability students, the successful pattern includes harder questions at both higher and lower levels and more critical feedback (Berliner, 1987; Good, 1988; Sadker & Sadker, 2003).

Whatever their age or ability, all students should have some experience with thought-provoking questions and, if necessary, help in learning how to answer them. To master critical thinking and problem-solving skills, students must have a chance to practise the skills. They also need time to think about their answers. But research shows that teachers wait an average of only one second for students to answer (Rowe, 1974). Consider the following slice of classroom life (Sadker & Sadker, 2003, p. 1128):

Teacher:	Who wrote the poem "Stopping by Woods on a Snowy Evening"? Tom?
Tom:	Robert Frost.
Teacher:	Good. What action takes place in the poem? Sally?
Sally:	A man stops his sleigh to watch the woods get filled with snow.
Teacher:	Yes. Emma, what thoughts go through the man's mind?
Emma:	He thinks how beautiful the woods are ... (She pauses for a second.)
Teacher:	What else does he think about? Joe?
Joe:	He thinks how he would like to stay and watch. (Pauses for a second.)
Teacher:	Yes—and what else? Rita? (Waits half a second.) Come on, Rita, you can get the answer to this. (Waits half a second.) Well, why does he feel he can't stay there indefinitely and watch the woods and the snow?
Sarah:	Well, I think it might be ... (Pauses for a second.)
Teacher:	Think, Sarah. (Teacher waits for half a second.) All right then—Mike? (Waits again for half a second.) John? (Waits half a second.) What's the matter with everyone today? Didn't you do the reading?

TABLE 5.7 Classroom Questions for Objectives in the Cognitive Domain

Thinking at different levels of Bloom's taxonomy in the cognitive domain can be encouraged by different questions. Of course, the thinking required depends on what has gone before in the discussion.

Category	Type of Thinking Expected	Examples
Knowledge (recognition)	Recalling or recognizing information as learned	Define ... What is the capital of ...? What did the text say about ...?
Comprehension	Demonstrating understanding of the materials; transforming, reorganizing, or interpreting	Explain in your own words ... Compare ... What is the main idea of ...? Describe what you saw ...
Application	Using information to solve a problem with a single correct answer	Which principle is demonstrated in ...? Calculate the area of ... Apply the rule of ... to solve ...
Analysis	Critical thinking; identifying reasons and motives; making inferences based on specific data; analyzing conclusions to see if supported by evidence	What influenced the writings of ...? Why was Ottawa chosen ...? Which of the following are facts and which are opinions ...? Based on your experiment, what is the chemical ...?
Synthesis	Divergent, original thinking; original plan, proposal, design, or story	What's a good name for ...? How could we raise money for ...? What would Canada be like if the Bloc Québécois were the official opposition?
Evaluation	Judging the merits of ideas, offering opinions, applying standards	Which prime minister was the most effective? Which painting do you believe to be better? Why? Why would you favour ...?

Source: Adapted from Sadker, M., & Sadker, D. (1986). Questioning skills. In J. Cooper (Ed.), *Classroom teaching skills: A Handbook* (3rd ed., pp. 143–160). Boston: D. C. Heath. Adapted by permission of D. C. Heath.

Very little thoughtful responding can take place in this situation. When teachers learn to pose a question, then wait at least three to five seconds before calling on a student to answer, students tend to give longer answers; more students are likely to participate, ask questions, and volunteer appropriate answers; student comments involving analysis, synthesis, inference, and speculation tend to increase; and the students generally appear more confident in their answers (Berliner, 1987; Rowe, 1974; Sadker & Sadker, 2003; Tobin, 1987).

This seems like a simple improvement in teaching, but five seconds of silence is not that easy to handle. It takes practice. You might try asking students to jot down ideas or even discuss the question with another student and formulate an answer together. This makes the wait more comfortable and gives students a chance to think. Of course, if it is clear that students are lost or don't understand the question, waiting longer will not help. When your question is met with blank stares, rephrase the question or ask if anyone can explain the confusion. Also, there is some evidence that extending wait times does not affect learning in university classes (Duell, 1994), so with advanced high school students, you may want to conduct your own evaluation of wait time.

If you call only on volunteers when selecting students to answer questions, you may get the wrong idea about how well students understand the material. Also, the same people volunteer over and over again. Many expert teachers have some systematic way of making sure that they call on everyone; they may pull names from a jar or check names off a list as each student speaks (Weinstein, 2003; Weinstein & Mignano, 2003). Another possibility is to put each student's name on an index card, then shuffle the cards and go through the deck as you call on people. You can use the card to make notes about students' answers or extra help they may need.

Responding to Student Answers. What do you do after the student answers? The most common response, occurring about 50 percent of the time in most classrooms, is simple acceptance—"Okay" or "Uh-huh" (Sadker & Sadker, 2003). But there are better reactions, depending on whether the student's answer is correct, partly correct, or wrong. If the answer is quick, firm, and correct, simply accept the answer or ask another question. If the answer is correct but hesitant, give the student feedback about why the answer is correct: "That's right, Chris, the Senate is part of the legislative branch of government because the Senate...." This allows you to explain the material again. If this student is unsure, others may be confused as well. If the answer is partially or completely wrong but the student has made an honest attempt, you should probe for more information, give clues, simplify the question, review the previous steps, or reteach the material. If the student's wrong answer is silly or careless, however, it is better simply to correct the answer and go on (Good, 1988; Rosenshine & Stevens, 1986).

Group Discussion

Group discussion is in some ways similar to the recitation strategy described in the previous section but should be more like the instructional conversations. A teacher may pose questions, listen to student answers, react, and probe for more information, but in a true group discussion, the teacher does not have a dominant role. Students ask questions, answer each other's questions, and respond to each other's answers (Beck, McKeown, Worthy, Sandora, & Kucan, 1996; Burbules & Bruce, 2001; Parker & Hess, 2001).

There are many advantages to group discussions. The students are directly involved and have the chance to participate. Group discussion helps students learn to express themselves clearly, to justify opinions, and to tolerate different views. Group discussion also gives students a chance to ask for clarification, examine their own thinking, follow personal interests, and assume responsibility by taking leadership roles in the group. Thus, group discussions help students evaluate ideas and synthesize personal viewpoints. Discussions are also useful

group discussion Conversation in which the teacher does not have the dominant role; students pose and answer their own questions.

when students are trying to understand difficult concepts that go against common sense. Many scientific concepts, such as the role of light in vision or Newton's laws of motion, are difficult to grasp because they contradict common sense notions. By thinking together, challenging each other, and suggesting and evaluating possible explanations, students are more likely to reach a genuine understanding.

Of course, there are disadvantages. Class discussions are quite unpredictable and may easily digress into exchanges of ignorance. Some members of the group may have great difficulty participating and may become anxious if forced to speak. In addition, you may have to do a good deal of preparation to ensure that participants have a background of knowledge on which to base the discussion. And large groups are often unwieldy. In many cases, a few students will dominate the discussion while the others daydream (Arends, 2001; Kindsvatter, Wilen, & Ishler, 1988). The Guidelines below give some ideas for facilitating a productive group discussion.

GUIDELINES

Productive Group Discussions

Invite shy children to participate.

EXAMPLES

1. "What's your opinion, Joel? We need to hear from some other students."

2. Don't wait until there is a deadly silence to ask shy students to reply. Most people, even those who are confident, hate to break a silence.

Direct student comments and questions back to another student.

EXAMPLES

1. "That's an unusual idea, Steve. Kim, what do you think of Steve's idea?"

2. "That's an important question, John. Maura, do you have any thoughts about how you'd answer that?"

3. Encourage students to look at and talk to one another rather than wait for your opinion.

Make sure you understand what a student has said. If you are unsure, other students may be unsure as well.

EXAMPLES

1. Ask a second student to summarize what the first student said; then the first student can try again to explain if the summary is incorrect.

2. "Jasdev, I think you're saying.... Is that right, or have I misunderstood?"

Probe for more information.

EXAMPLES

1. "That's a strong statement. Do you have any evidence to back it up?"

2. "Tell us how you reached that conclusion. What steps did you go through?"

Bring the discussion back to the subject.

EXAMPLES

1. "Let's see, we were discussing ... and Sarah made one suggestion. Does anyone have a different idea?"

2. "Before we continue, let me try to summarize what has happened so far."

Give time for thought before asking for responses.

EXAMPLE

1. "How would your life be different if television had never been invented? Jot down your ideas on paper, and we will share reactions in a minute." After a minute: "Hiromi, will you tell us what you wrote?"

When a student finishes speaking, look around the room to judge reactions.

EXAMPLES

1. If other students look puzzled, ask them to describe why they are confused.

2. If students are nodding assent, ask them to give an example of what was just said.

- What is direct instruction?
- Distinguish between convergent versus divergent and high-level versus low-level questions.
- How can wait time affect student learning?
- What are the uses and disadvantages of group discussion?

Apply to Practice

- What are some alternatives to seatwork?
- Give examples of convergent and divergent questions in your subject area.

We have been looking at instructional planning and some basic teaching formats associated with teacher-led, or direct, instruction. Now we turn to formats associated with teaching that is student-centred.

Connect & Extend

To your teaching
If you have observed in a primary grade, would you say the teacher made good use of direct, teacher-led approaches to instruction? Why or why not?

STUDENT-CENTRED TEACHING: EXAMPLES IN READING, MATHEMATICS, AND SCIENCE

What do we know about good teaching in student-centred instruction? Table 5.8 lists some student-centred teaching practices, which reflect constructivist views of learning described earlier in this chapter. It is clear that a teacher's knowledge of the subject is critical for teaching (Borko & Putnam, 1996). Part of that knowledge is pedagogical content knowledge, or knowing how to teach a subject to your particular students (Shulman, 1987). In the past decade, researchers have made great progress understanding how students learn, or construct understandings,

ENHANCING YOUR EXPERTISE WITH TECHNOLOGY

Questioning Techniques

Andrew was marking his 30th year as an administrator in his K–12 school district. He had hired and supervised hundreds of teachers at every level, kindergarten through grade 12. He had chaired dozens of committees that worked to keep the district current with modern curriculum standards, effective academic programs, and innovative instructional strategies. Early in his administrative career, Andrew observed that one of the major characteristics of expert teachers—whether they ran a teacher-centred classroom or a student-centred classroom—was the effective use of questions during lessons or learning activities. As he developed his expertise as an administrator, Andrew began to devote at least some part of a job interview with a prospective teacher or a post-observation teacher conference to questioning techniques and strategies.

The complex nature of questions and questioning techniques and strategies is reflected in the number of hits a web search engine provides for these terms. (Many of the pages and sites are designed for the corporate world. Questioning techniques are important for the employee selection process, planning business strategies, and for determining the needs of customers.) The two sites discussed here focus on different aspects of questioning and complement each other.

The Questioning Toolkit (**http://www.fno.org/nov97/toolkit. html**), sponsored by *The Educational Technology Journal*, defines and illustrates the many types of questions that arise in classroom discourse. It examines the different tasks that different kinds of questions can accomplish. For example,

in a stimulating learning environment, students and teachers are likely to pose a variety of organizing, hypothetical, probing, planning, and provocative questions. Expert use of the different types of questions can significantly enhance the level of cognitive activity of all those involved.

The University of Illinois at Champaign-Urbana offers an online booklet titled *Effective Classroom Questioning* (**http://www.oir.uiuc. edu/Did/docs/QUESTION/quest_ foreword.htm**). This booklet focuses on the use of questions as they pertain to Bloom's taxonomy, and explains the differences between open and closed questions and higher- and lower-order questions. It has an excellent section that considers important components of questioning such as wait time, instructor attitude, and student participation.

TABLE 5.8 Constructivist Teaching Practices

Constructivist teachers:

1. encourage and accept student autonomy and initiative;
2. use raw data and primary sources, along with manipulative, interactive, and physical materials;
3. use cognitive terminology when framing tasks—e.g., "classify," "analyze," "predict," and "create";
4. allow student responses to drive lessons, shift instructional strategies, and alter content;
5. inquire about students' understandings of concepts before sharing their own understandings of those concepts;
6. encourage students to engage in dialogue, both with the teacher and with one another;
7. encourage student inquiry by asking thoughtful, open-ended questions and encouraging students to ask questions of each other;
8. seek elaboration of students' initial responses;
9. engage students in experiences that might engender contradictions to their initial hypotheses and then encourage discussion;
10. allow wait time after posing questions;
11. provide time for students to discover relationships and create metaphors.

Source: Adapted from Brooks, J. G., & Brooks, M. G. Becoming a constructivist teacher. In J. G. Brooks & M. G. Brooks. (1995). *In search of understanding: The case for constructivist classrooms* (pp. 101–118). Alexandria, VA: Association for Supervision and Curriculum Development. Copyright © 1995 by ASCD. Reprinted with permission.

Connect & Extend

To your own philosophy
Can different formats, such as lecture or seatwork, be used in the service of different models, such as direct instruction or constructivist approaches?

about different subjects (Mayer, 1992a). Below we describe approaches to teaching reading, mathematics, and science that are based on these recent research findings.

Learning to Read and Write

For years, educators have debated whether students should be taught to read and write through code-based (phonics, skills) approaches that relate letters to sounds and sounds to words or through meaning-based (whole language, literature-based, emergent literacy) approaches that do not dissect words and sentences into pieces but instead focus on the meaning of the text (Goodman, 1986; Smith, 1994; Stahl & Miller, 1989; Symons, Woloshyn, & Pressley, 1994; Vellutino, 1991). The best approach to teaching reading and writing balances strategies from both code-based and meaning-based approaches. After all, we want our students to be both fluent and enthusiastic readers and writers (Bus & van Ijzendoorn, 1999; Pressley, 1998).

Focus on Meaning. Informed by theory and research in the fields of emergent literacy and developmental psychology, advocates of meaning-based approaches, such as whole language, believe that becoming literate is a natural process—much like mastering your native language—that begins long before children enter school. Also, consistent with cognitive and constructivist views of learning, whole language advocates believe that children actively create understandings of what it really means to read and to write by engaging in authentic reading and writing activities. Finally, they stress social aspects of learning to read and write. They emphasize how important it is for parents and teachers to model literate behaviour for developing readers and writers. From this **whole language perspective**, learning to read and write during the elementary-school years is part of a

whole language perspective A philosophical approach to teaching and learning that stresses learning through authentic, real-life tasks; it emphasizes using language to learn, integrating learning across skills and subjects, and respecting the language abilities of student and teacher.

continuum of learning that begins at birth and continues through adulthood (Chapman, 1997). Teachers have to be astute observers of students' literacy development to determine the supports or resources students need to learn.

In many whole language classrooms, teachers and students set goals and design curriculum together. In writing, for instance, students and teachers identify a purpose and an audience. For example, students might decide to write letters to the mayor of their city about her recycling policy. Using such activities is consistent with Lev Vygotsky's (1978) view that "writing should be incorporated into a task that is necessary and relevant for life. Only then can we be certain that it will develop not as a matter of hand and finger habits but as a really new and complex form of speech" (p. 118). Marilyn Chapman, at the University of British Columbia, agrees: "Children develop knowledge about writing primarily in the context of its purposeful use" (1997, p. 31). She also observes that the two main purposes for writing are to communicate with others and to facilitate students' thinking and learning.

Another hallmark of meaning-based approaches to instruction is their emphasis on integrating language processes—speaking, listening, reading, writing—across curricula and on teaching language and literacy skills in the context of meaningful curricular activities. Whole language advocates design instruction according to the belief that speaking, listening, reading, and writing processes are "integrated, mutually reinforcing ... activities" (Gunderson, 1997, p. 226) that develop concurrently (Chapman, 1997). They also hold that specific skills are better taught in a context of meaningful activities rather than in isolation.

Clearly, whole language approaches to instruction have much to commend them. John Shapiro (1994), at the University of British Columbia, argues that children who experience whole language approaches do become effective readers and writers:

> Their vocabulary increases, they employ varied strategies in word recognition, their comprehension abilities range from simple literal recall to more sophisticated judgments about authors' intent, they read for pleasure and information, and, perhaps more importantly, they have positive attitudes toward reading [and writing]. (pp. 458–459)

But is whole language the whole story?

Students Need Knowledge about the Code. There are now two decades of research demonstrating that skill in recognizing sounds and words supports reading. Keith Stanovich, at the Ontario Institute for Studies in Education, has conducted numerous studies that show that being able to identify many words as you read does not depend on using context to guess meaning (Stanovich, 1993/1994; Stanovich, West, & Freeman, 1984). In fact, it is almost the other way around—knowing words helps you make sense of context. Identifying words as you read is a highly automatic process. The more fluent and automatic you are in identifying words, the more effective you will be in getting meaning from context (Vandervelden & Siegel, 1995). It is the poorest readers who resort to using context to help them understand meaning (Pressley, 1996).

Many studies support the code-based position. For example, three different groups reported in the *Journal of Educational Psychology* (December 1991) that alphabetic coding and awareness of letter sounds are essential skills for acquiring word identification, so some direct teaching of the alphabet and phonics is helpful in learning to read. Stanovich (1993/1994) acknowledges that it is possible to "overdo the teaching of phonics," but he also contends that "some children in whole language classrooms do not pick up the alphabetic principle through simple immersion in print and writing activities, and such children need explicit instruction in alphabetic coding" (p. 285).

Being Sensible about Reading and Writing. The results of high-quality studies indicate that:

- Whole language approaches to reading and writing are most effective in preschool and kindergarten. Whole language gives children a good conceptual basis for reading and writing. The social interactions around reading and

Contemporary learning theories have sought to understand how students learn different subjects in different ways and how teaching methods might be adapted to these differences.

writing—reading big books, writing shared stories, examining pictures, discussing meaning—are activities that support literacy and mirror the early home experiences of children who come to school prepared to learn. Whole language approaches seem to improve students' motivation, interest, and attitude toward reading and help children understand the nature and purposes of reading and writing (Graham & Harris, 1994; Shapiro, 1994).

- Phonemic awareness—the sense that words are composed of separate sounds and that sounds are combined to say words—in kindergarten and grade 1 predicts literacy in later grades. If children do not have phonemic awareness in the early grades, direct teaching can dramatically improve their chances of long-term achievement in literacy (Pressley, 1996).

- Excellent primary school teachers balance their explicit teaching of decoding skills and their whole language instruction (Adams, Treiman, & Pressley, 1998; Vellutino, 1991; Wharton-McDonald, Pressley, & Mistretta, 1996). The Center for the Improvement of Early Reading Achievement (CIERA) has generated 10 research-based principles regarding early literacy development. These are outlined in Table 5.9.

If students need help cracking the code, give them what they need. Don't let ideology get in the way. You will just send more students to private tutors—if their families can afford it. But don't forget that reading and writing are for a purpose. Surround students with good literature and create a community of readers and writers.

The above discussion applies to reading and writing in the early grades, but what about the later years when comprehending texts becomes more demanding?

Learning and Teaching Mathematics

Stop/Think/Write

Think back to the ways that you were taught mathematics. What were your math classes like in elementary school? High school?

Some of the most compelling support for constructivist approaches to teaching comes from mathematics education. Critics of direct instruction believe that traditional mathematics instruction often teaches students an unintended lesson—that they "cannot understand mathematics," or worse, that mathematics doesn't have to make sense, you just have to memorize the formulas. Arthur Baroody and Herbert Ginsburg (1990, p. 62) give this example:

Sherry, a junior high student, explained that her math class was learning how to convert measurements from one unit to another. The interviewer gave Sherry the following problem:

To feed data into the computer, the measurements in your report have to be converted to one unit of measurement: metres. Your first measurement, however, is 150 centimetres. What are you going to feed into the computer?

Sherry recognized immediately that the conversion algorithm taught in school applied. However, because she really did not understand the rationale behind the conversion algorithm, Sherry had difficulty in remembering the steps and how to execute them. After some time she came up with an improbable answer (it was less than 1 m). Sherry knew she was in trouble and became flustered. At this point, the interviewer tried to help by asking her if there was any other way of solving the problem. Sherry responded sharply, "No!" She explained, "That's the way it has to be done." The interviewer tried to give Sherry a hint: "Look at the numbers in the problem, is there another way we can think about them that might help us figure out the problem more easily?" Sherry grew even more impatient, "This is the way I learned in school, so it has to be the way."

TABLE 5.9 Improving Early Reading Achievement

CIERA (the Center for the Improvement of Early Reading Achievement) has reviewed the research on learning to read and distilled the best findings into these 10 principles. You can read the expanded version of the principles online at **http://www.ciera.org/library/instresrc/principles.**

1. **Home language and literacy experiences** support the development of key print concepts, and a range of knowledge prepares students for school-based learning. Programs that help families initiate and sustain these experiences show positive benefits for children's reaching achievement.

   Examples: Joint reading with a family member, parental modelling of good reading habits, monitoring homework and television viewing.

2. **Preschool programs** are particularly beneficial for children who do not experience informal learning opportunities in their homes. Such preschool experiences lead to improved reading achievement, with some effects lasting through grade 3.

   Examples: Listening to and examining books, saying nursery rhymes, writing messages, and seeing and talking about print.

3. **Skills that predict later reading success** can be promoted in kindergarten and grade 1. The two most powerful of these predictors are letter-name knowledge and phonemic awareness. Instruction in these skills has demonstrated positive effects on primary-grade reading achievement, especially when it is coupled with letter-sound instruction.

   Examples: Hearing and blending sound through oral renditions of rhymes, poems, and songs, as well as writing messages and in journals.

4. **Primary-level instruction** that supports successful reading acquisition is consistent, well-designed, and focused.

   Examples: Systematic word recognition instruction on common, consistent letter-sound relationships and important but often unpredictable high-frequency words, such as *the* and *what*; teaching children to monitor the accuracy of their reading as well as their understanding of texts through strategies such as predicting, inferencing, clarifying misunderstandings, and summarizing; promoting word recognition and comprehension through repeated reading of text, guided reading and writing, strategy lessons, reading aloud with feedback, and conversations about texts children have read.

5. **Primary-level classroom environments** in successful schools provide opportunities for students to apply what they have learned in teacher-guided instruction to everyday reading and writing.

   Examples: Teachers read books aloud and hold follow-up discussions, children read independently every day, and children write stories and keep journals. These events are monitored frequently by teachers, ensuring that time is well spent and that children receive feedback on their efforts. Teachers design and revise these events based on information from ongoing assessment of children's strengths and needs.

6. **Cultural and linguistic diversity** among children reflects the variations within their communities and homes. This diversity is manifest in differences in the children's dispositions toward and knowledge about topics, language, and literacy.

   Examples: Effective instruction includes assessment, integration, and extension of relevant background knowledge and the use of texts that recognize diverse backgrounds. Build on the children's language when children are learning to speak, listen to, write, and read English. When teachers capitalize on the advantages of bilingualism or biliteracy, second-language reading acquisition is significantly enhanced.

7. **Children who are identified as having reading disabilities** profit from the same sort of well-balanced instructional programs that benefit all children who are learning to read and write, including systematic instruction *and* meaningful reading and writing.

   Examples: Intensive one-on-one or small-group instruction; attention to both comprehension and word recognition processes; thoroughly individualized assessment and instructional planning; extensive experiences with many types of texts.

8. **Proficient reading in grade 3 and above** is sustained and enhanced by programs that adhere to four fundamental features:

   Features: (1) deep and wide opportunities to read; (2) acquiring new knowledge and vocabulary, through wide reading and through explicit instruction about networks of new concepts; (3) emphasizing the influence on understanding of kinds of text (e.g., stories versus essays) and the ways writers organize particular texts; and (4) assisting students in reasoning about text.

9. **Professional opportunities** to improve reading achievement are prominent in successful schools and programs.

   Examples: Opportunities for teachers and administrators to analyze instruction, assessment, and achievement; to set goals for improvement; to learn about effective practices; and to participate in ongoing communities that deliberately try to understand both successes and persistent problems.

10. **Entire school staffs**, not just grade 1 teachers, are involved in bringing children to high levels of achievement.

    Examples: In successful schools, reading achievement goals are clear, expectations are high, instructional means for attaining goals are articulated, and shared assessments monitor children's progress. Even though they might use different materials and technologies, successful schools maintain a focus on reading and writing and have programs to involve family members in their children's reading and homework. Community partnerships, including volunteer tutoring programs, are common.

Source: Adapted from CIERA. (2002). Improving the reading achievement of America's children: 10 research-based principles. Retrieved April 1, 2005, from http://www.ciera.org/library/instresrc/principles. Copyright © Center for the Improvement of Early Reading Achievement, University of Michigan School of Education. Reprinted with permission.

Connect & Extend

To the research

Another example of how students solve mathematics problems by applying rules appears in Merseth, K. K. (1993). How old is the shepherd? An essay about mathematics education. *Phi Delta Kappan, 74*, 548–554. Merseth cites findings from research showing that three out of four students will produce some numerical answer to the problem: There are 125 sheep and 5 dogs in a flock. How old is the shepherd? Here is how one child reached an answer; notice that logic and reasoning play a role: "125 + 5 = 130 ... this is too big, and 125 – 5 = 120 is still too big ... while 125/5 = 25. That works! I think the shepherd is 25 years old!"

Connect & Extend

To other research

Gersten, R., & Chard, D. (1999). Number sense: Rethinking arithmetic instruction for students with mathematical disabilities. *Journal of Special Education 33*, 18–28.

Peterson, P., Fennema, E., & Carpenter, T. (1989). Using knowledge of how students think about mathematics. *Educational Leadership, 46*(4), 42–46.

Klein, P. D. (2000). Elementary students' strategies for writing-to-learn in science. *Cognition and Instruction, 18*, 317–348.

Sherry believed that there was only one way to solve a problem. Though Sherry knew that 100 centimetres was 1 metre and that shifting the "invisible" decimal at the end of 150 to the left increased the unit size in metric measurements, she did not use this knowledge to solve the problem informally and quickly. Her beliefs prevented her from effectively using her existing mathematical knowledge to solve the problem. Sherry had probably been taught to memorize the steps to convert one measurement to another. How would a constructivist approach teach the same material?

The following excerpt shows how a grade 3 teacher, Ms. Coleman, uses a constructivist approach to teach negative numbers. Notice the use of dialogue and the way the teacher asks students to justify and explain their thinking. The class has been considering one problem: $-10 + 10 = ?$ A student, Marta, has just tried to explain, using a number line, why $-10 + 10 = 0$:

Teacher: Marta says that negative ten plus ten equals zero, so you have to count ten numbers to the right. What do you think, Harold?

Harold: I think it's easy, but I don't understand how she explained it.

Teacher: OK. Does anybody else have a comment or a response to that? Tessa? (Peterson, 1992, p. 165)

As the discussion progresses, Ms. Coleman encourages students to talk directly to each other:

Teacher: You said you don't understand what she is trying to say?

Chang: No.

Teacher: Do you want to ask her?

Chang: What do you mean by counting to the right?

This dialogue reveals three things about learning and teaching in a constructivist classroom: the thinking processes of the students are the focus of attention; one topic is considered in depth rather than attempting to "cover" many topics; and assessment is ongoing and mutually shared by teacher and students.

Jere Confrey (1990b) analyzed an expert mathematics teacher in a class for high school girls who had difficulty with mathematics. Confrey identified five components in a model of this teacher's approach to teaching. These components are summarized in Table 5.10.

Learning Science

We have seen a number of times that by high school many students have "learned" some unfortunate lessons in school. Like Sherry, described in the preceding section, they have learned that math is impossible to understand and you just have to apply the rules to get the answers. Or they may have developed misconceptions about the world, such as the belief that the Earth is warmer in the summer because it is closer to the sun.

Many educators note that the key to understanding in science is for students to directly examine their own theories and confront the shortcomings (Hewson, Beeth, & Thorley, 1998). For conceptual change to take place, students must go through six stages: initial discomfort with their own ideas and beliefs; attempts to explain away inconsistencies between their theories and evidence presented to them; attempts to adjust measurements or observations to fit personal theories; doubt; vacillation; and finally conceptual change (Nissani & Hoefler-Nissani, 1992). You can see Piaget's notions of assimilation, disequilibrium, and accommodation operating here. Students try to make new information fit existing ideas (assimilation), but when the fit simply won't work and disequilibrium occurs, then accommodation or changes in cognitive structures follow.

TABLE 5.10 A Constructivist Approach to Mathematics: Five Components

1. Promote students' autonomy and commitment to their answers.

   Examples:

   - Question both right and wrong student answers.
   - Insist that students at least try to solve a problem and be able to explain what they tried.

2. Develop students' reflective processes.

   Examples:

   - Question students to guide them to try different ways to resolve the problem.
   - Ask students to restate the problem in their own words; to explain what they are doing and why; and to discuss what they mean by the terms they are using.

3. Construct a case history of each student.

   Examples:

   - Note general tendencies in the way the student approaches problems, as well as common misconceptions and strengths.

4. If the student is unable to solve a problem, intervene to negotiate a possible solution with the student.

   Examples:

   - Based on the case study and your understanding of how the student is thinking about a problem, guide the student to think about a possible solution.
   - Ask questions such as, "Is there anything you did in the last one that will help you here?" or "Can you explain your diagram?"
   - If the student is becoming frustrated, ask more direct, product-oriented questions.

5. When the problem is solved, review the solution.

   Examples:

   - Encourage students to reflect on what they did and why.
   - Note what students did well and build confidence.

Source: From Confrey, J. (1990). What constructivism implies for teaching. In R. Davis, C. Maher, & N. Noddings (Eds.), *Constructivist views on the teaching and learning of mathematics.* Monograph 4 of the National Council of Teachers of Mathematics, Reston, VA. Copyright © 1990 National Council of Teachers of Mathematics. Adapted with permission.

The goal of **conceptual change teaching in science** is to help students pass through these six stages of learning. The two central features of conceptual change teaching are:

- Teachers are committed to teaching for student understanding rather than "covering the curriculum."
- Students are encouraged to make sense of science using their current ideas—they are challenged to describe, predict, explain, justify, debate, and defend the adequacy of their understanding. Dialogue is key. Only when intuitive ideas prove inadequate can new learning take hold (Anderson & Roth, 1989).

> **conceptual change teaching in science** A method that helps students understand (rather than memorize) concepts in science by using and challenging the students' current ideas.

Conceptual change teaching has much in common with cognitive apprenticeships, inquiry learning, and reciprocal teaching—with scaffolding and dialogue playing key roles (Shuell, 1996). The Guidelines on page 476, adapted from Hewson, Beeth, and Thorley (1998), give some ideas for promoting conceptual change.

How would these guidelines look in practice? One answer comes from Michael Beeth's study of a grade 5 classroom. Table 5.11 is a list of learning goals that the teacher presented to her students. In this classroom, the teacher typically began instruction with questions such as, "Do you have ideas? Can you talk about them? Bring them out into the open? Why do you like your ideas? Why are you attracted to them?" (Beeth, 1998, p. 1095). During her teaching, she constantly asked questions that required explanation and justifications. She summarized the students' answers and sometimes challenged, "But do you really believe what you say?" Studies of the students in the teacher's classroom over the years showed that they had a sophisticated understanding of science concepts.

Teaching for Conceptual Change

Encourage students to make their ideas explicit.

EXAMPLES

1. Ask students to make predictions that might contradict their naive conceptions.
2. Ask students to state their ideas in their own words, including the attractions and limitations of the ideas for them.
3. Have students explain their ideas using physical models or illustrations.

Help students see the differences among ideas.

EXAMPLES

1. Have students summarize or paraphrase each other's ideas.
2. Encourage comparing ideas by presenting and comparing evidence.

Encourage metacognition.

EXAMPLES

1. Give a pretest before starting a unit, then have students discuss their own responses to the pretest. Group similar pretest responses together and ask students to discover a more general concept underlying the responses.

2. At the end of lessons, ask students, "What did you learn?" "What do you understand?" "What do you believe about the lesson?" "How have your ideas changed?"

Explore the status of ideas. Status is an indication of how much students know and accept ideas and find them useful.

EXAMPLES

1. Ask direct questions about how intelligible, plausible, and fruitful an idea is. That is, "Do you know what the idea means?" "Do you believe it?" "Can you achieve some valuable outcome using the idea?"
2. Plan activities and experiments that support and question the students' ideas, such as showing successful applications or pointing out contradictions.

Ask students for justifications of their ideas.

EXAMPLES

1. Teach students to use terms such as *logical*, *consistent*, *inconsistent*, and *coherent* in giving justifications.
2. Ask students to share and analyze each other's justifications.

Conceptual change teaching in science focuses teachers' and students' attention on students' understanding rather than on "covering the curriculum." Dialogue is key.

TABLE 5.11 One Teacher's Learning Goals for Conceptual Change Teaching

The teacher in one grade 5 class gives these questions to her students to support their thinking about science:

1. Can you state your own ideas?
2. Can you talk about why you are attracted to your ideas?
3. Are your ideas consistent?
4. Do you realize the limitations of your ideas and the possibility they might need to change?
5. Can you try to explain your ideas using physical models?
6. Can you explain the difference between understanding an idea and believing in an idea?
7. Can you apply the words *intelligible* and *plausible* as standards for evaluating your ideas?

Source: Adapted from Beeth, M. E. (1998). Teaching science in fifth grade: Instructional goals that support conceptual change. *Journal of Research in Science Teaching, 35,* 1093.

Canadian researchers Wolf-Michael Roth and Michelle McGinn add that a key to unlocking opportunities for students to construct understandings in science (and mathematics) is posing better problems (Roth & McGinn, 1997). Usually, the problems students are given to solve are uncluttered with the complexities that enrich the real world. Too often, problems have prefigured answers where "students' tasks are to disclose what the texts (or problems) hide ... as *the* solution" (pp. 19–20) rather than learn how to do science. Roth and McGinn suggest that teachers invite students to bring problems from outside school into the classroom. Then, teachers should support students as students frame hypotheses and explore methods to investigate them. This places problems in context so that students' experiences from outside school are joined with experiences of doing science. This model, called *open inquiry*, transforms what students do to resemble what scientists do. The result? Students construct understandings about science that are genuine rather than textbookish (Roth & Bowen, 1995; Roth & Roychoudhury, 1993).

Connect & Extend

To the research
White, B. Y. (1993). TinkerTools: Causal models, conceptual change, and science education. *Cognition and Instruction, 10,* 1–100.

Lapadat, J. C. (2000). Construction of science knowledge: Scaffolding conceptual change through discourse. *Journal of Classroom Instruction, 35,* 1–14.

Criticisms of Constructivist Approaches to Subject Teaching

Constructivist approaches have done much to correct the excesses of tell-and-drill teaching. Some positive outcomes from constructivist teaching are better understanding of the material, greater enjoyment of literature, more positive attitudes toward school, better problem solving, and greater motivation (Harris & Graham, 1996; Palincsar, 1998). But total reliance on constructivist approaches that ignores direct teaching of skills can be detrimental for some children. For example, Harris and Graham (1996) describe the experiences of their daughter Leah in a whole language, progressive education school, where the teachers successfully developed their daughter's creativity, thinking, and understanding.

> Skills, on the other hand, have been a problem for our daughter and for other children. At the end of kindergarten, when she had not made much progress in reading, her teacher said she believed Leah had a perceptual problem or a learning disability. Leah began asking what was wrong with her, because other kids were reading and she wasn't. Finally, an assessment was done. (p. 26)

The testing indicated no learning disability, strong comprehension abilities, and poor word attack skills. Luckily, Leah's parents knew how to teach word attack skills. Direct teaching of these skills helped Leah become an avid and able reader in about six weeks.

Ernst von Glasersfeld (1995), a strong advocate of constructivist teaching in mathematics, believes that it is a misunderstanding of constructivism to say that memorization and rote learning are always useless. "There are, indeed, matters that can and perhaps must be learned in a purely mechanical way" (p. 5). Classrooms that integrate constructivist teaching with needed direct teaching of skills are especially good learning environments for students with special needs. Careful ongoing assessment of each student's abilities, knowledge, and motivations, followed by appropriate support, should ensure that no students are lost or left behind (Graham & Harris, 1994).

Check Your Knowledge

- What is a balanced approach to teaching reading and writing?
- Describe constructivist approaches to mathematics and science teaching.

Apply to Practice

- How would you assess students' conceptions about the science topics you will teach?

BEYOND THE DEBATES TOWARD OUTSTANDING TEACHING

In spite of the criticisms and debates, there is no one best way to teach. Different goals require different methods. Direct instruction leads to better performance on achievement tests, whereas the open, informal methods such as discovery learning or inquiry approaches are associated with better performance on tasks requiring creativity, abstract thinking, problem solving, and self-regulated learning. In addition, the open methods are better for improving attitudes toward school and for stimulating curiosity, cooperation among students, and lower absence rates (Walberg, 1990). According to these conclusions, when the goals of teaching involve problem solving, creativity, understanding, and mastering processes, many approaches besides direct instruction should be effective. This view is in keeping with Tom Good's conclusion that teaching should become less direct as students mature and when the goals involve affective development and problem solving or critical thinking (Good, 1983a).

Below we describe teaching practices that promote self-regulated learning, a highly effective form of learning that was introduced in Chapter 9.

Teaching toward Self-Regulated Learning

Most teachers agree that students need to develop skills and attitudes for independent, lifelong learning—that is, self-regulated learning, or SRL. Fortunately, there is a growing body of research that offers guidance on how to design tasks and structure classroom interactions to support students' development of and engagement in SRL (Neuman & Roskos, 1997; Many, Fyfe, Lewis, & Mitchell, 1996; Perry, 1998; Tuner, 1995; Wharton-McDonald, Pressley, Rankin, Mistretta, Yokoi, & Ettenberger, 1997). This research indicates that students develop academically effective forms of SRL when teachers involve them in complex, meaningful tasks that extend over long periods of time, much like the math and science activities we described in the previous section on student-centred, constructivist approaches to teaching. Also, to develop SRL, students need to have some degree of control over their learning processes and products (e.g., choices), and it helps them work collaboratively with and seek feedback from peers. Finally, since self-monitoring and self-evaluation are key to effective SRL, teachers can help students develop SRL by involving them in setting criteria for evaluating their learning processes and products and giving them opportunities to make judgments about their progress toward those standards.

Complex Tasks. We use the term *complex* to refer to the design of tasks, not their level of difficulty. From a design point of view, tasks are complex when they address multiple goals and involve large chunks of meaning, as projects and thematic units do. Furthermore, complex tasks that extend over long periods of time engage students in a variety of cognitive and metacognitive processes and allow for the production of a wide range of products (Perry, VandeKamp, Mercer, & Nordby, 2002; Wharton-McDonald et al., 1997). For example, a study of Egyptian pyramids might result in the production of written reports, maps, diagrams, and models.

Research indicates that the most motivating and academically beneficial tasks for students are those that challenge but don't overwhelm them (Rohrkemper & Corno, 1988; Turner, 1997). Complex tasks need not be overly difficult for students. See the Reaching Every Student below for a description of how one

REACHING EVERY STUDENT
From Other-Regulation to Self-Regulation

Carol, a grade 2 student, had difficulty finding facts and then transforming those facts into meaningful prose. Carol's teacher, Lynn, also characterized her as "a very weak writer." Carol had problems with the mechanics of writing, which, according to Lynn, held her back.

Over the course of the school year, Lynn involved her grade 2 and 3 students in three writing projects about animals. Through these projects, she wanted students to learn how to: (a) do research, (b) write expository text, (c) edit and revise their writing, and (d) use the computer as a tool for researching and writing. For the first report, the class worked on one topic together (chipmunks). Students did the fact finding and writing together because Lynn needed to show them how to do research and write a report. Also, the class developed frameworks for working collaboratively as a community of learners. When students wrote the second report (on penguins), Lynn offered them many more choices and encouraged them to depend more on themselves and on one another. Finally, for the third report, students conducted a self-regulated

research project and wrote about an animal of their choosing. Now that they knew how to do research and write a report, they could work alone or together and be successful at this complex task.

Carol worked with a student in grade 3 who was doing research on a related topic. He showed Carol how to use a table of contents and offered advice about how to phrase ideas in her report. Also, Carol underlined words she thought were misspelled so that she could check them later when she met with Lynn to edit her report. Unlike many students who are low achieving, Carol was engaging with meaningful tasks and content and learning strategies for SRL. Carol was not afraid to attempt challenging tasks, and she was confident about her ability to develop as a writer. Reflecting on her progress across the school year, Carol said, "I learned a lot from when I was in grade 1 because I had a lot of trouble then."

Source: Perry, N. & Drummond, L. (2003). Helping young students become self-regulated researchers and writers. *The Reading Teacher, 56,* 298–310.

student who is low achieving benefited from her engagement with complex, meaningful tasks.

Importantly, complex tasks provide students with information about their learning progress, require them to engage in deep, elaborative processing and problem solving, and help them develop and refine cognitive and metacognitive strategies (Bruning, Schraw, & Ronning, 1995; McCaslin & Good, 1996; Turner, 1997). Furthermore, succeeding at such tasks increases students' self-efficacy and intrinsic motivation (McCaslin & Good, 1996). Rohrkemper and Corno (1988) advised teachers to design complex tasks that provide students with opportunities to modify the learning conditions or themselves to cope with challenging problems: "[L]earning to cope with and modify stressful situations ... is an important outcome of education; its deliberate promotion in a supportive classroom environment is a valuable educational goal" (p. 299).

Control. Teachers can share control with students by giving them choices. When students have choices (e.g., about what to produce, how to produce it, where to work, who to work with), they are more likely to predict a successful outcome and consequently increase effort and persist when difficulty arises (Turner & Paris, 1995). Also, by involving students in making decisions, teachers invite them to take responsibility for learning by planning, setting goals, monitoring progress, and evaluating outcomes (Turner, 1997). These are qualities of highly effective, self-regulating learners.

Giving students choices creates opportunities for them to adjust the degree of challenge particular tasks present (e.g., they can choose easy or more challenging reading materials, determine the nature and amount of writing in a report, supplement writing with other expressions of learning). But what if students make poor academic choices? Highly effective teachers who support self-regulated learning carefully consider the choices they give to students. They make sure that students have the knowledge and skills they need to operate independently and make good decisions (Perry & Drummond, 2002). For example, when students are learning new skills or routines, teachers can offer choices with constraints (e.g., students must write a minimum of four paragraphs, but they can choose to write more; they must demonstrate their understanding of an animal's habitat, food, and babies, but they can write, draw, or speak their knowledge).

Also, highly effective teachers teach and model good decision making. For example, when students are choosing partners, teachers ask them to consider what they need from their partner (e.g., shared interest and commitment, perhaps knowledge or skills that they need to develop). When students are making choices about how best to use their time, teachers ask, "What can you do when you're finished?" "What can you do if you are waiting for my help?" Often, lists are generated and posted, so that students can refer to these while they work. Finally, highly effective teachers give students feedback about the choices they make and tailor the choices they give to suit the unique characteristics of particular learners. For example, they might encourage some students to select research topics for which resources are readily available and written at a level that is accessible to them. Or they might encourage some students to work collaboratively to ensure that they have the support they need to be successful.

Collaboration. Nancy has observed that the most effective uses of cooperative/collaborative relationships to support SRL are those that reflect a climate of community and shared problem solving (Perry & Drummond, 2002;

Perry, VandeKamp, Mercer, & Nordby, 2002). In these contexts, teachers and students actually co-regulate one another's learning (McCaslin & Good, 1996), offering support to each other, whether working alone, in pairs, or small groups. This support is instrumental to individuals' development and use of metacognition, intrinsic motivation, and strategic action (e.g., sharing ideas, comparing strategies for solving problems, identifying *everyone's* area of expertise). Importantly, teachers who support self-regulated learning spend time at the start of each school year teaching routines and establishing norms of participation (e.g., how to give constructive feedback and how to interpret and respond to peers' suggestions). One teacher Nancy worked with said that instruction aimed at SRL "takes a lot of time but it is time well spent." Once routines and patterns of interaction are established, students can focus on learning, and teachers can attend to teaching academic skills and the curriculum.

Self-Evaluation. Evaluation practices that support SRL are non-threatening. They are embedded in ongoing activities, emphasize process as well as products, focus on personal progress, and help students interpret errors as opportunities for learning to occur. In these contexts, students actually seek challenging tasks because the cost of participation is low (Paris & Ayres, 1994). Involving students in generating evaluation criteria and in evaluating their work also reduces anxiety that often accompanies assessment, since it gives students a sense of control over the outcome. Students can judge their work in relation to a set of qualities they and their teachers identify as "good" work. They can consider the effectiveness of their approaches to learning and alter their behaviours in ways that enhance learning (Winne & Perry, 2000).

In classrooms where teachers support SRL, Nancy has observed both formal and informal opportunities for students to evaluate their learning. One student teacher asked grade 4/5 students to submit reflections journals with the games they designed with a partner or small group of collaborators in a probability and statistics unit (Perry, Phillips, & Dowler, 2004). These journals described students' contributions to their group's process and product and included reflections on what the students learned from participating. The student teacher took these reflections into account when she evaluated the games. More informally, teachers ask students, "What have you learned about yourself as a writer today?" "What do good researchers and writers do?" "What can we do that we couldn't do before?" Questions such as these, posed to individuals or embedded in class discussions, prompt students' metacognition, motivation, and strategic action, the components of SRL.

Check Your Knowledge

• How can teachers support self-regulated learning in their classrooms?

Apply to Practice

• Plan a complex task and then identify the opportunities it presents for students to engage in SRL.

Teaching toward SRL incorporates many of the beliefs and behaviours associated with highly effective teachers. Moreover, more than a quarter century of research indicates that SRL leads to success in school and beyond.

SUMMARY

Characteristics of Effective Teachers (pp. 146–147)

What are the general characteristics of good teachers?

Teacher knowledge of the subject is necessary but not sufficient for effective teaching; being more knowledgeable helps teachers be clearer and more organized. Teachers who provide clear presentations and explanations tend to have students who learn more and who rate their teachers more positively. Teacher warmth, friendliness, and understanding seem to be the traits most strongly related to positive student attitudes.

Teacher Expectations (pp. 147–151)

What are some sources of teacher expectations?

Sources include intelligence test scores, sex, notes from previous teachers and the medical or psychological reports found in cumulative folders, ethnic background, knowledge of older brothers and sisters, physical characteristics, previous achievement, socioeconomic class, and the actual behaviours of the student.

What are the two kinds of expectation effects, and how do they happen?

The first is the self-fulfilling prophecy, which occurs when the teacher's beliefs about the students' abilities have no basis in fact, but student behaviour comes to match the initially inaccurate expectation. The second is a sustaining expectation effect, which occurs when teachers are fairly accurate in their initial reading of students' abilities and respond to students appropriately. The problems arise when students show some improvement but teachers do not alter their expectations to take account of the improvement. When this happens, the teacher's unchanging expectation can sustain the students' achievement at the expected level. In practice, sustaining effects are more common than self-fulfilling prophecy effects.

What are the different avenues for communicating teacher expectations?

Some teachers tend to treat students differently, depending on their own views of how well the students are likely to do. Differences in treatment toward low-expectation students may include setting less challenging tasks, focusing on lower-level learning, giving fewer choices, providing inconsistent feedback, and communicating less respect and trust. Students may behave accordingly, fulfilling teachers' predictions or staying at an expected level of achievement.

Planning: The First Step in Effectively Teaching (pp. 151–160)

What are the levels of planning, and how do they affect teaching?

Teachers engage in several levels of planning—by the year, term, unit, week, and day. All the levels must be coordinated. Accomplishing the year's plan requires breaking the work into terms, the terms into units, and the units into weeks and days. The plan determines how time and materials will be turned into activities for students. There is no single model of planning, but all plans should allow for flexibility. Planning is a creative problem-solving process. Experienced teachers know how to accomplish many lessons and segments of lessons. They know what to expect and how to proceed, so they may not continue to follow the detailed lesson-planning models they learned during their teacher-preparation programs. Their planning may appear less formal. However, effective teachers plan for instruction.

What is an instructional objective?

An instructional objective is a clear and unambiguous description of your educational intentions for your students. Mager's influential system for writing behavioural objectives states that objectives ought to describe what students will be doing when demonstrating their achievement and how you will know they are doing it. A good objective has three parts—the intended student behaviour, the conditions under which the behaviour will occur, and the criteria for acceptable performance. Gronlund's alternative approach suggests that an objective should be stated first in general terms, then the teacher should clarify by listing sample behaviour that would provide evidence that the student has attained the objective. The most recent research on instructional objectives tends to favour approaches similar to Gronlund's.

Describe the three taxonomies of educational objectives.

Bloom and others have developed taxonomies categorizing basic objectives in the cognitive, affective, and psychomotor domains. In real life, of course, behaviour from these three domains occurs simultaneously. A taxonomy encourages systematic thinking about relevant objectives and ways to evaluate them. Six basic objectives are listed in the cognitive domain: knowledge, comprehension, application, analysis, synthesis, and evaluation. A recent revision of this taxonomy keeps the same cognitive processes but adds that these processes can act on four kinds of knowledge—factual, conceptual, procedural, and metacognitive. Objectives in the affective domain run from least committed to most committed. At the lowest level, students simply pay attention to a certain idea. At the highest level, students adopt an idea or a value and act consistently with that idea. Objectives in the psychomotor domain generally move from basic perceptions and reflex actions to skilled, creative movements.

Teacher-Directed Instruction
(pp. 160–171)

What is direct instruction?

Direct instruction is appropriate for teaching basic skills and explicit knowledge. It includes the teaching functions of review/overview, presentation, guided practice, feedback and correctives (with reteaching if necessary), independent practice, and periodic reviews. The younger or less able the students, the shorter the presentation should be, with more cycles of practice and feedback.

Distinguish between convergent versus divergent and high-level versus low-level questions.

Convergent questions have only one right answer. Divergent questions have many possible answers. High-level questions require analysis, synthesis, and evaluation—students have to think for themselves. Low-level questions assess remembering, understanding, and applying. The best pattern for younger students and for lower-ability students of all ages is simple questions that allow a high percentage of correct answers, ample encouragement, help when the student does not have the correct answer, and praise. For high-ability students, the successful pattern includes harder questions at both higher and lower levels and more critical feedback. Whatever their age or ability, all students should have some experience with thought-provoking questions and, if necessary, help in learning how to answer them.

How can wait time affect student learning?

Teacher responses to answers should not be too hasty in most cases and should provide appropriate feedback. When teachers learn to pose a question, then wait at least three to five seconds before calling on a student to answer, students tend to give longer answers; more students are likely to participate, ask questions, and volunteer appropriate answers; student comments involving analysis, synthesis, inference, and speculation tend to increase; and the students generally appear more confident in their answers.

What are the uses and disadvantages of group discussion?

Group discussion helps students participate directly, express themselves clearly, justify opinions, and tolerate different views. Group discussion also gives students a chance to ask for clarification, examine their own thinking, follow personal interests, and assume responsibility by taking leadership roles in the group. Thus, group discussions help students evaluate ideas and synthesize personal viewpoints. By thinking together, challenging each other, and suggesting and evaluating possible explanations, students are more likely to reach a genuine understanding. However, discussions are quite unpredictable and may easily digress into exchanges of ignorance.

Student-Centred Teaching: Examples in Reading, Mathematics, and Science
(pp. 171–180)

What is a balanced approach to reading and writing?

The best approach to teaching reading and writing balances strategies from both code-based and meaning-based approaches. There is extensive research indicating that skill in recognizing sounds and words—phonemic awareness—is fundamental in learning to read. Research also indicates that children are motivated to learn when they are surrounded by good literature and read and write for authentic purposes. Highly effective primary teachers use a balanced approach combining authentic reading and writing with skills instruction when needed.

Describe constructivist approaches to mathematics and science teaching.

Constructivist approaches to teaching mathematics and science emphasize deep understanding of concepts (as opposed to memorization), discussion and explanation, and exploration of students' implicit understandings. Many educators note that the key to understanding in science is for students to directly examine their own theories and confront the shortcomings. For change to take place, students must go through six stages: initial discomfort with their own ideas and beliefs; attempts to explain away inconsistencies between their theories and evidence presented to them; attempts to adjust measurements or observations to fit personal theories; doubt; vacillation; and finally conceptual change.

Beyond the Debates Toward Outstanding Teaching
(pp. 180–183)

How can teachers support self-regulated learning in their classrooms?

Students develop academically effective forms of SRL when teachers involve them in complex, meaningful tasks. Such tasks present opportunities for students to control their learning processes and products (e.g., by embedding choices) and monitor and evaluate their progress toward learning objectives. Teachers can support students' SRL by asking questions that require students to think deeply about learning and by teaching and modelling effective learning strategies. Also, working with and receiving feedback from peers supports SRL.

KEY TERMS

BECOMING A PROFESSIONAL

Reflecting on the Chapter

Can you apply the ideas from this chapter on teaching to solve the following problems of practice?

Preschool and Kindergarten

- You have a well-supplied science corner in your class, but your students seldom visit it. When they do, they don't seem to take advantage of the learning possibilities available with the manipulatives. How would you help students benefit from the materials?

Elementary and Middle School

- Your school administrator wants sample lesson plans for each of the subjects you teach. What would you include in the plans to make them useful for you?

- You are given a math workbook and text series and told that you must use these materials as the basis for your math teaching. What would you do to incorporate these materials into lessons that help students understand mathematical thinking and problem solving?

Junior High and High School

- Identify three instructional objectives for a lesson in your subject to be used in a mixed-ability grade 10 class. How would you make these learning objectives clear to your students?

Check Your Understanding

- Be familiar with Bloom's taxonomy in the cognitive domain, including examples of verbs that fit each level of the domain.

- Be familiar with the teaching functions of direct instruction.

- Know the differences between convergent and divergent questions and between high- and low-level questions.

Your Teaching Portfolio

Think about your philosophy of teaching, a question you will be asked at most job interviews.

What is your approach to planning? How will you match teaching approaches to learning goals?

Add some ideas for family involvement in homework from this chapter to your portfolio.

Teaching Resources

Include a summary of the cognitive, affective, and psychomotor taxonomies in your teaching resources file.

Add Table 5.3 ("A Revised Taxonomy in the Cognitive Domain") to your file.

Include Table 5.6 ("Active Learning and Teacher Presentations") in your file.

If you will teach elementary school, include Table 5.9 ("Improving Early Reading Achievement") in your file.

What Would They Do?

Here is how two practising teachers responded to the teaching situation presented at the beginning of this chapter about implementing a student-centred curriculum.

Carole Thomas Mandel
Whitney Public School
Toronto, Ontario

A student-centred curriculum is one that develops knowledge, skills, and independent thinking. In the student-centred classroom the teacher acknowledges the different ways children learn. The key to understanding and implementing a truly student-centred curriculum lies in achieving a balance between child-initiated and teacher-directed experiences. With diverse teaching materials and learning practices in place, and with parents and others acting as partners in the children's education, teachers and administrators can readily respond to parental complaints and other issues that have arisen about the new curriculum.

The good news is that there's a lot to celebrate. Many students appear to be more engaged in learning. However, some appear lost. As in any classroom, there can be a number of reasons why some students experience learning challenges. And so, rather than oppose a new curriculum that's been well planned in terms of both time and money, these reasons need to be carefully investigated. The school support team, including non-teaching professionals and parents, is the first place to seek guidance in helping a student who's experiencing unusual or exceptional difficulty. Modifications and adaptations to the curriculum (perhaps formalized in an Individual Education Plan) and remedial support during classroom time are normally suggested and then implemented by the classroom and sometimes resource room teachers.

Students' written work is now longer and more creative, an achievement everyone should celebrate. This hallmark, however, is set against a drop in standardized test scores, which tends to dismay parents. But parents need to be informed that standardized tests are only one method of evaluation and assessment. Equally valid—and for many educators even more valid, since standardized tests tend to assess what a student knows, or has memorized, on a given day—are the many other methods of evaluation and assessment in which classroom teachers are continually engaged. There needs to be a balance, then, between standardized tests and the ongoing and often more authentic classroom assessments. These assessments include, for example, clearly delineated rubrics attached to assignments (so that students and parents have a clear understanding of what's required to successfully complete them) and opportunities for student self-evaluation. They also involve regular reporting to parents in the form of oral and written reports that include anecdotal comments and achievement levels. However, with parents complaining that they have to hire private tutors or buy commercial programs to help teach their children the basics, more needs to be done beyond a fair and balanced approach in the use of different types of assessment.

The lower standardized test scores have to be addressed by implementing ways for students to improve without detracting from student-centred learning. After the test results are received, teachers should be encouraged to use this information as they plan their future test-preparation lessons. They can also make sure that students know how to use all the test material. Teachers need to provide opportunities to model, practise, and solve test-type questions throughout the year and for practice tests to be completed before testing. During information or curriculum evenings, teachers can map out what they've identified as areas of weakness. Homework that's at least partially reflective of the type of work that appears on standardized tests can be assigned, with a note to parents indicating this and encouraging home support. Hopefully, as test scores improve they'll be viewed as a valuable but incidental index that effective student-centred education is taking place.

Parental concerns about children not getting the basics also need to be validated. For students to successfully progress year by year they need the basics, which usually refer to such knowledge and essential skills as science facts, grammar rules, reading vocabulary, and math computations. And since these are often included in standardized tests, improving test scores and giving greater attention to effective, perhaps more step-by-step instruction of the basics are by no means mutually exclusive. A consistent, schoolwide approach to teaching the basics could easily be implemented, and could include something as straightforward as all teachers using the same math textbook series and support materials (just as levelled books were initially purchased with the goal of progress and consistency). Extra assistance in the classrooms can come from parent volunteers, and home support can also be sought. Teachers' websites can further communicate with parents and students, with reminders, for example, to review basic facts on a regular basis. As always, a balance must be maintained among teacher-directed instruction, the usually more open-ended student-initiated projects, and learning experiences that lend themselves readily to parental support (such as learning multiplication facts).

The planning and purchase of materials for the new student-centred classroom are parts of effective teaching and learning, but they are not the whole. Teachers have received professional development by taking workshops and much has been invested in quality children's literature, math manipulatives, and reading corners, etc. These are all good things. However, all good teachers know that in order to deliver the most effective, student-centred curriculum, a middle ground needs to be found. This includes open and positive responses to issues in education today, including a plan to improve standardized test results. Implicit in the student-centred curriculum is the belief that all children can learn but that sometimes support is needed; the need to implement a variety of instructional as well as assessment methods; and the acknowledgment that teachers must connect with parents and others involved in the school community as partners in the children's education.

Shannon Smith
Algonquin Public School
Brockville, Ontario

I would communicate with the parents and indicate to them my commitment to providing a positive learning experience for their children. I would welcome parents into my classroom and ensure that they are well informed of the educational processes taking place. In addition, I would take the parents' complaints directly to my principal and ensure that she is aware that parents are expressing concern about the new curriculum. The principal and the staff of the school should be involved in these decisions. I would back my principal and demonstrate my strong commitment to student learning and to the school as a whole.

Past experiences have given me the opportunity to implement creative educational strategies. As a teacher, I hope to motivate students by ascertaining their inner strengths and abilities and discovering what truly inspires them, and to create knowledge with students rather than simply passing it on. I believe in hands-on learning experiences. Through my teaching experience thus far, I have found facilitating, rather than dictating, to be a highly beneficial style of teaching. Students should be given power over their own education. If students construct their own learning experiences they will not only retain the information longer, but they will also become more confident in their abilities.

Through my commitment to learning, I hope to improve on my teaching skills to effectively teach and encourage children. I would reflect on my program by using numerous assessment techniques and then modify my program according to the needs of my students. I would make time for students who require additional instruction. In the past I have assisted students during lunch and recess to ensure that concepts are fully understood. I adapt materials, teaching techniques, and activities to meet the particular needs of my students. I hope to instill a love of learning through providing challenging and creative learning experiences.

Chapter 6
Psychology and the Workplace

Chapter 6

Psychology and the Workplace

If you ask people why they work, you will probably get some strange looks—and no wonder! Most of us don't have a choice. We have to work in order to survive. We did note that for most people, work is not a four-letter word; we can get a lot more from our work than just a paycheck. But that's not the point of this chapter. We're not asking why people work. Instead we're trying to find out what motivates us to work well, to do the best job we are capable of doing. We're concerned here with ways to get people to work more productively, to enhance their feelings of satisfaction and involvement, and to increase their commitment to their organization. This is one of the major problems facing organizations today.

Employers have made tremendous strides in applying the findings of industrial-organizational (I-O) psychology to recruit, select, and train their workers and to provide effective leadership. But none of these functions can improve the quality of the work being performed if employees are not motivated to do the best job possible.

The study of motivation is important to you for two reasons. First, as a consumer you are often the victim of dissatisfied workers who produce faulty products or who process your requests improperly. Second, you will likely spend one-third to one-half of your waking hours at work for 40 to 45 years. That is a long time to feel frustrated, dissatisfied, and unhappy, especially since these feelings will carry over to your family and social life and affect your physical and emotional health.

Psychologists have studied motivation, job satisfaction, job involvement, and organizational commitment. They have proposed various theories to explain employee motivation—why people behave as they do on the job. Some of these theories emphasize the impact of factors in the workplace. Other theories focus on personal characteristics. The theories have stimulated a great deal of research and have spawned a number of techniques to modify work behavior. Thus, they may provide options for making your work life more satisfying and fulfilling.

We discuss here two types of motivation theories: content theories and process theories. Content theories focus on the importance of the work itself and the challenges, growth opportunities, and responsibilities work provides for employees. These theories deal with the content of motivation, that is, with the specific needs that motivate and direct human behavior. Process theories do not focus directly on work but rather deal with the cognitive processes we use in making decisions and choices about our work.

CONTENT THEORIES OF MOTIVATION

We describe four content models: achievement motivation theory, needs hierarchy theory, motivator-hygiene (two-factor) theory, and job-characteristics theory.

People high in the need for achievement are motivated to excel. They derive satisfaction from working hard to accomplish their goals.

Achievement Motivation Theory

We mentioned the need for achievement, or **achievement motivation,** as a characteristic of successful executives. This desire to accomplish something, to do a good job, and to be the best typifies many people, not only business leaders. People who have a high degree of the need for achievement derive great satisfaction from working to accomplish some goal, and they are motivated to excel in whatever task they undertake.

Since the early 1950s, achievement motivation has been studied intensively by David McClelland and his colleagues (Atkinson & Feather, 1966; McClelland, Atkinson, Clark, & Lowell, 1953). Their research, conducted in several countries, shows that successful business managers consistently display a high need to achieve, regardless of the culture. For example, in Poland, which was then a Communist country, the level of concern for achievement was almost as high as in the United States. McClelland concluded that the economic growth of organizations and societies can be related to the level of the achievement need among employees and citizens (McClelland, 1961).

McClelland's research identified three major characteristics of people who have a high need to achieve:

1. They favor a work environment in which they are able to assume responsibility for solving problems.
2. They tend to take calculated risks and to set moderate, attainable goals.
3. They need continuing recognition and feedback about their progress so that they know how well they are doing.

Achievement motivation
The theory of motivation that emphasizes the need to accomplish something, to do a good job, and to be the best.

Studies have shown a high positive correlation between the achievement motivation scores of executives and the financial success of their companies. Research also shows that managers high in the need to achieve display more respect for their subordinates. These managers are more receptive to new ideas and are more accepting of participative management programs than are managers low in the need to achieve. Need achievement is positively related to subsequent promotions among middle- and upper-level managers. Also, both men and women entrepreneurs have been found to score significantly higher in the need to achieve than men and women employees who are not entrepreneurs.

Research suggests two types of goals—mastery and performance—that can satisfy the need for achievement (Barron & Harackiewicz, 2001). Mastery refers to developing competence and self-satisfaction through acquiring knowledge and skills. Performance goals involve developing competence by performing better than other people, such as co-workers, who are in the same situation. Both types of goals can be satisfied by doing one's job to the best of one's abilities.

However, a study of 170 employees of an energy company in the Netherlands showed that employees with a strong mastery orientation were more effective on the job than were those with a strong performance orientation. Also, those with a high mastery orientation established higher-quality leader-member exchanges (LMXs) with their supervisor, which, in turn, were linked to higher job satisfaction and intrinsic motivation. In contrast, employees with a strong performance orientation established lower-quality LMXs and correspondingly were lower in job satisfaction and intrinsic motivation (Janssen & Van Yperen, 2004).

In general, achievement motivation theory provides a plausible explanation for the motivation of some employees and is considered to have widespread application in the workplace.

Needs Hierarchy Theory

Needs hierarchy theory
The theory of motivation that encompasses physiological, safety, belonging, esteem, and self-actualization needs.

Abraham Maslow developed the **needs hierarchy theory** of motivation in which human needs are arranged in a hierarchy of importance (Maslow, 1970). According to Maslow, we always want what we do not yet have. Consequently, the needs that we have already satisfied no longer provide any motivation for our behavior and new needs must rise to prominence. Once we have satisfied our lower-level needs, we can pay attention to higher-level needs. The needs, from lowest to highest, are as follows:

- *Physiological needs:* The basic human needs, including food, air, water, and sleep, and the drives for sex and activity
- *Safety needs:* The needs for physical shelter and for psychological security and stability
- *Belonging and love needs:* The social needs for love, affection, friendship, and affiliation that involve interaction with and acceptance by other people
- *Esteem needs:* The needs for self-esteem and for esteem, admiration, and respect from other people
- *Self-actualization need:* The need for self-fulfillment, for achieving our full potential and realizing our capabilities

These needs should be satisfied in the order presented. People who are hungry or who fear for their physical safety are too busy attempting to satisfy these needs to be concerned about self-esteem or self-fulfillment. In times of economic hardship, when jobs are scarce, most people are so intent on survival that they cannot attend to higher needs such as self-actualization. However, once we reach a sufficient level of physical and economic security, we can move on; that is, we will be motivated to satisfy the next level of needs.

The belonging needs can be important motivating forces on the job. Workers can develop a social support network and a sense of belonging through interactions with co-workers. Esteem needs can be satisfied by buying a bigger house or car, which contributes to the feeling that we are successful, and through on-the-job rewards such as praise from the boss, a promotion, an office with a window, or a reserved parking space. To satisfy the self-actualization need, employees should be provided with opportunities for growth and responsibility so that they can exercise their abilities to the utmost. A routine and boring job will not satisfy the self-actualization need, no matter how high the salary.

Maslow's theory has received little research support and is judged to have low scientific validity and applicability. Its complexity makes it difficult to test empirically. However, the self-actualization concept became popular with managers and executives who accepted this high-level need as a potent motivating force.

Motivator-Hygiene (Two-Factor) Theory

The **motivator-hygiene (two-factor) theory,** which deals with both motivation and job satisfaction, was proposed by Frederick Herzberg. The theory has inspired a great deal of research, although the results have not been consistently supportive. The scientific validity of the theory is low, yet it has led many organizations to redefine the way many jobs are performed in order to increase employee motivation (Herzberg, 1966, 1974).

According to Herzberg, there are two sets of needs: the motivator needs, which produce job satisfaction, and the hygiene needs, which produce job dissatisfaction. The *motivator needs* (the higher needs) motivate employees to high job performance. Motivator needs are internal to the work itself. They include the nature of the individual job tasks and the worker's level of responsibility, achievement, recognition, advancement, and career development and growth. The motivator needs are similar to Maslow's self-actualization need. They can be satisfied by stimulating, challenging, and absorbing work. When these conditions are met, job satisfaction will result. However, when these conditions are not met—when work is not challenging—the result is not necessarily job dissatisfaction.

Job dissatisfaction is produced by the *hygiene needs* (the lower needs). The word *hygiene* relates to the promotion and maintenance of health. Hygiene needs are external to the tasks of a particular job and involve features of the work environment, such as company policy, supervision, interpersonal relations, working conditions, and salary and benefits. When the hygiene needs are not satisfied, the result is job dissatisfaction. However, when the hygiene needs are satisfied, the result is not necessarily job satisfaction, merely an absence of dissatisfaction. The hygiene needs are similar to Maslow's physiological, safety, and belonging needs. Both Maslow and Herzberg insisted that these lower needs be satisfied before a person can be motivated by higher needs.

Herzberg's theory focused attention on the importance of internal job factors as motivating forces for employees. If the motivator needs stimulate employees to perform at their best and to develop a positive attitude toward the job, then

Motivator-hygiene (two-factor) theory
The theory of motivation that explains work motivation and job satisfaction in terms of job tasks and workplace features.

Job enrichment An effort to expand the scope of a job to give employees a greater role in planning, performing, and evaluating their work.

why not redesign the job to maximize opportunities to satisfy motivator needs? This effort, called **job enrichment,** expands jobs to give employees a greater role in planning, performing, and evaluating their work, thus providing the chance to satisfy their motivator needs. Herzberg suggested the following ways of enriching a job:

1. Remove some management controls over employees and increase their accountability and responsibility for their work, thus increasing employee autonomy, authority, and freedom.
2. Create complete or natural work units where possible—for example, allow employees to produce a whole unit instead of one component of that unit. This policy increases the likelihood that employees will regard their work as meaningful within the total organizational process.
3. Provide regular and continuous feedback on productivity and job performance directly to employees instead of through their supervisors.
4. Encourage employees to take on new, challenging tasks and to become experts in a particular task or operation.

All these proposals have the same goals of increasing personal growth, fulfilling the needs for achievement and responsibility, and providing recognition. Proper job enrichment, therefore, involves more than simply giving the workers extra tasks to perform. It means expanding the level of knowledge and skills needed to perform the job.

This was demonstrated in a study involving 1,039 employees of a glass manufacturing plant. The research showed that job enrichment programs significantly increased their sense of self-efficacy—their belief in their ability to do their jobs (Parker, 1998). The program, which offered opportunities for greater accountability, responsibility, and autonomy, enhanced the employees' feelings of adequacy, efficiency, and confidence that they were performing their jobs well.

Job-Characteristics Theory

Job-characteristics theory The theory of motivation that states that specific job characteristics lead to psychological conditions that can increase motivation, performance, and satisfaction in employees who have a high growth need.

The job enrichment movement led two psychologists to ask which specific job characteristics could be enriched. J. Richard Hackman and G. R. Oldham developed the **job-characteristics theory** of motivation based on their research on objective measures of job factors that correlated with employee satisfaction and attendance (Hackman & Oldham, 1976, 1980). Evidence suggested that certain characteristics influence behavior and attitudes at work, but these characteristics do not influence all employees in the same way. For example, the research documented individual differences in the need for growth. People with a high growth need were found to be more affected by changes in job characteristics than were people with a low growth need. Also, changes in these job characteristics did not seem to influence employee attitudes and behavior directly but were filtered by the employees' cognitive processes—that is, their perceptions of the changes.

The presence of certain job characteristics causes employees to experience a positive emotional state when they perform their job well. This condition motivates them to continue to perform well, on the expectation that good performance will lead to good feelings. The strength of an employee's motivation to perform well depends on the strength of the need to grow and develop. The stronger the need, the more one will value the positive emotional feelings that result from good job performance. Thus, the job-characteristics theory states that specific job characteristics lead to psychological conditions that lead, in turn, to higher motivation, performance, and satisfaction—if employees have a high growth need to begin with.

The core job characteristics identified by Hackman and Oldham are as follows:

1. *Skill variety:* the extent to which workers use various skills and abilities on the job. The more challenging a job, the more meaningful it will be.
2. *Task identity:* the unity of a job—that is, whether it involves doing a whole unit of work or completing a product instead of making only part of a product on an assembly line.
3. *Task significance:* the importance of a job to the lives and well-being of co-workers or consumers. For example, the job of aircraft mechanic affects the lives of more people in a more significant way than does the job of postal clerk.
4. *Autonomy:* the amount of independence employees have in scheduling and organizing their work.
5. *Feedback:* the amount of information employees receive about the effectiveness and quality of their job performance.

Jobs can be redesigned to maximize these characteristics in a manner similar to that proposed earlier by Herzberg:

- Combine small, specialized tasks to form larger work units; this enhances skill variety and task identity.
- Arrange tasks in natural, meaningful work units to make the worker responsible for an identifiable unit; this enhances task identity and task significance.
- Give workers responsibility for direct contact with clients or end users; this enhances skill variety, autonomy, and feedback.
- Give workers authority, responsibility, and control over the job tasks; this increases skill variety, task identity, task significance, and autonomy.
- Arrange for workers to learn regularly how well they are performing the job; this increases feedback.

Hackman and Oldham developed the Job Diagnostic Survey (JDS) to measure three aspects of the theory: (1) employees' perceptions of the job characteristics, (2) employees' level of the growth need, and (3) employees' job satisfaction. The JDS is a self-report inventory consisting of short descriptive phrases about the various job characteristics. Respondents rate how accurately each statement describes their job. A revised version, using positively worded items only, has been found to be more valid than the original version.

The job-characteristics theory continues to stimulate research. Studies on job enrichment programs based on this theory have been more supportive and have shown that adding challenge, complexity, and responsibility to some jobs results in greater employee satisfaction, self-efficacy, and motivation (Campion & Berger, 1990).

As you can see, the content theories of motivation we have described share a common core or central concept. They focus on enlarging, enriching, or redefining jobs to provide greater employee responsibility. They note the importance of opportunities for growth, self-actualization, personal achievement, and increased motivation through increasing the amount of accountability, challenge, control, and autonomy at work. Enlarging the scope of a job can provide personal satisfaction and greater motivation to perform well. Boring and routine jobs can be stultifying and decrease satisfaction and motivation. You might keep this in mind when you apply for your next job.

PROCESS THEORIES OF MOTIVATION

We describe three process models: valence-instrumentality-expectancy (VIE) theory, equity theory, and goal-setting theory.

Valence-Instrumentality-Expectancy (VIE) Theory

Valence-instrumentality-expectancy (VIE) theory
The theory of motivation that states that people make choices that are based on their perceived expectations that certain rewards will follow if they behave in a particular way.

The **valence-instrumentality-expectancy (VIE) theory,** originated by Victor Vroom, asserts that people make choices that are based on their perceived expectancy that certain rewards will follow if they behave in a certain way (Vroom, 1964). In the workplace, employees will choose to perform at the level that results in the greatest payoff or benefit. They will be motivated to work hard if they expect this effort to lead to positive outcomes such as a promotion or pay raise and if those outcomes will be instrumental in leading to other desired results.

The psychological value, or valence, of the reward varies with the individual. In other words, our personal perception of the importance of the outcome determines its strength to us as a motivator. A high salary and increased responsibility have a positive valence for many people. Dangerous working conditions have a negative valence for most people. The outcome may not be as satisfying as we expected, but it is the level of expectancy that determines whether we will work hard to obtain that outcome.

The three facets of the VIE theory are related as follows:

1. Employees must decide whether they expect certain job behaviors—such as coming to work on time, following safe procedures, or improving productivity—to have a high probability of leading to a particular outcome (expectancy).
2. Employees must determine whether that outcome will lead to other outcomes—for example, whether a good attendance record leads to a bonus (instrumentality).
3. Employees must decide whether those outcomes have sufficient value to motivate them to behave a certain way (valence).

Think of your own experience in school. If you have decided that getting high grades in the courses you take in your major is important, then that outcome has a high valence for you. If you're not so concerned about your grades in your other courses, then earning high grades in them has a low valence for you. If you want high grades in your major, you have probably developed the expectancy that attending classes, studying hard, and doing more than the minimum requirements will be instrumental in achieving your goal. These calculations are not

Newsbreak   Driven by the Work Ethic

On September 8, 1995, a baseball player made history. He did it by showing up for work. Cal Ripken, Jr., showed up for work 2,131 times, every time his team, the Baltimore Orioles, played a major league baseball game.

The 42,000 fans in Oriole Park at Camden Yards stadium went wild the night Ripken broke the previous record, held by Lou Gehrig, for the longest streak of consecutive games played. The President of the United States witnessed the historic moment and praised Ripken's discipline, determination, and constancy. A television reporter summed up the excitement that gripped the nation when he described Ripken as "a paragon of the work ethic."

The *work ethic* is a term we hear a lot, and it has been a guiding rule and way of life for generations of American workers. It drives, pushes, goads, and motivates people to work hard like Cal Ripken, to do the best job they can, to be on time, and to show up for work every day. If you are curious about the great driving force of the 19th and 20th centuries that led to unimagined heights of industrial, agricultural, and commercial productivity and economic success, then the work ethic is where you should begin. In most progressive economies, work is not a four-letter word.

It wasn't always that way. There was a time when people were not motivated to perform a job well, or even to do it at all. To the ancient Greeks and Romans, there was nothing noble about work. It was a curse of the gods that brutalized the mind and ruined an otherwise good day. The early Hebrews agreed. Work was a punishment from God, although it was also a necessary evil, a way of improving society and atoning for sin.

The early Christians put a more positive spin on work, viewing it as a way to serve God by sharing the proceeds of one's work with people who were less fortunate. Wealth was a means to charity. Work became holy, and idleness sinful.

But it was John Calvin, the 16th-century French Protestant leader, who gave us the ultimate work ethic. Work alone pleases God, he declared, but to achieve that end, work must be methodical and disciplined. "Not leisure and enjoyment but only activity serves to increase the glory of God."

To Calvin, and others who refined what came to be called the Protestant work ethic, work was an emblem of faith. And so was wealth. It was OK to make a lot of money and not feel guilty about it, as long as you did not enjoy it. Old-fashioned, puritanical, nose-to-the-grindstone toil for its own sake became the motivation that drove millions of people to work hard all their lives and to feel virtuous for doing so. And it still drives many of us each and every day to do the best job we can. And to show up for every game.

Sources: R. Todd. All work, no ethic. *Worth Magazine,* January 1996, pp. 78–84; J. Bair & S. J. Sherer. What happened to the work ethic? *College Park Magazine,* Fall 1995, pp. 18–22.

difficult for most of us to make. Indeed, we may not even be aware of them, but they motivate us and guide our behavior nonetheless.

The VIE theory has received a great deal of research support. It appears to agree with personal experience and common sense. The greater our expectation of receiving a reward, assuming it is of sufficient value, the harder we will work for it.

Equity Theory

Equity theory The theory of motivation that states that our motivation on the job is influenced by our perception of how fairly we are treated.

J. Stacy Adams advanced the **equity theory,** the notion that motivation is influenced by our perception of how equitably or fairly we are treated at work (Adams, 1965). He proposed that in any work environment—whether office, shop, factory, or classroom—we assess our inputs (how much effort we put into the work) and our outcomes (how much reward we receive for the work). We calculate, perhaps unconsciously, the ratio of outcome to input and mentally compare it with what we believe are the ratios for our co-workers. If we think we are getting less than other people, the feeling of tension or inequity that results motivates us to act, to do something to bring about a state of equity. If we perceive that we are receiving the same ratio of reward-to-effort that others are receiving, then a state of equity exists.

Other psychologists have extended the equity theory, suggesting three behavioral response patterns to situations of perceived equity or inequity (Huseman, Hatfield, & Miles, 1987; O'Neil & Mone, 1998). These three types are benevolent, equity sensitive, and entitled. The level of reward received by each type affects motivation, job satisfaction, and job performance.

Benevolent persons, described as altruistic, are satisfied when they are underrewarded compared with co-workers and feel guilty when they are equitably rewarded or overrewarded. Equity-sensitive persons (the type described by the equity theory) believe that everyone should be rewarded fairly. They feel distressed when underrewarded and guilty when overrewarded. Entitled persons believe that everything they receive is their due. They are satisfied only when they are overrewarded and are distressed when underrewarded or equitably rewarded.

It seems intuitively correct to state that if we believe we are being treated fairly in comparison to others, in accordance with our expectations, then we will be motivated to maintain our level of job performance. In contrast, if we think we are being treated unfairly, then we will try to reduce that inequity by reducing our level of performance. Consider the example of major league baseball players (infielders and outfielders). If they have their salaries cut or lose at arbitration during their first year as free agents, they are likely to perform at lower levels during the following season. They may reduce their inputs (batting averages and runs batted in) if they believe that their outcomes (salaries) are too low.

Not all research is supportive of the equity theory, but some studies have shown that employee perceptions of inequity are linked to increased levels of resentment, absenteeism and turnover, and burnout (see, for example, Cropanzano & Greenberg, 1997; Van Dierendonck, Schaufeli, & Buunk, 2001).

Goal-Setting Theory

Goal-setting theory The theory of motivation based on the idea that our primary motivation on the job is defined in terms of our desire to achieve a particular goal.

Developed by Edwin Locke, **goal-setting theory** has a commonsense appeal and is clearly relevant to the workplace. Locke argued that our primary motivation in a work situation is defined in terms of our desire to achieve a particular goal (Locke, 1968; Locke & Latham, 1990). The goal represents what we intend to do at a given time in the future. For example, we may set the goal of graduating from college with honors, achieving the highest sales record in the company, or getting a pay raise within a year so we can buy a new house.

Setting specific and challenging performance goals can motivate and guide our behavior, spurring us to perform in more effective ways. Research has shown that having goals leads to better performance than not having goals. Specific goals are more powerful motivating forces than general goals. Goals that are difficult to attain are greater motivators than goals that are easy to attain. However, difficult goals may spur greater motivation toward attaining the goals at the expense of other behaviors, such as helping co-workers. This type of behavior has the potential for reducing overall organizational effectiveness. In addition, goals that are too difficult, perhaps beyond our capabilities, are worse than having no goals in terms of their impact on motivation and job performance.

An important aspect of the goal-setting theory is individual goal commitment, which is defined in terms of the strength of our determination to reach our goal. A meta-analysis of 83 research studies confirmed that goal commitment has a strong positive effect on the level of our task performance (Klein, Wesson, Hollenback, & Alge, 1999). Goal commitment is influenced by three types of factors: external, interactive, and internal. The external factors that affect goal commitment are authority, peer influence, and external rewards. Complying with the dictates of an authority figure such as a boss has been shown to be an inducement to high goal commitment. Goal commitment increases when the authority figure is physically present, supportive, and trusted. Peer group pressure and external rewards such as pay increases also strengthen goal commitment.

The interactive factors that influence our commitment to reaching our goals are competition and the opportunity to participate in setting goals. These factors have been shown to be an inducement to setting higher goals and to working harder to reach them. Internal cognitive factors that facilitate goal commitment are self-administered rewards and our expectation of success. Commitment to the goal is reduced when our expectation of achieving it declines.

Other personal and situational factors have been related to high goal commitment. These include the need for achievement, endurance, aggressiveness, and competitiveness (so-called Type A behavior), success in achieving difficult goals, high self-esteem, and an internal locus of control. In addition, a meta-analysis of 65 studies found that two of the Big Five personality factors are related to performance motivation, as described by the goal-setting theory. People who score high in conscientiousness and low in neuroticism display high levels of goal-setting-induced motivation (Judge & Ilies, 2002).

The goal-setting theory has generated considerable supportive research. Setting goals has been found to produce substantial increases in employee output. In general, the motivating effects of setting goals are strongest for easy tasks and weakest for more complex tasks. These effects generalize across a variety of organizations, jobs, and tasks. I-O psychologists reviewing 35 years of research concluded that "goal-setting theory is among the most valid and practical theories of employee motivation in organizational psychology" (Locke & Latham, 2002, p. 714).

The process theories are concerned with factors and processes internal to the employee. Instead of focusing on characteristics of the work itself, as with content theories, process theories deal with our thoughts and perceptions about our jobs, our calculations about what we stand to gain in return for our efforts, and the decisions we make based on those calculations. We can be motivated to perform at high levels by our expectations of getting the greatest benefit (VIE theory), by how fairly we perceive we are rewarded relative to our co-workers (equity theory), or by setting challenging goals to strive for (goal-setting theory). Or perhaps we can be motivated by some combination of all of them, at different times and in different situations. Process theories share the common theme that how we perceive the work situation will determine how motivated we are to perform at a high level in that situation.

Interest in work motivation theories has shifted since the 1990s, away from developing new theories and more toward extending, empirically testing, and applying proposed ideas in the workplace. The number of purely theoretical articles published in the leading behavioral science journals declined considerably, while the number of empirical studies increased (Steers, Mowday, & Shapiro, 2004). Does it follow that theories of work motivation are no longer a focus of I-O psychology? No. Although the theories described here have some limitations, most are useful in describing some aspect of employee motivation. The diversity of ideas derived from these theories, which are now being tested in and applied to the workplace, shows the progress we are making in understanding the multiple facets of employee motivation (see Locke & Latham, 2004).

JOB SATISFACTION: THE QUALITY OF LIFE AT WORK

Job satisfaction Our positive and negative feelings and attitudes about our jobs.

Job satisfaction refers to the positive and negative feelings and attitudes we hold about our job, and it is the most frequently studied independent variable in I-O psychology (Kinicki, McKee-Ryan, Schriesheim, & Carson, 2002). It depends on many work-related factors, ranging from our assigned parking space to the sense of fulfillment we get from our daily tasks. Personal factors can also influence job satisfaction. These factors include age, health, length of job experience, emotional stability, social status, leisure activities, and family and other social

Assembly-line workers tend to have low job satisfaction. Routine, repetitive work offers little opportunity for personal growth and development.

relationships. Our motivations and aspirations, and how well these are satisfied by our work, also affect our attitudes toward our jobs.

For some employees, job satisfaction is a stable, enduring characteristic, independent of the features of the job. Changes in job status, pay, working conditions, and goals have little effect on the job satisfaction of these people. Their personal tendency toward happiness (satisfaction) or unhappiness (dissatisfaction) varies little over time and circumstances.

I-O psychologists have suggested, based on research conducted with twins, that attitudes toward work and the satisfactions we expect from it may have a hereditary component. In other words, these feelings may be influenced more by our genetic endowment than by features of the work environment. Nevertheless, it is clear that some people are generally more satisfied with life and, thus, with their work. People who have positive attitudes toward their work are likely to have positive feelings about their personal and family life.

So it is generally accepted that job satisfaction and life satisfaction are positively related, but which one causes the other? Or are both influenced by some third factor? To explore this relationship, a sample of 804 employees, selected to be representative of the U.S. workforce, was interviewed and given questionnaires to assess job and life satisfaction. The results showed a positive and reciprocal relationship between job and life satisfaction in the short term; that is, each one influenced the other. Over time, however, the impact of life satisfaction on job satisfaction was significantly stronger, indicating that general life satisfaction may be the more influential of the two factors. This conclusion was supported in a study of 479 police officers. For them, life satisfaction was influenced more by nonwork factors than by satisfaction with their jobs (Hart, 1999). However, it does not follow that attempts to improve job satisfaction are useless. Remember that the two are interrelated. Job satisfaction still has an effect on life satisfaction.

Measuring Job Satisfaction

The approach used most often to measure employee attitudes is the anonymous questionnaire, typically distributed to employees through the company's e-mail network. Because participation is voluntary, not all workers will complete a questionnaire. There is no way of knowing which employees responded and which did not, or how those who failed to respond differ from those who did respond. It might make a difference if more good workers than poor workers completed the questionnaires.

Two popular attitude surveys are the Job Descriptive Index (JDI) and the Minnesota Satisfaction Questionnaire (MSQ). The JDI contains scales to measure five job factors: pay, promotion, supervision, the nature of the work, and the characteristics of one's co-workers. It can be completed in 15 minutes and has been published in several languages. The MSQ is a rating scale for various levels of satisfaction and dissatisfaction, ranging from very satisfied to very dissatisfied. It covers 20 job facets including advancement, independence, recognition, social status, and working conditions. The MSQ takes 30 minutes to complete; a ten-minute form is also available. These questionnaires have high construct validity.

Personal interviews are sometimes used in conjunction with the questionnaires. In these interviews, employees discuss aspects of their jobs with supervisors or interviewers from the organization's human resources department. Another method of measuring job attitudes is the sentence-completion test. Employees

TABLE 6–1

Level of Satisfaction with Individual Job Facets

Job Facet	Percentage of Employees Expressing Satisfaction
Interest in work	58
Quality of supervisor	55
Commute	55
Vacation policy	51
Job security	50
Sick leave	47
Health plan	40
Wages	37
Flexible work hours plan	37
Promotion policy	22

Source: Survey reported in *St. Petersburg (FL) Times,* August 22, 2002.

are presented with a list of phrases to complete. For example, "My job is _____." or "My job should be _____." In the critical-incidents technique for evaluating job satisfaction, employees are asked to describe job incidents that occurred at times when they felt very good or very bad about their jobs.

Job Facet Satisfaction

Many I-O psychologists suggest that data on overall job satisfaction may not be an adequate measure of the full range of employees' positive and negative attitudes toward all aspects of the work situation. Employees may be satisfied with certain conditions and dissatisfied with others. For example, you may like your work and be comfortable in your office but dislike your boss or your company's health insurance program. A national survey of 5,000 employees at all levels in a variety of occupations found that their satisfaction with specific job facets varied from 22 percent to 58 percent, as shown in Table 6–1.

A single measure of overall job satisfaction fails to make distinctions among these factors. For this reason, psychologists are focusing on measuring more specific facets or aspects of job satisfaction. Some facets appear to apply to all types of jobs and organizations, whereas others are present in only certain job categories.

Job Satisfaction Data

Every year the Gallup Poll organization asks a representative sample of U.S. workers the following question: On the whole, would you say you are satisfied or dissatisfied with the work you do?

The results show consistently that only 10 to 13 percent of the workers questioned each year say that they are dissatisfied with their jobs. Thus, the majority of people are assumed to be satisfied with their jobs. However, when more specific questions are asked about job satisfaction, the results are different. For example, when factory workers are asked if they would like to change jobs, many say yes, even though they claim to be satisfied with their present jobs. When people say they are satisfied, they often mean that they are not dissatisfied. Therefore, when we consider the data on job satisfaction, we must examine the kinds of questions that are asked.

Some job satisfaction studies survey a representative national sample of workers. Others deal with targeted populations, such as the workers in a particular industry, or with specific facets of job satisfaction. Job satisfaction varies with type of occupation. For example, assembly-line workers are significantly less satisfied with their jobs than are office workers. Managers in government agencies are significantly less satisfied than are managers in private industry and business.

Employees of companies on *Fortune* magazine's list of 100 best companies to work for in the United States report high levels of job satisfaction that tend to remain stable over time. Research also shows a high correlation between these employees' positive attitudes toward their companies and the companies' financial performance. The more satisfied workers seem to be, the better is the organization's economic health (Fulmer, Gerhart, & Scott, 2003). To find out more about the top 100 companies and to learn how the ratings were determined, go to the Web site www.greatplacetowork.com.

Impact of Personal Characteristics

Many characteristics of the job and the workplace affect job satisfaction. By redesigning job and work environments, it is possible for management to increase job satisfaction and productivity. Jobs can be redesigned to maximize opportunities to satisfy the needs for achievement, self-actualization, and personal growth. Jobs can be enriched to enhance the motivator needs and the core job characteristics, and to provide higher levels of responsibility.

Personal characteristics linked with job satisfaction include, among others, age, gender, race, cognitive ability, job experience, use of skills, job congruence, organizational justice, personality, job control, and occupational level.

Age. In general, job satisfaction increases with age; the lowest job satisfaction is reported by the youngest workers. This relationship holds for blue-collar and white-collar employees and for men and women employees. Many young people are disappointed with their first jobs because they fail to find sufficient challenge and responsibility. Why does job satisfaction tend to increase with age when the typical reaction to our first job is often disappointment? Three possible explanations have been suggested:

1. The most strongly dissatisfied young workers may drop out of the workforce or change jobs so frequently in their search for satisfaction that they are no longer counted in surveys. This means that the older the sample of employees studied, the fewer dissatisfied people are likely to be included.
2. A sense of resignation develops in some workers as they grow older. They may give up looking for fulfillment and challenge in their work and seek these satisfactions elsewhere. Therefore, they tend to report less dissatisfaction with their jobs.
3. Many older workers have greater opportunities to find fulfillment and self-actualization on the job. Age and experience usually bring increased confidence, competence, esteem, and responsibility. In turn, these feelings lead to a greater sense of accomplishment. In other words, older workers are more likely to have better jobs than are younger workers.

Gender. The research evidence about possible differences in job satisfaction between men and women employees is inconsistent and contradictory. Psychologists have found no clear pattern of differences in job satisfaction. It may not be gender, as such, that relates to job satisfaction as much as the group of factors that vary with gender. For example, women are typically paid less than men for the same work, and their opportunities for promotion are fewer. Most women employees believe that they have to work harder and be more outstanding on the job than men employees before they receive comparable rewards. Obviously, these factors can influence a person's satisfaction.

Race. In general, more White than non-White employees report satisfaction with their jobs. However, before a person can be concerned with job satisfaction, he or she must have a job. Although there is a large, thriving middle class among Black and ethnic minority employees, large numbers of people who want to work are unemployed, are employed irregularly, or are too discouraged to seek employment. Many who have full-time work are confined to low-level jobs that offer marginal pay and little opportunity for advancement or fulfillment. Thus, the primary concern for many workers is not satisfaction but finding a job that pays a decent wage.

Cognitive Ability. Cognitive ability does not appear to be a significant determinant of job satisfaction, but it may be important when related to the type of work a person chooses. For many jobs, there is a range of intelligence associated with high performance and satisfaction. People who are too intelligent for their work may find insufficient challenge, which leads to boredom and dissatisfaction. A survey of 12,686 U.S. workers, a majority of whom were African-American or Hispanic, showed that the more intelligent people held jobs with high interest and challenge. People whose jobs were not sufficiently challenging for their level of intelligence reported great dissatisfaction with their work (Ganzach, 1998).

A factor sometimes related to intelligence is level of education. Some studies have shown that education has a slight negative relationship to job satisfaction. The higher the level of formal education, the more likely a person is to be dissatisfied with the job. One explanation is that better-educated persons have higher expectations and believe that their work should provide greater responsibility and fulfillment. Many jobs do not satisfy these expectations. Employees with college degrees are somewhat more satisfied with their jobs than employees who attended college but did not graduate. This finding may be related to the fact that many higher-level positions are open only to college graduates.

Job Experience. During the initial stage of employment, new workers tend to be satisfied with their jobs. This period involves the stimulation and challenge of developing skills and abilities, and the work may seem attractive just because it is new. This early satisfaction wanes unless employees receive feedback on their progress and tangible evidence of their achievements. After a few years on the job, discouragement is common, often being brought on by the feeling that advancement in the company is too slow.

Job satisfaction appears to increase after a number of years of experience and to improve steadily thereafter. The relationship between job satisfaction and length of work experience parallels the relationship with age. They may be the same phenomenon under different labels.

Use of Skills.   A common complaint, particularly among college graduates in engineering and science, is that their jobs do not allow them to exercise their skills or apply the knowledge acquired during their college training. Surveys of engineers show high dissatisfaction with job facets such as pay, working conditions, supervisors, and opportunities for promotion. Other studies show that people are happier at work if they have the chance to use their abilities. Interviews with workers on an automobile assembly line in Sweden revealed that a major factor in their job satisfaction was the opportunity to perform their work at a high level of quality (Eklund, 1995). When working conditions or the actions of co-workers interfered with work quality, job satisfaction declined.

Job Congruence.   **Job congruence** refers to the match between the demands of a job and the abilities of the employee. The higher the congruence—the closer the fit between a person's skills and attributes and the job's requirements—the greater the job satisfaction. Conversely, a poor fit between job demands and personal skills reduces the potential for job satisfaction.

Job congruence The match between our abilities and the requirements of our jobs.

Organizational Justice.   Organizational justice refers to how fairly employees perceive themselves to be treated by their company. When workers believe they are being treated unfairly (a perceived lack of organizational justice), their job performance, job satisfaction, and organizational commitment are likely to decline. Under these circumstances, employees also report higher levels of stress, and they are more likely to file grievances or seek other jobs. Employees who work for large organizations or for companies with an authoritarian culture are likely to have a low opinion of the level of organizational justice in their workplace. Participation in decision making can contribute to an increase in organizational justice (Schminke, Ambrose, & Cropanzano, 2000).

Personality.   Research suggests that employees who are more satisfied in their work are better adjusted and more emotionally stable. Although the relationship seems clear, the cause-and-effect sequence is not. Which comes first, emotional stability or job satisfaction? Emotional instability or job dissatisfaction? Emotional instability can cause discontent in every sphere of life, and prolonged job dissatisfaction can lead to poor emotional adjustment.

Two personality factors related to job satisfaction are alienation and locus of control. Employees who feel less alienated and who have an internal locus of control are more likely to be high in job satisfaction, job involvement, and organizational commitment. A meta-analysis of 135 studies of job satisfaction confirmed the positive relationship between internal locus of control and job satisfaction. The study also found that high self-esteem and self-efficacy, and low neuroticism, are significantly related to high job satisfaction (Judge & Bono, 2001).

Two dimensions of the Type A personality are also related to job satisfaction. *Achievement striving* (the extent to which people work hard and take the work seriously) is positively related to job satisfaction and job performance. *Impatience/ irritability* (intolerance, anger, hostility, and a sense of time urgency) is negatively related to job satisfaction. The higher the impatience score, the lower the job satisfaction.

Job satisfaction appears to be highest among employees with a high degree of social and institutional trust, that is, those who believe that people and organizations are basically fair and helpful and can be trusted.

Job satisfaction was also found to be high among employees who scored high on the factors of conscientiousness and positive affectivity (which corresponds to extraversion in the Big Five personality factor model) and low on negative affectivity (neuroticism in the Big Five model) (Brief & Weiss, 2002; Ilies & Judge, 2003; Judge, Heller, & Mount, 2002).

An unusual research program studied the self-evaluations of 384 employed adults, including psychological measures of self-esteem, self-efficacy, locus of control, and neuroticism. This long-term study assessed these factors in childhood and again in adulthood. People who scored high in esteem and efficacy and low in neuroticism, and showed an internal locus of control, showed significantly higher job satisfaction in their middle adult years than did people who scored in the opposite direction. Thus, personality factors measured in childhood showed a direct relationship to job satisfaction measured some 30 years later (Judge, Bono, & Locke, 2000).

Job Control. Based on our earlier description of motivational theories, you might predict that people who can exercise greater control over their job duties will be more highly motivated to perform well and will experience greater satisfaction. This prediction was supported in a study of 412 customer service center workers in England. Those who scored high on a questionnaire called the Job Control Scale were found, one year later, to have better mental health and higher levels of job performance and job satisfaction than did those who reported a low level of job control (Bond & Bunce, 2003).

Occupational Level. The higher the occupational or status level of a job, the higher the job satisfaction. Executives express more positive job attitudes and feelings than do first-line supervisors, who, in turn, are usually more satisfied than their subordinates are. The higher the job level, the greater is the opportunity for satisfying motivator needs. Also, high-level jobs offer greater autonomy, challenge, and responsibility. Satisfaction of Maslow's esteem and self-actualization needs also increases with each level in the organizational hierarchy.

Job satisfaction varies with job category. High job satisfaction is more likely to be reported by entrepreneurs (self-employed persons) and by people in technical, professional, and managerial jobs. The least satisfied employees are in manufacturing and service industries and in wholesale and retail businesses.

Losing Your Job

There can be no job satisfaction without a job. I-O psychology research confirms the obvious. Losing one's job or being laid off is stressful for employees and their families. In Japan, layoffs are considered so traumatic that they are called *kubi kiri*, which means "beheading." Specific consequences of layoffs can include feelings of guilt, resentment, depression, and anxiety about the future, as well as physical complaints, alcohol abuse, drug abuse, divorce, spouse and child abuse, and thoughts of suicide.

Employees with higher-level jobs appear to suffer more greatly from unemployment. Employees with lower-level jobs seem to be more adaptable. Executives, managers, and professionals tend to become defensive and self-critical. Losing a job typically leads to significant changes in lifestyle, expectations, goals, and values. The psychological contract these employees believed they had with their employer has been breached. The unwritten agreement stating that if they worked hard and

Unemployment can lead to anxiety that may persist even after a new job has been found.

showed loyalty to the company, then the company would respond with job security, pay raises, and promotions, can no longer be relied upon. Many people who have lost their jobs feel a sense of betrayal. A study of 756 employees who lost their jobs found that over a two-year period the feeling of loss of personal control was especially harmful. In many cases it led to chronic physical health problems and impaired emotional functioning (Price, Choi, & Vinokur, 2002).

Negative reactions to layoffs can be minimized if management is honest with employees about the reasons for the dismissals. Well-informed employees are more likely to view the layoffs as fair, to continue to speak positively about the company, and to express no intention of suing for wrongful termination. Finding a new position typically reverses the negative effects of losing one's job. However, the nature of the new job relative to the old one can make a difference. A study of 100 workers found that those who were dissatisfied with their new job continued to experience most of the negative effects associated with being dismissed from their previous job (Kinicki, Prussia, & McKee-Ryan, 2000).

A survey of 202 adults who had lost their jobs showed that those who began job-hunting immediately did not improve their chances of finding a new job. Those who waited to begin their job search until they had dealt with such negative emotions as depression and low self-esteem appeared more secure and confident and less nervous during their subsequent job interviews. The people who waited also reported higher job satisfaction with their new jobs than did those who began their job search right away (Gowan, Riordan, & Gatewood, 1999).

When large-scale layoffs occur in an organization, the employees who have kept their jobs are also affected. Often they worry that they will be among the next to be dismissed. A report for the U.S. Department of Labor noted that half of the layoff survivors questioned reported increased job stress, lower morale, and reduced job commitment. Also, 60 percent reported greatly increased workloads because workers remaining on the job still had to meet production goals even though there were fewer workers. Also, the layoff survivors reported a decrease in feelings of commitment to the organization since their friends and co-workers had been dismissed (Shah, 2000).

Newsbreak

Grades Slipping? Maybe It's Not Your Fault

How good are you at assessing your parents' moods? Can you sense when they seem worried or upset about something, like maybe losing a job?

Psychologists have learned that children from ages ten to 17 are keenly aware when their parents experience feelings of insecurity about their work. For example, when children believe that their fathers are uneasy about their work situation, the children's attitudes toward their school-work will change and their grades are likely to drop. However, this effect was found only with fathers' jobs. When mothers experienced job insecurity, the children did not seem to be affected.

At Queen's University in Canada, psychologists investigated this situation in college students, even though they were no longer living with their parents at home. Would college students pick up on their parents' job anxiety and insecurity even though they didn't see or talk to them every day? And if so, would their own work, their academic performance, be altered?

The subjects in this experiment were 120 undergraduates under the age of 21. A questionnaire surveyed their perception of their parents' level of job security. A sample question was the following: *My mother/father can be sure of his/her present job as long as he/she does good work.* Two other questionnaires were administered. One measured cognitive functioning, and the other measured the student's level of identification with his or her parents.

Parents were asked to complete a questionnaire about their perceived level of job security. It included such items as this: *I am not really sure how long my present job will last.*

The results showed that college students were sensitive to their parents' feelings about their work, even though they no longer had daily contact with them. Like the younger children studied, the college students' grades fell with a decline in their parents' job security. Again, the effect was greater with fathers than with mothers. However, students who indicated a greater level of identification with their mothers were more likely to show a decline in grades than were students who identified more closely with their fathers.

So if you're a parent, remember that being laid off, or even fearing a lay-off, can have consequences for your children. And if you're a college student, maybe you should think twice before calling home and asking Mom or Dad how they're doing at work.

Source: J. Barling, A. Zacharatos, & C. G. Hepburn (1999). Parents' job insecurity affects children's academic performance through cognitive difficulties. *Journal of Applied Psychology, 84,* 437–444.

A survey of 283 employees in a company undergoing a major reorganization showed that their sense of job insecurity, from worry about being laid off, was related to a decrease in their organizational commitment and an increase in their stress levels and health problems. Employees who reported a high sense of job involvement experienced health problems and greater stress than did employees who were less involved with their jobs (Probst, 2000). A study of 1,297 workers in Finland reported that those who were concerned about being downsized experienced decreased levels of work motivation and well-being and a high level of stress. Even rumors about the possibility of company downsizing were sufficient to cause measurable increases in stress (Kalimo, Taris, & Schaufeli, 2003). A meta-analysis of more than 28,000 employees in 50 samples found that feelings of job insecurity correlated highly with health problems, negative attitudes toward their employer, and expressed intention to seek employment elsewhere (Sverke, Hellgren, & Naswall, 2002).

JOB SATISFACTION AND ON-THE-JOB BEHAVIOR

We have described several factors that influence job satisfaction. Now let us consider those aspects of our behavior at work that can be affected by our level of satisfaction.

Productivity.   Ample research has demonstrated a strong and significant relationship between job satisfaction and job performance: The higher the reported satisfaction, the higher the level of performance (see, for example, Judge, Thoresen, Bono, & Patton, 2001). When 4,467 employees, 143 managers, and 9,903 customers of a restaurant chain were surveyed, the results showed that employee satisfaction affected not only customer satisfaction but also the restaurant's level of profitability. When employees reported high job satisfaction, so did customers, who were then likely to spend more money at the restaurant (Koys, 2001).

Most job satisfaction research has focused on individual employees. More recently, I-O psychologists have turned their attention to collective measures of job satisfaction, that is, the satisfaction level of a business unit such as a work team, section, or department. A meta-analysis of 7,939 business units in 36 companies demonstrated that employee satisfaction at the collective level was positively related to customer satisfaction and loyalty, and to employee productivity and safety on the job. High collective job satisfaction was also related to reduced turnover rates (Harter, Schmidt, & Hayes, 2002).

Prosocial and Counterproductive Behavior.   High job satisfaction has been related to **prosocial behavior,** that is, to helpful behavior directed at customers, co-workers, and supervisors to the benefit of employees and their organization. Does it follow that low job satisfaction is related to antisocial actions or to counterproductive behavior that may thwart organizational goals? Negative employee behavior can interfere with production and lead to faulty products, poor service, destructive rumors, theft, and sabotaged equipment. Employees may view these behaviors as a way of striking back at an organization because of real or imagined grievances.

Studies have shown a positive relationship between job dissatisfaction and counterproductive behavior for workers over the age of 30. This does not mean that older workers engage in more negative behaviors than do younger workers; the frequency of negative behaviors is higher for employees under 30. What the research indicates is that only in older workers has counterproductive behavior been related to job dissatisfaction.

Prosocial behavior
Behaviors directed toward supervisors, co-workers, and clients that are helpful to an organization.

Absenteeism.   Absenteeism is widespread and costly for organizations. On any given workday in the United States, up to 20 percent of employees do not show up for work. Absenteeism costs businesses more than $30 billion a year.

Absenteeism has plagued industry since the invention of machines. In textile mills in Wales in the 1840s, the absenteeism rate was approximately 20 percent. During the two-week period following each monthly payday, absenteeism often reached 35 percent. Throughout the 19th century in England, workers typically took off Mondays—"Saint Monday," they called it—to recover from weekend drinking bouts. Factory owners levied stiff fines and dismissed many workers, but that had no impact on attendance.

Much of industry's absenteeism data come from self-reports. Suppose you were filling out a questionnaire dealing with your job performance. One of the questions asked how many days of work you missed over the past year. Would you answer accurately? Or would you underreport the number of times you were absent? Would you be tempted to say that you missed only two days when the actual number was nearer to ten? Studies with diverse groups of workers consistently demonstrate the underreporting of absences by as much as four days a year. Managers also tend to underreport the extent of absenteeism in their work groups. About 90 percent of employees claim to have above-average attendance records. Clearly, many of us are less than honest about admitting the amount of time we lose from work.

If self-report absenteeism data are sometimes inaccurate, then why not use a company's personnel records to get a true indication of the absenteeism situation? That's a good idea in theory, but it does not work well in practice. Many companies do not compile attendance data in any systematic fashion. For managers and professional employees, such as engineers and scientists, such data are rarely collected at all. So when you read a study about absenteeism and learn that the data come from self-reports, you know that the actual number of absences is likely to be higher.

Not surprisingly, the more liberal an organization's sick-leave policy, the higher its absenteeism rate. Absenteeism is also high in companies that do not require proof of illness, such as a physician's note. High-paying manufacturing industries have higher absenteeism rates than do low-paying industries. The more money employees earn, the more likely they are to feel entitled to take time off. Workers in routine jobs often have a higher absence rate than workers in more interesting, challenging jobs.

Societal values may foster absenteeism, as is evident in variations in absentee rates for different countries. In Japan and Switzerland, where job attendance is considered to be a duty, absenteeism rates are low. In Italy, where societal attitudes toward work are more permissive, companies routinely hire 15 percent more workers than needed to make sure that enough people report to work each day to maintain operations.

Management often contributes to an organizational climate that appears to condone absenteeism by failing to enforce company policy. If management is believed to be lenient and unconcerned about absences, some employees will take advantage of the situation. Economic conditions can influence absenteeism rates. In general, when a company is in the process of laying off workers, absenteeism rates decline. Absenteeism increases when the overall employment rate is high, a time when workers feel more secure about their jobs. Also, younger workers are far more likely to take unauthorized time from work than are older workers.

Personal factors can also influence absenteeism. For example, a study of 362 blue-collar workers for an automobile manufacturer in Australia found that those who scored high in positive affectivity (which includes characteristics such as a high activity level, enthusiasm, sociability, and extraversion) had a significantly lower rate of absenteeism on the job than did those who scored low in positive affectivity (Iverson & Deery, 2001). Research on 323 health service workers in England showed that work-related psychological distress and depression correlated significantly with absenteeism rates. Employees who reported greater levels of distress were far more likely to have greater absenteeism than were those who reported less job-related distress (Hardy, Woods, & Wall, 2003).

Research has also suggested that absenteeism can be reduced through a company-sponsored program of rewards and recognition for good attendance records. A garment manufacturer established a program of monthly, quarterly, and annual rewards for low absenteeism rates. For example, employees who did not miss work for a period of a month had their names posted with a gold star. Good attendance for longer periods qualified workers for more expensive gifts such as gold necklaces or penknives. Absenteeism under this program declined significantly from its former level, and employees reported a high degree of satisfaction with the incentive system (Markham, Scott, & McKee, 2002).

Turnover. Turnover is also costly for organizations. Every time someone quits, a replacement must be recruited, selected, trained, and permitted time on the job to gain experience. Evidence relating high turnover to high job dissatisfaction is strong. Studies have shown that both intended and actual turnover can be attributed to dissatisfaction with various aspects of the job such as low pay or poor leadership.

Organizational commitment is strongly related to turnover. The greater a person's commitment to the job and the company, the less likely he or she is to quit. Age, however, does not seem to be a factor that affects turnover. Turnover is higher in times of low unemployment and expanding job opportunities than it is in times of high unemployment and limited opportunities. When people perceive that the economic climate is good and the economy is growing, they find it easier to consider changing jobs in the hope of increasing their job satisfaction.

Jobs that require a high level of creativity tend to be high in challenge, complexity, and autonomy and low on organizational control and supervision. A survey of 2,200 employees showed that people in highly creative and challenging jobs reported higher job satisfaction and lower turnover intentions than did people whose jobs did not offer these characteristics (Shalley, Gilson, & Blum, 2000).

There is a crucial difference between absenteeism and turnover. Whereas absenteeism is almost always harmful to the organization, turnover is not necessarily so. Sometimes it is the unsatisfactory employees who leave the company. I-O psychologists distinguish between *functional turnover*, when poor performers quit, and *dysfunctional turnover*, when good performers quit.

And what about involuntary turnover, such as downsizing or a RIF (reduction in force), when a number of employees are terminated usually as a cost-cutting measure? We noted above that such layoffs have harmful effects not only on the employees who have lost their jobs, but also on the employees who remain with the company. A study of 31 work units of a national financial services company showed that involuntary turnover events had a significant negative effect on the job performance and productivity of the remaining workers. Thus, downsizing was related to the organization's level of productivity (McElroy, Morrow, & Rude, 2001).

MOTIVATION, JOB SATISFACTION, AND PAY

Considerable research has demonstrated a positive relationship between pay and job satisfaction. Pay also affects job and organizational performance. For example, a study of 333 hospitals in California found that high pay among hospital staff members, including physicians and nonphysicians in all job categories, resulted in high positive patient care outcomes and high financial performance for the hospital (Brown, Storman, & Simmering, 2003).

Perceived Pay Equity

The perceived equity or fairness of one's pay can be more important than the actual amount. Survey respondents who believed that people with similar qualifications earned more than they did reported dissatisfaction with their pay. They thought they were being paid less than they deserved. It is not surprising, then, that people who think their salaries are higher than those of their colleagues are likely to be more satisfied with their pay. You may recognize this as a real-world example of the equity theory of motivation, discussed earlier in this chapter.

Most of us develop personal standards of comparison that are based on the minimum salary we consider acceptable, the pay we believe our job deserves, and the amount we think our co-workers are being paid. Thus, satisfaction with pay is determined by the discrepancy between our standards and our actual salary.

Of course, as we have seen, for some groups in American society there is little pay equity, either actual or perceived. In general, women are paid less than men for the same or similar work, and many ethnic minority employees are paid less than Whites. Also, you might think that a family member CEO of a family-controlled company would have a higher salary than a CEO who is not a member of the family of a family-controlled company. A study of 253 family-owned companies over a four-year period revealed, however, that CEOs who were family members actually received lower pay and bonuses than CEOs who were not related to the family (Gomez-Mejia, Larraza-Kintana, & Makri, 2003).

Merit Pay

Merit pay A wage system in which pay is based on level of performance.

Merit pay, or pay for performance, means that the better-performing workers in an organization are paid more than the less productive workers. This wage system is fine in theory but does not translate well to the realities of the workplace. I-O psychologists have studied various influences on the size of the pay raises given under merit pay plans. They have found widespread disagreement among managers about the behaviors that they consider important in making decisions about a worker's pay increase. A worker in one department might receive a sizable raise for job behaviors that bring no recognition in another department. Supervisors who receive substantial pay raises tend to recommend larger raises for their subordinates than do supervisors who receive smaller pay raises.

Pay raises are also related to the degree to which managers rely on their subordinates' expertise and support and whether managers consider such dependence a threat. For example, a manager who is low in self-esteem may want subordinates to provide praise or positive feedback and therefore may be reluctant to give them low pay increases. The manager may fear that if subordinates do

Newsbreak

Unequal Pay for Women, and for Men, Too

Patti Landers was delighted when she got a job as an engineer with the Boeing Company in her home town of Seattle, Washington. Working at Boeing was a family tradition; her father, brother, and husband all had jobs with the aircraft manufacturer. Years before, her grandparents had also worked there. It seemed like a great opportunity, and it was, until Patti compared the amount of her paycheck with what the men in her family were earning—and found a big, big difference. She felt cheated, so she and 37 other women filed a sex discrimination lawsuit against the company.

Boeing denied the allegation that women were paid less than men for doing the same work. But *Business Week* magazine obtained more than 12,000 pages of company documents showing that Boeing had conducted several internal studies that confirmed that men were paid more than women for the same job. Yet Boeing still fought the lawsuit, even though their own documents—which they had taken the trouble to hide in a secure room with an electronic cipher lock—proved that they had known about the pay inequities for ten years.

If the company loses the suit, which has grown to a class-action suit on behalf of 28,000 women employees of Boeing, it could cost the company more than $1 billion, far more money than they saved by paying women workers less than men. A company spokesperson insisted, however, that Boeing was committed to "equal rights."

Company policies such as these are nothing new. The majority of businesses have typically paid women less than men for performing the same or similar jobs. What is new is a study showing that *both women and men* who manage work groups composed mostly of women are paid less than those who manage work groups composed mostly of men.

A study of 2,178 managers in 512 companies demonstrated that in work groups that are 40 to 50 percent female, the managers are paid substantially less than when their work groups have a majority of males. As the percentage of female employees in a work group increases, the pay of their manager decreases. The researchers concluded that pay is unequal for men, too, if the group they manage is composed mostly of women.

Sources: S. Holmes (April 26, 2004). A new black eye for Boeing: Internal documents suggest years of serious compensation gaps for women. *Business Week,* pp. 90–92; C. Ostroff & L. Atwater (2003). Does whom you work with matter? Effects of referent group gender and age composition on managers' compensation. *Journal of Applied Psychology, 88,* 725–740.

not receive a sufficient salary, they will withhold their support or reduce their productivity to make the manager look bad.

There is also evidence that not everyone who receives a merit pay increase reacts to it positively. The effects of merit pay raises were studied over an eight-month period among more than 1,700 hospital employees at all levels from housekeepers to physicians. The effect of the pay increases on employee motivation and job performance was greater among employees who scored low in positive affectivity than among employees who scored high in positive affectivity. In other words, greater pay for better performance was considered to be of greater value by employees who were more introverted and pessimistic and less energetic. Perhaps they needed the recognition and appreciation of the merit pay raise more than did those whose higher positive affectivity (greater energy and optimism) were more independent of the circumstances of their employment (Shaw, Duffy, Mitra, Lockhart, & Bowler, 2003).

Wage-Incentive Pay Systems

Wage-incentive system The primary pay system for production workers, in which the more units produced, the higher the wage.

There are also problems with **wage-incentive systems,** the primary pay scheme for production workers. Through a time-and-motion analysis of a production job, an average or standard number of units produced in a given time can be determined. The wage-incentive system is based on this rate. In theory, the system provides an incentive for high job performance—the more units produced, the higher the wage—but it seldom works in practice. Many work groups establish their own standard for a good shift's production. Regardless of the incentive offered, they will not produce more but will spread out the work to comfortably fill the hours. Surveys show that most workers prefer a straight hourly payment system.

JOB INVOLVEMENT AND ORGANIZATIONAL COMMITMENT

Closely related to motivation and job satisfaction is job involvement; that is, the intensity of a person's psychological identification with the job. Usually, the higher one's identification or involvement with a job is, the greater the job satisfaction. Job involvement is related to several personal and organizational variables.

Personal Factors

Personal characteristics important in job involvement are age, growth needs, and belief in the traditional work ethic. Older workers are usually more involved with their jobs, perhaps because they have more responsibility and challenge and more opportunity to satisfy their growth needs. Older workers are also more likely to believe in the value of hard work. Younger workers, typically in entry-level positions, hold less stimulating and challenging jobs.

Because growth needs are important in job involvement, it follows that the job characteristics most relevant to job involvement are stimulation, autonomy, variety, task identity, feedback, and participation, the characteristics that allow for the satisfaction of the growth needs.

Social factors on the job can also influence job involvement. Employees who work in groups or teams report stronger job involvement than employees who work alone. Participation in decision making is related to job involvement, as is the extent to which employees support organizational goals. Feelings of success and achievement on the job enhance one's level of job involvement.

The relationship between job involvement and job performance is unclear. Employees with high job involvement are more satisfied with, and more successful at, their jobs. Their rates of turnover and absenteeism are lower than those of employees with low job involvement. However, we cannot state with certainty that high job involvement correlates with high performance.

Another variable allied with motivation and job satisfaction is organizational commitment—that is, the degree of psychological identification with or attachment to the company for which we work. Organizational commitment has the following components:

- Acceptance of the organization's values and goals.
- Willingness to exert effort for the organization.
- Having a strong desire to remain affiliated with the organization.

Organizational commitment is related to both personal and organizational factors. Older employees who have been with a company more than two years and who have a high need to achieve are more likely to rate high in organizational commitment. A meta-analysis of 3,630 employees in 27 separate studies showed that the longer a person had been employed by a company, the stronger was the link between organizational commitment and job performance. The researchers suggested that taking measures to increase organizational commitment early in new employees could lead to better job performance (Wright & Bonett, 2002). Scientists and engineers appear to have less organizational commitment than do employees in other occupational groups. In addition, government employees have lower organizational commitment than do employees in the private sector. Government employees are also likely to be lower in job satisfaction.

Organizational Factors

Organizational factors associated with high organizational commitment include job enrichment, autonomy, opportunity to use skills, and positive attitudes toward the work group. Organizational commitment is influenced by employees' perception of how committed the organization is to them. The greater the perceived commitment to employees, the higher the employees' expectations that if they work to meet organizational goals, they will be equitably rewarded.

A study of 746 employees of a university showed that those who scored high in organizational commitment were more dedicated to a company-sponsored program designed to improve work quality than were those who scored low in organizational commitment (Neubert & Cady, 2001). There is also a positive relationship between perceived organizational support and organizational commitment, diligence, innovative management, job performance, and attendance. Organizational commitment is positively related to the amount of support received from supervisors and co-workers and to the degree of satisfaction with supervisors (Bishop & Scott, 2000; Liden, Wayne, & Sparrowe, 2000).

Studies have confirmed a positive relationship between organizational justice and organizational commitment. People who believe their employer treats them fairly are more likely to feel a commitment to the company than are people who believe they are being treated unfairly (Simons & Roberson, 2003).

Gender seems to be related to organizational commitment. The more women employees in a work group, the lower the commitment of the men. With women, however, the reaction is the opposite. The more men there are in a work group, the higher the level of organizational commitment among the women.

Job satisfaction is related to workplace conditions. For some employees, an exercise facility at the workplace fosters a positive attitude toward the job.

Types of Commitment

I-O psychologists have identified three kinds of organizational commitment: affective or attitudinal commitment, behavioral or continuance commitment, and normative commitment (Esnape & Redman, 2003; Meyer & Allen, 1991). In *affective commitment*, the type we have been discussing, the employee identifies with the organization, internalizes its values and attitudes, and complies with its demands. Affective commitment correlates highly with perceived organizational support, as was shown in research with 333 retail employees studied over a two-year period and 226 employees studied over a three-year period (Rhoades, Eisenberger, & Armeli, 2001). The results demonstrated that perceived organizational support was a primary factor in the development of affective commitment.

A review and meta-analysis of more than 70 studies also found a strong positive link between perceived organizational support and affective commitment (Rhoades & Eisenberger, 2002). A study of 211 employee-supervisor dyads showed that supervisor support and recognition was related to perceived organizational support, which, in turn, was related to organizational commitment (Wayne, Shore, Bommer, & Tetrick, 2002). The importance of supervisor support in increasing perceived organizational support was also demonstrated in a study of 493 retail sales employees. That study also found that high perceived organizational support was strongly related to reduced turnover (Eisenberger, Stingchamber, Vandenberghe, Socharski, & Rhoades, 2002).

Other research involving 413 postal workers found a reciprocal relationship between perceived organizational support and affective commitment, which suggests that each factor strengthens the other. The more employees believe their company cares for them and supports their needs, the more strongly they identify with the company and internalize its values and attitudes, and vice versa (Eisenberger, Armeli, Rexwinkel, Lynch, & Rhoades, 2001).

In *behavioral commitment*, the employee is bound to the organization only by peripheral factors such as pension plans and seniority, which would not continue if the employee quit. There is no personal identification with organizational goals and values. Research suggests that affective commitment is positively related to job performance, but behavioral commitment is negatively related to job performance.

Normative commitment involves a sense of obligation to remain with the employer, a feeling that develops when the employees receive benefits such as tuition reimbursement or specific skills training.

Organizational Citizenship Behavior

Organizational citizenship behavior involves putting forth extra effort, doing more for your employer than the minimum requirements of your job. It includes such behaviors as "taking on additional assignments, voluntarily assisting other people at work, keeping up with the developments in one's field or profession, following company rules even when no one is looking, promoting and protecting the organization, and keeping a positive attitude and tolerating inconveniences at work" (Bolino & Turnley, 2003, p. 60).

Good organizational citizens are model employees whose behavior can help ensure the success of an organization. Studies in a variety of businesses—including insurance agencies, paper mills, and fast-food restaurant chains—have demonstrated that employees who are high in organizational citizenship behaviors are more productive and offer better service, which is related to higher customer satisfaction and greater company profits (see, for example, Bolino & Turnley, 2003; Koys, 2001; Walz & Niehoff, 2000).

Some research has shown that people who display organizational citizenship behaviors score high on the factors of conscientiousness, extraversion, optimism, and altruism. They are also team-oriented. A study of 149 nurses in Canada found a strong cognitive component to organizational citizenship behavior. Good organizational citizens based their behaviors on deliberate rational calculations as to how they would benefit from displaying such behaviors on the job (Lee & Allen, 2002). Essentially, they seemed to be saying, "What's in it for me if I behave this way on the job?" But consider this: How much of our motivation, job satisfaction, and job involvement are influenced by pragmatic (some would say, self-serving) calculations?

Summary

Content theories of motivation deal with internal needs that influence behavior. Process theories focus on cognitive processes involved in making decisions. **Achievement motivation** theory posits the need to accomplish something and to be the best in whatever one undertakes. **Needs hierarchy theory** proposes five needs (physiological, safety, belonging, esteem, and self-actualization), each of which must be satisfied before the next becomes prominent. **Motivator-hygiene theory** proposes motivator needs (the nature of the work and its level of achievement and responsibility) and hygiene needs (aspects of the work environment such as pay and supervision). An outgrowth of motivator-hygiene theory is **job enrichment,** the redesign of jobs to maximize motivator factors.

Job-characteristics theory proposes individual differences in growth needs and suggests that employee perceptions of job characteristics influence motivation.

The **valence-instrumentality-expectancy (VIE) theory** describes a person's perceived expectation of the rewards that will follow certain behaviors. **Equity theory** deals with the ratio of outcome to input and how equitably that ratio compares with those of co-workers. **Goal-setting theory** suggests that motivation is defined by one's intention to achieve a particular goal.

Job satisfaction can be measured through questionnaires and interviews. It may be partly an inherited characteristic reciprocally related to overall life satisfaction. Job facet satisfaction refers to individual aspects of the job that can influence employee attitudes. Job satisfaction increases with age, length of job experience, and occupational level. Sex differences in reported job satisfaction are inconsistent. Job satisfaction appears unaffected by cognitive ability, assuming one's job is sufficiently challenging. Other factors affecting job satisfaction include **job congruence,** organizational justice, use of skills, personality, and control. Losing one's job can be damaging to self-esteem and health. Large-scale layoffs also affect those workers remaining on the job.

Research shows a significant relationship between job satisfaction and job performance. The higher the job satisfaction, the higher the performance, a relationship that holds for individuals and for business units such as work teams. Job satisfaction can result in **prosocial behavior;** job dissatisfaction can lead to counterproductive behavior that interferes with organizational goals. Absenteeism is higher among younger workers and in companies with liberal sick-leave policies. Absenteeism is high in low-status jobs and in high-paying jobs and can be caused by low positive affectivity and high levels of stress and depression. Turnover is allied with low job involvement, low organizational commitment, poor promotion opportunities, and dissatisfaction with pay and supervision. In functional turnover, low performers quit; in dysfunctional turnover, high performers quit.

There appears to be a positive relationship between pay and job satisfaction. An important factor in pay satisfaction is its perceived equity and relationship to job performance. Blue-collar workers on **wage-incentive systems** and managers on **merit pay** systems report pay dissatisfaction. Merit pay can lower work motivation because of perceived unfairness; one's true abilities may not be sufficiently rewarded.

Job involvement (intensity of psychological identification with work) is related to job satisfaction. Involvement is affected by personal characteristics such as age, growth needs, and belief in the work ethic, and by job characteristics such as level of challenge and opportunity for employee participation.

Organizational commitment is related to motivation and satisfaction and is greater among older employees and those high in achievement motivation. Also contributing to organizational commitment are job enrichment, autonomy, perceived organizational support, organizational justice, and a positive attitude toward the work group. Three types of commitment are affective commitment, behavioral commitment, and normative commitment.

Organizational citizenship behavior involves doing more for your employer than the job requires. It can lead to higher job performance and can be influenced by personality and by self-serving decisions.

achievement motivation
equity theory
goal-setting theory
job-characteristics theory
job congruence
job enrichment
job satisfaction

merit pay
motivator-hygiene (two-factor) theory
needs hierarchy theory
prosocial behavior
valence-instrumentality-expectancy
   theory
wage-incentive systems

1. Explain the differences between content theories and process theories of motivation. Give an example of each. What do these types of theories have in common?
2. What two types of goals can satisfy the need for achievement?
3. Describe the characteristics of people who are high in the need for achievement.
4. What are the needs in Maslow's needs hierarchy theory? Which needs can be satisfied on the job?
5. Distinguish between motivator needs and hygiene needs. Describe how each type affects job satisfaction.
6. How would you enrich the job of an automobile assembly-line worker?
7. In what ways does the motivator-hygiene theory differ from the job-characteristics theory? In what ways are they similar?
8. Give an example of how the VIE theory can be applied to your job as a student.
9. According to equity theory, what are three ways of responding to perceived equity or inequity? Which way best describes you?
10. Can goal-setting theory be applied to the workplace? If so, give an example of how it would work.
11. How can I-O psychologists measure job satisfaction? What personal characteristics can influence our level of job satisfaction?
12. Describe some effects of losing one's job. How does job loss affect the company employees who were not laid off?
13. What is prosocial behavior? How does it relate to job satisfaction?
14. Discuss the relationship between job satisfaction and job performance for individual employees and for work groups.
15. Why is it difficult to conduct research on absenteeism? What organizational policies may contribute to a high absenteeism rate?
16. Distinguish between functional turnover and dysfunctional turnover.
17. How does a merit pay system differ from a wage-incentive pay system? What are the problems with each of these approaches?
18. What is the difference between job involvement and organizational commitment?
19. Discuss personal and organizational factors that can influence organizational commitment.
20. Describe three types of organizational commitment.
21. What is organizational citizenship behavior? Give two examples of organizational citizenship behavior and tell what you think motivates it.

Additional Reading

Brown, M., & Heywood, J. S. (Eds.) (2003). *Paying for performance: An international comparison.* Armonk, NY: M. E. Sharpe. Discusses the use of pay-for-performance systems to encourage employee productivity in eight Western industrialized countries. Notes cultural differences as well as potential dysfunctional consequences of implementing such systems. Also considers the use of bonuses, promotions, tax breaks, seniority, and profit-sharing as part of an incentive package.

Dessler, G. (1999). How to earn your employees' commitment. *Academy of Management Executive, 13*(2), 58–67. Describes how modern organizations must clearly communicate the organization's mission, guarantee organizational justice, and support employee development.

Ellingson, J. E., Gruys, M. L., & Sackett, P. R. (1998). Factors related to the satisfaction and performance of temporary employees. *Journal of Applied Psychology, 83,* 913–921. Discusses job satisfaction among temp employees (a large but rarely studied subject group) and relates it to whether the decision to undertake temporary work is voluntary or involuntary.

Fraser, J. A. (2001). *White collar sweatshop: The deterioration of work and its rewards in corporate America.* New York: W. W. Norton. Assesses trends in the U.S. corporate workplace based on interviews with employees from entry level through upper management representing all major industries. Suggests from this anecdotal evidence that American workers are overworked, undervalued, struggling to balance work and family demands, vulnerable to job loss, and facing fewer opportunities for promotion.

Ganzach, Y. (1998). Intelligence and job satisfaction. *Academy of Management Journal, 41*(5), 526–539. Reviews research on the relationship between cognitive variables, level of education, and job satisfaction as affected by the complexity of the job.

Greenberg, J., & Cropanzano, R. (Eds.) (2001). *Advances in organizational justice.* Stanford, CA: Stanford University Press. Reviews research, theories, and practical implications of organizational justice, defined as the study of people's perceptions of fairness in their organization. Recognizes differences in perceptions among various ethnic groups and supervisory levels.

Hart, P. M. (1999). Predicting employee life satisfaction. *Journal of Applied Psychology, 84,* 564–584. Reports on personality correlates (such as neuroticism, extraversion, and job satisfaction) that relate to overall life satisfaction in a group of police officers.

Lawler, E. E., III. (2000). *Rewarding excellence: Pay strategies for the new economy.* San Francisco: Jossey-Bass. A model for pay systems recognizing the interdependence of several factors: global competition, changing technology, employee skills and knowledge, organizational structure, business strategies, and rewards for individual and team performance. Notes the importance of an appropriate reward system for attracting, developing, and retaining outstanding employees.

Wright, T. A., & Cropanzano, R. (2000). Psychological well-being and job satisfaction as predictors of job performance. *Journal of Occupational Health Psychology, 5*(1), 84–94. Analyzes the idea that the so-called happy worker is a more productive worker. Relates happiness (psychological well-being) and job satisfaction to job performance.

Chapter 7
Consumer Psychology

Chapter 7

Consumer Psychology

THE SCOPE OF CONSUMER PSYCHOLOGY

There is no escaping the influence of consumer psychology. Pick up a magazine, turn on the radio or TV, go online, or drive down a billboard-lined road, and almost everywhere you will be bombarded by thousands of advertising messages every day. Your phone company sends advertising flyers with your monthly bill. The supermarket prints ads on the back of your cash register receipt. Theaters showing popular films also run commercials. Public buildings post ads on the inside of the stall doors in the restrooms.

Banks run ads on their ATMs and spew out money-saving coupons with your cash. Office buildings install high-resolution color monitors in elevators to beam ads to the captive audience. Cable TV presents a running band across the bottom of the screen to show news headlines, sports scores, weather and traffic reports, and—you guessed it—ads! Supermarket checkout lines, gas pumps, the post office, doctors' offices—you'll find high-tech ads running wherever people have to wait.

Scented paper forces us to smell a product, even if we do not look at the ad for it. Aromas of perfumes, chocolates, detergents, and the leather upholstery of the Rolls-Royce automobile fill the glossy pages of our magazines. More than a billion scent strips a year are distributed, creating severe problems for people who suffer from allergies. Thanks to microchips the size of a grain of salt, it is possible to hear advertisements in print. Several years ago, a popular brand of vodka spent $1 million on a Christmastime ad that played "Jingle Bells" when readers turned the page. The company claimed that the ad produced the largest holiday season sales in its history.

It is not possible for us to pay attention to or respond adequately to all the messages directed toward consumers, nor should we, if we want to maintain our sanity. We do not consciously perceive the majority of the messages around us, but even if we remain unaware of the details of many ads, we are certainly aware that the process of advertising is ongoing, and many of us don't like it. A large-scale nationwide survey conducted in 2004 for the American Association of Advertising Agencies yielded results that did not make the ad agencies happy. Here are a few of the findings (Elliott, 2004):

1. 54 percent of those surveyed said they deliberately avoided products that overwhelmed them with advertising.
2. 60 percent said their opinions about advertising were much more negative than they were a few years ago.
3. 61 percent reported that the amount of advertising they were exposed to was "out of control."

4. 69 percent expressed interest in products and services that would help them eliminate or block ads.

5. 45 percent said that the amount of advertising and marketing detracted from the quality of everyday life.

Although it is true that advertising can annoy us, it can also inform and entertain us. Ads tell us about new products, new models of current products, product specifications and pricing, places to purchase the product, and sales. Some ads are attractive, clever, and funny. Advertising is part of daily life and a major topic of research for industrial-organizational (I-O) psychologists.

Indeed, consumer behavior has been of interest to I-O psychologists since the beginning of the field. It was the study of consumer behavior that launched I-O psychology. Industrial psychology dates from the early-twentieth-century work of Walter Dill Scott on advertising and selling. In 1921 John B. Watson, founder of the behaviorist school of psychology, began to apply his ideas about human behavior to problems in the business world. He proposed that consumer behavior could be conditioned—and, therefore, predicted and controlled—just like any other kind of behavior. He brought the experimental and survey methods to marketing and he insisted that advertisements should focus on style and image rather than substance and fact. He also pioneered the use of celebrity endorsements.

Since those early days, the field has continued to expand in scope and influence. In the late 1960s, the Association for Consumer Research was founded and the first consumer behavior textbooks were published. The Society for Consumer Psychology was founded in 1960 as Division 23 of the American Psychological Association. Besides psychology, researchers in the field of consumer behavior come from sociology, anthropology, economics, and business administration.

RESEARCH METHODS

Most consumer psychology research relies on the techniques, such as laboratory experiments and surveys, and is conducted in various settings, such as university laboratories, downtown intersections, homes, shopping centers, the offices of manufacturers and advertising agencies, and online.

Surveys and Public Opinion Polls

The premise underlying the use of surveys is simple—that is, most people can and will express their feelings, reactions, opinions, and desires when somebody asks them. This assumption holds whether we are trying to determine reactions to a new brand of peanut butter or to a presidential candidate. We have only to recall how accurately most preelection polls have predicted election results or how successfully new products have been introduced on the basis of market testing to know that the survey method often works well. However, there have also been spectacular failures to predict election results or to forecast a product's success. Table 7–1 shows advantages and disadvantages of different survey techniques.

Part of the difficulty is the complex and changeable nature of human behavior. Some people will tell a pollster on Friday that they intend to vote Republican

TABLE 7-1

Advantages and Disadvantages of Various Survey Techniques

	Mail	Telephone	Personal Interview	Online
Cost	Low	Moderate	High	Low
Speed	Slow	Immediate	Slow	Fast
Response rate	Low	Moderate	High	Self-selected
Geographic flexibility	Excellent	Good	Difficult	Excellent
Interviewer bias	N/A	Moderate	Problematic	N/A
Interviewer supervision	N/A	Easy	Difficult	N/A
Quality of response	Limited	Limited	Excellent	Excellent

Source: L. Schiffman & L. Kanuk (2004), *Consumer Behavior* (8th ed.). Upper Saddle River, NJ: Prentice Hall, p. 351.

and then will change their mind and vote Democrat on Tuesday. Respondents may tell an interviewer that they drink expensive imported beer, but a glance inside their refrigerator would reveal cans of some generic "lite" brand. They may have claimed to drink the imported brand because they thought it would make them appear sophisticated.

Searches of trash cans have revealed that on the average people drink twice the amount of beer and liquor than they report in consumer surveys. Survey respondents consistently underreport the amount of junk food they eat and over-report the amount of fresh fruit and diet soft drinks they consume. People tend to respond to surveys and polls with statements they believe will enhance their status, and on such vagaries elections are lost and manufacturers go bankrupt.

A survey of 2,448 people who had received mail-order catalogs reported that 10 percent of those who had purchased products from the company said they had *never* purchased anything from that company. In addition, 40 percent of those who had made no purchases reported that they had, indeed, bought something. Whatever the cause of such false responses—memory lapses or deliberate distortions—the results highlight the problem of inaccurate responses to survey questions (Woodside & Wilson, 2002).

Other research on survey methods found that for mail surveys, sending postcards to potential respondents that contained a contact telephone number to establish the survey's validity significantly increased the response rate over simply mailing the survey without advance notice or contact information (McPheters & Kossoff, 2003).

It has become increasingly difficult to conduct telephone surveys. Response rates have declined significantly since the development of Caller ID systems and the federal "Do Not Call" registry. Research has shown that 43 percent of those who own answering machines or subscribe to Caller ID services screen their calls and tend not to answer those whose names they do not recognize. The tendency to screen calls is higher among ages 18–29, single persons, African-Americans, and people with young children at home. The behavior is

Much consumer psychology research relies on surveys. Shoppers may be asked about the products they are using, how often they purchase them, and why they have chosen a particular brand.

also higher in large cities and their surrounding suburbs than in smaller cities and towns (Tuckel & O'Neill, 2002).

Therefore, many market researchers are turning to online surveys, which have become a fast and less expensive way to obtain data on consumer behavior and attitudes. Web sites have been developed that offer incentives (such as the chance to win a vacation or a television set) to respond to a survey online. One survey site, www.GreenfieldOnline.com, has signed up 1.2 million respondents by advertising on various Web sites.

In 2000 only 10 percent of all market research surveys were carried out online. By 2003 that had increased to 23 percent; by 2006 the figure is estimated to reach 33 percent. The Consumer Reports organization conducted its first annual product survey in 2003, reaching four million online subscribers. The return rate was 25 percent, compared to 14 percent in previous years when questionnaires were sent by mail. The cost of the online survey was half that of the mailed surveys (Jackson, 2003).

Focus Groups

A widely used type of survey involves **focus groups,** which are small samples of consumers who meet in groups of eight to 12 to describe their reactions to a product, package, or ad, or to the ideas and issues being promoted by a political candidate. Members of focus groups are usually paid for their participation and are selected to match the profile of the average voter or consumer of a particular type of product. For example, only pet owners would be selected for a focus group to test an ad for dog food. Only mothers of infants would be chosen to evaluate a new disposable diaper. Focus groups can be structured on the basis of age, income, educational level, or any other variable relevant to the product.

Focus groups A method of surveying public opinion through the paid participation of eight to 12 group members who meet to describe their reactions to a product or advertisement or to specific issues.

Newsbreak   How to Make a Living from Focus Groups

You can make a living from focus groups—if you tell them what they want to hear! Read this article from a popular magazine and draw your own conclusion.

"I have been many men in my career as a focus-group member. For a travel study, I was a hardy adventurer who'd backpacked through Mongolia. For a deodorant group, I claimed a glandular problem that caused me to sweat profusely, no matter the conditions. . . . It all began when I woke up to my status as a card-carrying member of the advertiser-horny 18-to-34-year-old, single-white-male segment of society. As such, my opinions are valuable. Focus groups pay serious money: anywhere from $75 to $300 an hour for sitting with a bunch of other guys and commenting on everything from alcohol packaging to the elastic waistband of your tighty-whities. These 'screenings' are constructed as theoretically perfect control groups, with men off the street full of fresh, unspoiled insights. To that end, most focus companies have a rule that no one can participate in a group more than once every six months. This is complete bunk. If you know how to game the system, you can do one of these a week, sometimes even more. . . . If [recruiters] ask you whether you've done [a focus group] in the past six months, just say no. They never check. If they ask you something off-the-wall, like 'Have you purchased a treadmill in the past year?' say yes; they wouldn't ask if that weren't the answer they wanted. If they ask you what brands you purchase most often, always name big ones: Sprint, Budweiser, Marlboro. They're representing either one of those companies or a smaller one trying to figure out how to steal you away. And, most important, let the recruiters lead you. Before you answer a question you're not sure about, pause for a couple of seconds. They'll tip their hand every time.

"Once you're actually in the group, it's vital to be as invisible as possible. If you're tagged as an 'outlier' who has opinions that don't jibe with an advertiser's research, it's less likely you'll be invited back. You are not a human; you are a demographic stereotype. So act manly: Refer to any pink product packaging as 'feminine' or 'wussy,' or mention that you're always 'tossing down a few after work with my buddies.' In one group for Johnnie Walker Black, it was obvious the marketers wanted us to consider their beverage upscale, for special occasions. Recognizing this, I made up a story about learning my best friend was engaged and telling him, 'It's Johnnie Walker time!' The interviewer looked like he wanted to hug me.

"It's also important to be vague. During the focus group on travel, the interviewer asked me if there were any countries I might have moral qualms visiting. The correct answer was 'Oh, none at all.' But I blurted out, 'South Africa,' sharing some underdeveloped thoughts I had about apartheid. The interviewer's face sharpened, and he began to pepper me with questions. I had forgotten the cardinal rule: They don't want your opinion; they want you to confirm what they already think. You're whatever they want you to be, baby."

Source: W. Leitch, Group thinker. *New York*, June 21, 2004.

Focus groups need to be structured differently for different segments of the population. For example, the approach suitable for groups of adolescents must be modified for the lesser attention span of children or the perceptual and cognitive differences of the elderly. A study of focus groups in Britain, whose members ranged in age from 60 to 88, showed that the older members responded better with shorter sessions, simpler and briefer questions, better lighting, larger-print materials, and familiar surroundings (Barrett & Kirk, 2000).

The focus group sessions are observed through one-way mirrors and video-taped for later analysis. The data produced by the focus groups—the comments and responses of the participants—are more qualitative than are those obtained from questionnaires in large-scale empirical surveys. Sometimes, focus group members are not asked direct questions but are observed as they try to use a new product. In a session to evaluate a disposable razor, observers found that many men cut themselves while shaving because the package directions were not clear.

As in surveys, focus group participants may distort their answers, saying what they think others want to hear—or what they want others to hear. Consider the focus group that was discussing ads for a company that performed surgical hair replacements (Lauro, 2000). The men in the group all insisted that they were not bothered, personally, by losing their hair, yet they were all wearing hats—on a hot day in Atlanta, Georgia! Their behavior may have been more truly reflective of their attitude about hair loss than what they said to others in the group, but how could we know for sure?

Virtual focus groups conducted online function in a similar way as face-to-face groups and offer the advantages of lower cost and greater efficiency. They can sample a more diverse group of people who might lack the time and transportation to come to a central meeting place for the focus group session.

The responses of members of actual and virtual focus groups may differ. Usually, in a face-to-face meeting, one person at a time expresses an opinion. Sometimes, one individual will dominate the group. In an online meeting, all participants have the chance to speak simultaneously and thus will tend to be less influenced by the opinions of others. When dealing with sensitive topics such as health issues, the privacy and anonymity of an online session enable people to speak more candidly (Collins, 2000).

Motivation Research

We cannot uncover all human motivations by asking questions that permit people to mask or distort their true intentions and feelings. To probe these deeper, hidden motivations, some psychologists use in-depth interviews and projective techniques. The pioneer in this field of motivation research was Ernest Dichter (1907–1992), a Vienna-born and trained psychologist who lived across the street from Sigmund Freud. Dichter emigrated to the United States in 1938. Building on Freudian psychoanalysis to discover unconscious motivations for neurotic behavior, he applied the approach to consumer behavior—why some people purchase particular products or decline to purchase other products.

Dichter's first success was with packaged cake mix, a product introduced around 1940. Everything needed to bake a cake was included in the box: sugar, flour, shortening, and dried egg. Just add water, stir, pour in a pan, and bake. The product promised a revolution in cake baking—an easy, quick, no fuss, and homemade cake with that just-baked aroma that never failed. The only problem was that consumers rejected it. Why? Dichter solved the problem for the General Mills company, using psychoanalytic techniques to uncover the real reason for customer resistance. Questioning a sample of female consumers, so-called typical homemakers of the day, he found that the women felt guilty about doing little or no work to bake a cake for their family. The solution? Give the consumer something to do, to help fulfill the urge to be creative. In this case, Dichter recommended that the company omit the dried egg and let the consumer add fresh eggs to the packaged mix. As a result, sales soared, Dichter became rich and famous, and his motivation research techniques became essential tools in the understanding of consumer behavior (see Schiffman & Kanuk, 2004; Smith, 2004; Stern, 2002).

We described some of these projective techniques namely, the Rorschach Inkblot Test, the Thematic Apperception Test, and the sentence completion test. The theory behind the use of projective techniques is the same whether they are applied to employee selection or to consumer behavior. When people are presented with an ambiguous stimulus, such as an inkblot, it is assumed that they will project their needs, fears, and values onto the stimulus in the act of interpreting it. A classic example of the use of projective techniques to study consumer behavior involved the reaction of low-income Southern women to a new brand of roach killer packaged in small plastic trays. Surveys showed that consumers said they believed the plastic trays were far more effective than the old-style sprays, yet they continued to buy the sprays. To determine the reasons for this inconsistency, groups of women were asked to draw pictures of roaches and to write stories about them. The researchers reported the following about the possible motivation of the female consumers:

> The results were very informative—all the roaches in the pictures were male, "symbolizing men who the women said had abandoned them and left them feeling poor and powerless." The women were said to be expressing their built-up hostility by spraying the roaches and watching them squirm and die!
> (Foxall & Goldsmith, 1994, p. 162).

Direct questioning would not have revealed this motivation.

In theory, the projective approach offers the same advantages as projective tests for employee selection, namely, the ability to reach deeper levels of motivation and to uncover feelings and desires that cannot be assessed by objective tests and questionnaires. However, projective tests are low in reliability and validity. There have been successful uses of projective techniques to study consumer behavior, but because the advertising industry does not publicize its failures, it is difficult to determine the extent of that success.

Observations of Shopping Behavior

Consumer surveys and the kinds of techniques used in motivation research share a basic weakness. They reveal only what people say they believe or will do. These expressed intentions do not always coincide with behavior. Because of this discrepancy, some consumer psychologists prefer to observe what people do when purchasing a product or when expressing their preference by selecting one brand over another. Common sense suggests that acceptance of a new product or advertising campaign will be reflected in subsequent sales figures. For example, if sales of a toothpaste brand double in the six months following an ad campaign, then the campaign must have been successful. However, unless all other variables capable of

Newsbreak	Are You a Minivan or an SUV?

Consumer researchers tell us that different products attract different kinds of people. This seems particularly true for the kinds of automobile we drive. A survey of 5,400 owners of minivans and sport utility vehicles revealed that what you drive tells the world a lot about your personality. And maybe that's why you chose it.

The research showed that SUV owners tend to be more restless, more devoted to pleasurable pursuits, less social, and more fearful of crime than are people who purchased minivans. Minivan owners tend to be more self-confident and sociable and more comfortable with the idea of being married and having children than are SUV drivers.

Both groups said they wanted to be "in control" of their vehicle, but they don't mean the same thing by that phrase. Minivan people want to be in control in terms of safety, the ability to maneuver well in traffic, and to park easily. SUV people want to be in control in the sense of dominating everyone around them.

It is not surprising, then, that SUV drivers have been found to be more aggressive and less concerned with behaving courteously to drivers of other vehicles. A French anthropologist who is a consultant to Ford, General Motors, and DaimlerChrysler said, "Sport utilities are designed to be masculine and assertive, often with hoods that resemble those on 18-wheel trucks and vertical metal slats across the grilles to give the appearance of a jungle cat's teeth. Sport utilities are designed to appeal to Americans' deepest fears of violence and crime."

SUVs are like weapons, he concluded, "armored cars for the battlefield." Their message is "Don't mess with me."

What do you drive? Hmmmmm?

Source: K. Bradsher. Was Freud a minivan or an SUV kind of guy? *New York Times,* July 17, 2000.

influencing sales were controlled, we cannot conclude with certainty that the new advertising program was solely or even partially responsible for the boost in sales.

Suppose the company's aggressive sales staff arranged for more prominent shelf display of the toothpaste during the six-month period. That increased visibility could have contributed to higher sales, independent of the ad campaign. Or suppose the company's leading competitor was faulted in a government report for adding an allegedly harmful ingredient to its toothpaste formula. That criticism could contribute to higher sales for all other toothpaste manufacturers. Thus, sales data can reflect factors other than the one being evaluated, and without adequate control over all possible influencing variables, we cannot determine precisely what caused any increase or decrease in sales.

The most direct way to investigate purchasing behavior is to site video cameras or place human observers in stores. Researchers have watched mothers with young children as they shopped for cereals and snack foods. More than 65 percent of the time, children ask for a particular product. And more than half the time, the mothers buy the products their children demand. This kind of data is especially valuable because it indicates that children, not adults, should be the target of ads for cereals and snack foods. Had the mothers been questioned directly in a survey, however, they might have said that *they* were the ones to choose these products, not wanting to appear to be dominated by their children, or perhaps not realizing the extent of their children's influence.

Another observation of purchasing behavior resulted in a change in how a product was stocked. Supermarket observers noted that while adults purchased dog food, dog treats were more often selected by children or older persons. However, dog treats were usually stocked on the upper shelves. Hidden cameras caught children climbing on the shelves to reach the dog cookies. Elderly women were observed using boxes of foil or other long objects to knock down a favorite brand of dog biscuit. By moving the dog treats to lower, more accessible shelves, sales improved almost overnight.

Although observations of actual purchasing behavior can be useful, they are costly and time-consuming. There are other problems as well. One relates to adequate sampling of shopping behavior. Stores in different locations (such as inner city versus suburban) attract customers with different needs and income levels. As you might expect, city and suburban shoppers preferred different kinds of stores, chose different types of products, and had differing amounts of disposable income for shopping.

Various types of shoppers can be found in the same store at different times of the day or week. People who shop in the evenings and on weekends may have different buying habits from those of people who shop during the day. The research design must compensate for this problem by providing for observations at an adequate sample of locations and shopping hours, but this increases the cost of the research.

Another problem with behavioral observations of purchasing behavior is the lack of experimental control over other influencing variables; this is a weakness of all types of observational research studies. In observing supermarket shopping patterns in urban and suburban locations, for example, it is difficult to determine whether the differences found are a function of socioeconomic level, ethnic composition, shelf arrangement, or inventory. All these factors could affect the outcome of the research. Despite such limitations, however, direct observation of shopping behavior has often revealed valuable marketing information that would have been difficult to obtain any other way.

Brand Identification and Preference Research

Consumer psychologists are also interested in how well shoppers recognize, identify, or recall specific product brands. Much of this research focuses on the ability to discriminate among competing brands of a product. When all recognizable cues are removed—such as product name and distinctive packaging—can consumers truly distinguish, say, one brand of cola from another? Studies consistently demonstrate that many people cannot discriminate among brands of products such as soft drinks, cigarettes, beer, and margarine. Researchers have concluded that many consumer preferences and loyalties are based on factors other than the product's taste or other intrinsic qualities.

Testing Reactions to Advertising

A major research activity of consumer psychologists is testing the effectiveness of advertising and promotional campaigns. The most direct approach is to ask people for their reactions to an ad. Does the ad make them want to buy the product? Do they believe the ad? Which of two ads for a product do they find more interesting? It is necessary that the respondents be a representative sample of the population for whom the product is intended. Using single men or elderly women to pretest an ad for baby food is not likely to yield useful results.

Aided Recall. The most popular technique to test advertising effectiveness is **aided recall,** which is used to determine the extent to which the contents of an ad can be remembered. Once an ad has appeared in a magazine or broadcast on radio or television, a sample of consumers is questioned, usually the following day, about whether they read the magazine or heard or saw the program in which the commercial appeared. If so, they are asked to tell as much of the selling message as they can recall. The interviewer asks specific questions about the nature of the ad; this aids the recall. However, a high rate of recall for an ad's message did not necessarily lead the consumer to purchase the product.

Aided recall technique A test of advertising effectiveness to determine the extent to which ad content can be recalled. The interviewer aids the recall by asking specific questions.

Recognition. Another technique for testing the effectiveness of ads is **recognition.** People who have seen a particular television program or magazine are shown copies of the ads and are questioned about them. Do the consumers recognize the ad and remember where they saw it? Do they recall the name of the product? Had they read the message? Unfortunately, people may say that they have seen an ad or commercial even when they have not. When researchers showed people ads that had not yet appeared in the media, some respondents claimed to have seen them. A comparison of aided recall and recognition techniques showed that recognition was the more sensitive measure of memory for TV commercials.

Recognition technique A technique for testing advertising effectiveness by asking people if they recognize a particular ad, where they saw it, and what they can recall about it.

Physiological Measures. Because TV commercials are designed to elicit an emotional response in viewers, physiological measures of those emotions are an effective way to measure a commercial's usefulness. For example, a group of consumers serving as research participants could be exposed to a variety of television commercials while their physiological responses are measured by electromyography (EMG), which detects changes in the electrical activity of the muscles. When applied to certain facial muscles, it measures a person's reaction to emotional stimuli. These consumers would be questioned some time later and asked to rate each commercial or ad on the basis of how much they liked it or how much pleasure (or other emotion) it aroused in them. If the results show that facial EMG data correlate strongly and positively with the ratings of the commercials, then the ads would be considered effective.

Sales Tests. Some psychologists argue that the only meaningful test of advertising effectiveness is whether it results in higher sales. However, we have noted the limitations of using sales data as a measure of advertising success. The **sales test technique** is designed to reduce those problems because it permits experimental control of extraneous variables. Sales tests have been found to be a highly accurate way of assessing the impact of advertising on sales.

Sales test technique A way of testing the effectiveness of an advertising campaign by introducing the new advertising in selected test markets.

Newsbreak

Coupons Make a Lot of Cents

It started in 1895, more than a hundred years ago, when Asa Chandler, of Atlanta, Georgia, distributed coupons for a free glass of Coca-Cola at his soda fountain. Today, an estimated 335 billion cents-off, free-product, and rebate coupons are distributed annually, an average of more than 3,000 for every U.S. household. We cut them out of newspapers and magazines or download them from the Internet and take them to stores to redeem for our purchases of toothpaste, headache remedies, cookies, and breakfast cereal. Pharmacies give them out for discounts on prescription drugs, department stores offer them for special sales, and cemeteries have dollars-off coupons for gravesites.

Coupons can save real money. The average family that uses coupons can count on saving approximately $700 a year, a substantial hourly payback rate for the time required to clip, assemble, and organize the coupons. Hardcore coupon users, who have been known to purchase several copies of the Sunday newspaper to get additional coupons, save even more money.

Most people still obtain their coupons from the Sunday newspapers and use them primarily at the supermarket, but that situation is changing rapidly as more people search for coupons online. It is easy to print them out at home and redeem them at stores and service providers such as travel agencies. In 2003 U.S. consumers downloaded 242 million coupons, an increase of 111 percent over the previous year. Although still a small share of the coupon market, the growth of online coupon delivery may soon reach and exceed coupon clipping from newspapers and magazines.

Online coupons provide a major benefit to marketers and researchers: instant personal information about the person who is downloading the coupon. For example, one company that issues coupons online is www.SmartSource. com. Users who log on to their Web site must register, providing details about themselves, family members, pets, income, and preferred stores. In return, they get free access to up to 35 coupons a day worth approximately $14. When they use a coupon, its code number tells the company who redeemed it, where it was redeemed, and for what product. That data cannot be obtained from a coupon cut out from a newspaper supplement.

So log on and get your coupons, but you'll give away a bit of your privacy. Do you think it's a fair trade?

Sources: No more clipping. *Newsweek,* April 1, 1996. It all started with a coupon for a free Coke. *St. Petersburg (FL) Times,* January 11, 1996. More consumers are clicking for online coupons. *St. Petersburg (FL) Times,* April 21, 2003.

In a sales test, an advertising campaign is introduced in selected test markets, such as a specific neighborhood, city, or other geographical area. Other locations, chosen to be as similar as possible to the test markets, serve as controls; the new advertising is not presented in these control areas. If the test and control areas are comparable, then any change in sales within the test areas can be attributed to the advertising campaign. The control over possible influencing variables is the major advantage of sales tests. The researcher is not measuring interest in an ad or what subjects say they remember, but whether they actually buy the product on the basis of the ad.

The use of sales tests for studying advertising effectiveness also has limitations. An adequate sales test is costly. It takes time to arrange, and it requires precise accounting of the purchasing behavior of a large number of people. Another problem involves the areas selected for the control group. By not exposing people in the control markets to the new ad campaign, the company risks losing sales to its competitors.

Coupon Returns.   The effectiveness of magazine and newspaper advertising can be tested by evaluating coupon returns. When coupons are returned to the manufacturer to obtain a product sample or to enter a contest, they provide a measure of reader interest. When coupons are used to purchase a product or receive a discount (cents-off coupons), they measure actual buying behavior. However, if the inducement to return the coupon is attractive, such as when a West Coast mail-order retailer offered a free pair of sweat socks to introduce a house brand, there is the danger that people will respond even though they have no interest in the product. Many people just want to get something free. There are also people who will return virtually any coupon because they like to get mail. It is difficult to determine how many coupon returns come from habitual coupon clippers and how many come from people genuinely interested in the product.

Coupon returns may indicate the attention-getting value of an ad, but they do not provide a direct measure of the ad's impact on sales. When coupons offer a reduced price for a product, they are effective in inducing people to change brands, at least temporarily. A price reduction obtained by redeeming a coupon at the supermarket promotes greater sales than an equivalent price markdown given at the store.

In one study, more than 900 shoppers were given questionnaires as they left various stores and asked to mail them to the researchers. The results showed that those who used coupons differed from those who did not. The high coupon users considered themselves to be smart shoppers, believed in the economic benefits of using coupons, were more price sensitive and value conscious, and were willing to invest the time required to obtain coupons in order to save money. High coupon users also reported that they enjoyed the shopping experience more than did low coupon users (Garretson & Burton, 2003).

THE NATURE AND SCOPE OF ADVERTISING

Let us examine some of the techniques the sellers of goods and services use to encourage, persuade, stimulate, or manipulate you, the consumer, to buy their products. There are several different types of advertising. Although the most frequently used is the direct sell type, designed to elicit an immediate response from the consumer, other advertising is created for different purposes.

Consumer Awareness.   Another type of advertising is designed to create consumer awareness of a new product, an improved product or package, or a price change. This advertising also tries to reinforce the brand name. Because so much purchasing behavior is linked to brand names, companies spend considerable sums creating and maintaining public awareness of company and product names.

This direct-sell ad promotes consumer awareness of the product and tries to establish an image of luxury and fun. (Courtesy of Ford Motor Company.)

VISITORS TO MS. GAWEL'S CLASSROOM FIND OUT JUST HOW WILD IT REALLY IS.

To help awaken them to the plight of the world's rainforests, Julie Gawel's students created one of their own.

Julie, an art teacher at Killough Middle School in Houston, Texas, designed the multi-disciplinary program for her students utilizing reading, writing, science, and art. After researching the rainforest environment, the students practiced drawing its inhabitants; learning about paint, color mixing, and texture in the process. Then they transformed their classroom with wall-size murals and papier-mâché trees filled with a menagerie of plants and wildlife.

Finally, the students invited parents and local business leaders to their rainforest, where the children made presentations and passed along the lessons they learned about conservation.

For teaching her students how to be wild about art – and the world's rainforests – Julie Gawel is our newest Good Neighbor Award winner.

State Farm is pleased to contribute $5,000 in her name to Alief Independent School District.

GOOD NEIGHBOR AWARD

STATE FARM INSURANCE COMPANIES
Home Offices: Bloomington, Illinois
www.statefarm.com

The Good Neighbor Award was developed in cooperation with the National Art Education Association.

Institutional advertising promotes the idea that the company is a good neighbor and community benefactor. (Reproduced by permission of State Farm Insurance Companies.)

Product Image. Some advertising tries to establish an image for a product or service. Many products cannot be distinguished from one another on the basis of ingredients or quality, so advertisers try to create differences in terms of images, symbols, or feelings. For example, an automobile must do more than provide transportation; a lipstick must provide more than color. It must, through its image, make the owners feel younger, sportier, or more attractive, or enhance their prestige and economic status. As the president of a firm that makes men's and women's fragrances said, "In the factory we make cosmetics. In the store we sell hope."

Institutional Advertising. The goal of institutional advertising is to persuade the public that the company is a good neighbor and community benefactor. An example is the campaign conducted by an oil company to promote highway safety rather than simply to sell its brand of gasoline. Companies advertise that their products are good for the environment, that they contribute a share of their profits to charities, or that they support Little League baseball teams. Institutional advertising can build public goodwill, boost sales, help recruit employees, improve employee morale, and drive up the price of the company's stock.

Informational Advertising. Some advertising comes under the heading of informational advertising when it enables consumers to make more intelligent purchasing decisions. The type of information provided in such an ad can include price, quality, performance data, components or contents, availability, nutritional information, warranties, and safety record. The use of informative advertising has increased from an average of 20 percent of all ads a decade ago to more than 65 percent today. Magazine ads tend to be more informative than television ads. More cable television commercials than network television commercials are of the informative type.

Advertising Placement. The outlets for advertising—of every type—have changed over the past several years. For example, McDonald's devotes one-third of its marketing budget to television ads, but only five years ago that figure was two-thirds. Many other companies are also cutting back on the money earmarked for TV advertising, spending it instead on other media outlets in an effort to reach more targeted audiences. For McDonald's, the money they used to spend on 30-second network spots now goes to closed-circuit sports programs piped into bars with a large Hispanic customer base, to ads in *Upscale* magazine (distributed to barber shops with a Black clientele), to in-store videos at Foot Locker, to print ads in women's magazines, and to pop-ups on Web sites such as Yahoo!. What happened to television advertising? Many consumers prefer to spend time in front of their computer instead of their TV set. And even when people watch television, they are more likely to ignore the commercials or zap past them with personal video recorders such as TiVo. Table 7–2 shows the growth in our lack of interest in TV ads for various consumer products (Bianco, 2004).

Types of Advertising Appeals

The major way in which an ad campaign can persuade you to buy a product is through its appeal—that is, what it promises to do for you. Look at some magazine ads. Which human needs or motivations does the product promise to satisfy? Psychologists have identified many human needs: the innate or primary needs, such as food, water, shelter, security, and sex; and the learned or secondary needs, such as power, status, achievement, esteem, and affiliation. These secondary motivations depend on our personal experiences and thus will vary from one person to another and one culture to another.

To sell their products and services, advertisers must identify the relevant needs and direct their messages toward the appropriate segment of the population. Most ads attempt to satisfy more than one need. For example, an ad for imported beer can promise to quench thirst (a primary need) and to satisfy the desires for status

TABLE 7–2

Interest in Various Types of Television Advertising

Product	Percent of Viewers Ignoring These TV Ads	Percent of Ads Skipped by Using Personal Video Recorders
Beer	5	32
Soft drinks	22	83
Fast food	45	96
Automobiles	53	69
Credit cards	63	94
Upcoming TV programs	75	94

Source: Business Week, July 12, 2004.

and belonging (secondary needs). Ads for mouthwash and deodorant promise to help us avoid embarrassing situations and thus be more likable. If we use the right cologne, we are assured by advertisers that we will find love and thus fulfill the needs for social support and self-esteem. Driving the right car can provide power, prestige, and achievement, along with the hope of attracting a mate. Advertisers use several techniques to appeal to these diverse human needs.

Celebrity Endorsements. A product endorsed by a celebrity entertainer or sports figure invites the audience to identify with that person's success. Celebrities are often used to sell products, although there is little published evidence of the impact of such endorsements on actual purchasing unless the celebrity is believed to be qualified to promote that product. A study of college students investigated the influence of celebrity status, attractiveness, trustworthiness, and perceived expertise on their expressed intentions to purchase particular items. Only the perceived expertise of the celebrities was positively related to buying intentions. For example, a tennis pro was considered to be a believable endorser of tennis rackets, a good-looking male movie star was an effective promoter of men's cologne, and a fashion model an appropriate spokesperson for a line of designer jeans.

Some celebrities endorse more than one product, which can cause problems for some sponsors or manufacturers. Research shows that as the number of products endorsed by a celebrity increases, ratings of the celebrity's credibility decrease significantly. In addition, attitudes toward the ads became significantly less favorable.

Positive and Negative Appeals. Advertising appeals can be positive or negative. The message can suggest that something good will happen to you if you use the product or that something unpleasant will happen if you don't use the product. An ad for deodorant soap can show a room full of happy people who are obviously desirable because they use the featured soap, or it can show a person sitting at home alone, dateless and dejected because he or she failed to bathe with the soap. A related approach is to make the person feel guilty for not buying the product, a tactic that is particularly effective with mothers of young children.

Negative appeals are effective for certain types of products, but they do not work when the consequences are overly unpleasant. Pictures of gruesome

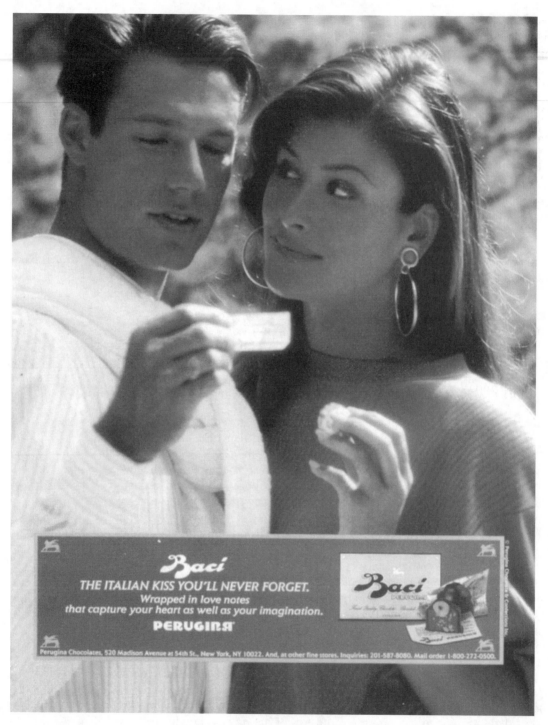

Some advertisers attempt to appeal to emotional needs and feelings such as affection, romance, and beauty. (Reproduced by permission of Perugina Chocolates.)

automobile accidents to promote safe driving or depictions of diseased lungs in antismoking campaigns have been shown to be ineffective. Such fear-laden appeals distract people from the message. The same holds true for guilt appeals. Research has shown that strong appeals are significantly less effective than moderate appeals in inducing feelings of guilt. A strong guilt appeal can easily generate anger toward the ad and the company that sponsored it. A frequently used approach combines both types of appeal, first showing the negative consequences of not using the product and then showing the positive consequences of using the product.

Whereas negative appeals may not be effective in advertising, shock appeals (ads that deliberately startle or offend the audience) may work. A series of three ads—one to inform, one to instill fear, and one to shock—were shown to 105 college students. The messages related to the use of condoms as a way to prevent HIV/AIDS. The shock ad showed a nude couple embracing; the message read "Don't be a f---ing idiot." The fear ad showed a driver's license with the expiration date circled; the message was "If you get the AIDS virus now, you and your license could expire at the same time." The information ad showed the acronym AIDS and the words "Acquired Immunodeficiency."

The results showed that the shock appeal produced significantly greater scores on recall, recognition, and attention paid to the message than the other types of appeals. Also, more people in the shock-ad group and the fear-ad group took AIDS-related informational materials from the items displayed on a table in the experimental treatment room (Dahl, Frankenberger, & Manchanda, 2003).

Implied Superiority. A widely used appeal is implied superiority, in which the superiority of one product over its competitors is not stated directly but is inferred by the consumer. For example, if all headache remedies take the same amount of time to bring relief, one company may claim that no competitor provides faster relief than its product. The claim is true—no one product is faster than another—but the phrasing may lead people to conclude that this brand is superior because it sounds as if it works faster. The ad also suggests indirectly that its claim is based on scientific research.

Trademarks

A familiar trademark can facilitate advertising effectiveness because it serves as a shorthand symbol of the feelings and images associated with the product (see Figure 7–1). Key aspects of the product come to be identified with and exemplified by the trademark. Most trademarks are brand names—for example, Coca-Cola, Kleenex, and Xerox. When a trademark is well established in the marketplace, it alone, without any other advertising message, can stimulate consumers to recall the product.

A survey of brand names and trademarks asked executives to rate them on the reputation, management strength, and investment potential of their companies. A second survey asked a random sample of more than 10,000 people to rate the brand names on product quality, corporate vision, and leadership. The rankings are shown in Table 7–3, in descending order of popularity. Only three names—Coca-Cola, Walt Disney, and Johnson & Johnson—appear on both lists. Otherwise, the companies selected by the executives are different from those

WAL★MART®

FIGURE 7–1. Trademarks. (Reproduced by permission of Wal-Mart Stores, Inc.; AT&T Corporation; and Toyota Motor Sales USA, Inc.)

selected by the random sample of consumers. Thus, it is clear that the "best" brand names depend on who is being asked to pick them.

Companies spend a great deal of time and money on the development of product trademarks and brand names. Identity consultants specialize in naming

TABLE 7–3

Rank Order of U.S. Companies by Reputation and Brand Name Recognition

By Executives	By Random Sample
Coca-Cola	**Johnson & Johnson**
Microsoft	**Coca-Cola**
Walt Disney	Hewlett-Packard
Campbell Soup	Intel
Johnson & Johnson	Ben & Jerry's
General Electric	Wal-Mart
FedEx	Xerox
Procter & Gamble	Home Depot
Hershey Foods	Gateway
Harley-Davidson	**Walt Disney**

and renaming products and companies. For example, California Airlines changed its name to AirCal when focus-group interviews revealed that the new name had greater consumer impact. Allegheny Airlines changed its name to USAir (now US Airways) to make it sound more like a national than a regional carrier.

Research can also tell manufacturers how recognizable their product name is to the consuming public and what it means to the target audience. This is especially crucial for U.S. companies marketing products in other countries. Sometimes a trademark can have an unintended, or unfavorable, meaning in another language. The Chevrolet Nova, named for a star that suddenly increases in brightness and energy, became in Spanish "no va," which means "doesn't go"—not a very good name for a car. Coca-Cola changed its product name in China when the company discovered that in Chinese, Coca-Cola meant "bite the wax tadpole." Pepsi had a similar problem. "Come alive with the Pepsi generation" translated into Chinese as "Pepsi will bring your ancestors back from the dead." Remember Kentucky Fried Chicken's "finger-lickin' good"? In Chinese it became "eat your fingers off." Oops. One U.S. airline boasted in Spanish-language magazines about the leather upholstery on its seats; in translation the message meant "sit naked." The Scandinavian vacuum cleaner company, Electrolux, pulled an ad that promised, "Nothing sucks like an Electrolux," when informed by their American distributors that this was not quite the image they wanted associated with their brand.

A trademark can be so effective that it comes to stand for all brands of a product. For example, "kleenex" is now used to mean any kind of facial tissue, "xerox" any type of photocopier, and "fedex" any express mail carrier. When this occurs, the company can lose its identifiability and its exclusive share of the market.

Trademarks that have worked successfully for years may have to be altered to reflect changes in the culture of the marketplace. The image of Betty Crocker, the fictional woman trademark for many General Mills's food products, was updated in 1996 to reflect the greater racial and ethnic diversity of the American population. The new Betty Crocker is a computer-generated hybrid of 75 real American faces. Designed to represent many races, she now looks multicultural, in an attempt to depict more accurately American society.

Product Image

Often allied with a product's trademark is its image—the ideas, thoughts, and feelings associated with the product's personality. The development of a successful product image, one with which consumers will want to identify, can bring a company from obscurity to prosperity. Indeed, the image can be more important than the qualities of the product itself.

Sometimes product image is transmitted by a symbol, such as the tiny alligator on some popular knit shirts. This symbol is supposed to convey the image of the person wearing the product. A now-classic study compared consumer perceptions of a person wearing a plain knit shirt and wearing shirts with alligator, fox, and polo player logos. The person wearing the plain shirt was judged to be self-confident, tolerant, satisfied, and friendly. The same person in the fox emblem shirt was described as self-confident, enthusiastic, and a leader. In the polo player shirt he was perceived as less self-confident, tolerant, enthusiastic, satisfied, and friendly than in any of the other shirts. In the alligator shirt, the same person was described as preppy but neither a leader nor a follower. The shirt was identical in all cases; the only difference was the logo (Swartz, 1983).

The most difficult problem in developing a product image is determining the qualities that will attract potential buyers. One technique for studying product image involves group interviews with selected samples of consumers in which they are questioned about their perceptions of various products. This in-depth approach attempts to elicit positive and negative feelings about the products.

A more objective approach involves the adjective checklist, which is what was used in the study of the shirts with the logos. Consumers are given a list of descriptive adjectives and phrases and are asked to select those that characterize their feelings about the product or their conception of the person who would buy the product.

Product Packaging

Another important aspect of an advertising campaign is the product's package, the part of the product that consumers see at the critical point of sale, the moment of deciding whether to purchase. Shoppers looking for a box of crackers on a supermarket shelf who are confronted by an array of competing brands may not remember the TV commercial they saw last night or the magazine ad they read last week. At the instant of purchase, the packaging may be the deciding factor.

There is an old saying about not judging a book by its cover, but many people make various decisions on just that basis. We often evaluate people by their clothing or their car, and we make similar judgments about the products we purchase. Consumer attitudes are often shaped not by the quality of an item but by the wrapping in which it is offered.

The most famous example is an early consumer study on the taste of coffee. Two groups of people were questioned. For one group, the coffee was poured from an ordinary electric coffeemaker. For the other group, the coffee was served from an ornately engraved antique silver urn. You guessed it. The consumers rated the taste of the coffee poured from the silver urn much higher than the coffee from the electric coffeemaker, though the coffee was the same in both cases. It was the container—the package—that accounted for the difference in the way people perceived the taste.

In other research on this concept, pills of two sizes were shown to groups of patients and physicians, who were asked to rate the potency of each drug. Both groups reported that they believed that the larger pill was the more potent. In fact, the larger pill was less than half as strong as the smaller pill.

Overall, the package must reinforce the product's image or personality as established by its advertising campaign. For example, a men's hair gel should not be packaged in a pink bottle with letters in script but in a sturdy box with bold stripes and colors. The design and matching of product and package can be determined through consumer research. Consumers may be asked to free-associate to the designs of current or proposed packaging, telling researchers the positive or negative images elicited by the designs. Surveys and projective techniques can also be used to determine packaging impact and preference.

Packaging is an expensive part of the manufacturing and marketing process, accounting for more than one-third of the cost of most supermarket items. For every dollar you spend on food, drugs, cosmetics, clothing, and electronics, approximately 35 cents goes for the container, not for what is in it.

Sex in Advertisements

The use of attractive and scantily clad models of both sexes is popular in advertising, so we might assume that their effectiveness is beyond question. However, the value of sexy images in ads has been accepted on faith, with little empirical research support. Sex appeal does have a high attention-getting value. Studies using the eye camera show that most consumers reading magazines, when confronted with several ads on a page, will immediately look at the ad that contains an element of sex. But what then? In general, the information in the ad that features provocative pictures of women is read more often by women than by men. Men look at the pictures, but women read the message, which usually means that the ad is communicating with the wrong audience. Similar results have been found with ads featuring pictures of attractive men; the messages are read more often by men than by women, again attracting the wrong audience.

More discouraging is research evidence suggesting a very low rate of recall for information that accompanies sexy illustrations. One company published two versions of a magazine ad, each containing a mail-in coupon for additional information. One ad showed a bikini-clad young woman; the other ad did not. Coupon returns were significantly higher for the ad without the sexy model.

Laboratory research supports these field observations. In one study, male subjects viewed several ads; some of the ads had sexy illustrations and some did not. The subjects were then shown the same ads with the brand names deleted and were asked to identify the product or advertiser. They were questioned again 24 hours later. There was no difference in the rate of recall for the sexy and nonsexy ads. After seven days, the subjects had forgotten significantly more of the sexy ads than the nonsexy ads.

A study in which 324 male and female adults were shown a sexually explicit or a neutral television program found that those who saw the sexy program had significantly lower recall and recognition scores for nine ads that were shown during the program than did those who saw the neutral program. In another experimental condition, those who watched a violent television program reacted similarly to the sexy-program group. Neither could recall or recognize the products advertised during the program as well as could those who watched the neutral program (Bushman & Bonacci, 2002).

It appears, then, that the wrong audience reads the messages accompanying sexy ads, and although many people enjoy looking at the ads, they are not likely to remember the product. However, advertisers continue to rely on the shock value, and their promotions—especially for fragrances, underwear, and jeans—grow more daring every year.

Effectiveness of Advertising Campaigns

The most important question for the seller is whether its advertising campaign is effective in increasing the sales of its product or service. In many cases, neither the advertising agency nor the company knows the answer, because effectiveness is difficult to determine. Further, companies are reluctant to go public with their failures and are apt to exaggerate their successes.

Research on television ad campaigns consistently shows that most people dislike commercials. Television viewers watch fewer than half the commercials broadcast. They leave the room during commercial breaks, turn off the sound or switch channels with the remote control device, and erase or fast-forward through commercials on video-recorded programs. A study of 360 television viewers in Hong Kong found that fully 81 percent avoided watching commercials (Tse & Lee, 2001).

Advertising agencies recognize that most people are not sitting through or paying attention to television ads. They describe viewers as "nomads," because they wander or surf from one channel to another. Consumer psychologists have described three types of viewers:

1. *Channel nomads:* people who surf from channel to channel looking for a program of interest. In New York City, viewers change channels on the average of every 3 minutes 26 seconds.
2. *Mental nomads:* people multitasking, concerned with other activities such as preparing dinner, talking on the phone, or playing with their children. Only occasionally do they glance at the TV set.
3. *Physical nomads:* people busy in other parts of the house who watch snatches of programs and commercials when they pass through the room containing the television set.

In laboratory test situations, where people watching TV commercials were unable to tune them out, channel surf, or leave the room, subjects typically misunderstood or forgot approximately one-third of what they had seen when questioned immediately after viewing the ads. A day later, the subjects had forgotten or misunderstood three-fourths of what they had seen. The figures were higher for magazine ads. Of course not everyone can avoid all commercials all the time. A study of advertising during the Super Bowl broadcast, where a 30-second spot can cost more than $2 million, showed that movies promoted in ads during the game grossed nearly 40 percent more than movies released at the same time but not advertised during the Super Bowl. In this instance, the ads were watched by enough people to more than pay for their cost (Yelkur, Tomkovick, & Traczyk, 2004). For current ratings of your favorite television programs, go to www.ytv.yahoo.com/nielsen/ and to learn about Internet ratings, see www.nielsen-netratings.com/.

You may have noticed that when you go to a movie theater nowadays, more ads are shown on the screen before the movie you paid to see even begins. A study of 14,400 people in South Africa who viewed commercials in movie theaters and on television, and 1,291,800 additional reviewers who reported on the same ads seen only in the theater, found that the recall rate for ads in the movie theaters was higher than the recall rate for ads shown on television. This result was the same for young adults (the primary movie audience) and for older adults. The researchers suggested that perhaps we pay more attention to ads in the theaters because we have little chance of avoiding them (Ewing, DuPlessis, & Foster, 2001).

A number of other factors can influence ad recall. For example, a telephone survey of 418 adults found that they were significantly more likely to remember an ad they had liked than an ad they had disliked. Whereas 65 percent of the subjects were able to describe ads they had disliked (which in itself is a respectable level of recall), more than 90 percent were able to describe ads they had liked (Stone, Besser, & Lewis, 2000).

How we feel about commercials in general can affect how well we remember them. In one study, the attitudes of 1,914 adults toward ads were measured first. Although 45 percent of the subjects believed that advertising was informative, 77 percent believed that ads were annoying and manipulative and that many

Some advertisers recognize the buying power of women for products that are beyond the scope of the traditional homemaker role. (Reproduced by permission of Samsonite Corporation.)

products failed to live up to their claims. These results tell advertisers that even people who think ads can be useful may also hold negative attitudes toward them. When these subjects were shown a series of magazine ads and asked on the following day to recall them, people with highly favorable attitudes toward advertising recalled significantly more of the ads they had seen than did people with highly unfavorable attitudes toward advertising (Mehta, 2000).

Racial identification can be a factor in our attitudes toward advertisements. A group of 160 Black adults participated in an experiment in which some of them viewed an ad featuring a White woman holding a garment bag and some viewed an ad featuring a Black woman holding the same bag. Their reactions were shown to depend on their level of identification with Black culture. Those with a high identification regarded the ad with the Black model more favorably. Those with a low identification with Black culture showed no preference for either model (Whittler & Spira, 2002).

Much research has been conducted on the effectiveness of magazine advertising. One study dealt with the controversial but widespread practice of advertisements for prescription drugs. A Gallup survey of 1,475 women over age 18, who described themselves as frequent magazine readers, showed that prescription ads were effective, especially among women who believed they had one of the symptoms described in the ad, which the drug claimed to cure. Half of those with such a symptom claimed to read the ads, and 43 percent reported that they asked their physicians about the medication. Older respondents had a higher rate of recall for the ad content and 62 percent of those surveyed, regardless of age, believed that prescription drug advertising provided vital information (Mehta & Purvis, 2003).

Mass-market advertising is a relatively recent, but rapidly growing, phenomenon in China. Research on the effectiveness of advertising there, conducted in a telephone survey of 825 adults ages 18–64, found that people in China held more positive attitudes toward ads than adults surveyed in the United States. A majority of the respondents (69 percent) reported that they found advertising to be informative, and 56 percent said they often used ads when making purchasing decisions. Younger people exhibited the most positive attitudes; they found advertisements to be entertaining and informative. Those with greater formal education held more positive attitudes toward advertising than did those with less education (Zhou, Zhang, & Vertinsky, 2002).

Advertising on the Web

The Internet is providing a new way for advertisers to spread their messages, although the effectiveness of their banner ads is still undetermined. To date, the effort is small, but it has the potential to grow. One survey reported that 40 percent of the people who use the Internet do so primarily for shopping. Even consumers who do not actually make purchases from Internet sites find it a good source of consumer information. Popular purchases include computers, books, flowers, music, travel services, and investment products. Yet for all the success stories, particularly around the Christmas shopping season, many companies have been disappointed by the response to their Web sites. A great deal more research is needed to identify the characteristics of potential Internet shoppers and the best ways to attract them.

One survey found that 85 percent of those who considered using, or actually used, online shopping reported frustration with the level of customer service.

TABLE 7–4

Reasons for Not Shopping Online

Reasons	Percent
Shipping charges	51
Cannot see and handle items	44
Cannot return items easily	32
Concern about credit card safety	24
Cannot ask questions	23
Takes too long to load screens	16
Worry about delivery time	15
Enjoy shopping in person	10

Source: W. Wells, J. Burnett, & S. Moriarty (2003). *Advertising: Principles and Practice* (6th ed.). Upper Saddle River, NJ: Prentice-Hall, p. 489.

Another 68 percent wanted to be able to contact a salesperson by e-mail or telephone but found that 40 percent of the shopping sites did not provide that capability. Some 51 percent said they cancelled an online purchase just before completion because the Web site requested too much personal information (Wells, Burnett, & Moriarty, 2003). Another survey cited several reasons some people refuse to shop online (see Table 7–4).

One consumer researcher sought to identify the types of direct-mail print ads that were likely to draw customers to commercial Web sites. Five different ads for a company that manufactured antique reproductions were mailed to 2,000 antique dealers, interior decorators, and designers. A Web address was included. The ads that produced the greatest number of hits were those that mentioned the Web address the greatest number of times. The ad that drew the fewest responses was the one that listed the Web address only once, at the end of the ad. The ad designed to look like a Web page, with a line of Web-like graphics across the top, drew the highest response rate (Bellizzi, 2000).

Research with groups of employed adults and college students on the design of Web pages has shown that complexity has a negative influence on advertising effectiveness. The simpler the Web page design, the higher was the stated intent to purchase the product displayed. Also, simpler Web pages engendered more favorable attitudes toward the company and the ad (Bruner & Kumar, 2000; Stevenson, Bruner, & Kumar, 2000).

A study of 311 adults who reviewed four hotel Web sites found that a high level of perceived interactivity with the site, as well as features such as a virtual tour of the facilities and an online reservation system, resulted in highly positive attitudes toward the companies and the sites. Web sites lacking these features did not receive positive ratings (McMillan, Hwang, & Lee, 2003).

An online survey of the purchasing behavior of 307 Internet users ages 16–40 showed that frequent Internet users bought books, CDs and other music products, electronic goods, and entertainment and travel services more often than did respondents who were infrequent Internet users. Age was not a factor in this study of Internet shopping behavior; older respondents purchased as many items as did younger respondents. Men were more likely than women to be more active buyers, and persons with higher incomes bought more items online than did those with lower incomes (Kwak, Fox, & Zinkhan, 2002).

An international study of 299 Internet users in 12 countries in Europe and South America, as well as the United States, found that consumer trust in a Web site was a major determinant in making the decision to purchase a product online. Trustworthiness was perceived to be higher when the site featured customer-service guarantees, reviews and testimonials from prior customers, and certification from an independent source such as a respected consumer organization (Lynch, Kent, & Srinivasan, 2001).

We noted that men shop online more frequently than women. This finding was confirmed in a questionnaire study of 227 adults over age 18 who had made at least one purchase online. The women in the sample shopped online less often and reported that they found online shopping to be less emotionally satisfying and less convenient than men did. Women were less trusting and more skeptical of Web site advertising claims than men were (Rodgers & Harris, 2003).

An international market research firm, Harris Interactive (www.harrisinteractive.com), suggests, on the basis of their survey results, six types of online shoppers (see Table 7–5).

Increasing amounts of research data are being published on the effectiveness of Web site advertising. In one study, pop-up questionnaires on 13 sites advertising and selling a variety of products were completed by more than 13,000 people who had logged on. The effectiveness of banner ads was measured by the length of the visit to the site and the number of clicks made to obtain additional information. The results showed that sites for so-called high-involvement products such as luxury cars provided more effective advertising (people spent more time on the site and clicked through more levels of information) than sites for low-involvement products such as baby diapers or diary products (Dahlen, Rasch, & Rosengren, 2003). Apparently, people will spend more time tracking down information on products that are more important, attractive, and desirable to them than on products that are merely functional.

This raises the question whether people who spend more time looking at ads on a Web site, or in any other medium, remember more of the ad content than do those who spend less time with the ad. A study conducted in New Zealand suggested yes. Some 149 university students were exposed to different ads on Web sites for various lengths of time (20 to 60 seconds per page). Then they were given aided recall and recognition tests on the ads they had just seen. The longer a person was exposed to a Web page containing an ad, the more likely they were to recall and recognize the ad after the exposure (Danaher & Mullarkey, 2003).

Personal interviews with 105 residents of Seoul, Korea, who used the Internet at least one hour per week, showed that their online time was greater for high-involvement products than low-involvement products; these results are similar to those of a study described earlier. Overall, however, the researchers did not find Internet ads to be as effective as television ads for enticing new consumers to consider luxury products. TV ads were more effective for all four products studied: luxury cars, expensive watches, fast food, and shampoo. Newspapers,

TABLE 7–5

Six Types of Internet Shoppers

E-bivalent newbies
Approximately 5% of the online shopping population, this group is the newest
to the Internet, is somewhat older, likes online shopping the least, and spends
the least money online.

Time-sensitive materialists
Approximately 17% of online shoppers, this group is most interested in
convenience and time-saving and is less likely to read product reviews,
compare prices, or use coupons.

Clicks and mortar
Approximately 23% of online shoppers, this group tends to shop online but
prefers to make purchases in stores, is more likely to include women
homemakers, expresses concerns about privacy and security when buying
online, and visits shopping malls more often than other groups.

Hooked, online, and single
Approximately 16% of online shoppers, this group is more likely to be young,
single men with high incomes, has used the Internet the longest, likes to play
games, download software, bank, invest, and shop online the most often.

Hunter-gatherers
Approximately 20% of online shoppers, this group is typically age 30–49 with
two children and most often visits Web sites that provide analysis and
comparison of products and prices.

Brand loyalists
Approximately 19% of online shoppers, this group is the most likely to connect
directly to the site address of a company they know, expresses the greatest
satisfaction with online shopping, and spends the most money online.

Source: Adapted from L. Schiffman & L. Kanuk (2004), *Consumer Behavior* (8th ed.). Upper
Saddle River, NJ: Prentice Hall, p. 70, after www.harrisinteractive.com.

magazines, and radio were also effective in enticing people to buy new products
(Yoon & Kim, 2001).

An overall measure of the effectiveness of Web site advertising is the number
of people who shop online. Although online purchases account for a smaller
percentage of sales than direct purchases in stores or from catalogs, the growth
rate for online shopping is increasing. Table 7–6 shows the annual growth rate in
sales for ten types of goods and services.

Fully half of today's online shopping occurs at work, from the office computer.
About one-third is done from home. Approximately 15 percent of online shopping
with U.S. companies comes from consumers in other countries, which indicates
the huge potential market for international online sales of American products and
services (Cappo, 2003).

Convenience and price are often cited as the major advantages of online shopping. A survey of 147 adults ages 22–44 confirmed these as the major reasons for
shopping online. The respondents also indicated that they were much more
likely to shop online for what are called "search goods," such as books or music,

TABLE 7–6

Fastest-Growing Categories of Consumer Online Spending

Category	2002 Sales	Percent Change from 2001
Furniture and appliances	$ 316,189,127	154%
Home and garden	899,882,381	101%
General services	201,415,914	80%
Sports and fitness	482,503,210	77%
Travel	14,773,387,316	71%
Event tickets	1,249,576,972	68%
Office	3,218,368,617	51%
Video games	121,492,909	47%
Computer hardware	4,662,862,978	45%
Movies and video	434,872,979	39%

where they can obtain information such as reviews, than for "experience goods," such as clothing, which shoppers prefer to feel or try on (Chiang & Dholakia, 2003).

Finally, Table 7–7 shows the relative advantages and disadvantages of advertising in the most frequently used media: direct mail, television, radio, periodicals, newspapers, and the Web. As you can see from the data, the Web has the potential for being the most effective source.

TABLE 7–7

Advantages and Disadvantages of Advertising in Different Media

Marketing Quality	World Wide Web	Radio	Newspaper	Periodicals	Television	Direct Mail
Large national audience	Yes	Maybe	Maybe	Maybe	Maybe	Yes
International exposure	Yes	No	No	Maybe	Maybe	No
Can be targeted to a specific audience	Yes	No	No	Maybe	No	Yes
Audience members can view ads at their convenience	Yes	No	Yes	Yes	No	Yes
Relative expense	Low	Medium	Medium	High	High	High
Instant customer interaction	Yes	No	No	No	No	No

Source: T. Kuegler (2000), *Advertising and marketing* (3rd ed.). Rocklin, CA: Prima Publishing.

CONSUMER BEHAVIOR AND MOTIVATION

Consumers can be influenced by marketplace factors other than advertising when they make their purchasing decisions. A store's atmosphere and cleanliness, the ease of parking, the length of the aisles—all these things can affect buyer behavior. For example, research on supermarket shopping behavior found that people will look down short aisles rather than walk down them. They are much more likely to walk down long aisles and to make more impulse buys as a result. In addition, the products more likely to be purchased on impulse are those displayed at the ends of the aisles and around the checkout lanes. You can readily see where manufacturers would want to shelve their products for maximum visibility.

Personal factors that affect consumer behavior include the standard biographical variables—age, sex, educational level, socioeconomic status, and ethnic origin—along with cognitive variables such as perceived time available for shopping, attitudes toward shopping, purpose of the shopping trip, and the shopper's mood and personality. For example, people who are self-conscious in public (overly concerned about the impression they make on others and what others think of them) tend to be concerned about the labels on the products they buy. Perhaps they believe that people will think more highly of them if they purchase national brands rather than store brands or generic brands of the same product.

Other factors that influence consumer behavior of interest to psychologists are brand placement, buying habits, brand loyalty, and the effect of product pricing.

Brand Placement

If you watch television or go to movies, it is impossible to avoid brand placement. When a film character drives a particular sports car or drinks a certain brand of beer, you are seeing an example of brand placement within the context of the story, rather than as a separate commercial or ad. A review of 112 hours of prime-time television programs showed an average of 30 brand placement appearances every hour (Avery & Ferraro, 2000). Advertisers like brand placement in movies, TV shows, and video games because they know the audience is not going to mute it, zap through it, leave the room, or channel surf the way they are likely to do when commercials come on. In addition, brand placement usually involves the use of the product by a popular star and thus can have the impact of a celebrity endorsement.

Studies have shown that when the lead character in a movie is shown using, driving, or drinking the product, viewer recall of that brand is increased. Viewers tend to evaluate the product more positively when a well-known actor appears to use the product. People also report that brand placement enhances their viewing experience because it makes the movie or television program seem more realistic (Yang, Roskos-Ewoldson, Roskos-Ewoldson, 2004).

In a study of 105 children ages 6–12, half were shown a brief film clip in which the Pepsi-Cola soft drink was mentioned and spilled on a table. The other group of children saw the same film clip but instead of Pepsi, unbranded food and milk were used. Then they were offered a choice between Coca-Cola and Pepsi-Cola, after which they were asked to describe the film clip. Significantly more of the children exposed to the brand placement selected Pepsi over

Newsbreak   Here's a Tip for You

Consumer psychologists try to amass as much information as possible about human behavior and motivation—where we shop, what we purchase, why we buy it, what ads we like, what ads turn us off. There's not much that escapes the scrutiny of consumer psychologists, even leaving a tip in a restaurant. To the people who serve meals and clear tables, the tips make up the bulk of their income. Therefore, the amount you decide to leave for their service is vital to them.

The money left on restaurant tables as tips totals more than $12 billion a year. Researchers have found that tipping has little to do with your opinion of the quality of the service you received and much more to do with the waiter's opinion of you! In other words, so researchers claim, we tip to please the waiter because we believe he or she is judging us. Do you buy that?

How do you decide on the size of the tip you leave at a restaurant? Do you tend to tip excessively? Do you tip only a token amount and hurry to leave before the waitperson notices? Here are several other factors that may influence the size of your tips:

- *How big was your bill?* The size of the tab you run up is the single best predictor of tip size. The larger the bill, the larger the tip.
- *How friendly was your server?* This should be the first thing a new server learns. The friendlier they are, the larger tip they receive. Waiters who smile and introduce themselves by name tend to make more money than those who do not. Also, waiters who crouch or bend down to your level while taking your order get better tips than those who remain standing. Women servers who draw smiley faces on the bill get higher tips than those who do not, but men servers who draw smiley faces get lower tips.
- *How professional was the service?* Studies show a weak relationship between customer evaluations of the quality of service and the size of the tip. Thus, friendliness may compensate for making a mistake with the order.
- *How attractive was the server?* As with many social activities, more attractive people fare better than less attractive people. In this case, they tend to receive somewhat larger tips, although the difference is not significant.
- *How many in your party?* Do you expect to leave a bigger tip when you are eating alone than when you're with a group? Tip size seems to decrease with the size of the party. Single diners leave an average of 20 percent of the bill. Two diners tip an average of 17 percent apiece. But when the group includes four or more, tip size drops to around 13 percent.
- *How often do you eat there?* Regulars at a restaurant tend to tip more than first-time customers or people who eat there only occasionally. Apparently, people feel differently about tipping when they expect to patronize the restaurant again.

> • *Cash or charge?* People who charge meals leave larger tips than those who pay cash. Perhaps it doesn't seem like "real money" when you're using plastic.
>
> A recent nationwide survey found that 30 percent of Americans do not know that it is customary to leave a 15 to 20 percent tip in a restaurant; they didn't have a clue about how much to leave for the server! A consumer behavior professor at Cornell University, who conducted the survey, was surprised by the results. He wrote that "a fair number of that 30 percent said 'I leave a buck or two.' I was shocked. I figured about 90 percent of the population would know that you leave 15 or 20 percent, and maybe there was that 10 percent of people living under a rock who didn't know." Hmm. How much do you tip?
>
> ------
>
> *Sources:* S. Daley, Hey, big spender. *Washingtonian Magazine,* May 1996, p. 194. W. Grimes, Tips: Check your insecurity at the door. *New York Times,* February 3, 1999. J. Sharkey, He parked your car. She retrieved it. Who gets a tip? *New York Times,* April 25, 2004.

Coke. This was true even for children who said they did not recall seeing Pepsi in the movie segment. Fewer younger children than older children were able to recall the brand they had seen, but there was no age difference in their choice of Pepsi over Coke. In this case, the brand placement was effective (Auty & Lewis, 2004).

Buying Habits and Brand Loyalty

Many of the stores in which we shop and the products we select are chosen on the basis of habit. Once we find a product we like, it is simpler to continue to buy it than to find a new one. To demonstrate the strength of shopping habits, one supermarket rearranged its display of canned soups. The soups had been grouped by brand name but were changed to alphabetical order by type of soup, thus intermixing all the different brands. Although signs were posted to explain the new arrangement, more than 60 percent of the customers were fooled. Habit led them to the space on the shelf where they had previously gotten the desired soups. When questioned, customers said that the soups had been stocked in their usual order. They were amazed to find the wrong cans in their shopping cart. When consumers shop in new stores, where habit does not automatically lead them to the shelf locations of their preferred products, they tend to buy many more different brands than in the past.

The design of an ad campaign to change persistent buying habits presents a challenge. Studies show that consumer loyalty to major brands can remain unchanged up to eight years. Sixteen brands that were top sellers in their product category in 1923 retained their primacy 60 years later: these included Campbell soup, Lipton tea, Kodak cameras, and Wrigley chewing gum. These findings reinforce the importance to advertisers of establishing brand preferences in childhood. Once committed, consumers tend to remain loyal to a particular brand for many years and to pass that loyalty on to their children.

It is sometimes difficult for researchers to distinguish between buying habits and brand loyalty. Both can be defined in terms of repeat purchase behavior, with the result that the consumer is relatively impervious to ads for competing brands. Some companies, notably airlines, hotels, and car rental agencies, have developed effective brand loyalty programs by offering a rising scale of rewards for repeat business. For example, airline frequent-flier plans offer rewards such as free flights, first-class upgrades, VIP check-in lines, early boarding, and sky-lounge memberships. These programs have been shown to be highly successful in inducing customer loyalty. Many people will make longer or more circuitous flight arrangements on their chosen airline just to accumulate additional miles.

A survey of 643 adults showed that the promise of a low to moderate reward for buying a product, in an effort to establish brand loyalty, was more cost-effective than the offer of a higher reward in return for an intention to purchase. This finding contradicted the results of a survey of 300 brand managers who believed that offering high rewards would be more cost-effective for their company in establishing brand loyalty (Wansink, 2003).

Product Pricing

The price of a product can be an important influence on buying behavior, independent of advertising and product quality. Consumers frequently use price as an index of quality on the assumption that the more an object costs, the better it must be. Some manufacturers capitalize on this belief and charge a higher price than their competitors do for a product of equal quality. Identical products, differing only in price, are often judged solely by their cost, with the more expensive product rated higher in quality.

Some consumers, however, do not consider price when shopping for certain items. Observations of supermarket shoppers reveal that most do not pay attention to price information when shopping for staples such as breakfast cereal,

Supermarket shoppers may judge certain products to be superior solely on the basis of price.

coffee, and soft drinks, and they cannot accurately report current prices. Because of different package weights and sizes, shoppers are often unable to make the calculations necessary to determine which of several brands is the best buy. When supermarkets provide unit pricing information, such as cost per serving or cost per item, some shoppers use this information in making purchasing decisions.

A popular technique to gain sales for a new product or package is to charge a low price as an introductory offer. The idea is that once shoppers purchase the product, they will continue to do so out of habit, even when the price is raised to the level of competing products. Research does not support this notion. Sales are usually high during the introductory price period but drop when the price is raised. In stores that do not lower the price during the introductory period, sales typically remain stable. Rebates are a more effective way of offering a price reduction as an inducement to purchase. A price decrease in the form of a rebate usually produces higher sales than an equal point-of-sale price reduction.

Advertising to Ethnic Groups

Research has identified important differences in consumer values, attitudes, and shopping behavior among people of different ethnic groups. Studies of Whites, Blacks, Hispanic-Americans, and Asian-Americans have documented preferences for various products. In many large cities, Blacks and Hispanics account for the majority of the residents, forming sizable markets with considerable purchasing power. Consumer Web sites for ethnic groups include www.nationalbcc.org, the National Black Chamber of Commerce, which offers discounts from major corporations and other benefits; www.blackplanet.com, which offers college databases and financial tools; www.starmedia.com, which offers Spanish-language shopping and travel services; and www.zonafinanciera.com, which provides banking, insurance, auto, and real estate services.

In 2002 Hispanics became the largest minority group in the United States; their population is expected to increase by 30 percent by 2010. The non-Hispanic White population is expected to increase only 6 percent during that time, and the Black population by less than 12 percent. The U.S. Census Bureau estimates that Hispanics will account for nearly one-third of the U.S. population by 2050.

Corporations such as Kraft, General Foods, and Pepsi-Cola have created special organizational units to develop advertising targeted to appeal to Hispanics. Studies show that as a group, Hispanics have positive attitudes toward advertising and rely on it, more than do other minority groups, to provide information about consumer products and services (Torres & Gelb, 2002). Recognizing this characteristic, Procter & Gamble spent $90 million in the year 2003 on advertising designed for Hispanic media outlets for a dozen products including toothpaste and laundry detergent. The company established a 65-member bilingual team to identify the needs and desires of Hispanic consumers. One result of this market research is the finding that Hispanic consumers like to be able to smell certain household products, such as toiletries and detergents. This has led the company to add new scents for this market (Grow, 2004). Market researchers have identified other characteristics of Hispanic shoppers (see Table 7–8).

TABLE 7–8

Characteristics of Hispanic-American Shoppers

- Prefer well-known or familiar brands
- Buy brands perceived to be prestigious
- Are fashion conscious
- Prefer to shop at smaller, more personal stores
- Buy brands advertised by their own ethnic group stores
- Tend not to be impulsive buyers
- Tend to clip and use cents-off coupons
- Prefer to purchase the products and brands their parents bought
- Prefer fresh or freshly prepared food items rather than frozen foods

Source: Adapted from L. Schiffman & L. Kanuk (2004), *Consumer behavior* (8th ed.). Upper Saddle River, NJ: Prentice Hall, p. 441.

Spanish-language television programs shown on the Telemundo network (owned by NBC) and the Univision network have been highly successful in reaching the greater Hispanic audience. Univision is the fifth most frequently watched network in the United States. Advertisers have learned that even Hispanics who are fluent in English prefer to watch Spanish-language programming, making them an ideal audience for advertisers. Spanish-language magazines such as *Latina, Urban Latino,* and *Glamour en Español* are popular outlets for advertising. General Motors spends more than $7 million annually for ads in such magazines. Kmart began a Spanish-language entertainment and lifestyle magazine, *La Vida,* with a circulation in excess of one million in ten key markets including Los Angeles and San Diego, California.

A major source of advertising to the Hispanic market is the telecommunications industry. As a group, Hispanic consumers spend more of their monthly household budget on cell phones and long-distance phone service, driven by the strong need to keep in touch with family members residing in other countries (Noguchi, 2004).

Blacks constitute nearly 13 percent of the U.S. population, making them also a desirable market with rapidly increasing purchasing power. During the decade of the 1990s, the buying power of Black consumers grew 73 percent, as more and more Blacks earned middle-class and upper-class incomes. Black consumers, more than any other group, demonstrate a high level of brand loyalty. Once a brand is selected, they are highly unlikely to switch to a competing grand.

Black households tend to spend a larger share of their income on food, clothing, entertainment, and health care than other groups. They also prefer to make more separate trips to grocery stores in the course of a week than do other groups. In general, Black consumers are more willing to pay more for what they consider to be products of higher quality. This includes a preference for high-fashion items and name-brand products that serve as a visible indicator of success. Blacks, in general, look to the media, movies, TV programs, and advertisements for cues as to which items of clothing, jewelry, and other products will define success in the mainstream culture (Schiffman & Kanuk, 2004).

Surveys of Black and Hispanic consumers show that both groups are attracted to upscale images and attributes of products and the stores in which they shop. For Blacks, unlike Hispanics, family and friends are an important reference point and source of information in making purchasing decisions. This indicates the value of word-of-mouth advertising and of showing images of friends and family using a particular product in the ads (Kim & Kang, 2001).

Surveys indicate a general level of distrust of advertising in the Black community. Because many people appear to believe that ads are designed for a White audience, Black adult consumers have greater trust in Black-centered media outlets as sources of information about consumer products. Consequently, major companies are spending millions of dollars designing ads to appeal to the Black community for Black-oriented print media, and radio and television programs. As with the Hispanic market, advertisers have learned that, contrary to the popular saying, one size does *not* fit all. An ad that may be highly successful with White consumers may fail to reach other groups.

The Asian-American community in the United States is approximately 4 percent of the population but is the fastest-growing segment. Asians have a reputation for being industrious, disciplined, and hard working, eager to achieve a middle-class lifestyle. Thus, they constitute another desirable market for advertisers. They tend to be better educated than the general population and to be more computer literate. About 60 percent of this group earns more than $60,000 a year; approximately half have professional positions in the workforce.

Asians tend to value high quality, to buy established and well-known brand names, and to remain loyal customers. They are a particularly diverse community of some 15 different ethnic groups with different buying and spending habits. Thus they can be expected to respond differently to advertising appeals. For example, almost 80 percent of the Vietnamese living in the United States were not born in this country; fewer than one-third of the Japanese community in the United States were not born here. Most Vietnamese prefer to use their native language and are highly committed to maintaining their cultural traditions. They do not like to make purchases on credit, because owing money in their culture brings disapproval. In contrast, Korean and Chinese people who have spent more years in the United States are highly agreeable to the use of credit as being the "American way" of being a good consumer in the marketplace (Schiffmann & Kanuk, 2004).

Advertising to Children and Adolescents

The 4-to-12 age group contains 35 million children with control over approximately $15 billion in disposable income. Fast-growing spending categories for these young consumers are shoes, clothing, breakfast cereals, candy, soda, and other snack foods. One explanation psychologists have advanced for the children's high degree of purchasing power is parental guilt. Consumer psychologists suggest that in single-parent families, in families with both parents employed outside the home, and in families in which parents have postponed childbearing until their thirties, the children have been indulged with more money to spend and more influence over family purchasing decisions.

Marketing to children uses techniques such as placing products on lower supermarket shelves, airing cartoon commercials on children's TV programs, and distributing in schools pencils, magazines, and book covers featuring a product's name or logo, but the primary way of reaching children in the marketplace is through electronic media.

Many teenage shoppers are responsible for household grocery purchases.

Children are exposed to an average of 40,000 television commercials annually. In the United States, children between the ages of two and 18 spend nearly 40 hours per week with some form of electronic media including television, computers, videos, movies, video games, cell phones, and radio. The average American child apparently spends more time staring at a screen than doing anything else (Levin & Linn, 2004).

Teenagers spend an estimated $30 billion a year on clothing, cosmetics, and other personal items such as videotapes, audiotapes, and CDs. They have also assumed responsibility for much household spending. Many adolescents compile the household grocery list, make decisions about specific brands, and do the family shopping. More than 60 percent of teenage girls and 40 percent of teenage boys are believed to do routine grocery shopping.

A study of nearly 200 teenagers found that half reported spending up to three hours a day watching television and one-third spent the same amount of time listening to the radio (LaFerle, Edwards, & Lee, 2000). Teenagers are also increasing their use of the Internet, spending more hours surfing the Web at home and at school. So much advertising is directed at adolescents about the importance of having the popular brand of shoes, jeans, cell phones, or cars that it has changed they way they view themselves and their interactions with peers and adults. One child psychologist noted that "By the time children reach their teens, a developmental stage when they're naturally insecure and searching for a personal identity, they've been taught that material possessions are what matter" (Kersting, 2004, p. 61). They define themselves, all too often, by the images they see in movies and on TV.

A survey of 329 college students ages 18–24 asked how informative they found the ads in different media. Television ads were ranked high in value for information, as were newspaper and magazine ads. Considering all media outlets, women in this sample found advertising to be more informative than men did (Wolburg & Pokyrwczynski, 2001).

Newsbreak

Does Advertising Exploit Children?

The answer is yes. In 2004 the American Psychological Association reported that ads directed at children under age eight should be restricted because young children tend to assume that what they see and hear is truthful and unbiased. And even advertisers admit that their marketing exploits children. The head of one ad agency said, "Advertising at its best is making people feel that without their product, you're a loser. Kids are very sensitive to that. If you tell them to buy something, they are resistant. But if you tell them they'll be a dork if they don't, you've got their attention. You open up emotional vulnerabilities, and it's easy to do that with kids."

Advertisers refer to a product's "nag factor"—how much they can get kids to nag their parents before they give in and purchase the product. One clinical psychologist reported that parents experience considerable emotional turmoil over how they should respond to such nagging. They feel guilty about surrendering and buying their children the junk food or violent video games the kids want, because the parents believe these things are bad for their children. And the parents feel guilty if they don't agree, thinking that maybe their decision will lead to a child's depression or anxiety or lowered self-esteem if he or she doesn't get the right shoes or backpack.

Advertisers also like to develop materialistic attitudes as early as possible, which, critics say, can lead children to grow up defining their self-worth in terms of their possessions instead of their personal qualities.

Now, how about that manipulation and deception, which critics charge is done on a massive scale? Psychologists agree that it happens, even though some of them help advertisers develop effective techniques to persuade children to buy products. As one psychologist put it, "The fake promise of popularity, success, and attractiveness that marketers routinely make for their products are such common lies that we have become inured to their dishonesty. Yet we know that when adults chronically deceive and manipulate a child it erodes the youngster's ability to trust others and to feel secure in the world."

Do children learn from a young age that advertising is not like real life and that they shouldn't take it seriously? Is this part of growing up, learning who and what to trust? And even if no psychologists were involved, wouldn't advertisers be doing the same thing? Here's the bottom line, according to the advertising industry: If companies did not use advertising ploys to sell products, they'd go out of business and would have to fire hundreds of thousands of employees, most of whom have children. Do you agree?

Sources: R. A. Clay, Advertising to children: Is it ethical? *Monitor on Psychology,* August 2000, 52–53; A. D. Kanner & T. Kasser (2000). Stuffing our kids: Should psychologists help advertisers manipulate children? *The Industrial-Organizational Psychologist, 38*(1), 185–187. Ads that target kids are unfair, studies say. *St. Petersburg (FL) Times,* February 24, 2004.

Advertising to Older Persons

Changing demographic trends have produced another important market for advertisers: working people over the age of 50. This consumer segment, growing in numbers and affluence, will, by the year 2020, constitute more than one-third of the population. The over-50 group now includes the first of the baby boomers, a market of 76 million consumers with a large disposable income that they are used to spending freely. People over 50 have half the discretionary income in the United States, and people over 65 have twice that of people between 25 and 34, in their prime earning years.

The over-50 age group represents a multibillion-dollar market for goods and services. Advertisers have responded to this trend by revising their image of older people in ads and by eliminating stereotypes about the older consumer. Ads featuring attractive older models now promote cosmetics, hair care products, luxury travel, automobiles, clothing, jewelry, health clubs, and investments.

Retired people over age 65 constitute a large market for clothing, home furnishings, travel, entertainment, and health care products and services. They tend to read more newspapers and magazines, and their television preferences include news and sports programs. Thus, they rely on mass media advertising and also use the Internet for shopping. There are more Internet users over age 50 than under age 20. The over-50 group tends to shop online for books, stocks, and computer equipment more frequently than the under-50 group. More than 90 percent of people over age 65 who have access to computers shop online. Older consumers are highly critical of ads suggesting that young people are the only ones who have any fun.

Advertising to the Gay Community

An increasingly vocal and visible consumer group, gay persons are better educated and more affluent than the general population. A survey of 20,000 homosexuals that was conducted by a Chicago opinion polling firm found that approximately 60 percent of gay men and women were college graduates, compared to about 20 percent of the U.S. population as a whole. As a large potential market of people with high discretionary incomes, they are increasingly coming to the attention of advertisers.

Interviews with 44 gay men in Canada found that they preferred making consumer purchases only from companies that were perceived as "gay positive." These were companies that advertised in gay media, supported gay and lesbian employee groups, and offered same-sex domestic-partnership benefits. These companies also supported the gay community at large—for example, by making corporate contributions to AIDS charities. In addition, the survey showed that these gay consumers actively boycotted companies perceived as being homophobic or practicing discrimination in hiring (Kates, 2000).

Another survey of 372 homosexuals in the United States confirmed their status as a better-educated and more affluent segment of the population, but these upscale characteristics applied more often to men than to women. The questionnaire responses indicated that these gay consumers preferred to read the *Wall Street Journal, Business Week, Fortune, Money, The New Yorker, Sports Illustrated,* and *National Geographic;* they were less likely to read *TV Guide* or *Readers' Digest.*

Television preferences included network news programs, CNN, "Late Night with David Letterman," and "60 Minutes." They rarely watched game shows, soap operas, or talk shows. This information tells companies where to target their ads. However, the survey also reported that the participants in this research claimed to have little use for advertising in making their purchasing decisions. They tended not to believe advertising in general and described most of it as condescending to homosexuals (Burnett, 2000). Note that the Web sites www.gay.com and www.planetout.com offer chat rooms, personal ads, shopping information, HIV information, investment opportunities, news, and links to gay-owned businesses.

Let us conclude by noting that manufacturers and advertisers respond to changing markets with new products and marketing techniques. Consumers should be aware of the varied nature of advertising—sometimes valuable and informative and sometimes manipulative and deceptive. As a consumer, you should remember one of history's oldest lessons: *caveat emptor*. Let the buyer—whether of ideas, political philosophies, values, theories, research findings, and even psychology textbooks—beware.

Summary

Consumer psychology studies consumer behavior through surveys, **focus groups,** motivation research, behavioral observations, and brand identification and preference research. Testing for advertising effectiveness is done through direct questioning, **aided recall** and **recognition,** physiological measures, **sales tests,** and coupon returns. Advertising types include direct sell, product image, consumer awareness, and institutional. Advertising appeals can be positive, negative, or mixed, or they may include celebrity endorsements. Many ads involve claims of implied superiority, which consumers tend to believe.

Trademarks can be effective advertising aids, as can the product image. Packaging can also be influential at the point of purchase. Sexy images are commonly used in ads; they attract people to the ads but do not seem to influence how much of the advertising message is recalled. Most people dislike TV commercials, avoid watching them, and fail to remember three-fourths of the ads they see. Internet advertising has increased; simpler Web page design is effective in getting people to purchase the advertised products, although some consumer resistance to online shopping still exists, typically related to shipping charges, credit card safety, and the inability to actually touch or see the product. Men shop more frequently online than women do. Trust in a Web site is also a factor in online shopping. People who spend more time looking at an online ad are more likely to recall the message and recognize the product.

Brand placement (having a product used by a character in a movie or TV program, for example) is effective in influencing consumer opinion about the product. Brand loyalty can render buyers immune to advertising for competing products. Product price is often used as an indication of quality.

Hispanic, Black, and Asian ethnic groups in the United States have become targeted audiences for advertising campaigns designed to appeal to their specific cultural needs and values; these can be seen most often in magazine ads and television commercials. Other groups likely to receive targeted ads include children, adolescents, elderly persons, and gay persons.

Key Terms

aided recall technique
focus groups

recognition technique
sales test technique

Review Questions

1. What did John B. Watson contribute to the study of consumer behavior?
2. Describe some of the results of the nationwide survey by the American Association of Advertising Agencies on popular opinions toward advertising.
3. What are the advantages of online consumer surveys over surveys conducted by telephone or in person?
4. Describe how focus groups are conducted. Discuss advantages and disadvantages of focus groups compared to surveys.
5. How did the study by Ernest Dichter on packaged cake mixes influence consumer research?
6. If you had the job of conducting research on the behavior of consumers shopping for cookies at supermarkets in your city, how would you design the project? What problems would you have to resolve in conducting this research?
7. Describe techniques used by consumer psychologists to test reactions to advertising.
8. How effective is the use of coupons in determining effectiveness of newspaper and magazine ads? What are the advantages of obtaining coupons online compared to cutting coupons out of the newspaper?
9. Which appeals are more effective in advertising: positive or negative appeals? Shock or fear appeals? Give an example of each type.
10. Describe the impact on consumer behavior of product packaging, product pricing, and the use of sex in advertisements.
11. What factors help us remember an ad we have seen? How effective are ads for prescription medications?
12. What are the advantages and disadvantages of advertising on the Web?
13. How do people who like online shopping differ from those who do not like online shopping?
14. What kinds of products are people more likely to purchase online? What are they least likely to buy online?
15. What is brand placement? How effective is brand placement when targeted at adults? At children?
16. How would you devise an ad campaign for upscale furniture if your target was the Hispanic consumer? The Black consumer? The Asian-American consumer? What media would you use for your ads?
17. Describe the major differences between the consumer behavior of Hispanics and of Blacks.
18. What characteristics define the Asian-American population in the United States?
19. Do you think it is ethical to advertise to children under the age of eight? Why or why not?
20. How do gay people appear to differ from nongay people in their consumer behavior?

Kasser, T., & Kanner, A. D. (Eds.) (2004). *Psychology and consumer culture: The struggle for a good life in a materialistic world*. Washington, D.C.: American Psychological Association. An in-depth psychological analysis of consumerism and its effects on people's lives and on society as a whole. Relates consumer behavior to ethnicity, childhood development, gender roles, work stress, and psychopathology.

Lewis, D., & Bridger, D. (2000). *The soul of the new consumer: Authenticity—What we buy and why in the new economy*. London: Nicholas Brealey. Market researchers present findings from consumer surveys on shopping experiences and television commercials. They describe the modern consumer as individualistic and well informed.

Longinotti-Buitoni, G. L. (1999). *Selling dreams: How to make any product irresistible*. New York: Simon & Schuster. The CEO of Ferrari North America describes his research on the emotional link between a product's image and its function. He applies his ideas to cars, hotels, magazines, beauty products, wines, clothing, and electronics.

Reichert, T., & Lambiase, J. (Eds.) (2003). *Sex in advertising: Perspectives on the erotic appeal*. Mahwah, NJ: Erlbaum. Attempts to answer questions about sex in advertising: What is it? Doses it work? Why is it so popular? How does it affect different consumer groups? How is it used by new media? What are its effects on society?

Simonson, I., Carmon, Z., Dhar, R., Drolet, A., & Nowlis, S. M. (2001). Consumer research. *Annual Review of Psychology, 52,* 249–275. Reviews theories of consumer behavior, social and cognitive influences, and research methods (including online behaviors, field experiments, and laboratory research).

Tourangeau, R., Rips, J. L., & Rasinski, K. (2000). *The psychology of survey response*. New York: Cambridge University Press. Summarizes and reviews research on the psychological mechanisms of the survey response. Shows how minor variations in the wording of survey questions can affect employee comprehension, judgment, and response.

Twitchell, J. B. (2001). *20 ads that shook the world: The century's most groundbreaking advertising and how it changed us all*. New York: Crown. A look back at classic ad campaigns for Coca-Cola, Volkswagen, Listerine, Nike, and Lydia E. Pinkham's Vegetable Compound, showing how a market can be created for a product we never knew we needed.

Underhill, P. (1999). *Why we buy: The science of shopping*. New York: Simon & Schuster. An urban geographer presents his findings based on 20 years of observations of shoppers in supermarkets, bookshops, and department stores.

Williams, J. D., Lee, W.-N., & Haugtvedt, C. P. (Eds.) (2004). *Diversity in advertising: Broadening the scope of research directions*. Mahwah, NJ: Erlbaum. Reviews research on diversity in advertising covering prejudice and discrimination, gender bias, language, group differences in information processing, social context, celebrity endorsements, ethnic identity and targeted marketing, culturally embedded ads, religious symbolism, and social values.

Additional Reading

Chapter 8
Engineering Psychology

Chapter 8

Engineering Psychology

CHAPTER OUTLINE

HISTORY AND SCOPE OF ENGINEERING PSYCHOLOGY

We have discussed various ways in which industrial-organizational (I-O) psychologists contribute to the organizational goals of increasing employee efficiency, productivity, and job satisfaction. We have seen how employees with the best abilities can be recruited and selected, trained for their jobs, and supervised and motivated effectively. We have also described techniques that can be applied to optimize the quality of work life and the conditions of the work environment. But we have mentioned only briefly a factor as influential as any of those discussed—the design of the machinery and equipment employees use to do their jobs and the workspaces in which those tasks are performed.

Tools, equipment, and work stations must be compatible with the workers who use them. We may think of this as a team operation, a person and a machine functioning together to perform a task that could not be accomplished by either working alone. If the person and the machine are to work smoothly in this person-machine system, they must be compatible so that each makes use of the strengths of the other and, where necessary, compensates for the weaknesses of the other.

Engineering psychology
The design of machines and equipment for human use, and the determination of the appropriate human behaviors for the efficient operation of the machines. The field is also called human factors, human engineering, and ergonomics.

This pairing of operator and machine is the province of **engineering psychology,** also called human factors, or human engineering. British psychologists use the term *ergonomics,* which is derived from the Greek word *ergon,* meaning "work," and *nomos,* meaning "natural laws." In conjunction with engineers, engineering psychologists apply their knowledge of psychology to the formulation of natural laws of work. Thus, engineering psychology is the science of designing or engineering machines and equipment for human use and of engineering human behavior for the efficient operation of the machines.

Until the 1940s, the design of machinery, equipment, and industrial plants was solely the responsibility of engineers. They made design decisions on the basis of mechanical, electrical, space, and size considerations. They paid little attention to the workers who would have to operate the machines. The machine was considered to be a constant factor, incapable of being changed to meet human needs. It was the employee who would have to adapt. No matter how uncomfortable, tiring, or unsafe the equipment was, the human operators—the only flexible part of the person-machine system—had to adjust, to make the best of the situation and fit themselves to the machine's requirements.

Adapting the worker to the machine was accomplished through time-and-motion study, a forerunner of engineering psychology, in which jobs were analyzed to determine how they could be simplified. Of course, this approach to designing machines while ignoring the needs of the people who operated them could not be maintained. Machines were becoming too complex, requiring levels of speed, skill, and attention that threatened to exceed human capacities to monitor and control them.

The weapons developed for use in World War II placed greater demands on human abilities, not only muscle strength but also sensing, perceiving, judging, and making split-second decisions. For example, pilots of sophisticated fighter aircraft were allowed little time to react to a dangerous situation, to determine a course of action, and to initiate the appropriate response. Radar and sonar operators also required high levels of skill. In general, the wartime equipment worked well, but mistakes were frequent. The most precise bombsight ever developed was not leading to accurate bombing. Friendly ships and aircraft were being misidentified and fired upon. Whales were mistaken for submarines. Although the machinery seemed to be functioning properly, the system—the interaction of the person and the machine—clearly was not.

It was this wartime need that spurred the development of engineering psychology, similar to the way the screening and selection needs of the army in World War I gave rise to mass psychological testing. Authorities recognized that human abilities and limitations would have to be taken into account while designing machines if the overall system was to operate efficiently. Psychologists, physiologists, and physicians soon joined engineers to design aircraft cockpits, submarine and tank crew stations, and components of military uniforms.

An example of this early work helped American pilots stay alive. At the time, there was no consistent or standard arrangement of displays and controls within the cockpits of different models of aircraft. A pilot used to one type of plane who was suddenly assigned to another would be confronted by a different set of displays and controls. The lever to raise the wheels in the new plane might be in the same place as the lever to operate the flaps in the old plane. Imagine trying to drive a car in which gas pedal and brake pedal are reversed. In an emergency you would probably step on what you thought was the brake pedal, but you would be stepping on the gas instead.

There was also no consistency in the operating characteristics of aircraft controls. Within the same cockpit, one control might be pushed upward to turn something on and another switched downward to turn something on. A number of separate controls with identical knobs were often placed close together so that a pilot whose attention was diverted would not be able to distinguish among the controls by touch alone. As these problems were recognized, they were corrected, but many pilots were killed because their machines had been designed poorly from the reference point of the pilot, whose job was to direct and control the aircraft's power.

Poor design has also led to other kinds of accidents. In 1979 a disastrous situation occurred at the nuclear power plant at Three Mile Island, Pennsylvania. The accident occurred during the night shift when the operators were less alert, but part of the problem involved a lack of attention to human needs. In the power plant's control room, instrument dials and controls had been placed too far apart. When operators detected a dangerous reading on one of the displays, valuable time was lost because the employees had to run to another part of the room to activate controls to correct the malfunction. To prevent a recurrence, the Nuclear Regulatory Commission ordered modification of nuclear power plant control rooms to consider the abilities of the human operators.

To deal with human factors in aircraft accidents, 66 percent of which can be traced to pilot error, the National Transportation Safety Board added engineering psychologists to its staff. Their job is to investigate pilot and crew fatigue, shift work schedules, health issues, stress, and equipment design, all of which can contribute to accidents.

Much human factors research has been conducted on passenger vehicles in an effort to make them safer. Variables studied include the brightness of automobile and motorcycle headlights; the position, color, and brightness of brake lights; and the layout of dashboard controls and displays. Since 1985, passenger cars driven in the United States must have a brake light mounted in the rear window. This requirement is a result of human factors research on 8,000 vehicles that showed that a high-mounted brake light reduced the incidence of rear-end collisions by 50 percent.

Engineering psychologists are studying ways to make license plates and traffic signs more legible and noticeable at night. They investigate the effects of alcohol on driver behavior and conduct research on driver reaction time—how drivers perceive and comprehend risky situations and make decisions about responding.

Another problem engineering psychologists are tackling is the effect on visibility of tinting or solar film on car windows. Research results show that the detection of objects, such as pedestrians or other cars, through the rear window while backing up is significantly reduced when that window is tinted. In some cases, a tinted window admits only half of the available light, a finding that has led many states to regulate the use of solar film for safe visibility. Older drivers are more affected by dark window tints than are younger drivers. One study found that drivers between the ages of 60 and 69 experienced a greater reduction in contrast sensitivity to light than did drivers between the ages of 20 and 29 (LaMotte, Ridder, Yeung, & DeLand, 2000).

Research by engineering psychologists has demonstrated that using cell phones while driving reduces reaction time, particularly among older drivers, and can lead to a higher accident risk among drivers of all ages. These and similar research findings are instigating state regulation of cell phone use.

Engineering psychologists contribute to the design of a variety of other products, including dental and surgical implements, cameras, toothbrushes, and bucket seats for cars. They have been involved in the redesign of the mailbags used by letter carriers. Why? Because more than 20 percent of letter carriers suffer from musculoskeletal problems such as low back pain from carrying mailbags slung over their shoulders. A mailbag with a waist-support strap, and a double bag that requires the use of both shoulders, have been shown to reduce muscle fatigue.

The most well-developed human factors programs in the United States and in several European and Asian nations are in the automobile, electronics, and food industries, as well as in the design of work stations for a variety of businesses. Some of the leading companies in applying human factors findings to their workplaces and products include General Motors, DaimlerChrysler, SAAB, Volvo, and IBM and other computer makers (see Hagg, 2003).

An analysis of the economic benefits to corporations of applying ergonomic research showed net gains between 1 and 12 percent over the cost of the human factors intervention. These financial gains almost always accrued in less than a year after incorporating human factors changes. One example is the introduction of the high-mounted brake light on automobiles, which cost the industry about $10 per car. The annual return on that modest initial investment has been approximately $434 million in lower car repair costs resulting from the 50 percent drop in rear-end collisions (Stanton & Baber, 2003).

Because the field of engineering psychology is a hybrid, it is not surprising that its practitioners have diverse backgrounds. The membership of the Human Factors and Ergonomics Society consists primarily of psychologists and engineers but also includes professionals from medicine, sociology, anthropology, computer sciences, and other behavioral and physical sciences. Over the past decade there has been a substantial increase in the number of masters-level psychologists undertaking careers in engineering psychology. The growth of the field remains dynamic, and its work extends to many types of organizations.

TIME-AND-MOTION STUDY

Time-and-motion study was an early attempt to redesign work tools and equipment and to reshape the way workers performed their jobs. It stemmed from the efforts of three pioneers who focused on ways to make physical labor more efficient.

The first systematic attempt to study the performance of specific job tasks began in 1898 when Frederick W. Taylor, the promoter of scientific management, undertook an investigation of the nature of shoveling at the request of a large U.S. steel manufacturer. Taylor observed the workers and found that they were using shovels of many sizes and shapes. As a result, the loads being lifted by each man ranged from 3½ pounds to 38 pounds. By experimenting with different loads, Taylor determined that the optimum shovel—the one with which workers were most efficient—held 21½ pounds. Lighter or heavier loads resulted in a decrease in total daily output. Taylor introduced shovels of different sizes for handling different materials—for example, a small one for heavy iron ore and a larger one for ashes. These changes may sound trivial, but Taylor's work saved the company more than $78,000 a year, an enormous sum at that time. With the new shovels, 140 men could accomplish the same amount of work that previously required 500 men. By offering an incentive of higher pay for greater productivity, the company allowed workers to increase their wages by 60 percent (Taylor, 1911).

Taylor's work was the first empirical demonstration of the relationship between work tools and worker efficiency. The next pioneers in the field were Frank Gilbreth, an engineer, and Lillian Gilbreth, a psychologist, who did more than anyone else to promote time-and-motion study. Whereas Taylor had been concerned primarily with tool design and incentive wage systems, the Gilbreths were interested in the mechanics of job performance. Their goal was to eliminate all unnecessary motion (Gilbreth, 1911).

It began when Frank Gilbreth at age 17 was working as an apprentice bricklayer. During his first day on the job, he noticed that the bricklayers made many unnecessary motions in doing their work. He thought he could redesign the job to make it faster and easier, and within a year he was the fastest bricklayer on the job. Once he persuaded his co-workers to try his methods, the entire crew was accomplishing far more work without becoming exhausted.

Gilbreth designed a scaffold that could be raised or lowered so that the worker would always be at a height convenient to the task. By analyzing the hand and arm movements involved in laying bricks and changing to the most efficient ones, he found that workers could lay 350 bricks an hour instead of 120. This increase in productivity was not brought about by forcing men to work faster but by reducing the number of motions needed for laying each brick from 18 to 5.

Frank and Lillian Gilbreth organized their household and their personal lives around the principles of time-and-motion economy. Every activity was scrutinized for wasted motion. For example, Frank Gilbreth always buttoned his vest from the bottom up because it took four seconds less than buttoning it from the top down. He used two brushes, one in each hand, to lather his face for shaving, a savings of 17 seconds. He tried shaving with two razors simultaneously but lost more time bandaging cuts than he had saved in shaving. The efforts to schedule the activities of the 12 Gilbreth children were recounted in a popular book and

Time-and-motion study
An early attempt to redesign work tools and to reshape the way workers performed routine, repetitive jobs.

Newsbreak | World's Greatest Woman Engineer

Lillian Moller thought she was so plain that no one would ever marry her, so she decided to have a career. This was an unpopular notion for a 22-year-old woman in the year 1900. She graduated from the University of California at Berkeley that year and was the first woman ever to be chosen as the school's commencement speaker. She stayed on at Berkeley to study for her PhD in English literature with a minor in psychology. In 1904 her plans were upset when she met a handsome, charismatic, wealthy owner of a construction company.

Frank Gilbreth was ten years older than Lillian. He lived in Boston, where Lillian and some friends had stopped on their way to Europe. When they returned, Frank was waiting at the dock with flowers. Before long, he traveled to California to meet her parents and set the date for the wedding. Frank wanted a wife, children, and all the pleasures of domesticity, but he also desired a partner for his work. At his urging, Lillian changed her major to psychology and enrolled in graduate school at Brown University. She started working alongside him at construction sites, climbing ladders and striding across steel girders high in the sky. A fearless and fast learner, Lillian was soon helping Frank with decisions that would make construction work more efficient. She encouraged Frank to give up the construction business and become a management consultant, so they could apply their ideas about work performance and efficiency to a broad range of jobs.

But the times decreed that women couldn't do such things. That was made clear to Lillian in many ways. In 1911, for example, Lillian and Frank wrote a book, *Motion Study*, but the publisher refused to list her as coauthor, claiming that a woman's name would detract from the book's credibility. The same thing happened a year later with their next book. In 1914 Lillian completed her PhD in psychology, but when she tried to publish her dissertation in book form, the publisher would not let her use her first name, insisting that hardheaded businessmen would never buy a book on the psychology of management that was written by a woman. (Consequently, the title page listed the author as L. M. Gilbreth.)

Twenty years later, with a thriving consulting business to run and 12 children to raise, Lillian Moller Gilbreth found herself a widow. She tried to carry on their work, but most of the business executives for whom she and Frank had done consulting work for many years now cut her off. They had been willing to tolerate her as a wife helping her husband but wanted nothing to do with her on her own.

If she could no longer apply time-and-motion study in the workplace, the business she and Frank had built, she decided to teach others how to do it. She organized workshops on industrial management, which attracted participants from many countries. These workshops, and the quality of the trainees she turned out, enhanced her reputation so that, eventually, business and industrial organizations began to seek her advice.

Over the years, Lillian Gilbreth became immensely successful and influential. She was awarded several honorary degrees, received appointments to presidential commissions, and won accolades from the male-dominated engineering community. One business leader called her "the world's greatest woman engineer." She and Frank earned an additional measure of fame when the movie *Cheaper by the Dozen* was made in 1950 about how they reared their 12 children according to the principles of time-and-motion study. (A remake of the movie, starring Steve Martin, was released in 2003.)

Lillian Gilbreth died in 1972, in her nineties, still working in the field of scientific management. She applied her ideas to problems of efficient work at home as well as in the factory. The next time you open your refrigerator, notice the shelves on the inside of the door. That was her idea. Does your trash can have a foot-pedal to operate the lid? That's easier to use than having to bend down to lift the lid, isn't it? That was her idea, too. Although these may seem like trivial examples to us today, Lillian Gilbreth's contributions in applying the principles of time-and-motion economy were so extensive that they touched everyday tasks not only at home, but in factories, shops, and offices, making work for everyone a little easier. Her influence and popularity remain secure, in the 21st century, through the publication of a new biography (Lancaster, 2004).

Source: R. M. Kelly & V. P. Kelly (1990). Lillian Moller Gilbreth (1878–1972). In A. N. O'Connell & N. F. Russo (Eds.), *Women in psychology: A bio-bibliographic sourcebook* (pp. 117–124). New York: Greenwood Press.

movie, *Cheaper by the Dozen*. To learn more about the life and work of Taylor, see www.netmba.com/mgmt/scientific/. For more about Frank and Lillian Gilbreth, see www.gilbrethnetwork.tripod.com.

Time-and-motion engineers (sometimes called *efficiency experts*) have applied the Gilbreths' techniques to many types of jobs, with the goal of reducing the number of motions required. The familiar operating room procedure of having nurses place each tool in the surgeon's hand is an outgrowth of time-and-motion analysis. Previously, surgeons sought out tools themselves, a practice that greatly increased operating time.

The next time you see a United Parcel Service truck stop to make a delivery, watch how the driver behaves. Every move has been dictated by time-and-motion analysis to ensure a fast delivery. Drivers carry packages only under their left arm, step out of the truck with their right foot, cover three feet per second when they walk, and hold their truck's keys with the teeth face up. Unnecessary and wasteful motions have been eliminated. These procedures allow the drivers to work faster and more efficiently without creating extra work and stress.

The most significant results of time-and-motion analysis have been with routine and repetitive work. In a typical motion study the worker's movements are recorded on video and analyzed with a view to modifying or eliminating inefficient and wasteful motions. (The same technique is applied by sports psychologists and coaches to analyze the performance of athletes.)

From years of research, psychologists have developed guidelines for efficient work. Some rules for increasing the ease, speed, and accuracy of manual jobs include the following:

1. Minimize the distance workers must reach to get tools and supplies or to operate machines.
2. Both hands should begin and end their movement at the same time. Movements should be as symmetrical as possible. The right hand should reach to the right for one item as the left hand reaches to the left for another item.
3. The hands should never be idle except during authorized rest breaks.
4. The hands should never do tasks that can be performed by other parts of the body, particularly legs and feet. A foot control can often be used, thus relieving the hands of one more operation.
5. Whenever possible, work materials should be held by a mechanical device, such as a vise, instead of being held by hand.
6. The work bench or table should be of sufficient height that the job can be performed when standing or when sitting on a high stool. Alternating positions relieves fatigue.

You might think that these guidelines for simplifying jobs would be received with enthusiasm. After all, the company reaps a greater output and employees' jobs are made easier. Although management has generally been pleased with the results of time-and-motion study, workers and labor unions have been suspicious, even hostile. They have argued that the only reason for time-and-motion study is to force employees to work faster. This would lead to lower pay and to dismissals because fewer workers would be needed to maintain production levels. These concerns do have some validity. Other worker complaints are that job simplification leads to boredom, to a lack of challenge and responsibility, and to low motivation, which is manifested in lower productivity.

Time-and-motion analysis is most applicable today for routine tasks such as assembly-line jobs. When operations, equipment, and functions are more complex and the total relationship between person and machine must be considered, a more sophisticated approach to the person-machine interaction is needed.

PERSON-MACHINE SYSTEMS

Person-machine system
A system in which human and mechanical components operate together to accomplish a task.

A **person-machine system** is one in which both components work together to accomplish a task. Neither part is of value without the other. A person pushing a lawnmower is a person-machine system. A person driving a car or playing a video game is a more complex person-machine system. At a more sophisticated level, an airliner and its crew of specialists, each responsible for a different operation, is a person-machine system. An air traffic control network includes a number of separate person-machine systems, each an integral part of the whole. If one part—mechanical or human—fails, all other parts of the system will be affected.

In all person-machine systems, the human operator receives input on the status of the machine from the displays. On the basis of this information, the

An airplane cockpit is a complex person-machine system. Displays present information on the machine's status. The flight engineer processes the information and initiates action by operating the appropriate controls.

operator regulates the equipment by using the controls to initiate some action (see Figure 8–1). Suppose you are driving a car on a highway at a constant speed. You receive input from the speedometer (a display), process this information mentally, and decide that you are driving too fast. Through the control action of easing your foot off the accelerator, you cause the computer-aided fuel injection system to reduce the flow of gasoline to the engine, which slows the speed of the car. This decrease in speed is displayed on the speedometer for your information, and so the process continues.

Drivers also receive information from the external environment, such as a sign noting a change in the speed limit or a slow car blocking your lane. You process this information and dictate a change in speed to the machine. Verification of the altered status of the machine—the new speed—is displayed on the speedometer. The principle is the same for even the most sophisticated person-machine systems. It is the total system that is the starting point for the engineering psychologist's job.

Person-machine systems vary in the extent to which the human operator is actively and continuously involved. In flying an airplane or controlling traffic at a busy airport, operators are necessary most of the time. Even when an airplane is on automatic pilot, the flight crew must be prepared to assume control in an emergency. In other person-machine systems, humans interact less extensively. Many large-scale production processes, such as those in oil refineries, are highly automated. Some products and components can be assembled entirely by

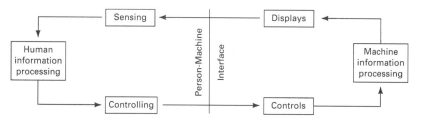

FIGURE 8–1. A person-machine system. (Adapted from "Human Factors in the Workplace" by W. C. Howell, 1991. In M. D. Dunnette and L. M. Hough (Eds.), *Handbook of Industrial and Organizational Psychology*, 2nd ed., vol. 2, p. 214. Palo Alto, CA: Consulting Psychologists Press.)

industrial robots. Although this automated equipment can operate itself, it cannot design, build, or maintain itself, or replace its own lightbulb. Humans remain important components of such automated manufacturing systems even when they are not directly or continuously operating the equipment.

Automation has complicated the task of engineering psychologists. Employees who are required to monitor automated equipment find that task to be more fatiguing and boring than the job of actually running a machine. Engineering psychologists must design monitoring equipment to keep observers alert and vigilant so that they can detect errors and malfunctions and respond immediately and appropriately.

In general, the definition and requirements of person-machine systems are the same, regardless of the degree of involvement of the worker with the machine. No one has yet developed a machine that can design, build, and maintain other machines. Humans are still vital to the system.

Allocating Functions

The initial step in the design of a person-machine system involves making decisions about the division of labor between the human operator and the machine. To do that, each step or process in the functioning of the total system must be analyzed to determine its characteristics: the speed, accuracy, and frequency with which it is performed and the stress under which it occurs. When this information is evaluated, the engineering psychologist can proceed to match the requirements of the system with the abilities of the person and of the machine. Each component—person and machine—has its advantages and its limitations.

Research by psychologists, physiologists, and physicians has provided considerable information about human strengths and weaknesses, revealing those functions for which humans are superior or inferior to machines. In general, machines are better than humans in performing the following functions:

1. Machines can detect stimuli such as radar wavelengths and ultraviolet light that are beyond human sensory capacities.
2. Machines can monitor reliably for lengthy periods as long as the stimulus in question is programmed or specified in advance for the machine.
3. Machines can make large numbers of rapid, accurate calculations.
4. Machines can store and retrieve huge amounts of information with a high level of accuracy.
5. Machines can apply greater physical force continuously and rapidly.
6. Machines can engage in repetitive activities with no performance deterioration as long as proper maintenance is applied.

Of course, machines are not perfect. They have several weaknesses and limitations.

1. Machines are not very flexible. Even the most sophisticated computer can do only what it is programmed to do. When the system requires the ability to adapt to changing circumstances, machines are at a disadvantage.
2. Machines cannot learn from errors or modify their behavior on the basis of past experience. Any change in operation must be built into the system or initiated by the human operator.

3. Machines cannot improvise. They are unable to reason or to examine unprogrammed alternatives.

Some engineers believe that they should automate every possible function in a person-machine system, relegating the operator to a peripheral role. However, fully automated systems can fail, sometimes with disastrous results. Consider modern mass transit systems. In some subway lines, drivers do not control the train's speed, nor do they bring it to a stop at station platforms. Those functions are computer controlled. In a study of the Metrorail system in Miami, Florida, trains fail to stop at stations 10 percent of the time, forcing the drivers to press an emergency button to stop the train quickly, usually overshooting the station platform. Without the driver to intercede, the train proceeds automatically to the next station, delivering its passengers to the wrong place. Drivers in this system have been reduced to being little more than monitors, acting only when the machine malfunctions. They say they find it hard to remain alert when they have so little to do. The job is boring, lacking challenge and responsibility, and it rarely requires the drivers to use their skills. As the operators become more dependent on the computer-controlled equipment, they become less capable of making crucial decisions in emergencies. No matter how thoroughly they have been trained, if their job skills are rarely used, those skills will deteriorate.

A similar problem has been found in passenger aircraft. Consider the different philosophies behind the design of the European-built Airbus and the U.S.-built Boeing 777. The Airbus is largely computer controlled and limits the actions pilots are allowed to take in flying the plane. In general, Airbus pilots are unable to override the computer. In the Boeing airplane, pilots can take the controls themselves at any time to negate or override the onboard computer. Nevertheless, all large passenger aircraft today have such efficient flight computers, navigational equipment, and automatic pilots that much of the human pilot's time is spent merely monitoring the informational displays rather than actively controlling and flying the plane. As a result, pilots can easily become bored and inattentive. The Federal Aviation Administration (FAA) has officially expressed concern that pilots' basic flying skills are deteriorating because they rely so much on automation. One could say that too many functions in modern aircraft are being allocated to the machine component of the system and not enough to the human.

A study of 27 commercial airline pilots found that half of them relied more on the *feel* of the airplane's controls when determining the appropriate action to initiate when ice built up on the wings, than on a status indicator that displayed the actual extent of the ice buildup. Thus, they placed more trust in their own judgment than in the machine's display of factual information (Sarter & Schroeder, 2001).

Research on 30 pilots from a major U.S. airline found that automated systems increasingly communicate only with other machine parts of the system, making decisions and initiating actions, without interacting with the human operator. In experimental tests in flight simulators, pilots under time pressure were unable to detect situations in which flight systems were initiating inappropriate or incompatible control decisions that could have harmful consequences for the aircraft. The human part of the person-machine system was being bypassed in critical decision-making situations (Olson & Sarter, 2001).

For information on a variety of issues in engineering psychology, see www. ergonomics.ucla.edu and www.ergonomics.org/uk/ (the home page of the Ergonomics Society).

Newsbreak   Who's Right—The Person or the Machine?

At 11:40 on the night of July 1, 2002, two aircraft were on a collision course over southern Germany. Unless one or both of them took evasive action immediately, they would collide in less time than it will take you to read this paragraph. One plane was a cargo jet with a crew of two. The other was a chartered airliner from Russia with 71 people on board, including 43 children. Both planes were equipped with computerized collision avoidance systems that had recognized the impending disaster and triggered audible and visible warnings in each cockpit with urgent instructions for the pilots.

The automated systems told the pilot of the cargo jet to descend to a lower altitude, an action he began to initiate. A similar system told the Russian pilot to climb to a higher altitude, but he hesitated, first contacting an air traffic controller to ask for additional instructions.

Two controllers were scheduled to be on duty that night, but one was taking a break while the other tried to keep track of the five aircraft in his sector. The controller also had a computerized alarm system, which at that instant could have provided him with the information that the two planes were on a collision course. But the system had been shut down for routine maintenance. There was no backup.

When the Russian pilot reported the alarm in his cockpit, the controller told him to descend, the opposite of what his warning system was telling him to do. So now, with 70 lives in his hands, he had two conflicting instructions: go up, or go down. Was he to believe the human—the air traffic controller—or was he to believe the insistent alarm from the machine? He chose to believe the human. At 11:43 the two planes smashed into each other. Everyone aboard was killed.

There is a postscript to this tragedy. Many months later, on February 26, 2004, the unfortunate air traffic controller answered a knock on the door of his house near Zurich, Switzerland. The visitor, whose wife and two children had died in the crash, stabbed the man to death.

Sources: G. Johnson, To err is human. *New York Times,* July 14, 2002; Revenge suspected as motive for killing of air controller, *Chechen Times,* February 26, 2004 (www.chechentimes.org/); Silence for slain air controller, BBC News, World Edition, March 5, 2004 (www.news.bbc.co.uk).

WORKSPACE DESIGN

The harmful effects of poor workspace design were seen in the U.S. Army's M-1 Abrams tank. The interior of a tank is the crew's workspace, and its design can influence job performance—in this case, the tank crew's fighting efficiency. The tank was designed without benefit of engineering psychology research and thus without regard for the needs and abilities of the crew. When the tank was tested, 27 of the

We don't buy just any seats. We design them.

GM begins with detailed studies of the human body. Biomedical research. The kind of comprehensive investigation of anatomy da Vinci undertook in the 1500s.

As a leader in the field of Human Factors Engineering, we design interiors scientifically to minimize the possible distractions from your driving.

It may take us two years and countless clay models to arrive at a more comfortable, durable seat for new GM cars and trucks. But we think it's worth it.

And we believe old Leonardo would have thought so, too.

We believe in taking the extra time, giving the extra effort and paying attention to every detail. That's what it takes to provide the quality that leads more people to buy GM cars and trucks than any other kind. And why GM owners are the most loyal on the road.

That's the GM commitment to excellence.

Engineering psychologists help design components for various workspaces. (Reproduced by permission of General Motors Corporation.)

29 test drivers developed such severe neck and back pains that they required medical attention. Also, the drivers were unable to see the ground in front of the tank for a distance of nine yards, making it difficult to avoid obstacles or to cross trenches.

When the engine and turret blowers were operating, more than half the tank's gunners, loaders, and drivers reported that they could not hear one another well enough to communicate because the noise of the machinery was too loud. All crew members reported visibility problems at their work stations. When drivers and tank commanders rode with an open hatch, they found that the front fenders had been so poorly designed that they did not protect the crew from rocks, dirt, and mud churned up by the tank's treads. It was obvious that the designers of the M-1 tank had given no consideration to the human factor, to the people who would have to operate the machine.

The effective design of the human operator's workspace, whether it is a bench for an electronic parts assembler, a display screen for a newspaper copywriter, or a locomotive cab for a driver, involves the following established principles from time-and-motion study and engineering psychology research:

1. All materials, tools, and supplies needed by the workers should be placed in the order in which they will be used so that the paths of the workers' movements will be continuous. Knowing that each part or tool is always in the same place saves the time and annoyance of searching for it.
2. Tools should be positioned so that they can be picked up ready for use. For example, for a job requiring the repeated use of a screwdriver, that tool can be suspended just above the work area on a coil spring. When the tool is needed, the worker can reach up without looking and pull it down ready for use.
3. All parts and tools should be within a comfortable reaching distance (approximately 28 inches). It is fatiguing for workers to change positions frequently to reach beyond the normal working area.

As an example of good workspace design, see Figure 8–2, which illustrates the work station of a radar operator or power plant monitor. Typically, the worker is seated before a panel or console of lights, dials, and switches. The job involves monitoring and controlling the operation of complex equipment. The monitoring console is designed so that operators can see and reach everything necessary for successful job performance without leaving their chair or reaching excessively beyond normal seated posture.

Another important consideration in workspace design is the size and shape of individual hand tools that must be used repeatedly. Applying engineering psychology principles can improve even basic tools such as hammers to make them easier, safer, and less tiring to use. Hand tools should be designed so that workers can use them without bending their wrists. Hands are less vulnerable to injury when the wrists can be kept straight. Engineering psychology principles applicable to the design of pliers are shown in Figure 8–3.

The proper design of hand tools affects productivity, satisfaction, and physical health. The continuous use of tools that require bending the wrist while working can lead to nerve injuries, such as carpal tunnel syndrome, caused by the repetitive motion. Carpal tunnel syndrome can be painful and debilitating. It is also prevalent among people who spend a great deal of time playing the piano, knitting, or playing video games, a finding that may influence your choice of hobbies.

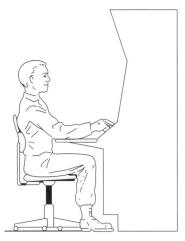
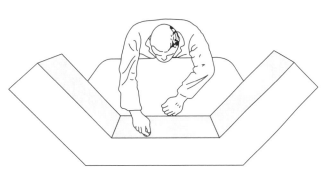

FIGURE 8–2. Monitoring console work arrangement. (From K. Kroemer, H. Kroemer, & K. Kroemer-Elbert, *Ergonomics: How to design for ease and efficiency,* 2nd ed., Upper Saddle River, NJ: Prentice Hall, 2000, p. 384.)

A study of 87 clerical employees in a municipal office building investigated the effects of redesigning the work stations to apply ergonomic principles. The human factors alterations were in four areas: seating, keyboards, computer relocations, and computer screen modifications. Some of the modifications included new chairs and chair cushions, back supports, wrist support pads, and glare guards for computer monitors. Most of the changes were simple and inexpensive yet they resulted in significant benefits to the workers in terms of decreased upper back pain and greater satisfaction with the design and efficiency of the work stations (May, Reed, & Schwoerer, 2004).

A branch of engineering psychology called **human anthropometry** is concerned with the measurement of the physical structure of the human body. Complete sets of body measurements have been compiled from a large, representative sample of the population in the performance of various activities. Specific data include height (standing and sitting), shoulder breadth, back height, chest depth, foot and hand length, knee angle, and so on (see Figure 8–4). These measurements are applied to the design of work areas to determine, for example, normal and maximum reaching distances, tool and desk height and arrangement, size and shape of seats, and viewing angles for video display terminals.

Human anthropometry
A branch of engineering psychology concerned with the measurement of the physical structure of the body.

FIGURE 8–3. Application of human factors principles to the design of pliers. (From "Ergonomics," 1986, *Personnel Journal, 65*(6), p. 99.)

Avoid short tool handles that press into the palm of the hand. The palm is very soft and easily damaged.

Avoid narrow tool handles that concentrate large forces onto small areas of the hand.

Tools and jobs should be designed so that they can be performed with straight wrists. Hands are stronger and less vulnerable to injury when the wrists are kept straight.

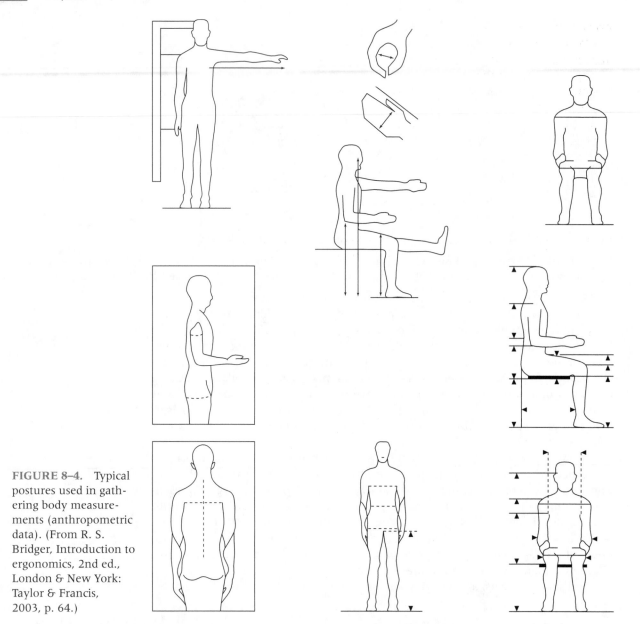

FIGURE 8–4. Typical postures used in gathering body measurements (anthropometric data). (From R. S. Bridger, Introduction to ergonomics, 2nd ed., London & New York: Taylor & Francis, 2003, p. 64.)

With the increasing globalization of the workforce, efficient design of work stations must consider that "average" body measurements and dimensions may vary with workers from different cultures. This was demonstrated in a study comparing anthropometric measurements of Chinese workers (to represent Asians) and German workers (to represent Caucasians). Chinese workers were typically found to have longer torsos and shorter legs than German workers, as well as larger heads and arms. Thus the same work stations, ergonomic chairs, tools, and uniforms would not be suitable for both groups (Shan & Bohn, 2003).

For the millions of people who work at a desk or work bench, the seats we use, if improperly designed, can cause back and neck pain and lead to fatigue, which, in turn, reduces productive efficiency. Research has been conducted on every conceivable aspect of the design of workplace seating, and guidelines are available for various kinds of jobs. For example, you may have noticed that seats are getting larger and wider—because we are! With the notable exception of seats in airplanes, the seats in stadiums, movie theaters, and subway cars have become roomier. The ferries crossing Puget Sound in Washington State used to hold 250 people in seats 18 inches wide. Because the operators had to install wider seats, each boat now carries only 230 people.

For an interesting, often humorous, look at bad human factors design of items from maps to toothbrushes, log on to www.baddesigns.com/index.shtml.

DISPLAYS: PRESENTING INFORMATION

In person-machine systems, operators receive inputs from the machine through the physical senses. For example, in driving a car you receive information on the operating status of the machine from visual displays (speedometer, temperature indicator, gas gauge) and from auditory displays (the chime alerting you to fasten your seat belt or remove the ignition key). More informally, you receive inputs tactually, such as when a balky engine causes the car to vibrate.

One of the earliest decisions to be made about the presentation of information in the design of a person-machine system is to select the most effective means of communication. Visual presentation of information, the mode most frequently used, is more appropriate in the following instances:

- The message is long, difficult, and abstract.
- The environment is too noisy for auditory messages.
- The auditory channels of communication are overloaded.
- The message consists of many different kinds of information that must be presented simultaneously.

The auditory presentation of information is more effective in the following instances:

- The information is short, simple, and straightforward.
- The message is urgent; auditory signals typically attract attention more readily than visual ones do.
- The environment is too dark or otherwise does not allow for visual communication.
- The operator's job requires moving to different locations. The ears can receive messages from all directions, whereas the eyes must be focused on the display to receive messages.

Visual Displays

A common error made in the visual presentation of information is to provide more input than the operator needs to run the system. For example, most drivers do not need a tachometer to indicate engine rpm. Although this may not be a major concern in a passenger car, in an airplane, where large amounts of vital information must be displayed, any unnecessary input adds to the display problem and is potentially confusing for the pilot. The engineering psychologist must ask:

Visual displays in an air traffic control tower present information in words, symbols, and graphics.

Is this information needed to operate the system? If the system can function without it, then that is one less item for the busy human operator to confront. If the information is vital to the operation of the equipment, what is the most effective way to display it?

Three types of visual displays commonly used in person-machine systems are quantitative, qualitative, and check reading.

Quantitative visual displays Displays that present a precise numerical value, such as speed, altitude, or temperature.

Quantitative Displays. **Quantitative visual displays** present a precise numerical value. In situations dealing with speed, altitude, or temperature, for example, the operator must know the precise numerical value of a condition of the system. A pilot must know if the altitude is, say, 10,500 feet, as dictated by the flight plan. An approximate indication of altitude instead of an exact one could lead the plane into the path of another aircraft or into a mountain in fog.

Five displays for presenting quantitative information and their relative reading accuracy are shown in Figure 8–5. You can see that the open-window display was read with the fewest errors. The vertical display was misread more than one-third of the time. These results, from a now-classic research study, were obtained from a laboratory experiment on instrument dial shapes in which subjects were required to read displays in a brief fixed time period.

A quantitative display that is easier to read than the open-window type is the digital display, or counter, in which actual numbers are shown. The familiar digital clock or wristwatch is an example of this type of display. Digital displays are common in electronic consumer products such as DVD players and microwave ovens.

Although digital displays can be read faster and with fewer errors than any other type of display, they cannot be used in all situations. If the information being presented changes rapidly or continuously, a set of numbers may not remain in place long enough to be read and processed by the human operator. Digital displays are also unsuitable when it is important to know the direction or the rate of change—for example, whether engine temperature is rising or falling, or whether it is rising rapidly or slowly.

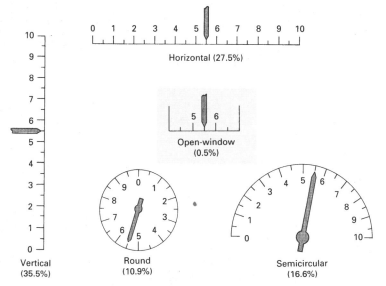

FIGURE 8–5. Percentage of errors in reading five types of quantitative display. (From "The Effect of Instrument Dial Shape on Legibility" by R. Sleight, 1948, *Journal of Applied Psychology, 32,* p. 177. Copyright 1948 by the American Psychological Association. Reprinted by permission.)

Qualitative Displays. **Qualitative visual displays** can be used when a precise numerical reading is not necessary. For example, most drivers do not need to know the precise temperature of their car's engine. All most of us want to know is whether the temperature is in the safe operating range. With many components of person-machine systems, the operator needs to know only whether the system is functioning within the proper range and whether the values are increasing or decreasing over time.

A typical qualitative display is shown in Figure 8–6. The operating ranges are often color coded with the dangerous, or hot, portion in red and the safe portion in green. Such a display permits quick, accurate verification of the system's status and reduces the amount of technical information the operator must absorb.

When several qualitative displays must be checked frequently, consistent patterning makes them easier to read accurately (see Figure 8–7). Placing the dials so that they always face the same way in the normal operating range makes it easier to scan the display and detect an abnormal reading. Unpatterned displays force the operator to read each dial separately. Patterned displays are used in aircraft cockpits, power plant control rooms, and automated manufacturing plants.

Check Reading Displays. **Check reading visual displays** are the simplest kind of visual display. They tell the operator whether the system is on or off, safe or unsafe, or operating normally or abnormally. For example, with the engine temperature gauge in your car, a warning light is sufficient to indicate whether you

> **Qualitative visual displays** Displays that present a range rather than a precise numerical value. They are frequently used to show whether components, such as engine temperature, are operating in the safe or unsafe range.

> **Check reading visual displays** Displays that tell the operator whether the system is on or off, safe or unsafe, or operating normally or abnormally.

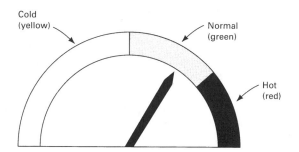

FIGURE 8–6. A qualitative visual display. (Adapted from *Human Factors in Engineering and Design* (p. 76) by E. J. McCormick, 1976, New York: McGraw-Hill.)

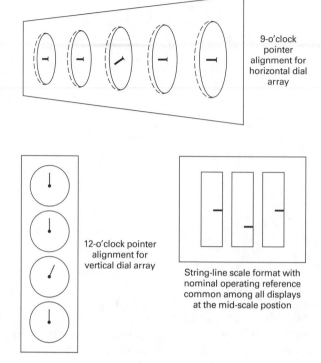

9-o'clock pointer alignment for horizontal dial array

12-o'clock pointer alignment for vertical dial array

String-line scale format with nominal operating reference common among all displays at the mid-scale postion

FIGURE 8–7. Patterned and unpatterned dial displays with pointers aligned for rapid reading. (From K. Kroemer, H. Kroemer, & K. Kroemer-Elbert, *Ergonomics: How to design for ease and efficiency,* 2nd ed., Upper Saddle River, NJ: Prentice Hall, 2000, p. 491.)

can continue to drive safely or should stop because the engine is in danger of overheating. This kind of display is sometimes referred to as "go/no go." Either the system is in condition to operate (to go) or it is not.

The most common check reading display is the warning light. When the light is not illuminated, the system is functioning satisfactorily. When the light comes on, it indicates a system malfunction serious enough to require the operator to take immediate corrective action.

Among the considerations in the design of warning lights is level of brightness. On a display panel that contains several sources of light, it is vital that a warning light be at least twice as bright as the background to get the operator's attention. Location of warning lights is also important. They should be centrally located within the operator's field of vision. Warning lights too far to one side of a console may not be noticed when the worker is paying attention to more centrally located displays and controls. Also, flashing lights attract attention more quickly than continuous warning lights.

Visual displays today include more than the familiar lights, dials, and gauges. Much information is displayed on video screens and in words, symbols, and graphics. The electronic flight information system used in aircraft and in air traffic control radar screens combines lines, numbers, and pictorial symbols to present precise information about location. Adding color to cockpit displays reduces errors and response times for aircraft crew members in reading and processing information.

Not all visual displays are high-tech. For example, the common push/pull door signs are used every day by millions of people entering and exiting stores, factories, and office buildings. Some doors need to be pushed, others pulled. To find out how best to display this basic information visually, so that users would follow directions accurately, a study was conducted using 60 subjects under laboratory conditions and 1,100 subjects in the real world. Eleven different kinds of

Newsbreak

Let Jack Do It

"In his 15 years on the job," wrote a reporter for the *New York Times*, "Jack has been trapped in coal mines and forced to lift and carry objects that could break his back, and once while pregnant—yes, pregnant—was stuffed into a car to see if he could fit behind the wheel and reach the pedals. Jack never complains, however, because Jack is a piece of software, a virtual reality representation of a person who can take on various forms. Jack can walk, avoid obstacles, reach, and lift. But if he cannot perform a certain task, an image of the character will signal a problem, sometimes by turning a body part a different color on a computer screen. Jack rolls with the punches so that we don't have to."

By wearing virtual reality helmets, real people, such as designers of cars or aircraft cockpits or work stations, can see through Jack's eyes as he becomes a driver or pilot, a factory worker or office manager. Thus, the engineering psychologists or human factors engineers can see how something works—or fails to work—before they actually build it.

For example, they might find out whether by reaching to change a radio station in your sports car, you could accidentally nudge the gear shift lever into neutral. They might find out whether the farmer driving the redesigned tractor has a clear view of the blades that are tilling the soil behind it. When the John Deere company learned that Jack couldn't see those blades from the new tractor cab, it was no big deal to change the design at that stage. But had the tractors already started rolling off the assembly line, it would have been tremendously expensive to redesign them.

Good ol' Jack never fails. And never gets tired or cranky or comes in late or stays home with the flu. And he costs only $25,000. In today's market, Jack's a bargain.

Source: Jack is put through the wringer so you won't be. *New York Times*, May 11, 2000.

signs were tested. The most effective signs (those quickly identified or eliciting the greatest compliance) combined a drawing of a hand with an arrow and the word push or pull displayed horizontally (see Figure 8–8). Even a simple visual display can be improved through engineering psychology research.

Auditory Displays

An **auditory display** can be more compelling than a visual display for the following reasons: (1) Our ears are always open, but our eyes are not; (2) we can receive auditory information from all directions; and (3) our visual sense is often taxed to capacity. Table 8–1 presents the major types of auditory alarms.

No matter how loud or effective an auditory alarm is, it is only as good as the human operator's response to it. We learned this from the case of the Russian airline pilot, described above, who chose not to believe what the auditory collision warning system told him to do. Ignoring alarm systems is not such unusual

Auditory displays Alarms or warning signals in person-machine systems. Auditory displays can be more compelling than visual displays.

Most effective (word plus symbol)

FIGURE 8–8.   Most effective and least effective door pull signs. (Adapted from T. J. B. Kline & G. A. Beitel, "Assessment of push/pull door signs: A laboratory and a field study." *Human Factors,* 1994, *36,* 688.)

Least effective (symbol only)

behavior; people often fail to respond properly. For example, a long-term study of employees monitoring the daily operation of nuclear power plants in Canada found that more than 50 percent of the alarms did not provide useful or meaningful information for the human operator, so that he or she could initiate some corrective action. These so-called "nuisance alarms" served only to add clutter or confusion to a critical and demanding job (Mumaw, Roth, Vicente, & Burns, 2000). A study of highly trained registered nurse-anesthetists in 24 surgical cases found that almost half of the auditory alarms from the medical equipment were ignored. No corrective

TABLE 8–1

Characteristics of Auditory Alarms

Alarm	Intensity	Attention-Getting Ability
Foghorn	Very high	Good
Horn	High	Good
Whistle	High	Good, if intermittent
Siren	High	Very good, if pitch rises and falls
Bell	Medium	Good
Buzzer	Low to medium	Good
Human voice	Low to medium	Fair

Note: Adapted from "Auditory and Other Sensory Forms of Information Presentation" by B. H. Deatherage, 1972. *Human Engineering Guide to Equipment Design,* Washington, D.C.: U.S. Government Printing Office.

action was taken because none was needed. The surgical team had learned that the warnings were probably nuisance alarms (Seagull & Sanderson, 2001).

Sometimes, even the most carefully designed person-machine system does not work as intended because the human operator violates the conditions under which the system is supposed to function. On the night of May 17, 1987, aboard the navy frigate USS *Stark* on duty in the Persian Gulf, a radar operator was monitoring a complex system that was tracking all nearby radar signals. The system had visual and auditory warning devices to alert the operator if hostile radar was detected. The system designers believed that with both visual and auditory displays, there was no way the operator could miss a warning. If the operator was looking away from the visual display screen, the auditory signal—a rapid beeping—would surely be noticed.

Yet, when hostile radar was detected that night and the visual warning signal flashed on the screen, the operator was looking away and the auditory signal failed to sound. That operator, or an operator from an earlier shift, had disconnected the auditory alarm because he found it to be annoying. Because the ship was in enemy territory, the alarm was beeping frequently, and the sailor had decided that it was a nuisance.

With the auditory alarm disabled and the visual warning signal unseen, a jet fighter plane from Iraq fired an Exocet missile at the USS *Stark*, killing 37 American sailors. In this case the equipment portion of the person-machine system functioned satisfactorily, but the human operator did not.

Auditory signals may be used to transmit complex information. One example is the shipboard use of sonar for detecting underwater objects. A high-frequency sound is transmitted from beneath the ship through the water. When it strikes a large enough object, the signal is reflected back to the ship and reproduced as the familiar pinging sound heard in old war movies. The job of interpreting the message or information that the sound conveys can be difficult. Extensive training is required to be able to discriminate among the sound's various qualities. With sonar, if the detected object is moving away from the ship, the reflected sound is of a lower frequency than is the transmitted sound. An object moving toward the ship provides a higher frequency of returning sound.

Humans can receive and interpret a variety of information through the auditory sense. We are capable of responding to formal signaling procedures (warning horns, whistles, and buzzers) and to informal cues (the misfire of a car engine, the wail of a miswound audiotape, or the beep of the computer that lost your term paper).

CONTROLS: TAKING ACTION

In person-machine systems, once the human operators receive input through the displays and mentally process that information, they must communicate some control action to the machine. They transmit their control decisions through such devices as switches, push buttons, levers, cranks, steering wheels, mouses, trackballs, and foot pedals. Engineering psychologists analyze the nature of the task to determine whether it involves, for example, turning on a light or activating some other system component. Does the task involve a fine adjustment, such as selecting one radio frequency from the spectrum of frequencies? Does it require frequent and rapid readjustment of a control, or is a single setting sufficient? How much force must the operator exert to accomplish the job? If the control must be activated in cold temperatures, will the wearing of gloves interfere with proper operation? If the control must be activated under low lighting conditions, can it be easily identified by shape alone?

Guidelines for Controls.   For a task that requires two discrete settings of a control, such as "on" and "off," a hand or foot push button is suitable. For four or more discrete settings, a group of finger push buttons or a rotary selector switch is preferred. For continuous settings, knobs or cranks are the best choice. For selecting elements on a computer display, devices such as a mouse, light pen, or touch pad can be used. A selection of controls and the actions for which they are appropriate are shown in Figure 8–9. In addition, controls should satisfy the following two criteria:

1. *Control-body matching.* Although some controls could be activated with the head or the elbow, most of them use hands and feet. It is important that no one limb be given too many tasks to perform. The hands are capable of greater precision in operating controls, and the feet are capable of exerting greater force.

FIGURE 8–9.   Control devices and the type of information they best transmit. (From M. S. Sanders & E. J. McCormick, *Human factors in engineering and design,* 6th ed., p. 261. New York: McGraw-Hill, 1987. Copyright 1987, McGraw-Hill Book Co. Used with permission.)

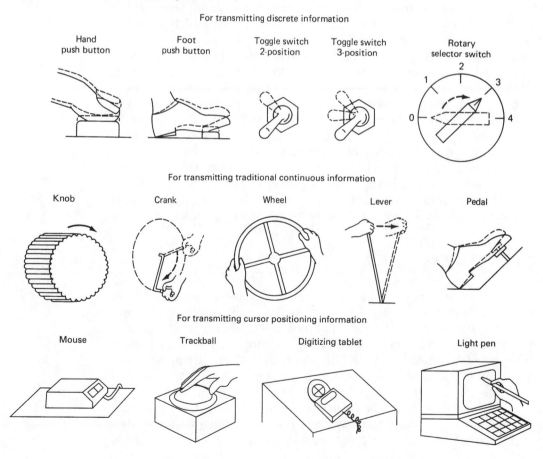

2. *Control-task compatibility.* A control action should imitate the movements it produces. For example, pulling an airplane's control column to the right pulls the plane to the right; the control movement and the machine's response are parallel. To lower aircraft flaps or landing gear, the control should move downward. Typically, we turn a control knob to the right (clockwise) to turn a machine on. Most people would have difficulty adjusting to a knob that turned to the left to activate a machine.

Combining Related Controls. Wherever possible, it is more efficient to combine controls that perform similar or related operations. For example, simple radios have three control functions—on/off, volume, and station selection—yet there are only two controls. The on/off and volume controls, which perform related functions, are combined to reduce the number of separate actions required of the human operator and to save space on the control panel.

Identification of Controls. Controls must be clearly marked or coded to assure their correct and rapid identification. Automobile manufacturers code instrument panels by using pictorial symbols to represent control functions (for example, a miniature wiper blade identifies the windshield wiper switch). On a crowded instrument panel, easily identifiable controls can minimize errors caused by activating the wrong control.

Shape coding means designing each knob on a console or control panel in a recognizably different shape (see Figure 8–10). This allows for rapid visual identification of the correct control and permits identification by touch in low-lighting conditions or when the eyes must focus elsewhere. Sometimes the control's shape symbolizes its function. In U.S. Air Force planes the landing flap control looks like a landing flap, and the landing gear control looks like a tire. Each control is unique in touch and appearance, and the control functions can be learned quickly. Standardizing the controls on all aircraft reduces the opportunity for pilot error.

Shape coding Designing knobs for control panels in recognizably different shapes so that they can be identified by touch alone.

Placement of Controls. Once the kind and shape of the controls have been selected, engineering psychologists determine their placement on the control panel. They also consider the control's relationship to an informational display. A primary requisite for control location is consistency or uniformity of placement.

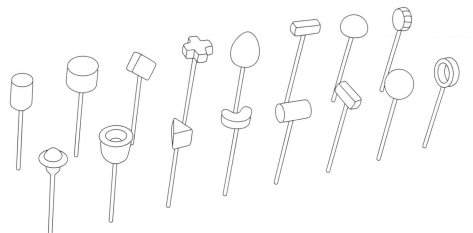

FIGURE 8–10.
Recommended handle shapes for coding. (From W. Woodson, B. Tillman, & P. Tillman, *Human factors design handbook,* 2nd ed., New York: McGraw-Hill, 1992, p. 439.)

For example, we expect the gas pedal to be located to the right of the brake pedal on automobiles, and for the Enter key to be on the right side of the keyboard. The greater the standardization of control arrangement, the easier and safer it is for people to work with different models of the same system. This sounds like common sense, but it took many years before engineering psychology research was accepted and for aircraft instrument panels to be standardized. This basic design principle is still being ignored in many consumer products.

Consider the kitchen range. Typically, there are four burners on top and four knobs on a panel to control the burners. However, there is little consistency in the relationship between control knobs and burners. A survey of 49 electric and gas ranges revealed six different knob-burner operating linkages. Although this does not create as serious a problem as lack of standardization in an airplane, it can lead to burns and other accidents. With a gas range, we receive immediate feedback when we turn a knob to activate a burner, but with an electric range, we could touch a burner, thinking it is cold, to find out it had been turned on.

In the global marketplace, where a product manufactured in one country may be sold in many others, human engineers must be aware of cultural differences that may influence the product's use, such as the linkage between displays and controls. For example, research subjects in Taiwan preferred a different burner-control link when operating a four-burner stove than subjects in the United States. They automatically reached for different knobs than the American subjects to operate the same burners. This probably reflected the Taiwanese practice of reading characters vertically and from right to left, whereas English-speaking people read horizontally and from left to right. Thus, the so-called natural approach to the use of these controls differed for people in the two cultures.

Controls that are associated with emergency functions must be placed in the normal line of sight where they can be distinguished from other controls. The operator should be able to reach emergency controls quickly. The controls should be protected with a cover or shield so that they cannot be activated accidentally.

When displays are associated functionally with controls—such as a dial that must be set by turning a knob—they should be placed as close together as possible. It is desirable to group related displays and controls according to function. For example, in an aircraft cockpit, displays and controls involving engine performance are grouped. When the order of operation is consistent, displays and controls can be grouped sequentially.

HUMAN FACTORS IN EVERYDAY LIFE

Research and application of ergonomics findings can be found in many areas of everyday life, from driving your car to using the voice menu in a telephone call. Human factors are no longer confined to tanks, airplanes, or work areas. The relatively new field of *telematics*, for example, refers to the wireless information technology you may already have in your car, such as a GPS navigation system, a satellite radio, or a built-in wireless phone. The automatic collision notification system, such as OnStar, that seems to know where your car is at all times and alerts authorities when your airbag deploys, is another example. Currently being researched are e-mail and Internet access for your car, Bluetooth support, and built-in PDAs. The obvious problem with these devices, however, is that they can distract the driver and lead to accidents. Engineering psychologists are involved with determining the nature and extent of these distractions and how best to equip the human operator to deal with them.

The use of cell phones while driving is also believed to be a major contributor to accidents, but the data are incomplete to date. Most jurisdictions do not yet require information on cell phone use in traffic accident reports. The currently accepted figure is that the chance of being involved in a car crash is 4.3 times greater when the driver is using a cell phone as when he or she is not using a cell phone.

Research on drivers in Japan showed that the primary cause of accidents was answering a call while driving. The second most frequent cause was placing a call while driving. Third was talking on the phone while driving. No significant differences were found between the use of handheld phones and hands-free phones. The nature of the distraction was found to be similar in both cases (Green, 2003).

Preliminary research on the GPS navigation system while driving in urban traffic showed that drivers were able to make visual-manual destination entries using a touch screen in an average time of 3.4 seconds. The average glance time at the screen to check on location was 1.32 seconds. The researchers of this study suggested that being able to enter destinations by voice activation rather than manual activation would simplify the driver's task and reduce the time the driver's attention would be focused on the screen (Chiang, Brooks, & Weir, 2004).

Studies conducted in automobiles on the road, as well as in a realistic laboratory driving simulator, showed that an auditory warning system that sounded when drivers were too close to the car ahead led these drivers to maintain a greater distance behind other cars and thus reduced the number of rear-end collisions by 50 percent (Ben-Yaacov, Maltz, & Shinar, 2002; Lee, McGehee, Brown, & Reyes, 2002).

Other human factors research has focused on telephone voice menu systems. A study of 114 research participants, ranging in age from 18 to over 60, found that older people had greater difficulty than younger people in identifying the menu choices they wanted. Providing a graphic aid with the recorded spoken instructions significantly improved the performance of older people in selecting the appropriate menu options (Sharit, Czaja, Nair, & Lee, 2003).

Desks and chairs for your school classroom have also been the subject of human factors research. Anthropometric measures of 180 primary school students (ages 7–12) in Greece found that the furniture was poorly designed for the use and comfort of the children. Chairs were too high and the seats and desks were too deep for the reach of most students. This situation led to uncomfortable and unnatural sitting postures, leading to slumping and pressure on the spine and back (Panagiotopoulou, Christoulas, Papanckolaou, & Mandroukas, 2004). These findings supported a similar study in Michigan in which 80 percent of the students (ages 11–14) had seats that were too high and deep and desks that were too high. Attention to the anthropometric measurements for children in these age ranges could have prevented much discomfort and harm.

Moving on to airplanes, have you noticed that passengers in first class often get leather seats while the rest of us in the rear of the plane have fabric-covered seats? Do you envy them? You shouldn't. A study conducted in Germany found that fabric upholstery was rated more comfortable because fabric breathes and leather does not. People are more likely to perspire in a leather-covered seat (Bartels, 2003).

And what about kitchen utensils, say ice cream scoops and spatulas? Ergonomics researchers have been working in that area, too. Research has shown that the physical stress of repeated scooping by employees of retail ice-cream shops can be reduced if the ice cream is kept no colder than minus 14 degrees Celsius.

Scooping is also less physically difficult if the edge of the scoop is sharpened at least once a month. In addition, the job was found to be easier when an antifreeze liquid was encapsulated within the scoop but as yet designers haven't found a way to keep the antifreeze from leaking onto the ice cream, which would not be good for business (Dempsey, McGorry, Cotnam, & Braun, 2000).

Ergonomics researchers in China found that spatulas used by restaurant cooks to turn over food while it is cooking can lead to carpal tunnel syndrome and other trauma disorders in the upper limbs. They tested spatulas with different handle lengths and various angles between the handle and the turning surface. Both factors significantly affected the twisting, or flexion, angle of the cook's wrist. The straighter the wrist could be held, the less physical strain occurred. From a human factors design viewpoint, then, the best spatula was found to be one that minimized the flexing of the wrist: 25 centimeters in length with a lift angle of 25 degrees. With a tool of those dimensions, the restaurant cooks were able to manage more food with less physical damage and pain (Wu & Hsieh, 2002).

These and similar research findings continue to be applied to transportation, furniture design, kitchen items, home workspaces, and other consumer products to make them more comfortable and efficient and to minimize discomfort from long-term use.

COMPUTERS

Millions of us use computers on the job and in everyday life. When the human engineering aspects of the design of computer terminals and computer furniture are ignored, the result is physical strain and discomfort. Concern about the effects of prolonged computer use on employee health stems from the 1970s when two employees of the *New York Times* reportedly developed cataracts, which they attributed to working at video display terminals. Many computer users have since complained of blurred vision, eyestrain, and changes in color perception. However, the National Academy of Sciences concluded that there is no scientific evidence that computers caused visual damage.

Engineering psychologists suggest that most employee complaints about visual disturbances result not from the terminals but from equipment components and from the design of the work station. Equipment factors identified as potential hazards include the color of the phosphor in the cathode ray tube, the size of the screen, the degree of flicker of the characters on the screen, and the rate at which characters are generated.

In addition, level of illumination and glare in the workplace can be sources of eyestrain. Antiglare coatings and shields can be applied to reduce the problems. The overall lighting of the work area can be reduced, and walls can be painted in darker colors. Fluorescent overhead lights can be replaced by indirect lighting. All these changes can enhance visual comfort for computer users.

There is evidence that people read more slowly from computer screens than from paper. Research is focusing on specific factors of the display and the user—such as length of time spent at the terminal—to explain this phenomenon. I-O psychologists suggest that slower reading speed may be related to the quality of the image on the screen (size, type style, clarity, and contrast with background).

Many people have a better understanding of what they read on paper than what they read on the screen. This was shown in a study of 113 college students who read and answered questions about two magazine articles. One group was presented with the material on paper; the other group read the articles on a computer. More readers of the paper version reported that the articles were interesting and persuasive than did the readers of the computer version. The readers of the paper version also showed a higher degree of comprehension of the content of the articles (Greenman, 2000).

Other complaints from computer users are fatigue and pain in wrists, hands, shoulders, neck, and back, all of which can be related to a lack of attention to human engineering concerns. For example, desks and chairs used with computer equipment are often poorly designed for jobs that involve sitting for long periods. The best chair is adjustable, enabling computer operators to adapt it to their height, weight, and posture. Periodically changing position can reduce fatigue, and this is easier to do with an adjustable chair. Desks with split and adjustable tops that hold keyboard and display screen components at different heights can also increase user comfort. Comparisons of the standard flat keyboard and the split adjustable keyboard, using experienced typists as subjects, have found no differences between the two designs in terms of their causing musculoskeletal pain. However, people who use a padded wrist rest report less pain in elbows and forearms than people who do not use a wrist rest.

A great deal of human factors research has been conducted on the design of computers and work stations. Some well-established guidelines are illustrated in Figure 8–11. For example, research findings indicate that a downward-sloping computer keyboard at an angle of 15 degrees decreases discomfort in the neck and shoulders. Locating the monitor too high or too low creates pain in the neck and lower back. Viewing angle has a significant effect on posture; an angle of approximately 17 degrees permits the best postural alignment of back, neck, and shoulders (see Psihogios, Sommerich, Mirka, & Moon, 2001; Simoneau & Marklin, 2001; Sommerich, Joines, & Psihogios, 2001).

Studies have also been conducted on the standard mouse, comparing it with other types of control devices. The mouse requires extensive movement of wrist

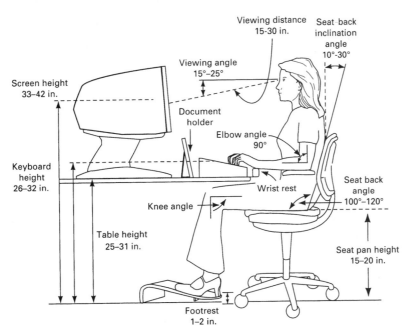

FIGURE 8–11. Guidelines for the design of computer work stations. (Adapted from M. S. Sanders & E. J. McCormick, *Human factors in engineering and design*, 6th ed., p. 358. New York: McGraw-Hill, 1987. Copyright 1987, McGraw-Hill Book Co. Used with permission.)

TABLE 8–2

Ergonomics Questionnaire on the Design of Work Stations

Employees answer YES or NO

1. Are you able to view your computer screen without tipping your head forward or backward?
2. Are you looking straight ahead at your screen?
3. Is your copyholder next to your screen and at the same height and distance from your eyes?
4. Can you easily view your work without leaning forward and hunching your shoulders and back?
5. Are the screen contrast and brightness levels set correctly for your visual comfort?
6. Is the screen free of glare, reflections, or white spots that might be caused by the surrounding work environment?
7. Can you avoid bending your neck or hunching your shoulders when you hold your telephone?
8. When you work at your desk or keyboard, is your elbow at about a 90-degree angle?
9. Are your wrists almost straight (in a neutral posture) as you work?
10. Is your work area free of sharp edges that might rub against your wrists or forearms?
11. Can you reach frequently used items (such as your mouse, files, coffee mug, or pen) without stretching?
12. Can you sit all the way back in your chair without feeling pressure against the back of your knees?
13. Does your chair provide good support for the lumbar region of your back?
14. Are your feet fully supported by the floor or by a foot rest?
15. Do you take mini-breaks during the workday to stand up, stretch, and focus your eyes on something far away?

Source: Adapted from Eastman Kodak Company (2004). *Kodak's Ergonomic Design for People at Work* (2nd ed.). New York: Wiley, p. 131.

and forearm. Research conducted in Sweden suggests that it is less comfortable to work with, and is related to lower productivity, than a virtual mouse shaped like the joystick used to play video games (Gustafsson & Hagberg, 2003). With the virtual mouse, the hand is maintained in a vertical position wrapped around the stick, with the thumb operating the click button. Thus, there is no strain on the muscles of the wrist and forearm.

The Ergonomics Group at the Eastman Kodak Company developed a questionnaire to determine the kinds of problems employees faced in their daily interaction with computers. The goal was to gather information from employees so that work stations could be redesigned to reduce fatigue, stress, and neuromuscular disorders (Eastman Kodak, 2004). So sit down in front of your computer, answer "yes" or "no" to the questions in Table 8–2, and see how you score.

Don't Take Your Laptop to Lunch

It happens every day. You've probably done it yourself. You're leaning over your computer, intent on surfing the Web or sending an e-mail, and you drop food on the keyboard. Chocolate chip cookie crumbs, pizza, cheese curls, or worse—coffee or soda—can destroy a computer. The high-tech wonders of the workplace, which have so transformed the way we live and do our jobs—these marvels of design and engineering—can be totally ruined by a diet cola. No joke! This is a serious problem as more and more people stay at their desks to eat lunch or take their laptops to the cafeteria.

All that food and drink is messing up today's sensitive electronics. At the ExecuSpace company in Chicago, a woman trashed a $1,000 digital telephone when she spilled iced tea on it. Sticky liquids with sugar are the worst. They jam keys and push buttons, clog openings, and also attract bugs. An exterminator in Chicago, whose business is obviously increasing, was quoted as saying, "We're seeing more and more cockroach, mice, and ant problems in [office] cubicles." To solve this growing problem, the Amherst-Merritt International company of Dallas, Texas, is marketing a computer condom. A simple plastic sheath, called the SafeSkin, keeps those nasty crumbs out of your keyboard.

But suppose you've already done the damage. Is it too late to save the mechanism? An official from Gateway advises, "Take the keyboard into the shower [unplugged, of course]. Give it a good going over with warm water. Let it sit upside down for two weeks. There's a slight possibility it will work again."

Source: Desk dining may be hazardous to office's health. *St. Petersburg (FL) Times,* April 18, 2000.

If your answers to all the questions were "yes," congratulations! You are working comfortably and are not experiencing computer-related physical problems. If you answered "no" to any of the questions, then something about your work area probably needs to be readjusted.

Summary

Engineering psychology is concerned with the design of tools, equipment, and workspaces to make them compatible with the abilities of employees. Psychologists consider the limitations and capacities of workers as well as the characteristics of the equipment to produce an efficient **person-machine system.** A precursor to engineering psychology was **time-and-motion study,** pioneered by Frederick Taylor and Frank and Lillian Gilbreth, which attempted to redesign tools and wage-incentive systems and to eliminate wasted motions on the job. Time-and-motion study is applied to routine jobs, whereas engineering psychology focuses on higher-level jobs involving more complex systems.

The initial step in designing a person-machine system is allocating functions between human operators and machines. Humans are superior in detecting a range of stimuli, detecting rare or low-level stimuli from a confusing background, sensing and recognizing unusual or unexpected stimuli, recalling relevant information, using past experiences in making decisions, responding quickly to diverse situations, using inductive reasoning, and showing flexibility in problem solving. Machines are superior to humans in detecting stimuli beyond human sensory powers, monitoring for long periods, calculating rapidly and accurately, storing and retrieving large amounts of data, applying physical force, and engaging in repetitive tasks with no performance deterioration.

Workspace design involves principles of motion economy as well as data from **human anthropometry** (measurements of the body's physical structure). Three types of visual informational display are quantitative, qualitative, and check reading. **Quantitative displays** provide a precise numerical value. **Qualitative displays** provide an indication of relative operating conditions. **Check reading displays** tell whether a system is operating normally or abnormally or whether it is on or off. **Auditory displays** can attract attention more readily than can visual displays because the ears receive sound from all directions.

Controls to initiate action must be compatible with the task and the worker's abilities. Controls should be combined for similar or related operations and must be easily identifiable. Control identification can be aided by pictorial symbols or by **shape coding.** Controls may have to be modified for users from different cultures. Engineering psychology research is being applied to daily life, from the impact of telematics (wireless information technology) in our automobiles to the design of classroom desks to the shape of ice cream scoops and cooking utensils.

Computers are person-machine systems that may cause problems for the human operator. Computer use can lead to a downgrading of human skills, job dissatisfaction, boredom, muscle strain, and pain, much of which can be eliminated by paying attention to human factors considerations in designing computer work stations.

Key Terms

auditory displays	qualitative visual displays
check reading visual displays	quantitative visual displays
engineering psychology	shape coding
human anthropometry	time-and-motion study
person-machine system	

Review Questions

1. Define *ergonomics* and describe its role and function in the workplace.
2. When did the field of human factors begin? How did its early efforts help save the lives of military pilots?
3. Give an example of how human factors research has reduced the chances of being involved in a car crash.
4. Who was Frederick Taylor and what did he do to improve the job of shoveling?
5. How did Frank and Lillian Gilbreth change the way jobs are performed?
6. How did the Gilbreths apply time-and-motion study to everyday life?
7. Describe several rules for increasing the ease, speed, and accuracy of manual jobs that developed from the findings of time-and-motion studies.

8. What is the relationship of displays, controls, and the human operator in a person-machine system? Give an example of a person-machine system.

9. What advantages do humans have over machines? In what ways are machines superior to humans?

10. How would you design a workspace for a person who is assembling and testing cell phones so that the job can be performed rapidly and safely?

11. What is *human anthropometry?* How is it applied to workspace design? How is it used in the field of transportation, such as subway cars?

12. Under what conditions is the visual presentation of information superior to the auditory presentation of information? Give an example that involves your automobile.

13. Describe three types of visual displays and note what kind of information is best displayed on each.

14. What are some problems with auditory alarm systems? How would you correct these problems?

15. What is the field of *telematics?* Why is it important in engineering psychology?

16. What has human factors research learned about (a) the use of cell phones while driving, (b) leather versus fabric seating, and (c) furniture for the classroom?

17. How would you design a study to determine the most efficient ice cream scoop to minimize muscle strain?

18. What factors should be considered in designing a computer work station?

19. What are the most frequent complaints from computer users?

20. Would you rather read a magazine article on your computer screen or printed on paper? Which format provides for faster reading and better understanding?

Additional Reading

Carroll, J. M. (1997). Human-computer interaction. *Annual Review of Psychology, 48,* 61–83. Reviews research and applications in the field of human-computer interaction focusing on the development of user-centered systems.

Chiles, J. R. (2001). *Inviting disaster: Lessons from the edge of technology.* New York: Harper Business. Describes dramatic incidents such as mine shaft explosions, chemical plant mishaps, sunken ships, drilling rig accidents, airplane crashes, and spacecraft disasters. Suggests that such events show a chain of human errors (mismanagement, fatigue, panic, carelessness, and insufficient training) in response to machine malfunctions.

Dekker, S. W. A. (2004). *Ten questions about human error: A new view of human factors and system safety.* Mahwah, NJ: Erlbaum. Deals with questions asked in accident investigations, policymaking, training, and research on human errors. Suggests models to deal with the complexities of these situations.

Lancaster, J. (2004). *Making time: Lillian Moller Gilbreth: A life beyond "Cheaper by the Dozen."* Boston: Northeastern University Press. A lively and detailed biography of Lillian Gilbreth, who combined marriage, motherhood, and a career in a so-called man's profession. A high-profile engineer and efficiency expert, she helped develop time-and-motion study and showed empathy toward workers. She served as an adviser on women's issues to five U.S. presidents. The daily problems she faced still resonate with working women today.

Meister, D., & Enderwick, T. P. (2002). *Human factors in system design, development, and testing.* Mahwah, NJ: Erlbaum. A comprehensive review of human factors issues from task analysis to formal experimentation.

Nelson, N. A., & Silverstein, B. A. (1998). Workplace changes associated with a reduction in musculoskeletal symptoms in office workers. *Human Factors, 40,* 337–350. Identifies workplace factors associated with hand/arm and neck/shoulder/back complaints among office workers.

O'Brien, T. G., & Charlton, S. G. (Eds.) (1996). *Handbook of human factors testing and evaluation.* Hillsdale, NJ: Erlbaum. A sourcebook on assessing the components of a person-machine system.

Shih, H. M., & Goonetilleke, R. S. (1998). Effectiveness of menu orientation in Chinese. *Human Factors, 40,* 569–576. An example of cultural differences in human factors applications. Studies reading and writing flow (for example, vertical versus horizontal) in the effectiveness of computer menus.

Chapter 9
Psychology and the Environment

Chapter 9

Psychology and the Environment

"British Columbia residents launch lawsuit over airport noise," "Residents protest new runway opening in Toronto area," "Community in Canada angered by barking dogs," "Canadian Native people disturbed by noise from military jets," "Vancouver police checkpoints to inspect noise levels of motorcycles." The list of headlines goes on and on. Airplanes, traffic noise, motorcycles, barking dogs, concerts—the world around us is making noise we don't want to hear. A few years ago, a hapless 67-year-old accordion player in Bronte, Ontario, was creating too much noise with his summer outdoor concerts, according to some nearby residents who filed complaints with the police. After playing on the same spot for 17 years, Ron Jensen was asked to turn down the volume and move to a new location, or risk being taken to court and charged with a noise bylaw violation.

Noise is not the only source of stress in our environment. Imagine living in an area described as Canada's worst toxic waste site and hearing that people who live where you do show particularly high rates of cancer. How would this affect you? This is the situation in which residents of Nova Scotia living near the Sydney Tar Ponds find themselves. For nearly a century, emissions and waste products from Sydney's Sysco steel plant have been dumped there. The high level of carcinogenic materials makes this one of Canada's most hazardous toxic sites. To find out how people are affected by living in such an environment, researchers at the University College of Cape Breton interviewed junior high school students attending a school near the Tar Ponds (O'Leary & Covell, 2002). The researchers found that these adolescents reported worrying about environmental issues and about their own health and that of their families— more so than students attending a school 40 kilometres away. Sadly, the adolescents who worried most about health also showed the highest level of depression. (Overall, depression levels were higher than the national average among both groups of adolescents. The researchers suggest that even the students who lived 40 kilometres away may have felt affected by this environmental hazard.)

As is apparent from the headlines and the study of Tar Ponds residents, our physical world is becoming an increasingly important source of stress. It is getting more

◀ As the human population increases, the physical world is becoming an increasingly important source of stress. Noise from airplanes, for example, is a common feature of urban life.

difficult to escape industrial pollutants and the noise caused by such modern conveniences as jetliners and heavy traffic, and, alas, even accordians. And just as our environment exerts stress on us, so we exert stress on our environment. Few problems are as pressing as the damage we are doing to the environment, including toxic waste, overflowing landfills, pollution, global warming, and the destruction of rainforests. In this module, we will consider the following questions: To what extent and under what conditions is the environment a source of stress? And how can social influence techniques be used to get people to behave in more environmentally sound ways?

The Environment as a Source of Stress

Looking back over the centuries, it is impressive to what extent we have learned to master the harsh environmental hazards that plagued our ancestors. Tragically, in many areas of the world, starvation and preventable diseases are still major causes of premature death. The irony is that at the same time as we have found ways to master the environment, we have created new environmental stressors that our ancestors did not have to face. Chief among these hazards is our phenomenal reproductive success.

Crowding as a Source of Stress

More than 6 billion human beings inhabit the earth—more people than the total number of all human beings who have ever lived before. The world's population is increasing at the rate of 250 000 people every day. At our current rate of growth, the world population will double by the year 2025 and double again at increasingly shorter intervals. At the same time, the food supply is dwindling and the number of malnourished people in the world is increasing (Sadik, 1991).

Even when there is enough food, overcrowding can be a source of considerable stress to both animals and human beings. When animals are crowded together, in either their natural environments or the laboratory, they reproduce more slowly, take inadequate care of their young, and become more susceptible to disease (Calhoun, 1973;

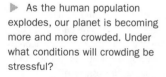 As the human population explodes, our planet is becoming more and more crowded. Under what conditions will crowding be stressful?

Christian, 1963). Studies of crowding in human beings show similar negative effects. As crowding increases in prisons, for example, disciplinary problems, suicides, and overall death rates increase (Paulus & Dzindolet, 1992; Paulus, McCain, & Cox, 1981). Studies at universities find that students living in crowded dorms (e.g., ones that have long corridors with common bathroom and lounge facilities) are more withdrawn socially and are more likely to show signs of learned helplessness than are students living in less crowded dorms (e.g., ones with smaller suites that have their own bathrooms; Baum & Valins, 1979; Evans, Lepore, & Schroeder, 1996; Kaya & Erkip, 2001). To give one last example, University of Saskatchewan researchers Debra Morgan and Norma Stewart (1998) found that elderly people suffering from dementia who were moved to a new special care unit where conditions were less crowded (e.g., private rooms compared to the old units with two to four beds per room) showed beneficial effects (e.g., decreases in disruptive behaviour such as resisting care and making antisocial remarks); in contrast, those who remained in the old units showed an increase in disruptive behaviour.

What is it about crowding that is so aversive? To answer this question, we must first recognize that the presence of other people is not always unpleasant. Many people love living in large cities. When Saturday night arrives, many of us are ready to join our friends for an evening of fun, feeling that the more people we round up, the merrier. This fact has led researchers to distinguish between two terms. **Density** is a neutral term that refers to the number of people who occupy a given space; a classroom with 20 students has a lower density of people than the same classroom with 50 students. **Crowding** is the subjective feeling of unpleasantness that results from the presence of other people; it is the stress we feel when density becomes unpleasant. Under some circumstances, the class with 20 students might feel more crowded than the class with 50 students.

CROWDING AND PERCEIVED CONTROL When will density turn into crowding? One factor, as you might expect, pertains to how people interpret the presence of others, including how much control they feel they have over the crowded conditions (Baron & Rodin, 1978; Schmidt & Keating, 1979; Sherrod & Cohen, 1979). If the presence of others reduces our feelings of control—for example, making us feel it is harder to move around as freely as we would like, or harder to avoid running into people we would just as soon avoid—then we are likely to experience a crowd as stressful. If we feel we have control over the situation—for example, if we know we can leave the crowd at any point and find solace in a quiet spot—then we are unlikely to experience it as stressful.

To test this hypothesis, Drury Sherrod (1974) asked high school students to work on some problems in a room that was jam-packed with other people. In one condition, he told the students that they were free to leave at any point: "In the past, some people who have been in the experiment have chosen to leave," he said. "Others have not. We would prefer that you do not, but that's entirely up to you" (Sherrod, 1974). Students in a second condition worked under identical crowded conditions but were not given the choice to leave at any point. Finally, students in a third condition worked in uncrowded conditions. After working on the initial set of problems, the participants were moved to uncrowded quarters, where they worked on a series of difficult puzzles.

At first, the students who were crowded—regardless of whether they had a sense of control—solved as many problems as did students who were not crowded. Initially, they were able to concentrate, ignoring the fact that they were shoulder to shoulder with other people. For students in the condition where they were not given the option to leave, however, the lack of control eventually took its toll. As seen in Figure 9.1, the

> The thing which in the subway is called congestion is highly esteemed in the night spots as intimacy.
> —Simeon Strunsky, journalist, 1954

Density the number of people who occupy a given space

Crowding the subjective feeling of unpleasantness that results from the presence of other people

▶ **FIGURE 9.1**

CROWDING AND PERCEIVED CONTROL

People who believed that they had control over the crowded conditions tried almost as hard on a subsequent task as people who were not crowded at all.

(Adapted from Sherrod, 1974)

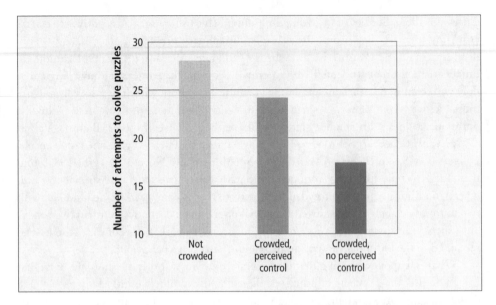

students who had no control over the crowded conditions in the first session tried to solve significantly fewer puzzles in the second session, as compared to students in the other two conditions. The students who had a sense of *perceived* control over the crowded conditions worked on almost as many difficult puzzles as the students who had not been crowded at all.

The moral? It is not crowding itself that causes stress but, rather, the feeling that one cannot control or escape crowded conditions. It might seem that this is much easier in some parts of the world than in others. If you live in a high-rise in New York City, for example, it would seem to be more difficult to avoid crowded conditions than if you live on a farm on Prince Edward Island. Similarly, homes and apartments are much smaller in Japan than in Canada, and to Canadians, at least, it might seem that it would be more difficult to escape crowded conditions in Japan. Yet even in areas where the density of people is quite high, norms develop to protect people's privacy and to allow them an escape from feelings of being overcrowded. Richard Brislin (1993) notes, for instance, that in Japan and in the slums of Mexico, both of which have a high density of people, norms about visiting people in their homes are different from those in North America. In Mexico, your home is respected as a sacrosanct place where you can be by yourself and escape the stress of crowded conditions; it is virtually unheard of for an individual to drop by someone else's house (Pandey, 1990). Similarly, the Japanese entertain in their homes much less than North Americans do; they are more likely to invite guests for a meal in a restaurant. The way in which people in different cultures gain control over crowding differs, but the need for control appears to be universal (Fuller et al., 1996). To examine whether density or perceived control is most likely to produce feelings of crowding, see Try It! on page 411.

CROWDING AND EXPECTATIONS As we have already discussed, the fact that a large number of people are in our environment doesn't necessarily mean that we feel crowded. What is important is how we perceive the situation. For example, we are likely to feel crowded when an environment contains more people than we expect. Vaske, Donnelly, and Petruzzi (1996) interviewed two kinds of visitors to the Columbia Icefields

try it!   When Do People Feel Crowded?

Over a period of a few days, observe people in a variety of situations in which crowding might occur, such as a university or college party, a busy bus stop, a line to enter a movie theatre or dining hall, or a rock concert. In each situation, make the following ratings:

1. What is the density of people in this setting? That is, how many people are there per square metre? (Obviously this will be hard to measure exactly, but make a rough estimate.)

2. How much control do people have in this situation? Specifically, how easily could they leave and find a less crowded setting, if they so desired? Rate your response, using the scale below.

In this situation, people seem to feel

| 1 | 2 | 3 | 4 | 5 | 6 | 7 | 8 | 9 |

very little control   complete control

3. How crowded do people appear to be? Specifically, how negative an experience is it to be in this setting?

People seem to find this setting

| 1 | 2 | 3 | 4 | 5 | 6 | 7 | 8 | 9 |

very unpleasant   very pleasant

After sampling several situations, see which predicts your answers to number 3 the best: the density of people (question 1) or how much control people feel (question 2). If you have had a course in statistics, you can compute the correlation coefficient between your answers to questions 1 and 3 and between your answers to questions 2 and 3, to see which one is bigger. If you haven't, just examine the pattern of answers and see whether your answers to question 3 seem to follow more your answers to question 1 or to question 2. Based on the research discussed in the text, it is likely that your answers to question 3 depended more on the amount of control people felt (question 2) than on the objective density of people in the situation (question 1).

in Jasper National Park—those who saw the glacier on a tour bus and those who explored the glacier on their own. Not surprisingly, visitors who arrived via tour bus encountered many more people on the glacier than did those who were on their own. However, the tour bus people didn't necessarily feel any more crowded than did the others. What determined feelings of crowding by both kinds of visitors was the number of people they *expected* would be on the glacier. If there were more people on the glacier than they had anticipated, the visitors felt crowded. This held true regardless of the visitors' country of origin (Canada, United States, Japan, Germany, or England).

CROWDING AND ATTRIBUTION Other factors also determine how aversive people will find crowded conditions. It is well known, for example, that the presence of others makes people physiologically aroused (Zajonc, 1965). Arousal can have intriguing consequences. It can lead to quite different emotions, depending on the attributions people make about the source of their arousal (Schachter & Singer, 1962). As a result, as we might expect, people's attributions for the arousal caused by crowding are an important determinant of how aversive crowding will be. If people attribute their arousal to the presence of the other people, they will interpret it as a sign that the setting is too crowded and will feel uncomfortable, cramped, and irritated. If they attribute the arousal to another source, they will not feel crowded (Aiello, Thompson, & Brodzinsky, 1983; Schmidt & Keating, 1979). If, for example, a student in a class of 300 people attributes her arousal to the stimulating and fascinating lecture she is hearing, she will feel less crowded than if she attributes her arousal to the fact that she feels like a sardine in a can.

CROWDING AND SENSORY OVERLOAD Finally, crowding will be aversive if it leads to **sensory overload** (Cohen, 1978; Milgram, 1970), which occurs when we receive more stimulation from the environment than we can pay attention to or process. Since other people are a key source of stimulation, one instance in which sensory overload can occur is when so many people are around that we cannot pay attention to everyone. For example, if a committee of 10 people was interviewing you for a job, you'd feel that you had to pay close attention to everything each interviewer said and did. The result? A severe demand would be placed on your attention system—and it would most likely have negative consequences for you.

Noise as a Source of Stress

Consider the lives of the people known as the Mabaan, who live in the Sudan in northeastern Africa, near the equator. When studied by Rosen, Bergman, Plester, El-Mofty, and Satti (1962), this culture was relatively untouched by modern civilization. The Mabaan lived in bamboo huts, wore little clothing, and thrived on a diet of grains, fish, and small game. Their environment was quiet and uncrowded, free of many of the stressors associated with modern urban life. There were no sleep-jarring noises from sirens and trucks, no traffic jams to endure at the end of the day, and little fear of crime. Rosen and his colleagues found that, compared to adults in the United States, the Mabaan had less hypertension (high blood pressure), less obesity, and superior hearing.

We cannot be sure, of course, that the absence of modern environmental stressors, such as the noise of urban life, was responsible for the excellent health of the Mabaan. Even if it were, we might not want to conclude that living in modern, urban areas is always stressful and inevitably causes health problems. Some people thrive in the hustle and bustle of a big city. Further, the identical event—such as loud music—can be enjoyable on some occasions but highly stressful on others. To understand why noise is bothersome at some times but not at others, we need to revisit a basic assumption of social psychology: it is not objective but subjective situations that influence people. The same stimulus, such as loud music, is interpreted as a source of pleasure on some occasions and as an annoying interruption on others. To understand when our environment will be stressful, then, we need to understand how and why people construe that environment as a threat to their well-being. Just as with crowding, noise is especially stressful when people feel that they cannot control it.

NOISE AND PERCEIVED CONTROL David Glass and Jerome Singer (1972) performed a series of studies to test the conditions under which noise is perceived as stressful. In a typical experiment, participants were given several problems to solve, such as complex addition problems, and a proofreading task. While they worked on these problems, they heard loud bursts of noise coming from various sources—a mimeograph machine, a typewriter, or two people speaking in Spanish. The noise was played at 108 decibels—about what you would hear if you were operating a riveting machine or were standing near the runway when a large commercial jet took off.

In one condition, the bursts of noise occurred at unpredictable lengths and at unpredictable intervals over the course of the 25-minute session. In a second condition, people

Sensory overload situations in which we receive more stimulation from the environment than we can pay attention to or process

Noise, *n.* A stench in the ear.... The chief product and authenticating sign of civilization.
—Ambrose Bierce, *Devil's Dictionary,* 1906

classic research

heard the same sequence of noises but were given a sense of control over them. The experimenter told participants that they could stop the noise at any point by pressing a button. "Whether or not you press the button is up to you," explained the experimenter. "We'd prefer that you do not, but that's entirely up to you" (Glass & Singer, 1972). A key fact to remember is that *no one* actually pressed the button. People in this condition heard the same amount of noise as people in the uncontrollable noise condition; the only difference was that they believed they could stop the noise whenever they wanted. Finally, a third condition was included wherein people worked on the problem in peace and quiet. After the 25-minute session was over, people in all conditions worked on new problems without any noise present.

Interestingly, the noise had little effect on people during the initial 25-minute session. As long as a task was not too complex, people could bear down and ignore unpleasant noises, doing just as well on the problems as people who worked on them in quiet surroundings. A different picture emerged, however, when people worked on problems in the next session, in which everyone could work in peace and quiet. As you can see in Figure 9.2, those who had endured the uncontrollable noises made significantly more errors during this session than did people who had not heard noises during the first session. In contrast, the people who heard the noises but believed they could control them did almost as well on the subsequent problems as those who heard no noise at all (see Figure 9.2). When people knew they could turn off the noise at any point, the noise was much easier to tolerate and did not impair later performance—even though these people had never actually turned it off.

Why did it take time for the noise to hurt people's performance, and why did this occur only in the condition where the noise couldn't be controlled? When people are initially exposed to uncontrollable, negative events, they often attempt to overcome them as best they can. But if negative uncontrollable events continue despite our best efforts to overcome them, learned helplessness sets in (Abramson, Seligman, & Teasdale, 1978; Wortman & Brehm, 1975; see Chapter 3). One consequence of learned helplessness is reduced effort, which makes it more difficult to learn new material. As a result, the participants who could not control the noise in the Glass and Singer (1972) experiment were

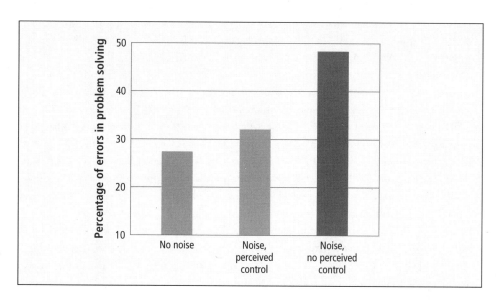

◀ **FIGURE 9.2**

NOISE AND PERCEIVED CONTROL

People who believed they could control the noxious noise did about as well on a subsequent task as people who heard no noise at all.

(Adapted from Glass & Singer, 1972)

able to deal with it and do well on the problems initially, but the lack of control they experienced eventually took its toll, causing them to do poorly on the second task. In contrast, participants who believed they could control the noise never experienced learned helplessness and thus were able to do well on the second set of problems.

Subsequent research conducted at the University of Manitoba underscores the importance of perceived control. Cramer, Nickels, and Gural (1997) found that participants who were told that there was nothing they could do to escape bursts of loud noise (78 decibels) resembling sirens of emergency vehicles did, in fact, feel more helpless than did those who were told they had some control. Interestingly, among those who were told that they had some control, helplessness was reduced to the same extent, regardless of whether participants were told that they had 25 percent, 50 percent, or 75 percent control. As the researchers put it, "A little control may go far to shield a person from feelings of helplessness, and additional control provides little extra protection" (Cramer, Nickels, & Gural, 1997).

NOISE AND URBAN LIFE Consider the case of Torontonian Robin Ward. In the fall of 1997, Ward had to quickly find a new home because of the dissolution of his marriage. He fell in love with a house in Rosedale and invested a substantial sum of money in repairs and renovations. While resting on his sofa on a Saturday afternoon the following spring, he was jolted upright by a tremendous, frightening roar. Three people wearing headphones were operating leaf blowers near his house. He rushed outside to confront them but apparently they couldn't hear a thing he said. This event triggered a series of attempts to force people in the neighbourhood using leaf blowers, lawn mowers, and weed eaters to stop making so much noise. But Toronto's noise bylaws did not adequately address noise created by such devices. The result? Ward found the noise so unbearable that he moved—although he still hopes one day to win the battle of the leaf blowers and return to his home.

As Robin Ward is well aware, in modern urban life, loud noises are often not controllable, and they last a lot longer than the 25-minute sessions in the Glass and Singer (1972) study. Several studies have shown that people who are exposed to real-life noises respond like the participants in the uncontrollable noise condition of Glass and Singer's study. For example, children who live near busy highways and airports have higher blood pressure, are more easily distracted, and do more poorly on reading tests than children who live in quieter areas (Cohen, Evans, Krantz, Stokols, & Kelly, 1981; Cohen, Glass, & Singer, 1973). These deficits are classic signs of learned helplessness.

Obviously, the researchers in these studies could not randomly assign children to live near or far from an airport. Whereas the researchers did their best to match the children on such variables as race, social class, and economic background, there is always the possibility that the children differed in some way other than their exposure to uncontrollable noise. Recently, the opening of a new airport in Munich, Germany, and the closing of the old airport provided a unique opportunity to study the effects of noise over time in the same neighbourhoods. Researchers gave reading tests to children who lived near the old airport—both before and after it closed, and to children who lived near the new airport—both before and after it opened (Hygge, Evans, & Bullinger, 2002). Confirming previous studies, the children who were exposed to aircraft noise did significantly worse on the reading tests than the children who were not. That is, the children who lived near the old airport before it closed did poorly on the reading test, as did the children who lived near the new airport after it opened.

Frequent, unpredictable noises are an unavoidable fact of urban life. Studies have shown that children who are exposed to constant noises have higher blood pressure, are more easily distracted, and are more likely to give up when working on difficult puzzles than other children.

This study also examined a new question—whether the effects of the aircraft noise are reversed when the noise ends. By a year after the old airport closed, the children who lived nearby were doing as well on the reading tests as children who lived farther away. This finding is encouraging, suggesting that attempts to reduce urban noise will pay off relatively quickly. Due in part to studies such as these, attempts have recently been made to reduce the amount of noise to which people are subjected—for example, by adding soundproofing materials to schools and devices to jet engines that make them less noisy (Bronzaft, 2002).

Toxic Environments as a Source of Stress

What did adolescents affected by the Tar Ponds in Nova Scotia identify as the greatest problem in their neighbourhood? Not peer pressure or bullying but—pollution. Clearly, even among 12- to 14-year-olds, living in a toxic environment creates stress. A study conducted with two communities in Ontario found that even nonhazardous landfill sites create stress and reduce well-being among residents (Wakefield & Elliott, 2000). These researchers found that decision-making processes (e.g., whether the government allowed public input, divisions in the community over the effects of the site) often created as much stress as the outcome itself.

Thus, it is clear that people are harming the physical environment in multiple ways. Changes in attitudes and behaviour are urgently needed to avoid environmental catastrophe. Social psychologists have studied a number of techniques involving social influence and social interaction that encourage people to behave in more environmentally sound ways (Geller, 2002; Oskamp, 1995; Sundstrom et al., 1996; Vining & Ebreo, 2002). We turn to these now.

Using Social Psychology to Change Environmentally Damaging Behaviour

We humans have been treating our planet like a large garbage can, rapidly filling up ground water and the atmosphere with all sorts of pollutants. When people lived in small groups of hunters and gatherers, they could get away with discarding their trash wherever they pleased. Now there are more than 6 billion of us (and counting), and we have developed toxic waste that will remain poisonous for centuries (Gilbert, 1990). For example, more than 360 chemical compounds have been identified in the Great Lakes. As a result, various species of fish are suffering from tumours, lesions, and reproductive difficulties. In fact, 7 of the 10 most highly valued species of fish in Lake Ontario have nearly disappeared (Great Lakes: Chemical hot spot, 2000). And on land, the discovery of hideous deformities on frogs has been traced to farmers' pesticide use. Researcher Martin Ouellet and a team of Canadian Wildlife Service biologists have examined nearly 30 000 frogs along the St. Lawrence River and have documented abnormalities such as a frog with an eye staring out of its back, a frog with 23 extra toes, frogs with missing eyes and limbs, and frogs whose altered DNA makes them appear to be male although they are female inside (Jacobs, 1998). Rates of deformity are dramatically higher on agricultural land that has been sprayed with pesticides or other chemicals, compared to land that has not been sprayed for decades. Sadly, these findings also have implications for humans. Research conducted in Canada, the United States, and Finland shows that farmers' children are more likely to have deformities such as missing fingers and toes and abnormal hearts, kidneys, and sexual organs than are children whose parents are not farmers (Jacobs, 1998).

Clearly, it is important to learn more about such environmental problems and to find ways of solving them. This will involve convincing people to treat the environment better. Naturally, you will recognize this as a classic social psychological question, in that it concerns how we can change people's attitudes and behaviours. Let's see what solutions social psychologists have come up with for the planet's pressing environmental problems.

> "
> The earth we abuse and the living things we kill, in the end, take their revenge; for in exploiting their presences we are diminishing our future.
> —Marya Mannes, 1958

▶ Pollution and waste hurt not only humans but also many other species.

"Help!"

Resolving Social Dilemmas

The first step is to realize that we are dealing with a classic social dilemma. A social dilemma is a conflict in which the most beneficial action for an individual will, if chosen by most people, have harmful effects on everyone. Of particular relevance to the environment is a variant called the *commons dilemma*—a situation in which everyone takes from a common pool of goods that will replenish itself if used in moderation but that will disappear if overused. Examples include the use of limited resources such as water and energy. Individuals benefit by using as much as they need but, if everyone does so, shortages often result. As with many social dilemmas, however, so many individuals act in their own self-interest that everyone suffers (Dawes, 1980; Kerr & Kaufman-Gilliland, 1997; Kortenkamp & Moore, 2001; Levine & Moreland, 1998; Pruitt, 1998).

Canada's National Parks face the dilemma of development for tourism, which potentially could destroy the very beauty that tourists are coming to see. Edgar Jackson (1987) found that people's views on preservation of land versus development of land for recreational purposes depended on the kinds of recreational activities they engaged in. In a survey conducted with residents of Calgary and Edmonton, he found that people who performed mechanized (e.g., snowmobiling) and consumptive (e.g., fishing) recreational activities more strongly favoured development. Those who preferred activities such as canoeing or hiking more strongly favoured preservation of the environment.

How can we resolve social dilemmas, convincing people to act for the greater good of everyone, rather than purely out of self-interest? Social psychologists have devised some fascinating laboratory games to try to answer this question. Imagine you arrive for a study and discover that there are six other participants you have never met. The experimenter gives you and the other participants $6 and says that each of you can keep the money. There is, however, another option. Each person can donate his or her money to the rest of the group, to be divided equally among the six other members. If anyone does so, the experimenter will double the contribution. For example, if you donate your money, it will be doubled to $12 and divided evenly among the six other participants. If other group members donate their money to the pot, it will be doubled and you will get a share. Think about the dilemma. If everyone, including you, cooperates by donating his or her money to the group, once it is doubled and divided up, your share will be $12— double what you started with. Donating your money is risky, however; if you are the only one who does so, you will end up with nothing, while having increased everyone else's winnings (see Table 9.1). Clearly, the most selfish—and safest—course of action is to keep your money, hoping that everyone else donates theirs. That way, you would make up to $18—your $6, plus your share of the money everyone else threw into the pot. Of course, if everyone thinks this way, you'll make only $6, because no one will donate any money to the group.

If you are like most of the participants in the actual study, you would keep your six bucks (Orbell, van de Kragt, & Dawes, 1988). After all, as you can see in Table 9.1, you will always earn more money by keeping your $6 than by giving it away (i.e., the winnings in the top row of Table 9.1 are always higher than the winnings in the bottom row). The only problem with this strategy is that because most people adopt it, everyone suffers. That is, the total pool of money to be divided remains low, because few people donate to the group, which would allow the experimenter to double the money. As with many social dilemmas, most people look out for themselves and, as a result, everyone loses.

Table 9.1	Amount of money you stand to win in the Orbell, van de Kragt, and Dawes (1988) experiment

You can either keep your $6 or donate it to the six other group members. If you donate it, the money will be doubled, so that each group member will receive $2. Most people who play this game want to keep their money, to maximize their own gains. The more people who keep their money, however, the more everyone loses.

Other people's decisions

	6 Keep 0 Give	5 Keep 1 Gives	4 Keep 2 Give	3 Keep 3 Give	2 Keep 4 Give	1 Keeps 5 Give	0 Keep 6 Give
Your Decision							
Keep Your $6	$6	$8	$10	$12	$14	$16	$18
Give Your $6	$0	$2	$4	$6	$8	$10	$12

(Adapted from Orbell, van de Kragt, & Dawes, 1988)

How can people be convinced to trust their fellow group members, cooperating in such a way that everyone benefits? It is notoriously difficult to resolve social dilemmas, as indicated by the effort required to get people to conserve water when there are droughts, recycle their waste goods, clean up a common area in a dormitory or apartment, or reduce the use of pesticides and thereby lower the production and visual appeal of produce.

In another condition of the experiment discussed above, John Orbell and his colleagues (1988) found an intriguing result. Simply allowing the group to talk together for 10 minutes dramatically increased the number of members who donated money to the group—from 38 to 79 percent. The increase in the number of donors led to a larger pool of money to be divided, from an average of $32 to $66. Communication works because it allows each person to find out whether the others are planning to act cooperatively or competitively, as well as to persuade others to act for the common good (e.g., "I'll donate my money if you donate yours") (Bouas & Komorita, 1996; De Cremer, 2002).

This finding is encouraging, but it may be limited to small groups that are able to communicate face to face. What happens when an entire community is caught in a social dilemma? When large groups are involved, alternative approaches are needed. One approach is to make people's behaviour as public as possible. If people can take the selfish route privately, undiscovered by their peers, they will often do so. However, if their actions are public, the kinds of normative pressures come into play, making people's behaviour more consistent with group norms. Some farmers might be tempted, for example, to allow runoff of fertilizers from their land if no one will find out about it, but if they believe they will become the object of derision and scorn of their neighbours, they will most likely refrain from doing so. Peer pressure can also be effective in the city. Scott (1999) found that residents of the Greater Toronto area recycled a higher number of products when they felt social pressure to do so. As one respondent remarked, [people] "feel they have to because their neighbours put out a Blue Box."

Another approach that benefits the entire group is to make it easier for individuals to monitor their own behaviour. A problem with some environmental social dilemmas is that it is not easy for people to keep track of how much of a resource they are using, such as water or electricity. During a drought, for example, people may be asked to conserve water, but it is not easy for them to monitor how many litres a day they are using. One pair of researchers reasoned that making it easy for people to keep track of their water use would make it easier for them to act on their concern for the greater good (Van Vugt & Samuelson, 1999). They compared two communities in the Hampshire region of England during a severe drought in the summer of 1995. The houses in one community had been equipped with water meters that allowed residents to monitor how much water they were consuming. The houses in the other community did not have meters. As expected, when people felt that the water shortage was severe, those in the metered houses consumed less water than those in the unmetered houses. Further, there was evidence that they did so not purely out of self-interest (i.e., using less water would save money) but also out of concern for the collective good. Therefore, one simple way to resolve an environmental social dilemma is to make it easier for people to monitor their consumption, which makes it easier for them to act on their good intentions (Van Vugt, 2001).

Reducing Litter

Compared to other environmental problems, littering may not seem to be all that serious. Most people seem to think it isn't a big deal to leave their paper cup at the side of the road instead of in a garbage can. Unfortunately, those paper cups add up. In California, for example, littering has increased steadily over the past 15 years, to the point where $100 million of tax money is spent cleaning it up every year (Cialdini, Kallgren, & Reno, 1991). The stuff we discard is polluting water systems, endangering wildlife, and costing us millions of dollars.

Littering is another classic social dilemma. Sometimes it's a pain to find a garbage can and, from an individual's point of view, what's one more paper cup added to the side of the road? As with all social dilemmas, the problem is that if everyone thinks this way, everyone suffers (Sibley & Lui, 2000). How can we get people to act less selfishly when they have that empty paper cup in hand?

One answer is to remind people of the social norms against littering. Robert Cialdini, Carl Kallgren, and Raymond Reno have pointed out that there are two important kinds of social norms that can influence whether people litter (Cialdini, Kallgren, & Reno, 1991; Cialdini, Reno, & Kallgren, 1990; Kallgren, Reno, & Cialdini, 2000; Reno, Cialdini, & Kallgren, 1993). First, there are **injunctive norms,** which are socially sanctioned behaviours—people's perceptions of what behaviour is approved or disapproved by others. For example, we may be in an environment where many people are littering but know that there is an injunctive norm against littering—most people disapprove of it. Second, there are **descriptive norms,** which are people's perceptions of how others are actually behaving in a given situation, regardless of whether the behaviour is approved or disapproved by others.

Focusing people's attention on either of these norms has been found to reduce littering. For example, Reno, Cialdini, and Kallgren (1993) conducted a field experiment to investigate the power of injunctive norms. As people left a local library and approached their cars in the parking lot, a confederate walked by them, picked up a fast-food bag that had been discarded on the ground, and put the bag in the trash. In a control condition, no bag was on the ground, and the confederate simply walked by the library patrons. When the patrons got to their car, they found a pamphlet on their windshield. The question was how many of these people would litter by throwing the pamphlet on the ground. Reno and colleagues hypothesized that seeing the confederate pick up the fast-food bag would be a vivid reminder of the injunctive norm—littering is bad, and other people disapprove of it—and hence would lower the participant's own inclination to litter. They

> We live in an environment whose principal product is garbage.
> —Russell Baker, 1968

Injunctive norms people's perceptions of what behaviour is approved or disapproved by others

Descriptive norms people's perceptions of how other people actually behave in a given situation, regardless of whether the behaviour is approved or disapproved by others

classic research

▶ Besides being unsightly, litter can cost millions of dollars to clean up. Social psychologists have found that emphasizing various kinds of social norms against littering is an effective way to prevent it.

were right. In this condition, only 7 percent of the people tossed the pamphlet on the ground, compared to 37 percent in the control condition. If you would like to try to replicate this effect in an experiment of your own, see Try It! below.

What is the best way to communicate descriptive norms against littering? The most straightforward way, it would seem, would be to clean up all of the litter in an environment to illustrate that "no one litters here." In general, this is true. The less litter there is in an environment, the less likely people are to litter (Huffman et al., 1995; Reiter &

try it! Reducing Littering Using Injunctive Norms

See if you can get people to pick up litter by invoking injunctive norms, using the techniques discovered by Reno, Cialdini, and Kallgren (1993). This exercise is easier to do with a friend who can unobtrusively observe if people littler. Here's how it works:

Find an environment in which people are likely to litter. In the psychology building at one of our universities, for example, the place where people pick up the student newspaper would be appropriate. The paper often comes with an advertising insert and, when people pick up the paper, they often discard the insert on the floor.

Next, plant a conspicuous piece of litter in this environment. Reno and colleagues (1993) used a fast-food bag stuffed with litter. Place it in a location where people are sure to see, such as near a doorway.

In one condition, wait until an individual enters the environment and is in full view of the piece of trash you have planted. Then, pick up the trash, throw it away, and go on your way. It is critical that the person realizes it wasn't *your* bag but that you decided to pick it up and throw it away anyway. In a second condition, walk by the trash, glance at it, and continue on your way without picking it up.

The observer should watch to see whether people litter; for example, whether they throw the paper's advertising insert on the floor or put it in a garbage can.

Reno, Cialdini, and Kallgren (1993) found that when people saw someone pick up another person's litter, they were much less likely to litter themselves. Did you replicate this effect? Why or why not?

Samuel, 1980). There is, however, an interesting exception to this finding. Cialdini and colleagues (1990) figured that seeing one conspicuous piece of litter on the ground, spoiling an otherwise clean environment, would be a better reminder of descriptive norms than seeing a completely clean environment. The single piece of trash sticks out like a sore thumb, reminding people that no one has littered here—except for one thoughtless person. In comparison, if there is no litter on the ground, people might not even think about the descriptive norm. Ironically, then, littering may be more likely to occur in a totally clean environment than in one containing a single piece of litter.

To test this hypothesis, the researchers stuffed students' mailboxes with brochures and then observed, from a hidden vantage point, how many of the students dropped them on the floor (Cialdini, Reno, & Kallgren, 1990). In the first condition, the researchers cleaned up the mailroom so there were no other pieces of litter to be seen. In the second condition, they placed one very noticeable piece of litter on the floor—a hollowed-out piece of watermelon. In the third condition, they not only put the water-melon rind on the floor but also spread out dozens of discarded brochures. As predicted, the lowest rate of littering occurred in the condition where there was a single piece of litter on the floor (see Figure 9.3). The single violation of a descriptive norm highlighted the fact that no one had littered except the one idiot who had dropped the watermelon rind. Now that people's attention was focused on the descriptive norm against littering, virtually none of the students littered. The highest percentage of littering occurred when the floor was littered with many brochures; here, it was clear that there was a descriptive norm in favour of littering, and many of the students followed suit.

Clearly, drawing people's attention to both injunctive and descriptive norms can reduce littering. Of the two kinds of norms, Cialdini and colleagues suggest that injunc-tive norms work better. Descriptive norms work only if everyone cooperates—for example, by keeping an environment relatively free of litter. This method is not perfect, however; if litter starts to accumulate, the descriptive norm becomes "See, lots of people litter here!" and littering will increase. In contrast, reminding people of the injunctive norm works in a wide variety of situations (Cialdini, [in press]; Reno, Cialdini, & Kallgren, 1993; Kallgren, Reno, & Cialdini, 2000). Once we are reminded that "people disapprove of littering," we are less likely to litter in virtually all circumstances.

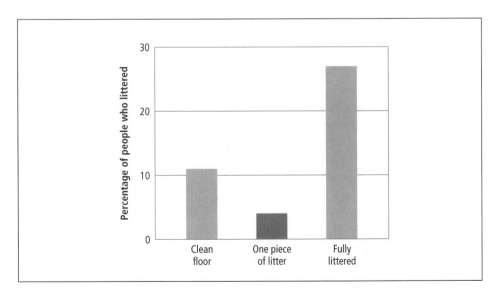

◀ **FIGURE 9.3**

DESCRIPTIVE NORMS AND LITTERING

Who littered the least—people who saw that no one else had littered, people who saw one piece of litter on the floor, or people who saw several pieces of litter? As shown in the figure, it was people who saw one piece of litter. Seeing the single piece of litter was most likely to draw people's attention to the fact that most people had not littered, making participants less likely to litter.

(Adapted from Cialdini, Reno, & Kallgren, 1990)

Conserving Water

Several years ago, during severe water shortages, the administrators at one campus of the University of California realized that an enormous amount of water was being wasted by students using the university athletic facilities. The administrators posted signs in the shower rooms of the gymnasiums, exhorting students to conserve water by taking briefer, more efficient showers. The signs appealed to the students' conscience by urging them to take brief showers and to turn off the water while soaping up. The administrators were confident that the signs would be effective because the vast majority of students at this campus were ecology-minded and believed in preserving natural resources. However, systematic observation revealed that fewer than 15 percent of the students complied with the conservation message on the posted signs.

The administrators were puzzled—perhaps the majority of the students hadn't paid attention to the sign? After all, a sign on the wall is easy to ignore. So administrators made each sign more obtrusive, putting it on a tripod at the entrance to the showers so the students needed to walk around the sign in order to get into the shower room. While this increased compliance slightly—19 percent turned off the shower while soaping up—it apparently made a great many students angry. The sign was continually being knocked over and kicked around, and a large percentage of students took inordinately *long* showers, apparently as a reaction against being told what to do. The sign was doing more harm than good, which puzzled the administrators even more. Time to call in the social psychologists.

Elliot Aronson and his students (Dickerson et al., 1992) decided to apply the hypocrisy technique used in an earlier study to increase condom purchases to this new situation. The procedure involved intercepting female students who were on their way from the swimming pool to the women's shower room, introducing the experimental manipulations, and then having a research assistant casually follow them into the shower room, where the assistant unobtrusively timed their showers. Research participants in one condition were asked to respond to a brief questionnaire about their water use, a task designed to make them mindful of how they sometimes wasted water while showering. In another condition, research participants made a public commitment, exhorting others to take steps to conserve water. Specifically, these participants were asked to sign their names to a public poster that read, "Take Shorter Showers. Turn Shower Off While Soaping Up. If I Can Do It, So Can YOU!" In the crucial condition—the hypocrisy condition—the participants did both; that is, they were made mindful of their own wasteful behaviour and indicated publicly (on the poster) that they were practising water conservation. In short, they were made aware that they were preaching behaviour they themselves were not practising. Just as in the condom study, participants who were made to feel like hypocrites changed their behaviour so they could feel good about themselves. In this case, they took very brief showers. Indeed, the procedure was so effective that the average time students in this condition spent showering was reduced to 3.5 minutes. The hypocrisy procedure has also been found to increase other environmentally sound practices, such as recycling (Fried & Aronson, 1995).

Other approaches may be necessary when attempting to increase water conservation on a wider scale. In Great Britain, Van Vugt (2001) adopted a social dilemma approach and hypothesized that people would be more likely to conserve water if they were charged for how much water they actually used (a variable tariff) than if they were simply charged a standard fee regardless of use (a fixed tariff). This hypothesis was supported in a nine-month field study tracking how much water was used in nearly 300 households,

In a study by Dickerson, Thibodeau, Aronson, and Miller (1992), university students who were made aware that they were advocating conservation behaviour they themselves were not practising changed their behaviour by taking shorter showers.

as well as in a laboratory study. These findings indicate that if there is a direct relation between how much we use a resource and how much we pay for it, we may be more motivated to reduce our consumption.

Finally, recent research suggests that social norms can also be useful in water conservation. In the previous section, we discussed research by Cialdini and colleagues in which descriptive norms were used to reduce littering. More recently, Robert Cialdini and his graduate students, Noah Goldstein and Vladas Griskevicius have examined whether descriptive norms can be used to encourage hotel patrons to re-use their towels (as described in Tracey [Dittman], 2005). This behaviour not only saves water but also reduces energy consumption and the use of toxic chemicals (e.g., detergents, bleaches). Specifically, the researchers posted signs in hotel rooms urging guests to re-use their towels. In addition, the signs focused on the benefits to the hotel ("Help the hotel save energy") or benefits to the environment ("Help save the environment") or invoked a descriptive norm "(Join your fellow patrons in helping to save the environment"). Remarkably, the use of a descriptive norm was the most effective—41 percent of the guests in this condition re-used their towel. In contrast, the compliance rate in the pro-environmental condition was significantly lower (31%); the benefit to the hotel message produced the lowest rate of compliance (20%) (Tracey, 2005). Thus, something as simple as telling people that others are performing pro-environment behaviours can promote positive social change.

Conserving Energy

Historically, we have felt perfectly content using as much energy as we needed, assuming that the planet had an infinite supply of wood, oil, natural gas, and electrical power. Indeed, according to research conducted with geography students at the University of Alberta, people favour the continued exploitation of such resources, with less support for the idea of energy conservation, development of solar power, and other alternatives (Jackson, 1985). To this day, Alberta continues to be one of the provinces most strongly opposed to the energy-conservation measures proposed in the Kyoto Accord. Regardless of one's views on this particular agreement, one thing is clear: There is not an unlimited supply of resources.

Can people be motivated to engage in energy conservation? Let's take private homes as an example. Through simple measures such as increasing ceiling, wall, and floor insulation; plugging air leaks; using more efficient light bulbs; and properly maintaining furnaces, the typical energy consumer could reduce the amount of energy used to heat, light, and cool his or her home by 30 to 75 percent (Williams & Ross, 1980; www.hydro.mb.ca/news/release/news_01_01_19b.shtml). The technology needed to increase energy efficiency currently exists and is well within the financial means of most homeowners. This technology would not only save energy, but also save the individual homeowner a great deal of money. Indeed, when McKenzie-Mohr, Nemiroff, Beers, and Desmarais (1995) interviewed residents of British Columbia, they found that both environmental concerns and cost-saving concerns predicted the use of energy-saving devices such as compact fluorescent bulbs and programmable thermostats. However, despite the fact that the societal and financial advantages of conservation have been well publicized, the vast majority of homeowners have not taken action (Hutton et al., 1986). Why not? Why have North Americans been slow to act in a manner that is in their economic self-interest? This lack of compliance has perplexed economists and policy makers, because they have failed to see that the issue is partly a social psychological one.

MAKING ENERGY LOSS VIVID The people's attention is typically directed to the aspects of their environment that are conspicuous and vivid. Elliot Aronson and his colleagues (Aronson, 1990; Aronson & Yates, 1985; Coltrane, Archer, & Aronson, 1986) reasoned that if the issue of energy conservation was made more vivid, people would be more likely to take action. To test this hypothesis, Aronson and his colleagues (Aronson & Gonzales, 1990; Gonzales, Aronson, & Costanzo, 1988) worked with several energy auditors in California. As in many U.S. states, California utility companies offer a free service wherein an auditor will come to people's homes and give them a customized assessment of what needs to be done to make their homes more energy efficient. What a deal! The problem was that fewer than 20 percent of the individuals requesting audits actually followed the auditors' recommendations.

To increase compliance, the Aronson research team trained the auditors to present their findings in a more vivid manner. For example, let's consider weather stripping. For most people, a small crack under the door didn't seem like a huge drain of energy, so when an auditor told them they should put in some weather stripping, they thought, "Yeah, big deal." Aronson and his colleagues told the auditors to make this statement more vivid:

> If you were to add up all the cracks around and under the doors of your home,
> you'd have the equivalent of a hole the size of a football in your living room
> wall. Think for a moment about all the heat that would escape from a hole that
> size. That's precisely why I'm recommending that you install weather stripping
> (Gonzales, Aronson, & Costanzo, 1988, p. 1052).

Similar attempts were made to make other problems more vivid; for example, referring to an attic that lacks insulation as a "naked attic that is like facing winter not just without an overcoat, but without any clothing at all" (p. 1052).

The results were striking. The percentage of homeowners who followed the vivid recommendations jumped to 61 percent. This study demonstrates that people will, in fact, act in a manner that is sensible in terms of environmental goals and their own economic self-interest, but, if old habits are involved, the communication must be one that is vivid enough to break through those established habits.

MAKING CONSERVATION COMPETITIVE Frans Siero and his colleagues have demonstrated another simple but powerful way to get people to conserve energy in the workplace (Siero et al., 1996). At one unit of a factory in the Netherlands, the employees were urged to engage in energy-saving behaviour. For example, announcements were placed in the company magazine asking people to close windows during cold weather and to turn off lights when leaving a room. In addition, the employees received weekly feedback on their behaviour; graphs were posted that showed how much they had improved their energy-saving behaviour, such as how often they had turned off the lights. This intervention resulted in modest improvement. By the end of the program, the number of times people left the lights on for example, decreased by 27 percent.

Another unit of the factory took part in an identical program, with one difference. In addition to receiving weekly feedback on their own energy-saving actions, they received feedback about how the other unit was doing. Siero and colleagues (1996) hypothesized that this social comparison information would motivate people to do better than their colleagues in the other unit. As seen in Figure 9.4, they were right. By the end of the program, the number of times people left the lights on had decreased by 61 percent. Clearly, engaging people's competitive spirit can have a significant impact on their behaviour.

Getting People to Recycle

To reduce the amount of garbage that ends up in landfills, many cities are encouraging their residents to recycle materials such as glass, paper, and aluminum. However, as you know, it

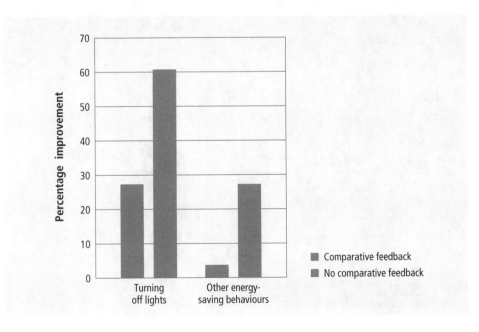

◀ **FIGURE 9.4**

EFFECTS OF COMPARATIVE FEEDBACK ON ENERGY-SAVING BEHAVIOUR

Two units of a factory were urged to conserve energy, and then received feedback about how their unit was doing. Only one of the units, however, received comparative feedback about how they were doing relative to the other unit. As seen in the graph, workers in this second unit improved their behaviour the most, especially by turning off the lights more.

(Adapted from Siero et al., 1996)

can be inconvenient to do so; in some areas you have to load your car with boxes of cans and bottles and drop them off at a recycling centre, which might be several kilometres from your house. Other cities have curbside recycling, whereby a truck picks up recycling materials that you put out on the curb on a designated day. Even then, though, you have to remember to separate your cans, bottles, and newspapers, and find a place to store them until pickup day. We therefore have another social dilemma—a behaviour (recycling) that, while good for us all, is effortful and unpleasant for individuals. As you might imagine, several social psychologists have turned their attention to ways of getting people to recycle more.

There have been two general approaches to this problem. First, some psychologists have focused on ways of changing people's attitudes and values in a pro-environment direction, with the assumption that behaviour will follow. This assumption is consistent with social psychological research on attitudes, which has found that under many conditions people's attitudes are good predictors of their behaviour. Indeed, several studies have found that people's attitudes toward recycling are good predictors of their recycling behaviour, suggesting that a mass media campaign that targets people's attitudes is a good way to go (Cheung, Chan, & Wong, 1999; Ewing, 2001; Oskamp et al., 1998; Scott, 1999).

Sometimes, though, we might fail to act consistently with our attitudes, despite our best intentions. Perhaps the recycling centre is too far away, or we just can't find the time to sort our trash, even though we know we should. Research conducted with residents of Cornwall, Ontario, found that a major reason why people failed to engage in pro-environmental actions was, "I just can't seem to make the effort to change my habits" (Pelletier et al., 1999).

▷ Social psychologists have identified several ways of increasing the likelihood that people will recycle materials such as bottles, cans, and newspapers. One way is to make it as convenient as possible; for example, by offering curbside pickup, as shown in this photo of the recycling service in Toronto.

Kurt Lewin (1947), one of the founders of social psychology, made the observation that big social changes can sometimes occur by removing small barriers from people's environments (Ross & Nisbett, 1991). In the context of recycling, it might be better to simply remove some of the hassles involved—such as by instituting curbside recycling—than to try to change people's attitudes toward the environment. Indeed, the results of studies on recycling conducted with residents of Edmonton (Wall, 1995) and four communities in the Greater Toronto area (Scott, 1999), as well as a 1991 Statistics Canada survey on the environment (Berger, 1997), all converge on the same conclusion—namely, that "people will take pro-environmental actions if they have access to a convenient way of doing so" (Berger, 1997). Increasing the number of recycling bins in a community, instituting curbside recycling, and allowing residents to mix materials instead of having to sort them have all been found to increase people's recycling behaviour (Domina & Koch, 2002; Ludwig, Gray, & Rowell, 1998; Schultz, Oskamp, & Mainieri, 1995).

The moral? There are two ways to get people to act in more environmentally sound ways. First, you can try to change people's attitudes in a pro-environmental direction; this will motivate them to act in environmentally friendly ways, even if there are barriers that make it hard to do so such as having to find a box for your bottles and cans, and then taking it to a recycling centre. It is often easier, however, simply to remove the barriers, such as by instituting curbside recycling and giving people containers. When it is easy to comply, many people will make an effort, even if they do not have strong pro-environmental attitudes. Now that you have read about several ways of changing people's behaviour in ways that help the environment, you are in a position to try them out yourself. See Try It! below.

try it! Changing Environmentally Damaging Behaviour

Use the techniques discussed in this chapter to change people's behaviour in ways that help the environment. Here's how to proceed:

1. Choose the behaviour you want to change. You might try to increase the amount that you and your roommates recycle, reduce the amount of energy wasted in your dorm, or increase water conservation.

2. Choose the technique you will use to change the behaviour. You might, for example, use the comparative feedback technique used by Frans Siero and colleagues (1996) to increase energy conservation. Encourage two areas of your dormitory to reduce energy use or to recycle, and give each feedback about how they are doing relative to the other area. (To do this, you will have to have an easy, objective way of measuring people's behaviour, such as the number of times lights are left on at night or the number of cans that are recycled.) Or you might try the hypocrisy technique used by Elliot Aronson and colleagues (1991) to increase water conservation,

whereby you ask people to sign a public poster that encourages recycling and have them fill out a questionnaire that makes them mindful of times they have failed to recycle. Be creative and feel free to use more than one technique.

3. Measure the success of your intervention. Find an easy way to measure people's behaviour, such as the amount they recycle. Assess their behaviour before and after your intervention. If possible, include a control group of people who do not receive your intervention (randomly assigned, of course). In the absence of such a control group, it will be difficult to gauge the success of your intervention; for example, if people's behaviour changes over time, you won't be able to tell if it is because of your intervention or some other factor (e.g., an article on recycling that happened to appear in the newspaper). By comparing the changes in behaviour in your target group to the control group, you will have a better estimate of the success of your intervention.

Summary

As we human beings continue to populate the earth at an alarming rate, our physical world is becoming a crowded, noisy, and toxic place in which to live. Social psychologists have focused on how people interpret and explain crowded conditions and noise. One key interpretation is how much perceived control people have over an event. The less control people believe they have, the more likely it is that the event will cause them physical and psychological problems. For example, if people in high-**density** settings feel they have a low level of control (i.e., they believe it is difficult to escape to a less dense setting), they will experience **crowding**—the subjective feeling of unpleasantness because of the presence of other people. People will also experience crowding if a space contains more people than they had expected. Crowding can be aversive if it leads to **sensory overload**, which occurs when the presence of other people places a severe demand on our attention system. In addition, the way in which people explain the causes of negative events (e.g., noise, crowding) is critical to how an event is interpreted, and therefore to how stressful it will be.

We also discussed the effects people are having on the environment and the ways in which social influence techniques can be used to get people to behave in more environmentally sound ways. This is not easy because many environmental problems are classic social dilemmas, wherein actions that are beneficial for individuals, if performed by most people, are harmful to everyone. Using proven techniques to change people's attitudes and behaviour, however, social psychologists have had some success in getting people to act in more environmentally sound ways. One technique is to remind people of both **injunctive** and **descriptive norms** against environmentally damaging acts, such as littering. Focusing people's attention on injunctive norms against littering—the idea that discarding garbage on the ground is not a socially accepted behaviour—is especially effective. Another is to arouse dissonance in people by making them feel that they are not practising what they preach—for example, that they are taking long showers even though they believe in water conservation. Finally, removing barriers that make pro-environmental behaviour difficult, such as by instituting curbside recycling and providing people with recycling bins, has been shown to be effective.

Thinking Critically

1. Suppose you were asked to help design a new dormitory at a university. Based on what you have learned about the stressful effects of crowding and noise, what design approach would you take?

2. Based on research on social dilemmas, how might you try to get the residents of a dormitory to recycle more and consume less energy and water?

3. Suppose you are the mayor of a mid-size town in Canada. You are running out of landfill space to deposit the town's garbage, and it is expensive to ship your garbage elsewhere. Based on what you have learned in this chapter, what might you do to get the residents of the town to recycle more in order to produce less garbage?

If You Are Interested

Cohen, S., Evans, G. W., Stokols, D. S., & Krantz, D. S. (1986). *Behavior, health, and environmental stress*. New York: Plenum. A detailed discussion of stress and human health, with a focus on studies the authors conducted on the effects of aircraft noise on children.

Komorita, S. S. & Parks, C. D. (1994). *Social dilemmas*. Dubuque, IA: Brown & Benchmark. A readable introduction to research on social dilemmas. Several examples relevant to environmental issues are used.

Suzuki, D., and McConnell, A. (2002). *Sacred balance: Rediscovering our place in nature* (2nd ed.). Mountaineers Books. A refreshing look at the relationship between human beings and the environment.

Wadleigh, Michael (Director). (1970). *Woodstock* [Documentary]. A documentary about the definitive rock festival; in addition to vintage rock and roll, the film shows some interesting crowd scenes. A fascinating application of research on crowding. When is a dense crowd of people pleasing, and when is it stressful?

Winter, D. D. H. (1996). *Ecological psychology: Healing the split between planet and self.* New York: Addison Wesley. Deborah Du Hann Winter argues that because environmental problems have been caused by human behaviour, beliefs, and values, they are directly related to psychology, and that the solutions will also be found in psychology.

Weblinks

www.snre.umich.edu/eplab

Environmental Psychology

This site contains an overview of environmental psychology.

www.conservationpsychology.org

Conservation Psychology

This site was recently launched by members of the American Psychological Association's Division 34 (Population and Environmental) and researchers from the Brookfield Zoo in Brookfield, Illinois. The site features the research of many environmental psychologists.

www.cbsm.com

Encouraging Pro-Environmental Behaviours at the Community Level

This site, developed by Dr. Doug McKenzie-Mohr, a Canadian environmental psychologist, focuses on changing environmental behaviours locally. Community leaders are encouraged to use simple but effective techniques, such as placing signs near light switches to remind people to turn off the lights when leaving a room. The site includes a number of articles and reports on promoting environmental behaviours within communities.

www.eltoroairport.org/issues/cornell-030498.html

Aircraft Noise and Kids

A paper is presented showing evidence that noise is detrimental to the health of children.

www.psychologymatters.org

Psychology Matters

On this site posted by the American Psychological Association, you can click on "environmentally friendly behaviors" to learn about psychological research aimed at protecting the environment.

Chapter 10
Military Psychology

Chapter 10
Military Psychology

In this chapter we consider the war room, which includes all topics traditional to the study of military psychology. Over the centuries tacticians and leaders have consistently used psychological concepts. While the execution of war changes with technology, many elements of the psychology of war do not. We consider the more general area of military psychology and discuss how psychology has been applied to practical problems such as assessment, selection, leadership, motivation, and morale. We show that the impact of the group is important not only for military precision, but also to ensure the emotional well-being of the soldier. We provide two scenarios that highlight very different applications of psychology. One of the scenarios illustrates how psychologists have been useful in improving the design of military machines, and reflects how psychology has influenced man-machine interactions. The other scenario shows how a psychologist's scholarly skills were put to use in a situation involving espionage.

The nature of conflict

In this section we first look briefly at the nature of conflict and conclude that we are an innately aggressive species. We then look at the distinction between the psychology of war and military psychology, our own area of interest, before proceeding to a recognition that the importance of psychological principles to warfare has a very long history.

We start out by concluding that we are a species that engages in violent behaviours against each other. We assault each other as individuals, and we assault each other as groups, whether as gangs, tribes, clans, religious groups, or nations. Some scholars argue that the absence of any other species of hominids is evidence that we, *Homo sapiens sapiens,* are an aggressive, combative, social animal—so much so that we wiped out our more docile 'cousin' species.

Wars start when we, side A, cannot agree with you, side B, over some issue, and are unable, or unwilling, to use non-aggressive communication to resolve our differences. Once having decided that aggressive conflict is the way forward, we form strategies, and execute a plan, or plans, that will, we hope, result in us winning the dispute. Necessary to our success is, of course, an assessment of risk and loss. We must decide how much we are willing to sacrifice, how many lives we are willing to lose in order to secure our victory. However, regardless of the victor, we want to ensure that we have the necessary means to win another conflict—should the need arise—or, at least, protect and defend what we may have left. We will call the general context in which the planning and development of strategies for conflict and for peace occur the war room.

The war room exists in the real world whenever there is a conflict, or a truce, between two or more identifiable groups of people. For example, a conflict between the armed forces of different nations and a conflict between two local gangs would both yield some strategy of aggressive tactics, goals, etc. We shall see that most of the input that psychologists have had in the war room has been motivated by large, military organizations. Not surprisingly then, many of the topics we discuss are more clearly relevant to formal military organizations, like combat psychology and personnel selection. However, some of the topics are relevant to conflicts and truces, regardless of the sizes of the group, such as the importance of good morale and the effects of propaganda.

The psychology of war versus military psychology

Before beginning our discussion of some of the more traditional topics found in the war room, we first need to distinguish between the psychology of war and military psychology. The psychology of war is concerned with all elements of combat; for example, tactics, performance fatigue, duty rotation, and weapon use. Psychological principles are applied within the context of a combative environment where casualties are anticipated. Given that casualties are anticipated, the psychology of war must by necessity include discussions of highly specific topics. For example, leaders and commanders expect their soldiers in combat to become desensitized to seeing dead bodies and hearing the cries of the wounded. In some sense, being among casualties is part of the job and the soldier must somehow become immune to the emotional effects that this might have. However, seeing one's best friend die is likely to have an entirely different effect on the soldier, and may require specialized psychological treatment.

In contrast, military psychology is much more general, and covers aspects of war *and* peace. The *Corsini Encyclopedia of Psychology and the Behavioral Sciences* (2001) defines it as 'the application of psychological principles and methods and military needs . . . military psychology is not so much a separate field of psychology, but rather is defined by its area of application: military personnel and organizations . . .' For example, military psychology would include the examination of the effects of the combat environment on the soldier, as well as research regarding the effects of environmental factors that are present in everyday, non-combat life, such has as the effects of having families on base, or the effects of reassignments.

In this chapter, we discuss issues that are traditionally considered under the general heading of military psychology, which by definition can include factors pertaining to combative environments.

The historical context of psychology and war

All scholars agree that modern military psychology is lodged firmly in the twentieth century, as we discuss below. However, we feel that it is essential to remember that, when we examine the war room, we are looking at a very old, surprisingly unchanged, real-world context. While the discipline of psychology may not have emerged until the late nineteenth century, the application of psychology to war has been common since the time of the ancients, and testimonials to this fact abound. There is Sun Tzu (*c*.500 BC), who considered open confrontation to be destructive ultimately, and instead advocated strategic manoeuvring so that you 'bend others without coming of conflict' (*The Art of Strategy*, p. 12, translated by R.L. Wing 1997). Sun Tzu argued that central tactical leadership and psychological manipulation were the elements of success: '[good leaders] lure through advantages, and take control through confusion' (ibid., p. 25). The importance of healthy morale among soldiers was noted by the Greek mercenary Xenophon two millennia ago: 'whichever army goes into battle stronger in soul, their enemies generally cannot withstand them' (quoted in Richardson 1978). This point was not lost, centuries later, on Napoleon, who claimed that 'Morale makes up three quarters of the game—relative balance of manpower accounts only for the remaining quarter' (Heidl 1967).

These quotes demonstrate that concepts of tactical leadership, strategic manoeuvres, and psychological manipulation were as relevant to past generals and leaders as they are to those operating in the twenty-first century. In this way, many topics pertinent to the war room remain as important today as they did 2000 years ago, in spite of the obvious changes in technology, weaponry, and combat practices. We admit that it is beyond the scope of this chapter to do justice to this fact. Nonetheless, we can still acknowledge that the leaders of ancient times knew the importance of psychological principles, and used them to secure victory and maintain peace, just as their modern, military counterparts continue to do.

Assessment, selection, and training

In this section, we consider the related topics of selection, assessment, and training. We look at the situations in which psychologists have been called upon to devise task analyses in order to ensure that the right soldier is selected for the right military task. We then look at how psychologists helped to discover the differences between good fighters and poor fighters, as well as identify the characteristics that make good leaders. Finally, we discuss the role psychologists have played in increasing the effectiveness of training. Modifications have included better opportunities to learn necessary skills and more realistic training programmers, such as those offered by simulations.

The First World War

The First World War was the starting point for modern military psychology as the Allied military forces needed fast answers to important questions. For example, there were the related problems of assessment and selection. Not everybody is equally well suited to join an army; and once in the army, not everyone is equally well suited to the same job. While these observations are obvious and probably universally accepted, the military still had the practical problem of discovering, in an efficient and speedy manner, the recruits who were unfit for military service. An obvious example was the problem of low intelligence. The military needed to know which recruits were of such low mental ability that they could not successfully engage in training. Another goal was to screen recruits so that the most appropriate recruits were allocated to each assignment. Yet another challenge was to devise the most efficient methods for training recruits, which would have to include not only training recruits to use weapons, but also preparing them of the realities of combat.

Psychologists were asked to help in these matters, to devise reliable and cost-efficient ways of assessing a recruit's abilities, to map these abilities to the most appropriate military job, and to develop effective training programmes. In this way, the First World War provided psychologists with their first formal opportunity to fit the worker to the job. In fact, many of the topics that we have already considered the 'The work room' first flourished in the context of the war effort, such as the application of task analyses. For example, the roles of a foot soldier require different physical and mental abilities from the roles of a vehicle driver. A psychologist's expertise in task analyses was invaluable. The psychologist could provide way of identifying the actions that the task required and could identify the abilities that were needed to perform those actions. In this way, the psychologist was essential in helping to devise tests that could discriminate those who were unsuitable. In fact, during the First World War psychologists dominated the business of assessing ability and aptitude.

Psychological expertise in research design and analysis also proved vital. Psychologists could devise a series of standard questions to discriminate between those recruits who would make good fighters and those who would make good pilots. However, without having expertise in research design and data analysis, we could not guarantee that our standardized test had any **reliability** and **validity**. Further, there was a limit to the extent to which the psychologist could *guarantee* an accurate prediction of a recruit's ability from performance on a standardized test.

Box 10.1   THE BEGINNINGS OF PERSONNEL SELECTION

The earliest psychological studies on job–worker match, personnel selection, and leadership, and the effects of the physical environment, were in direct response to military questions that arose from conflicts during the First World War. Robert M. Yerkes, who was then president of the American Psychological Association, assembled leading psychologists to help in the war effort, in particular to help with the enormous task of assessing and selecting recruits. Under Yerkes's guidance, these psychologists developed a selection programme that assessed the mental suitability of recruits for different military jobs. The resultant standardized tests, the Army Examinations Alpha, for those recruits who could read, and the Army Examinations Beta, for those recruits who could not read, were used to screen about one million recruits. This early work with the military served as the starting point for many popular areas of psychological enquiry, especially those that are now considered under the traditional headings of organizational and occupational psychology.

Sir Frederic Bartlett, in *Psychology and the Soldier* (1927), addressed this issue directly when he cautioned against over-interpreting a recruit's fitness to perform a military task on the basis of his performance on examination tests alone. He concluded that it was relatively easy to devise tests that identified the unfit; however, it was much more difficult to be confident in decisions about the 'fit' candidate. Bartlett pointed out that examination tests, whether they measure mental abilities or practical skills, do not reliably take into account other factors that may have an effect on a recruit's ability to perform a military task. Bartlett cited an example where a recruit's condescending attitude towards his fellow recruits, and his lack of social cohesion with his *primary group,* resulted in '[his] high intellectual capacity. . .[being] prevented. . .from finding expression' (Bartlett 1927, p. 35).

Barlett felt that there were many factors that must be considered if selection and training are to be effective; among them is the person's **temperament**. Temperament does not reflect a single trait and is determined by a variety of personality factors, like a person's ability to tolerate change and ambiguity, their amicability and popularity, their ease in new situations, and so on. As Bartlett stated 'when a man presents himself for entry to any important social group in his country, the records of his intelligence rating and of his temperamental make-up ought to be as readily available as his ordinary health records. If these were made seriously at the proper time, the problems of building and training an efficient army would be considerably simplified' (Bartlett 1927, p. 37).

The Second World War

By the time of the Second World War, psychologists were major players in the recruitment, assessment, selection, and training of military personnel. Not surprisingly, as technological advances changed the manner in which war was conducted, selection tests had to change, becoming progressively more sophisticated. This meant that problems of allocation, namely how to match the recruit to the job, took priority. For example, as artillery equipment became more complex, the aptitudes and abilities of those who would be controlling them changed accordingly. Unlike rifles, some of these new weapons, such as anti-aircraft batters and aircraft guns, required collaborative efforts between groups of individuals. As a consequence, much of the selection and assessment procedures during the Second World War classified recruits not only on the basis of their ability to learn new tasks, but also in terms of their ability to work with others, and under stressful situations.

The Second World War also marked a change in the training of recruits. For example, during the First World War, the major model for training a soldier was through an apprenticeship, or **vicarious learning**. The novice soldier watched the experienced soldier and received tuition when necessary. In this way the novice learned what things needed doing, the sequence of actions required, and so on. This type of learning is compatible with the notion of *on-the-job training*, and is effective in that we all learn much of our everyday skills through social, vicarious learning. However, this type of learning is more likely to be successful when the person has repeated opportunities to learn, and is not under stress. Obviously, the conditions of war do not afford either to the newly enlisted recruit.

The psychologist was in an ideal position to provide some advice on how to improve training. At the forefront of any military training are two goals. One is to equip the recruit with some mastery of the skills necessary to perform his military duties, and the second is to prepare the recruit for the conditions of war. Fortunately, many psychological concepts could be directly translated into military training. For example, the importance of feedback on performance was introduced in the so-called quick-kill training method. A quick-kill training method has targets of silhouettes pop up unexpectedly and the soldier has to make quick decisions as to whether to fire or not. One of the basic principles of learning theory is that feedback (i.e. knowing how well you perform) improves performance. Applying this helped to promote target accuracy. When training programmes were reworked to include sound psychological principles, the recruit had a better opportunity to improve his military skills, and to be prepared for some of the conditions of combat.

The Korean War

By the time of the Korean War, there was sufficient evidence to suggest that careful selection, followed by adequate training, could dramatically improve the effective use of military resources. In particular, the earlier work of Marshall (1950), who showed that only a proportion of men actually fire against the enemy (see Box 10.2), indicated clearly that the killing effectiveness of military units could be enhanced dramatically if the appropriate people were recruited and selected. To this end, much attention was given to identifying those individuals who had an aptitude, or ability, to be good fighters. While there were a few studies undertaken, the research conducted by the Human Resource Research Office (HRRO; an organization that was funded by the Army) is considered the more reliable.

Who makes a good fighter?

Researchers at the HRRO first focused on identifying the two groups of soldiers that they would be comparing: a *good* fighter group and a *poor* fighter group. (Note that this is

Box 10.2   ACTIVE COMBAT

One of the most important psychological studies that emerged from the Second World War is that of S.L.A. Marshall, who systematically examined the behaviour of combat troops, in his 1950 book *Men Against Fire*. Significantly, Marshall reported that only a small, consistent percentage of fighting soldiers actually ever fired at the enemy. Depending upon his sample, this varied from 15 to 30 percent, with the latter only occurring in exceptional companies. These estimates stayed surprisingly constant, regardless of the type or length of combat action in question. Generally, if a man were to pull the trigger, he would do so from the start of his combat experience and continue to do so until the end. Importantly, the difference between fighters and non-fighters was not their courage, as the non-fighters were as likely to expose themselves to danger as their counterparts who pulled the trigger. Marshall's work highlighted how essential it is to consider the individual soldier's psychological make-up.

different to Marshall's earlier comparison of *fighters* versus *non-fighters*.) The initial assessment of whether someone was a good or poor fighter was based on verbal reports, commendations, and first-hand reports from other men. Researchers found that good fighters exposed themselves more to enemy fire than poor fighters. However, even when being exposed to the same amount of fire, a good fighter systematically behaved differently to a poor fighter. They assumed leadership when necessary (e.g. when the designated leader is not operative), they engaged in aggressive acts outside the normal role of a leader (e.g. attacking another unit offensively), or they performed a supporting role (e.g. protecting another injured soldier while medical help is called). In contrast, poor fighters physically withdrew from engagement (e.g. when under fire they refused to return fire), psychologically withdrew from engagement (e.g. obeyed orders only at gunpoint), showed signs of mental dissociation (e.g. saw or heard things that were not there), and became emotionally labile (e.g. trembled and cried).

Soldiers in the two groups were asked to complete roughly eighty-six psychological tests, and consistent differences were found. Good fighters scored higher in terms of leadership, as assessed in terms of poise, spontaneity, extroversion, independence, and freedom from anxiety. Good fighters were also more likely to engage in adventurous activities or sports and body-contact games. The researches noted that *differences in masculinity* were among the most significant ones that they found between good and poor fighters.

Box 10.3   TASK MAINTENANCE

A related topic, which still poses one of the most important problems in today's military operations, regards skills maintenance. That is, how often does a person need to have a refresher course in order to maintain his level of skill? This is by no means a straightforward question as the answer requires at least three things. One, some task analyses must be performed in order to determine the necessary component skills to complete the task (e.g. to fire a rifle). Two, there would have to be some breakdown of the differential rates at which these components are learned to a stable level. For example, aiming accurately to hit your target may be more difficult to learn that pulling the trigger once you have aimed. Three there would need to be a similar breakdown of the differential rates at which these components are forgotten. For example, the skills necessary to aim accurately may require more practice to maintain than the skills necessary to pull the trigger. Given the increasing complexity of the skills required to operate technologically advanced weaponry, it is not surprising that psychologists continue to be vital in the context of military training.

Box 10.4   PROBLEMS WITH RELIABILITY AND VALIDITY

Such was the success of these standardized tests that many of them have been applied to other contexts, such as education and aptitude testing. Nonetheless, we need to be cautious about what we conclude from this early research. For one, the sheer number of psychological tests employed, and the possibility of extensive **covariability** among them, requires us to take a conservative view. For example, whenever there is a large number of tests, researchers must be concerned with increases in **experiment-wise error rates.** Simply put, the more tests we conduct the more likely it is by chance alone that we will accept a finding as significant when it is not. This problem certainly exists with the HRRO research, given that more than eighty tests were used. Second, there is the real question of covariability among the different tests used. For example, the tests used to assess leadership may have examined factors that were highly correlated with other measures used to assess emotional stability. Therefore, we may simply be measuring different components of the same factor. Furthermore, while the data are reliable and consistent, there is no unifying psychological explanation for the findings. We need to stress this, as the presence or absence of a coherent psychological explanation is essential to good applied psychological research. Without a unifying theory, we run the risk of accepting and acting on findings for which we have no real understanding.

Good fighters were also more intelligent, although there is a caveat to this. There was ample documentation that, as a group, combat soldiers were significantly *less* intelligent than men in other military branches, a problem that still confronts the Army today. Perhaps smarter people do their best not to get assigned to the front line! Nonetheless, the researchers concluded that the intelligent combat soldier made a better fighter than his non-intelligent counterpart. Perhaps related to this, good fighters preferred humour that was witty and sarcastic rather than simply telling jokes. Finally, good fighters were more emotionally stable, and less prone to anxiety or depression.

We cannot overestimate the importance of the early HRRO findings. Most crucially, many of the psychological tests identified could be administered *before* an individual engaged in combat, and this was highly advantageous to the military. The HRRO data were also important in helping to refine how soldiers got allocated to assignments. For example, the proportion of good fighters in a unit, relative to average or poor fighters, could now be manipulated. This in turn would have an impact on the effectiveness of different military operations. For these reasons, the research by the HRRO is one of the most important examples of applying psychology to the war room.

Who makes a good leader?

A related problem to the selection of a good fighter is the problem of selecting a good military commander and leader. This problem was particularly acute during the Second World War, and especially in the UK, where the normal methods of obtaining officer candidates (i.e. recruiting officers exclusively from public schools) became impractical. Some highly creative procedures were adopted to determine a candidate's leadership and command qualities, such as problem-solving situations rather than standardized question-answering sessions. These novel procedures included giving candidates real-life scenarios in which no solutions were obvious and where group cooperation was essential.

One of the most famous examples of a problem scenario is cited by Shelford Bidwell (1973, p. 112 ff.). The candidates were told that they had to make their way across a shark-infested river using only an oil drum, a plank, a piece of rope, and a few other tools. Candidates were observed in terms of how they performed, whether they emerged as

Box 10.5   ARE LEADERS BORN OR MADE?

The debate between nature and nurture is particularly relevant to a discussion of the selection of leaders. Are leaders born with the ability to lead, or can we make someone a leader by training them properly and putting them in the right situations? The question centres around the issue of whether the characteristics of an individual, be they personality traits, mental abilities, or emotional intelligence, are determined by genetic influences (i.e. nature), or by environmental and situational factors (i.e. nurture). As is often the case with psychological debates, there is evidence for both sides of the debate. Studies with twins are particularly popular in this context as they provide built-in controls for heredity and environmental factors. **Monozygotic twins** (i.e. identical twins) who are reared together show greater similarities on certain traits, like achievement, than **dyzygotic twins** (i.e. non-identical or fraternal twins), who are reared together. Such data support the view that nature determines who they will be and how they will act. On the other hand, identical twins who are reared together show greater similarities in achievement levels than identical twins who are reared apart. This provides evidence that environmental factors influences the person's development. The correct answer is undoubtedly a combination of both.

leaders, and whether they showed flexibility in their problem solving and united the group's efforts. This method of selection proved successful and is still used today.

After the Second World War, psychologists were more directly involved in identifying the psychological characteristics that made for a good leader and commander. Psychologists discovered that a good leader is aggressive and good at problem-solving. They communicate clearly and explain reasons for commands. They demand a high level of performance from subordinates, explicitly reward good performance, and deal with failure constructively and without threat. A good leader is also able to mediate and dissipate tension between members of the group. Finally, a good leader identifies the outstanding qualities of his subordinates and uses them to best effect (i.e. assigns the most appropriate person to each task).

However, one of the most startling findings to emerge was that non-combat leadership and combat leadership required different characteristics and abilities. For example, a good non-combat leader was rigid with respect to rules, athletic, physically imposing, and tactful. This was not the case with a good combat leader. Highlighting these differences enabled the military to distinguish between the leaders needed during combat and those who were more useful during times of peace.

SUMMARY

By the end of the Korean War, assessment, selection, and training were major factors in determining the combat behaviour of both individual soldiers and their units. In this section we have reviewed research on soldiers' experience in combat zones and shown how these findings provided the basis for developing more sophisticated selection and training procedures. We have illustrated how better selection, through the development of standardized tests, allowed the right soldier to be assigned to the right military job. We have also shown that through better training, the soldier is better equipped to perform his tasks, thereby ensuring that he is more efficient and effective at his job. Improvements in training included better identification of the requisite skills that need to be mastered, and more realistic opportunities to engage in practice, such as in simulations.

This leads us directly to our next topic—the soldier's morale. Giving more opportunities to practice skills, and more realistic situations under which to practice, understandably improves the morale of the fighting soldier and his unit. Training prepares the solider; and being prepared reduces the soldier's apprehension and unease about going into combat. However, the best selection and training in the world is useless if the soldier is unwilling to fight—has little 'heart'. The soldier must be willing to sacrifice and endanger himself, and must be willing to engage in hostile activities when directed to do so or when the situation demands it. To be truly effective, the soldier must be motivated to fight.

Morale and the fighting spirit

The morale of a soldier is a topic that has long captured the attention of students of military psychology. Morale is a complex concept and it is not easy to provide a clear-cut definition, as it is best seen as a combination of related factors. There are both situational and psychological factors that influence morale and these interact with each other. One of the most important psychological components is the soldier's motivation to fight.

While ancient leaders may have appreciated the vital importance of good morale, it has taken some time for modern military leaders to realize this. For example, leaders of the nineteenth century considered rigid discipline and routine to be more effective in producing effective soldiers than positive incentives like the promise of getting a few days leave. In fact, despite the extensive breakdown in morale after the First World War (notably in Russian and Austro-Hungarian armies), the formal study of morale did not emerge until well into the Second World War.

Components of morale

Morale is not an easy concept to define. Part of the difficulty is that it is a psychological term that covers many levels of explanation. There are physical and situational factors that will affect a soldier's morale. For example, if we are fighting in terrain that is highly unfamiliar and treacherous, and we are outnumbered, we may suffer from low morale simply because we are at a clear disadvantage relative to our enemy. Similarly, if we are starved of proper food, or rest, out morale will be lower than the morale of soldiers who are well fed and physically rested. Physical factors can be environmental, such as the climate, and also institutional, such as poor tactics and management of supplies to troops.

At the same time, there are internal or psychological factors that contribute to the soldier's morale. These, too, are complex as they may be emotional, physical, and mental. Although the influence of emotions is not always easy to predict, there is clearly an affective or emotional component to morale. For example, we could argue that extreme fear is unlikely to yield high morale on the battlefield. However, there are many instances where soldiers, out of sheer fear for their lives and a desire to live, fought the enemy ferociously. Their morale, and willingness to fight to the death, was supported by their instinct for self-preservation.

Then there is the person's physical state, or vitality, which will be affected by a number of things such as sleep loss, fatigue, and arousal levels. These obviously interact

Box 10.6   PEER-GROUP INFLUENCE

The work of Asch (1956) is one of the most cited empirical demonstrations of the power of groups on an individual's behaviour. Asch's experiment involved the use of *confederates* who pretended to be students in a psychology class, and a naive participant (i.e. a student who was unaware of the purpose of the experiment). Asch presented two lines, one that was clearly longer than the other, and asked each student to say if the two lines were equivalent. Each of the six or seven confederate 'students' agreed that the lines were of equal length. The last person to be asked was the naive participant. Asch documented that naive participants were often persuaded to agree with the group's decision, and conclude that the two lines were equivalent, in spite of the evidence of their eyes. Although there are criticisms of this experiment, Asch's findings nonetheless provide startling evidence for the impact that the group, and its values, can have on the individual. The military applications of this finding are important. People can be led into seeing, believing, and behaving a certain way, in spite of what their senses tell them!

with situational factors and institutional responses from the military. For example, institutional responses to promote good morale include rest and leave, and appropriate rotations, where limits are imposed on the length of combat duty that a soldier must serve before he receives a change in duties.

A definition of morale would also need to include some description of mental components. We would want to consider cognition generally, such as the soldier's ability to be vigilant during a watch, to identify a target correctly, or to remember the correct sequence of actions when under stress. We would also need to consider what are called the **hot cognitions**, or beliefs the person holds, since morale is influenced by beliefs. For example, wars are conducted for reasons, although the ones that are given explicitly are not necessarily the real reasons for the conflict. Still, if a soldier believes in the reasons, the justness of the cause for the fight, his motivation will be greater than if he *does not* believe in the cause. These beliefs are 'hot' because they are ones to which the person ascribes great personal significance. Hot beliefs underlie how we feel about ourselves and how we understand the world, and dictate how we relate to others. Psychologists are all too aware that horrible atrocities can be committed in the name of extreme feelings of patriotism and religious fervour, when cognition is at its hottest.

Morale is also influenced by how the individual interacts *with* the world. In this instance, group cohesiveness, and feelings of belonging to his primary fighting group, will be important. A soldier who is highly committed to the group's common goal, and has bonded well with his group, will have higher morale. The power of the relationship between the individual soldier and his group cannot be underestimated as a protection against the conditions of war, as we shall see.

Motivation

In this section we consider how aggressive combat behaviour can be understood in terms of innate drives and personality traits. We also consider explanations that view aggressive behaviour as learned, and explore what incentives or rewards might be useful in motivating the soldier.

One of the most important aspects of morale is the soldier's motivation. While morale and motivation are closely linked, there are important differences. For example, the concept of morale has been largely restricted to discussions of military environments, and to a lesser extent, working environments. In contrast, motivation is a psychological concept that has been extensively studied by psychologists and has formed a major part of many theories of animal and human behaviour.

The topic of motivation is so central to the study of psychology as a whole, that we cannot consider it fully here. Essentially, the question of motivation is the question of *why?* Why does the soldier obey commands, why is the soldier willing to fight? The answer depends so which conflict we choose to examine. For example, Genghis Khan told his troops that 'The greatest pleasure in life is to defeat your enemies, to chase them before you, to rob them of their wealth, to see those dear to them bathed in tears, to ride their horses...' (quoted in Bidwell 1973, p. 20). This suggests that the opportunity to be aggressive and to pilfer was sufficient to motivate the ancient soldier. While the modern military may claim to deplore such glorification, they too, realize that *aggression* is a powerful motivator on the battlefield.

Why are soldiers motivated by aggression?

How can we explain why normally placid individuals are able to commit aggressive acts when commanded to do so during war? As before, there are many different types of possible explanation. Biological explanations were originally developed in the context of animal behaviours. Concepts like **drives** and innate tendencies were common. Examples of drives includes feeding, drinking, and some social behaviour, like hierarchical dominance in social groups and mating. These explanations focused on the need for the animal to disperse energy associated with the drive.

Although psychologists continue to study the biological basis for emotions, with the development of sophisticated technology, psychologists can now examine the physiological and neurological factors that underlie emotional behaviours like aggression. For example, the limbic system (i.e. the thalamus, hypothalamus, amygdala, and hippocampus) has been implicated as important for the expression of many basic drives (e.g. hunger, thirst, and sex) as well as being responsible for the control of emotions like fear and rage. Similarly, new techniques have helped to describe the function of chemical

Box 10.7   THE ORIGINS OF AGGRESSION

Konrad Lorenz was renowned for developed the study of **ethology**. Ethologists observe animal behaviour in the animal's natural habitat, under natural conditions with little or no intervention. Ethology is in direct contrast to an **experimental methodology**, where the psychologist deliberately manipulates or alters various aspects of the environments in order to observe the effects of these components on behaviour. Lorenz viewed aggressive behaviour in human beings as an innate drive, much like our need to eat, sleep, and drink. His description is analogous to the idea of a reservoir, where drive builds up and the animal needs to release this stored up energy periodically. For Lorenz, soldiers are motivated to be aggressive because they have an innate drive to do so. Some soldiers have higher drives than others, or bigger reservoirs, and so are more likely to fight than other soldiers. This significance of this view to military psychology is enormous, as it suggests that some people are more aggressive due to their biological make-up and hence would make better soldiers than other people.

alterations in neurotransmitter substances (e.g. epinephrine (also known adrenalin), GABA (-aminobutyric acid), and glutamate) in emotions such as anxiety, fear, and rage. Such research will go some way towards helping us to understand the biological basis underlying a soldier's motivation to fight. However, there are important ethical issue that need considering. For example, there is the worrying possibility that we may be in a position, in the near future, to turn someone into a good fighting machine simply by giving him the appropriate cocktail of drugs.

Explanations of individual differences in aggression and motivation are also concerned with inherited components of aggression. For example, the military has long been known to attract a particular type of personality, one who is more rule-bound, more conservative, and more inflexible in outlook. That is, the classic *authoritarian personality*. The authoritarian personality is more likely to conform to institutional regulations and procedures, more likely to adapt better to group demands and more likely to be socialized with respect to training. Interestingly, studies have shown that good commanders are more rigid in terms of routines and regulations and expect high levels of conformity from their subordinates.

Other explanations propose that aggressive behaviour is a learned characteristic, subject to the laws of reinforcement, as developed by Skinner and Pavlov. We have already discussed **social learning theory**, which argues that our social behaviour is learned. According to such theories, a person will be motivated to fight given the appropriate reinforcement. This leads us to consider what a soldier might regard as *incentives* or rewards for fighting.

Internal and external motivators

There are two classes of motivator, internal and external. Internal motivators serve as incentives because of their inherent value to the person. An example of an internal motivator is the desire for higher *self-esteem*. Our self-esteem is positively associated with our feelings of pride and satisfaction in how we act, or how well we behave in a situation. Some psychologists, like Abraham Maslow, have argued that self-esteem and self-satisfaction are as strong internal motivators of human behaviour as the most basic of needs, such as hunger or safety. A soldier who has pride and self-satisfaction in performing his

---

Box 10.8   MORALE AND PUBLIC SUPPORT

We should note that the public's attitudes towards military action affect morale. If there is little public support, this will have a negative effect on the psychological states of those engaged in military action. A modern example of this is Vietnam and the impact that the peace movement had on combat soldiers and veterans returning to the USA. In recent conflicts unprecedented access to combat manoeuvres has been given to the media. Modern communications and technology now ensure that public dissent is transmitted to combat soldiers more rapidly than ever before. This is a factor that will need to be considered in future conflicts, particularly when public support is lacking. However, even when the public does support a course of military action, soldiers often feel that they do not receive the recognition for their actions that they deserve. Military historians note that soldiers throughout all major conflicts have felt that the public remained largely ignorant of the conditions and consequences of war. Some studies of the Second World War have shown that combat soldiers returned home with a sense of being owed some status in the post-war world. More often than not, these expectations were never realized, leading to feelings of bitterness and betrayal.

duties will have higher self-esteem. His higher self-esteem, in turn, would be associated with increased motivation.

Examples of external motivators are awards or promotions that a soldier receives, or group recognition of his performance in combat. The attractiveness of certain external rewards has changed. Five hundred years ago the prospect of plunder may have been a sufficient incentive for the soldier to fight. Even today, the promise of material gain is sufficient for some soldiers, as when mercenary fighters are recruited. However, monetary or materialistic gain is not as powerful an external reward to the modern soldier as is external recognition, be it from the military itself, or from the public. A hero's welcome is a greater incentive to fight than the promise of more money.

Not surprisingly, most studies show that external rewards, such as peer recognition, self-pride, or increased autonomy (as in having more recreational leave) can seldom outweigh internal motivators. Internal rewards have more significance to the individual and are more intrinsically valuable. Most modern military institutions now recognize that a soldier who is fighting to achieve some internal reward or goal will endure more hardship than will a soldier who is fighting simply for money, or external recognition.

Identification with the primary group

In this section we discuss how the soldier's identification with the group influences morale. We then examine the different psychological roles that individuals must perform in order to keep combat units effective. Finally, we look at how the individual's emotional relationships within the group can provide some protection against the horrors of war.

Military historians uniformly note that while beliefs and other motivators are important, it is often the more intimate feelings of friendship and comradeship that instill the will to fight. It is the primary group that sets and reinforces standards of behaviour, such as fighting or following military procedure. At the same time, individuals in the group, such as a 'buddy', provide emotional support and companionship during times of stress. Studies from the Second World War, the Korean War, and Vietnam all confirm the critical function that friendship plays in supporting the soldier.

A soldier's feelings of belonging to his group develop as a consequence of many factors. For example, close spatial proximity and the ability to have intimate conversations with at least one other trusted comrade will encourage a soldier's bond to his group. Equally, more intimate relationships between members of the group, as with buddies, increase group cohesion, as individual soldiers come to rely on and trust each other more.

Research conducted after the Korean conflict was concerned with understanding the *inter-personal dynamics* between members of the same primary fighting units. Anecdotal evidence often suggested that different members of the group fulfilled different roles. For example, a soldier might choose to share a night-watch with person A because the person was a good marksman and was highly dependable under stress. However, the same soldier might choose person B with whom to go on leave because person B was more likeable and a closer confidante. Such observations led military psychologists to conclude that different psychological functions must be fulfilled in order for the group to be effective, and for group cohesion.

Psychological roles within the combat group

From these anecdotal findings, psychologists began to understand that a good fighting unit is supported by the quality of the human relationships its individual members have with each other. For example, the American psychologist, Rodney Clark, identified five psychological duties that must be fulfilled in order for a combat group to operate (Clark 1953). One was managing the group; for example, ensuring that the supplies and provisions were distributed equitably. Another was defining and maintaining group norms, which involved making sure that all members of the unit were clearly told what was and what was not acceptable behaviour. This included initiating discussions to resolve conflicts and explicitly stating what was expected from each member of the group. Modelling was another function that had to be fulfilled, where senior members operated as role models for junior group members. Related to this is the fourth function of teaching. As we have already discussed, teaching through demonstration, or vicarious learning, was one way in which a novice soldier could learn. The teacher had to be a person who was perceived by the other group members as having sufficient knowledge to be an expert; the teacher also had to be good at communication, so that he could present the information in a way that other group members could understand. Finally, someone had to take responsibility for containing the emotional conflicts that would inevitably arise between group members. Clark suggested that this function was more than just being able to listen or sympathize. Rather, this function seemed to be more akin to therapy. People who served this function had an ability to sense 'when and individual's desires were in conflict with the welfare of the group . . .' and helped the individual to '. . .adjust his conflicting efforts to harmonize with the squad's goals' (Clark 1953).

We can see that some of the functions are likely to be fulfilled by the formal leader of the group. For example, managing the group is likely to be done by higher ranks, or those people who have organizational responsibilities to perform managerial duties. In contrast, men from lower ranks are equally likely to fulfil other functions, such as containing emotional conflict by being someone's buddy, or teaching a junior soldier how to rest during breaks in firing.

The emotional consequences of combat

There is no doubt that all soldiers suffer from demoralized feelings and fear at some time. However, one factor that mediates these negative emotions is the soldier's bond with his group. When a soldier feels that he belongs to the group, he is better protected against intense and prolonged combat reactions. It seems as through being with others in the same boat, even if it is a lousy boat, is some comfort and helps the soldier deal with the emotional consequences of war. In fact, reports of psychiatric breakdowns or **combat trauma** were less likely when the soldier felt strongly attached to his primary fighting group. The group, and the bond it afforded, provided the soldier with some resilience in dealing with the emotional battering that war inflicts.

Of course, there is a negative consequence of being attached to your fighting comrades. The prospect of your best friend dying or being injured from enemy fire is an entirely realistic possibility; and, when this happens, the emotional impact is so considerable that some soldiers cannot continue, and suffer symptoms of combat trauma. There are a variety of reasons why soldiers suffer combat trauma, and the symptoms are equally varied. However, we defer discussion of combat trauma here, since the treatments that military psychiatrists developed for combat trauma have had an enormous impact on the treatment of trauma in the general population. For this reason, we consider combat trauma and combat psychiatry in 'The treatment room'.

SUMMARY

We have considered some of the traditional topics that have been central to the application of psychology in the war room. We have shown that psychologists were essential in developing methods of assessments, selection, and allocation and that their involvement directly affected military campaigns. These early efforts, like mapping the worker to the job, served as the basis for much of the later work done in non-military working environments. We suggested that the questions posed by these early researches in the context of war and combat highlighted debates that are still central to psychology today, such as the biological basis of emotions and the effects of nature versus nurture. We illustrated how psychologists used basic principles derived from learning theory, particularly notions like reinforcement and incentives, not only to improve training and performance, but also to sustain the soldier's morale and motivation. We also considered how important the soldier's affiliation to his fighting group is in ensuring well-being and emotional resilience.

SCENARIO ONE

THE ROLE OF PSYCHOACOUSTICS IN THE DEVELOPMENT OF AUDITORY WARNING SIGNALS

This first scenario looks at the problem of designing auditory warning signals on aircraft. This work is derived from a series of studies conducted by Dr Roy Patterson and his research team. It is an excellent example of applied psychology that combines the field of human *ergonomics*, including issues regarding man-machine compatibility, with theories of perception. This scenario illustrates the effectiveness of experimental methodology and design in addressing questions that have great significance in the context of the war room.

Every military action requires resources, including personnel, and combat tactics reflect this fact. To ensure their effective use, risk assessments are conducted to determine whether the benefits of the action outweigh the costs to resources. Human life is simply another resource in combat and military leaders must ultimately decide what are acceptable losses. They acknowledge that a certain number of people on both sides will be injured or killed in order to achieve their objectives. These losses are judged to be acceptable as they are the unavoidable consequence of combat action. The military feels that it can justify them to the public, and to the loved ones of those who are lost.

However, military personnel also die, not through combat, but through failure or error on the part of the military (e.g. through so-called 'friendly fire'). These losses are unacceptable, as they can be avoided or averted. Unacceptable losses pose a serious problem for military leaders. The public is not as easily swayed into believing that the people who lost their lives due to the negligence of the military died for 'a good and just cause'.

The following scenario provides an example of how unacceptable losses were reduced through the input of a group of psychologists. It is a wonderful illustration of how psychologists and psychological theories can directly influence the safety of military personnel through the development of more user-friendly machines.

What was the situation?

After the Korean conflict, war technology became significantly more advanced. The highly sophisticated technology on board the new helicopters required the crew to assimilate a considerable amount of diverse information and to perform many tasks at once. That is, the environment was **multi-modal**, with different sounds, lights, and background noises. The workload was distributed across all members of the crew, so that the safety and success of any mission was reliant on a number of people performing different operations in certain sequences. This meant that it was essential for the crew to communicate information accurately with each other.

Very soon, it became apparent that signals warning of danger (i.e. that required immediate action) needed to override all other perceptual information. In response to these requirements, designers adopted a visual warning system, and this served as a prototype for all warning systems on certain types of military helicopter up to the mid-1980s. For example, flashing yellow lights were used to signal that the craft was descending to a dangerously low height.

Unfortunately, there are various factors that render a visual warning system less than optimal. First consider how we might get people to attend to visual information. We could flood the environment, as occurs with strobe-lighting effects. Under these conditions, the ambient light is flashing so dramatically that our attention cannot help but be alerted. Unfortunately, it would be very difficult to read flight-deck instruments accurately if the ambient light were pulsating! Another way to attract attention is with flashing lights. The rhythmic pulsation of light is salient, particularly under the light conditions of a flight deck. However, in order for the signal to capture our attention we need to be *facing* it. If our back is to the signal, or if we have our heads down looking at something else, we might not see the signal and this could lead to disaster.

Next, let us consider what happens during an emergency on a flight deck. As already mentioned, the members of the flight crew are doing more than one task at any time and this is particularly the case in an emergency. In psychological terms, they will be **parallel processing** or **serial processing** (see Box 10.9), will be engaged in a **multi-task situation**, and are likely to be in a state of heightened alertness and anxiety.

Significantly, the crew will be focusing on other visual information, such as instruments that need to be monitored. Last but not least, the act of flying itself relies primarily

Box 10.9   SERIAL AND PARALLEL PROCESSING

The distinction between serial and parallel processing is an important one for psychologists. Many of the early theories of attention, such as that of Donald Broadbent (1958), argued that people could do more than one thing at once through rapid serial processing: attention and its processes would be switched from one task to the other. These types of models suggest that attention can become 'bottlenecked', with too much information resulting in only a subset being processed. In contrast, modern theories of perception and cognition, such as those of Hinton and Anderson (1981) and Barnard and Teasdale (1991) argue that information is processed in parallel across different information units. The limitation of the person to do, or attend to, multiple tasks is determined not only by the amount of information, but also the quality of the information processing involved.

Box 10.10   THE PREIMITIVE WARNING SYSTEM

Psychologists who study hearing argue that the auditory modality is far superior to the visual modality as a perceptual warning system. Patterson (1990) points out that hearing is a primitive warning sense. For example, the sound of our enemy rustling through the foliage will reach us far faster than the sight of our enemy. Patterson also notes than an auditory warning signal does not require the pilot's attention. The pilot can be engaged in another visual task, or can be quietly taking a rest with their eyes closed; in either case, an auditory warning will be detected. As Patterson clearly argues, the military needed to consider the psychology of hearing and examine how the brain processes auditory information. If they had, they would have seen that the question was not whether helicopters should have auditory warning systems, but rather how they could construct warning sounds that would promote the best and most reliable detection.

on vision, and even during night flights most of the flight panel is visual. Thus the crew would be processing a huge amount of visual information in the course of their normal duties, let alone under emergency conditions. A visual warning signal would be in stiff competition with other visual information for the crew's attention; and this would increase the chances of the crew not attending to the warning signal in sufficient time to avert disaster.

Sadly, this proved true when a helicopter came down, killing all personnel. It appeared that while the pilots were looking for landfalls within fog, they had been able to ignore the flashing yellow light signalling that the craft had descended dangerously low. Subsequent military investigations concluded that if the warning signals had been auditory, the accident could have been avoided.

Eager to avoid any future disasters, the military decided to produce an auditory warning signal that would not fail to dominate attention. They decided to model their warning system on the ambulance siren, which cuts through all other traffic sounds and noise by sheer volume. Importantly, because it uses the auditory modality, a siren does not require the driver to be oriented to it spatially, so it will not interfere with the act of driving itself, which is dominated by vision. Given the similarity of the conditions between driving and flying, the military decided that this type of auditory signal would ensure that the crew could not ignore the warning. In addition to the visual warning system, new helicopters were therefore fitted with auditory signals that would dominate all other perceptual information. For economic reasons, high-frequency tones were selected for the majority of warning signals, with the major distinctions between the different signals being their absolute frequency (pitch) and their intensity (loudness).

Why was the psychologist involved?

The new design, using auditory and visual warnings, solved the problem of the fight crew ignoring the warning signals. Unfortunately, it introduced new and equally disturbing concerns, and the number of incident reports that cited problems with the new warning system increased. After a sufficient number of complaints, and near-miss disasters, the military decided to enlist the help of applied psychologists who were experts in the area of human hearing. Through collaboration with private companies, government departments, and research councils, the psychologists agreed to address the flights crews' complaints. One of these regarded the level of the auditory warning. Pilots had complained that some of the warnings were so loud that it was impossible for them to hear anything else, which made communicating information to each other difficult. Ironically, pilots claimed that often their first action was to *turn off* the warning system, so that the flight crew could talk to each other and find out what the problem was!

A second complaint was that warnings were not always easy to discriminate from other sounds that shared the same **spectral characteristics**, such as when turbines or pumps became worn (see Box 10.11). Members of the crew were uncertain whether the sound they were hearing was a warning signal, or just a normal part of the background noise of the aircraft. A third problem was that the warning signal reached its highest intensity immediately, going from a completely quiet situation to full volume. This had the consistent effect of startling the pilots so that they could not respond to the situation with composure and objectivity. When we are startled, our natural reaction is to experience muscular tension and prepare for an immediate response. The problem is that if a pilot reacts too rapidly, their reaction is likely to be incorrect because they have insufficient information, which is why instantaneous reactions are always *discouraged* in pilot training.

A fourth criticism was that there were too many warning signals. For example, on some aircraft, there were as many as fifteen different auditory warning signals, from those signalling evacuation procedures to those associated with over-speed problems. Crews therefore had difficulty learning which sound signaled which danger. Furthermore, the majority of warning signals were of high frequency. This was a problem because the human ear is designed to discriminate between changes in sounds rather than absolute sounds. To compound the problem even further, when two or more warning signals came on simultaneously, their combined sound made it difficult for the pilots to recognize the component signals involved.

What psychological concepts are relevant?

Concepts developed from the discipline of **psychoacoustics** were of obvious relevance. The study of psychoacoustics combines experimental methodologies developed from psychology with an understanding of the anatomy and physiology of the ear, to explain how people process and perceive auditory information from the environment. In this case, the psychologists felt that the problems were related to same fairly basic theoretical concepts

---

Box 10.11   THE WAY WE HEAR

We perceive sound as a pattern of changes in the pressure of air. Our hearing system is designed to tell us about three things: wavelength, amplitude, and location. Wavelength, or **frequency**, refers to the time it takes for the sound wave to complete one cycle. This is generally measured in cycles per second, or **Hertz**, also known as **Hz**. Humans are sensitive to frequencies between 30 and 20,000 Hz. High-frequency sounds, such as screams, have very short cycles, whereas low-frequency sounds, such as Buddhist chants, have very long cycles. Any complex sound, such as that produced by a musical instrument, is a combination of many simpler sounds.

Each component sound will have a particular frequency, or cycle, and can be thought of as having **spectral characteristics**. Amplitude is the size of the wave, as would be measured as the loudness or intensity of the sound. Sounds of greater amplitude are louder than sounds of smaller amplitude. Generally, intensity or power is referred to in **decibels** or **dB**. Finally, we are sensitive to the location of the sound as those that are closer to our ear are processed quicker and received faster by the brain. The ability to utilize differences in the speed in the processing of auditory information is the basis for the *echo-location* used by some species of mammals.

regarding how people detect patterns of sound, how they learn to associate meaning to patterns of sounds, and how they remember them.

The first problem was to produce a warning sound that would be easily detected above the background noise of the helicopter. Flying an aircraft is a noisy business with multiple sounds coming from outside the aircraft as well as the engines and the flight deck itself. Similar problems have been addressed by psychologists interested in how we single out, and selectively attend to, one perceptual feature when there are many other things going on in the environment that are competing for our attention. Although there are many possible answers, we shall turn to **signal detection theory**, one of the most familiar explanations to arise from the work of *psychophysics*.

Signal detection theory operates on the assumption that people detect a target, in this case the warning sound, from a background of non-target sounds, as a consequence of two independent processes. One process relies on differences between the sensory features of the target and non-targets, such as the spectral characteristics of the sound (see Box 10.11). The overlap between the sensory features of the target and the non-target is assessed by d'. This is a measure of the ratio that reflects the difference between target and background, and ranges from zero to one. The smaller the ratio, the more similar the target and background, and consequently the more difficult it is for us to detect the difference. For example, suppose you are asked to press a button when you hear speaker A (the target), but not when you hear speaker B (the non-target). If both of the speakers are men, you will find it more difficult to distinguish between the two than if speaker A is a women and speaker B is a man. Part of the reason for this is that the two male voices share more perceptual features.

The second process has to do with how readily we are able to *accept* that the sound we are hearing is the target. This process involves us making a decision and is related to the level of certainty we have to reach in order to decide that this is the target and not some random noise. This is measured by beta ( ), and is referred to as our *criterion*. Typically, criteria are discussed in terms of whether they are lax or strict. For example, suppose we are given the task of identifying a song by the first four notes of its music-a task commonly used in television game shows. If we have a lax criterion, we may decide that we only need two notes to identify the song. However, if we have a strict criterion, we may want to wait until all four notes have been played. These decisions have nothing

Box 10.12   THE CLASSIC AREA OF PSYCHOPHYSICS

The area of psychoacoustics belongs to the more general area of psychophysics. Psychophysics attempts to explain the processes of perception through analyses of molecular sensory processing of the five main sensory systems (i.e. vision, hearing, touch, smell, and taste). In particular, discussions focus on how information from our physical environment is translated, or *transduced*, into information that can be understood and processed by our brain. Psychologists interested in psychophysics would be concerned with descriptions of *sensory receptors*. They examine how sensory receptors detect the presence of physical events in the external world, how they convey the occurrence of physical events to the brain, and how they process this information so that the brain can receive it. Through the use of experimental methodology, psychophysics provides a level of explanation that is based around descriptions of sensory receptors and action potentials. This level of description is different from that provided by more cognitive approaches. For example, a cognitive theory may not only discuss sensory receptors, but also consider non-sensory aspects involved in perception, such as the effects that emotion or memory might have on our perceptual abilities.

to do with the sensory information but with how willing we are to accept that we have heard a target, given the amount of information we have received.

Regardless of their explanatory framework, the psychologists knew that it was essential for the perceptual features of the warning signals to be distinctive from the background sounds of the flight deck and sounds of flying. The original designers had dealt with this problem by selecting a very high-frequency sound and making it very loud: one hundred decibels. What they had failed to take into account was the fact that sounds over eighty-five decibels are generally quite unpleasant, particularly at high frequency. The psychologists knew that they needed to examine closely the perceptual features of the warning signals in the context of the environment under which the crew was operating. Their main focus was how to increase the perceptual distinctiveness of the warning signal. In order to do this, the psychologists would have to analyse the nature of the competing sensory information on the flight deck, in particular the spectral characteristics of other sounds common to a flight deck (e.g. engine noise and rotor-blade sounds).

Analysing the spectral characteristics of the other sounds would also address another criticism, which was the problem of detecting a meaningful pattern of sound. In psychological terms, the problem is how we assign meaning to sensory information. To put it another way, how do we combine bits of sensory information into whole objects, or patterns? A good example from the visual modality is the three-lines/triangle. This well-known figure consists of three straight lines arranged to form the outline of a triangle, but with the corners not joined. If we ask most people what they see when they look at this figure, they will respond with 'a triangle'. However, what are actually present are three disjointed lines. So, how is it that we are able to *see* a triangle where none exists? According to **Gestalt** theory, we take the sensory information that is present, and then actively impose some organization or structure on it in order to *see* something meaningful. We fill in the spatial gaps, and using our knowledge about objects, and about triangles in particular, impose structure so that the three lines become a set of lines forming a triangle. Of course, our ability to impose this organization on the figure is aided by the fact that the three lines are angled in such a way that is consistent with how they would look as a triangle. According to Gestalt theorists, the organization inherent in the sensory information and our ability to impose our own organization on the environment allows us to *perceive* a meaningful object, where, in fact, there is none.

In the case of auditory information, we associate certain temporal patterns, or rhythms, with whole units or sets. For example, the sound series, da-da-da, da-da-da, is perceived by most people as two sets of triplets. In this way, we would use rhythm to indicate a set, or whole. Unfortunately, the warning signals did not make use of any distinct temporal patterns. Because the sounds comprising the warning signals lacked any inherent structure, the crew failed to recognize them as *a set of sounds that meant something*. The psychologists knew that if the warning signals had contained better structure, such as a recognizable rhythmic temporal pattern, the crew would have been better able to distinguish this systematic pattern from the random patterns of noise and sound around them.

Another issue was that the large number of auditory warnings meant that the pilots were experiencing perceptual confusion. It became difficult for them to tell whether warning A or warning K was occurring. Additionally, the pilots found it difficult to learn and remember so many different warning signals. There are two separate issues that the psychologists felt needed considering, and both were relevant to psychological concepts regarding learning and memory. First, the crew had to recognize a large number of signals. The psychologists realized that the crew had not been allowed to learn each signal to a stable level so that they could recognize them automatically and without hesitation. Furthermore, given that the crew only heard the warning signals occasionally (i.e. during an emergency) the large number of signals was clearly going to stretch the crew's ability to remember them all, particularly during states of high emergency and stress.

The second problem was that the crew was also required to learn and remember what each signal meant. Learning to associate two things together is an area that has been studied extensively by psychologists. One feature that can make learning associations easy or hard is the extent of *class* or *set similarity*. Learning theorists have long argued that, when two or more sets or patterns are to be learned, the more similar the two sets are, the more difficult it is to distinguish one from the other. For example, suppose you are learning two lists of **paired-associate** items and your task is to remember which list contained a particular pair. In one, set A, you are presented with a series of word–word pairs, like train-black. After learning set A, you are asked to learn set B, in which you are presented with a different series of word-word pairs such as plane-white. If you are then asked to identify whether a word pair came from set A or set B, you will experience some difficulty, as the two sets share significant properties. However, if set B has number-world pairs, like 7-blue, your task would be much easier, as the set similarities would be greatly reduced.

The psychologists could immediately see why this principle needed to be taken into account. As the majority of signals shared similar properties (e.g. most were high-frequency), this made it difficult for the crew to learn and remember the specific association between signal and emergency condition. The psychologists knew that they needed to find a set of signals that not only would be easy to learn and remember, but could also be easily distinguished from each other.

What did the psychologists do?

The psychologists decided that they would approach the problem by devising a research programme whereby observational studies would be combined with experiments involving flight crew and pilots. For example, the problem of deciding what was the appropriate level of intensity for warning signals was addressed by first analysing the spectrum of components of a flight deck, and their corresponding intensity levels. This provided an indication of the level of intensity at which background sounds were operating, which would have to be surpassed if the warning signal was to be detectable. Analyses of flight-deck noise also provided critical information about similarities between the sensory characteristics of the warning signals and other fight-deck noises. This could provide an initial way of addressing the problem that pilots had in distinguishing the warning signal pattern from other rhythmic patterns.

Bearing in mind that anything louder than one hundred decibels would be uncomfortable and distracting, the psychologists plotted background noise on the flight deck. From this, they developed a model that predicted the appropriate range of intensity levels that would maintain the distinctiveness of a warning, and still be acceptable to the listener. The psychologists then conducted experiments with pilots in flight. The pilots were given six different warning horns and were asked to select the one they felt was the most appropriate. Interestingly, the pilots selected the warning horns that corresponded to the levels that were predicted by the psychologists' model.

The problem of learning and remembering the different warning signals was addressed by another set of experiments. Naive listeners were asked to learn and remember a set of ten auditory warning signals that were drawn from flight decks in aircraft. Some of the warning signals shared spectral characteristics (i.e. frequencies), some shared similar temporal characteristics (i.e. rhythm or pulse-repetition rate), whereas others shared both spectral and temporal characteristics. By varying the type and extent of similarity, psychologists could advise how to create warning signals that were not only easy to learn, but also easy to remember.

The data from the naive listeners proved fascinating. First, the listeners had relatively little trouble in learning six warning signals. However, once the number of signals exceeded six, the learning rate declined sharply and listeners found the task much more difficult. The psychologists knew that these results could not be translated directly to the flight-deck situation, as they were using naive listeners who were unaccustomed to the task of identifying different sounds. However, they felt that these results certainly reinforced the view that aircraft with more than ten warning signals may be putting undue stress on the flight crew.

Equally informative were the analysis of the types of error that the listeners made. It was very interesting that the most confusion seemed to occur when there were temporal similarities between the signals. That is, signals with vastly different spectral components but sharing the same rhythm were often confused. Again, although the psychologists were aware that they could not apply their results directly to the flight-deck situation, the importance of rhythmic patterns in the recognition of signals was underlined. Their results clearly demonstrated that the potential for confusion could be reduced dramatically by introducing more variation in the temporal patterns of warning signals. On the basis of these data, the psychologists conducted a subsequent study with helicopter pilots. Pilots were given the standard set of ten signals used previously, and a new set of ten signals that introduced variability between the temporal patterns of the signal. The data showed that the learning and retention rates for the newly devised set of signals far exceeded those of the standard set, and that the confusion rate was much lower.

Another problem that the psychologists felt was essential to address related to the time needed for a warning to reach its full intensity. The psychologists knew that the majority of warnings came on at full intensity, producing the highly undesirable effect of startling the crew. The psychologists addressed this problem by developing a model of a prototype warning sound. The prototype served to identify what might be optimal features in terms of the onset and offset of a warning, the intensity or loudness of the warning, and its rhythm or pulse pattern. The prototype was made of a sound pulse with distinct spectral features and a pulse pattern was used to provide a distinctive rhythm. The pattern of pulses was a basic grouping of four clustered pulses followed by two, irregularly spaced pulses, which completed over a few seconds. Each pulse could be manipulated to have different on/off contours; for example, rounded contours meant that the onset and offset of the sound was slow, and sharp contours reflected abrupt onset and offset.

On the basis of this prototype, the psychologists were able to develop a warning that could capture the crew's attention without risking a startle response. They suggested that, in an emergency situation, the first burst of a warning-sound pattern should be at a relatively moderate level, one that was audible but would not interfere with any necessary actions that might be required. The successive bursts of pulses after the initial pulse would quickly increase in intensity and then recede again slowly as the pulse pattern concluded. The psychologists believed that this envelope of amplitude differences, with its pattern of sudden up then down, would give the impression of movement, of first moving forward rapidly and then receding slowly, and that this apparent motion would draw the crew's attention. The pattern would then be repeated for a second time, with a gap of a few seconds. In the event that some action had been taken, the pitch, level, and speed of warning bursts would be lowered, so as to indicate less urgency, and should be repeated after four or five seconds. Importantly, gaps in the bursts would allow the crew to communicate with each other. If, however, no action were taken after the first pattern, successive patterns would be introduced at increasingly higher pitch, intensity, and speed. This would ensure that they would override any ongoing speech and would demand immediate attention.

How was the psychologists' input assessed?

This is one example where applied research was not only well received, but also acted upon. On the basis of both the spectral modelling and the behavioural data, the psychologists devised a set of warning signals that adddressed all of the criticisms of the old system. The new, modified set of warning signals were first tested on flight crews. The result indicated that the new set substantially increased the chances of the flight crew responding appropriately to emergency situations. The military was delighted with the results and lives were unquestionably saved as a result of the psychologists' input.

SCENARIO TWO

ASSESSING THE USEFULNESS OF LIE DETECTORS

Our second scenario has espionage as its backdrop. As the nature of war has changed, so too has the nature of peace. The end of what was known as the Cold War helped to lesson the immediate worry of major nuclear conflict between two or more superpowers. However, while there may have been an overt change in the relationship between traditional opponents, there was an increase in what might be called covert operations. Covert operations include such things as special operations, intelligence units, and other techniques of psychological warfare. These covert operations, as their name implies, are conducted largely outside the awareness of the general public. To be most effective, they must also be kept secret from our allies, national partners, and political adversaries.

As we have already discussed, one of the most pressing problems that has consistently confronted the military is how to select the right person for the right job (see above, pp. 138-45). Indeed, we saw that this was a problem for virtually every branch of modern military organizations, from deciding who should be a ground soldier to who should be leading a battalion of men. A similar, perhaps more pressing problem existed when considering special operations. Special operations require special skills and abilities. Modern military leaders realize the seriousness of the problem of selection, and invest considerable amounts of energy and resources into utilizing standardized tests that would highlight candidates' aptitudes, as relevant to the job.

For example, suppose we want to select people to do a special job, such as to infiltrate a counter-insurgency cell. We can assume that there are going to be certain characteristics, or aptitudes, that will make for better, or poorer, agents. These might include the person's general level of anxiety: given the stealthy nature of the task, we would want people who maintain a level of clam and clear thinking under pressure. We might also want to select people who show few outward reactions when they are lying, and select people who are convincing in their false portrayals. It would make sense for us to devise some means of assessing whether our prospective candidates had these qualities, and determine how much these qualities affected how well different people did the job.

This next scenario demonstrates how things can go wrong when this approach is not adopted. It outlines how a government bureau responsible for intelligence and counter-intelligence ignored the hard-learned lessons of the military. As a consequence, the government was put in a highly compromising situation, and national security was put at risk.

What was the situation?

In the late 1980s the British Civil Service, in consultation with the military, established a network of counter-intelligence units. One unit, Unit Z, had the task of listening to chatter, or eavesdropping, on radio communication between members of a known guerrilla organization, the Freedom Fighters. The Freedom Fighters had been responsible for a few gruesome attacks on key government buildings in which many casualties occurred. They were regarded as a serious threat to national security. Unit Z was expected to monitor and collate all information, and report regularly to the appropriate branch of military intelligence. Different teams of five listeners, spread over eight-hour shifts, were responsible for maintaining constant surveillance.

As the team members were Civil Servants, they were selected for the job on the basis of their scores on traditional Civil Service tests. These tests are fairly comprehensive examinations that assess general world knowledge, general intellectual competence, as well as general reading and comprehension skills. Unfortunately, the traditional Civil Service tests did not seem to address any traits that might be relevant to tasks involved in counter-intelligence, such as loyalty, discretion, and the willingness to engage in deception. Provided that the person had an acceptable level of intellectual competence, and signed the appropriate documents regarding official secrets, they could work at Unit Z, regardless of any other individual characteristics or personality traits they might possess.

Over the course of a month's listening sessions, the team pieced together information that the present government was planning to sell arms illegally to the Freedom Fighters, and furthermore was engaged in clandestine talks with those directly responsible for the

Box 10.13 STANDARDIZED TESTS AND SPECIAL OPERATIONS

The tests use by the Civil Service measure general intellectual abilities, but would not be considered as *psychological*. This is because the tests had no measure of validity or reliability, and were not **standardized tests**. In contrast, the military has made extensive use of standardized psychological tests in selecting those involved in special operations, like counter-insurgency operations. For example, the *Minnesota Multiphasic Personality Inventory* (MMPI) has been use to assess characteristics deemed preferable, or essential, to do a job. These identify such things as propensity to complain about minor aches and pains, and how concerned the person is about right and wrong. The ideal candidate would be someone with high pain thresholds and someone who operated more from pragmatism than from high morals. As outlined by Peter Watson, in his book *War on the Mind* (1980), the use of standardized tests has led to further developments in terms of a 'constellation of reaction', which identify a good agent from a poor agent. These included fear of injury, lack of social responsibility, and uneasiness about the unknown, to name a few.

attacks. The Freedom Fighters, in return, were providing the government with information about a neighbouring nation, suspected by the international community of developing nuclear weapons. The reality of the government's hypocrisy had a significant impact on one of the team, who had lost someone close to them in one of the attacks. After much consideration, the team member decided that her only option was to declare what she knew to the major television networks and national newspapers. A second member of the team, who found the hypocrisy equally difficult to accept, joined her in revealing the contents of the communication.

A highly publicized trial ensured where both were convicted of breaching national security and sentenced to imprisonment. Not surprisingly, the government was concerned on two levels. The first was getting some idea of how many other people currently working in counter-intelligence units would be likely to defect in this manner. The second was putting into place an adequate screening process that would identify applicants who were likely to defect from those who were likely to remain loyal and discrete.

The then head of the bureau of the Civil Service responsible for counter-intelligence units was something of an amateur psychologists and had some knowledge about polygraphs (lie-detector tests). The head decided that all members currently employed in the counter-intelligence units would be required to take an obligatory polygraph test to determine their loyalty to the government. On the basis of the results, the employee could be discharged from duties. Additionally, all new applicants would be required to take a lie-detector test and, if they failed, they would be prohibited from working in counter-intelligence, if not from the Civil Service itself.

The members of the units were appalled at the suggestion. In the first instance, many were aware that polygraph techniques yield mixed results in criminal and forensic cases, and questioned the use of such techniques. Further, unit staff were not allowed union membership in order to prevent them from taking industrial action. This meant that, should any member be unfairly dismissed as a result of an unreliable test, there would be no means for that person to appeal against the management's decision. In essence, unit members could be fired on the basis of a faulty test, and would have no recourse. Faced with these circumstances, teams across different units began to meet and considered their options, which for the first time included the possibility of industrial action. The Civil Service was confronted with a major uprising. Unfortunately, the head was a particularly stubborn woman, and she refused to be persuaded to give up her idea of using the polygraph.

Why was the psychologist involved?

In order to prevent a complete breakdown within the branch, junior ministers convinced the head that she should attempt to find ways of improving the reliability of the polygraph. She agreed and placed one junior minister in charge of finding an expert. The junior minister contacted a national governing body for psychologists and enquired directly about experts in polygraph techniques.

Once an expert psychologist had been contacted, a meeting was arranged between the psychologist, the head, senior members of the branch of the Civil Service in question, and the junior minister who had made the initial enquiries. An agreed agenda was established rapidly. The psychologist's general objective was to address the feasibility of polygraph security screening in the intelligence and security agencies. In particular, the psychologist was charged with providing a summary of the extant literature, including recommendations and conclusions regarding any future work. The psychologist also was asked to address the question of whether any research could be conducted that would highlight how polygraphic techniques could be made more reliable in the detection of deception, especially with reference to screening. Finally, the psychologist was asked to provide some indication of the margin of error in polygraph techniques, and how the techniques could be improved so as to reduce this error.

What psychological concepts are relevant?

Not surprisingly, there are many mainstream psychological concepts that could be applied to this problem. The notion that we can devise a technique that will tell us when someone is lying and when they are telling the truth makes certain basic assumptions about human behaviour. The first, and most obvious, is that psychological states are associated or correlated with physiological and physical symptoms. For example, we when get angry we often experience body heat and our faces turn red. Similarly, in the case of deception, we assume that the psychological state of lying, or deliberately deceiving, is associated with certain changes in our psychological reactions.

The scientific discipline that supports the development of such notions is referred to as *psychophysiology*. Psychophysiology is concerned with the underlying psychological mechanisms that govern human behaviour. In the case of the polygraph, issues surrounded the peripheral indices of activity in the **autonomic nervous system** (ANS), that part of the central nervous system that controls unconscious bodily activity. Autonomic activity can be triggered in at least two ways. Each response has a different pattern. One is triggered by attentional reactions to novel, unexpected, interesting, or meaningful external events. This type of response is generally referred to as an **orienting reaction** (**OR**), and serves to direct the person's attention to what is happening and what is likely to happen next. A good example of this is when we are engrossed in the act of reading and we hear a sudden, loud noise: generally, we look up in response and orient ourselves in the direction of the sound because the noise is unexpected and surprising. The OR is measurable through virtually all bodily systems, from the humble blinking of an eyelid to patterns of heartbeat and breathing. The same type of response can also be elicited when the person is confronted with painful, emotive, or fear-provoking external events, and serves to prepare the person for either the **fight-or-flight reaction**, also known as the **defence reaction** (DR). A good example, and one often quoted in psychology textbooks, is proffered by William James in his article "What is an emotion?" (1884), where he cites the defence reaction we might have were we to encounter a bear in the countryside! While both OR and DR share similar properties, there are differences in the patterns of changes that accompany each. This means that when we are surprised we exhibit a different pattern of psychological behaviours than when we are frightened or repulsed.

Once we accept that a DR is associated with particular pattern of change in the ANS, we can see a theoretical explanation behind how the polygraph might work. Let us assume that the DR, and its particular pattern of physiological change, is in response to fear, or other negative emotions. Let us also assume that the act of deception is stressful and hence negative. Taken together, we see that the polygraph can detect those changes that are related to the person experiencing a frightening or negative event, which lying while being tested would be assumed to fulfil!

For everything to work, we would need some **baseline measurement** of the person's reaction to what we know are negative events, against which to compare the physiological patterns to questions where we suspect the person may be lying. Every polygraphic technique assumes that all of us have *something* to hide. The job of the examiner is to discover these things about the examinee and use them as the basis for control questions. Importantly, this is done with the full agreement of the person, so that certain factors, like surprise, can be ruled out. Control questions will be associated with identifiable changes in the heart, lungs, and electrodermal system; and these serve as the basis to compare the person's reactions to questions where it is suspected that the person is lying.

For example, suppose we want to know whether someone is telling the truth about stealing a car. We would first find out about other known negative events. We might ask the examinee 'is there anything you ever stole, no matter how small?' Once we know these other negative, autobiographical details, we develop control questions. We know that the event occurred and we know that when asked the question, if the person answers 'yes', he is responding truthfully. We would then compare the psychophysiological changes that accompanied the truthful answer with subsequent questions about stealing the car. If the two are similar, we can conclude that the person is telling the truth.

One of the most crucial elements to the polygraph being an accurate assessment tool is that the examinee must believe that the polygraph is infallible. In fact, this is an essential part of the examiner's job-to convince the person that the polygraph is an accurate and reliable way to tell whether someone is lying. If the examinee believes that the test is a reliable index of whether he is being truthful, he is more likely to have detectable physical reactions to lying, as he assumes that the examiner will know anyway! This shows the strong interaction between cognition, in this case our beliefs, and our emotional reactions.

Thus far, we have assumed that people's reactions when lying are uniform, that all of us respond in the same way, with the same set of patterns of ANS responses. In fact, research in the early 1950s and 1960s demonstrated clearly that the various peripheral indices of autonomic activity are poorly correlated (e.g. Lacey et al. 1953; Engel 1960). Further, the indices tend to be arranged in a pattern that is determined more by the constitution and previous experience of the individual examinee than the truthfulness of the replies. Autonomic specificity exists not only between individuals, but also between different situations. This means that the same person might produce a different pattern of responding over different situations.

Box 10.14   PHYSIOLOGICAL CHANGES AND EMOTION

While there is little disagreement that some form of physiological change accompanies our different emotional states, the question still remains as to whether these physiological changes are unique or specific to the emotional state we are experiencing. William James (1884) was of the view that each emotion could be associated with specific bodily changes. In fact, emotion, according to James, was simply our experience of these different physiological states, so that our emotional reactions were merely bodily changes in blood pressure and so on. While there is some evidence to support James' contention that different classes of emotions are associated with different physiological patterns, there is some doubt as to whether all emotions that we experience can be distinguished on the basis of their unique bodily processes. In contrast to James, modern cognitive approaches put emphasis on the interpretative, or attributional nature of our emotional experiences. For example, according to Teasdale and Barnard (1993) our emotions are, in part, the result of our ability to evaluate our current bodily states in the context of current goals or needs.

Related to this is the concept of **habituation**. Habituation refers to the phenomenon where an individual's reactivity to an event becomes lessened through learning. Effectively, the novelty of an event becomes less when the event, or a similar event, is repeated. As the novelty decreases so too does our reaction to the event. The ANS learns that the event is 'old' and is less reactive to it, particularly when the event is associated with neutral, or mildly noxious, consequences. Habituation, which is one of the most basic types of learning, is as subject to individual differences as our initial reactivity to novel, negative stimuli.

Importantly, individual differences in reactivity and habituation seem to be governed by factors that are normally considered to pertain to personality. For example, people who are labelled as neurotic, either by questionnaire or by clinical examination, are more labile and show a different pattern of habituation than people who are not identified as neurotic. Other personality factors known to influence psychophysiological responses include sensation seeking, suggestibility, and gender. In fact, some psychologists have argued that the diversity of electrodermal responses is itself a personality factor.

What did the psychologist do?

The psychologist sought to provide a comprehensive review of all the relevant scientific literature and research, and to determine its viability and the need for further work. The psychologist always kept as his point of reference the application of the polygraph to pre-employment and in-service screening. He first conducted a number of computer searches within the open professional and scientific literature. Eliminating materials that were purely polemical, but retaining commentaries that represented informed opinion, the psychologist derived a literature base of over 370 papers and articles dealing with scientific aspects of polygraphy.

He developed three sections to include in his final report. The first section provided a theoretical and scientific perspective of the field of polygraphy, which was designed to help the naive reader understand the issues involved in evaluation. This included a historical review of the field and outlined guidelines for interpreting any controversial issues that arose regarding evaluation, such as issues of reliability, accuracy, and validity. The second, main section reviewed the literature in sufficient detail so that the reader had a firm appreciation of the types of procedure used in the investigation of the polygraph, and the empirical sources for any controversies or agreements. The final section dealt with the difficult question of how to improve on the reliability and accuracy of polygraphic techniques. The psychologist, by necessity, had to draw on the empirical findings of the scientific literature. However, this final section contained more of the psychologist's own, professional opinion, albeit one that was informed by the scientific literature. This final section also included an overview of the issues that were raised by the scientific literature.

These three sections formed the bulk of the final report that was presented. In addition, the final report contained a summary and recommendations on three separate issues. One regarded whether the government should adopt the polygraph as a reliable and accurate in-service or pre-employment tool. Another considered whether any research might be usefully commissioned to determine the validity of techniques for the detection of deception with specific reference to screening. Finally, a third addressed the extent to which any margins of error inherent in the techniques could be corrected by improving testing procedures.

On the basis of his review, the psychologist concluded that, as an instrument of detection, the polygraph lacked sufficient accuracy, and fell short of the standards set by conventional psychometric tests. He also suggested that any research directed at understanding the causal mechanisms behind the inaccuracy, or individual differences in reactivity or habituation, would not be prudent, as such research would require long-term investments and be unlikely to improve accuracy. However, the psychologist did feel that some efforts could be made in improving current testing procedures, primarily by examining the effectiveness of different examiners. He pointed out that much of the discrepancy between laboratory and field studies seemed to lie in the skill of the examiner.

To this end, the psychologist suggested that research could be usefully applied towards scientifically examining current practice that existed within an established service, such as an US Federal Agency. Through rigorous observation and controlled tests of trained examiners, such studies could throw light on the processes underlying polygraphy, although no research could be expected to provide a precise estimate of the practical efficacy of polygraph techniques. In fact, the psychologist's firm conclusion was that nothing in the polygraph literature led to the expectation that accuracy of detection could be improved substantially.

How was the psychologist's input assessed?

The psychologist delivered his report to the head of the branch, who in turn presented the formal report to the Prime Minister and the Cabinet. The Prime Minister, in turn, reported the conclusions of the study to the House of Commons. The informed decision of the government was that polygraph techniques are not sufficiently reliable to justify their usage in assessing or screening for security risk.

ADDITIONAL READING

Dixon, N.F. (1976) *On the Psychology of Military Incompetence*. Jonathan Cape, London. This is a serious and searching attempt to explain, in psychological terms, the frequency of disasters in the course of military history. The author served in the military for a number of years before training as a psychologist.

Watson, P. (1980) *War on the Mind: the Military Uses and Abuses of Psychology*. Penguin Books, New York. A careful consideration of the positive and negative aspects of psychology in warfare.

QUESTIONS

Scenario one

1   Do you think the psychologists had an obligation to report the findings publicly? Why?

2   What specific psychological problems might you expect an air crew to demonstrate after an otherwise avoidable accident had occurred?

Scenario two

1   How did reviewing the literature assist the psychologist in making his recommendations about the polygraph?

2   If you were to build a machine that could reliably detect a lie, what behaviours would you want it to measure?